The Mammoth Book of
THE WEST

The Mammoth Book of
THE WEST

The Making of the American West

Jon E. Lewis

CARROLL & GRAF PUBLISHERS, INC.
New York

Carroll & Graf Publishers, Inc.
19 West 21st Street
New York
NY 10010-6805

First published in the UK by Robinson Publishing 1996

First Carroll & Graf edition 1996
This new edition published 2001

ISBN 0–7867–0864–6

Printed and bound in the EU

Jon. E Lewis was born in 1961. His previous books include the best-selling The Mammoth Book of How It Happened: An Eyewitness History of the World, Eyewitness the 20th Century and Eye-witness D-Day. Other titles in the Mammoth series are The Mammoth Book of Soldiers at War, The Mammoth Book of Life Before the Mast, The Mammoth Book of Endurance and Adventure, The Mammoth Book of War Letters and Diaries, The Mammoth Book of True War Stories, The Mammoth Book of Modern War Stories, The Mammoth Book of Battles, The Handbook of SAS & Elite Forces and The Mammoth Book of Private Lives.

Contents

Introduction   xi

Part I
The Way West

Prologue   3
Into the Wilderness   10
The Clash of Empire   14
Daniel Boone and the Bluegrass   20
The Revolution in the West   24
The Voyage of Lewis and Clark   34
Pike's Progress, Long's Labour   44
Of Mountain Men and Furs   50
"And Remember the Alamo"   62
Pioneers Across the Plains   77
The Donner Tragedy   96
Westward With God   103
The Gold Rush   112
Motive Power   128

Part II
The Trampling Herd

Prologue   147
The Cradle of the Cattle Kingdom   149
On the Trail   155
Babylons of the Plains   171
"Oh, To Be a Cowboy"   181
Bonanzaland   196
Billy the Kid   206
Snow, Sheep and Blood   222

Part III
The Lawless Land

Prologue   251
The Outlaw Breed   268
Jesse James and His Men   280
Frontier Lawmen   294
The Legend and Life of Wyatt Earp   303
Texas Rangers, Pinkerton Detectives   313
Wild, Wild Women   329

Part IV
The Indian Wars

Prologue   339
War Comes to the Land of Little Rain   345
The Great Sioux Uprising   353
Sand Creek   359
Red Cloud's War   367
Blood on the Grasslands   381
The Struggle for the Staked Plains   405
Little Big Horn   415
Geronimo, Apache Tiger   431
Ghost Dancers   450

Part V
The Last Days of the West

Prologue   459
Settling the Great Plains   462
The Wild Bunch   479
The Saga of Tom Horn   489
Wild West Shows and Rodeos   495

Afterword: The West in the Movies   503
Appendix I: Chronology of the American West   515
Appendix II: Bibliography   529
Appendix III: The American Indian Nations of
   North America   545
Index   551

Introduction

The American West was a time, and a place. But above all, it was a state of mind.

For pioneers staring, hip-cocked, into the virgin land of the setting sun, the West represented a new start, a future of endless possibilities, a place where a man or woman might make something of themselves. Wrote Helen Carpenter in her diary on 26 May 1857, the day she began her journey across the plains in an ox wagon: "Ho – for California – at last we are on the way – only seven miles from home (which is to be home no longer) yet we have really started and with good luck may some day reach the 'promised land'."

The promised land of the West did not always turn out to be the Eden of pioneer expectations. "Oh, the trees, the trees," lamented one settler in Kentucky, faced with the awesome task of clearing the looming, claustrophobic forest. Yet, whether they liked it or loathed it, those who endured life on the remote frontier became transformed, even as they transformed the land around them. They became less urbane, less European in outlook. The frontier mentality thus formed was independent, optimistic, eager for material success, and scornful of rank, pretension, and class. Nearly all travellers to the New World noted these pronounced traits. The English writer Anthony

Trollope, visiting the USA in the early 1860s, commented in his *North America* (1862) that "there is an independence which sits gracefully on their [the Americans'] shoulders, and teaches you at first glance that the man has a right to assume himself your equal."

This frontier spirit was born long before men and women moved to settle the big, rolling lands beyond the Mississippi. Although the decades 1860–1890 are often equated with "the American West", the frontier, the moving edge of settlement into the "wilderness", began on the Eastern side of the Appalachians in the seventeenth century. The final sweep of settlement, the conquering of trans-Mississippi America, was but the finale of a process which had been hundreds of years in the making. Many of those who homesteaded the Great Plains were the descendants of farmers who had toiled on land of the Eastern coastal belt. And pioneers nearly always went West, not North or South, so keeping within familiar climatic zones. New Englanders stuck to the upper reaches of the West; Virginians and Carolinians headed for Alabama, and then crossed the Mississippi into Louisiana, Arkansas, and Texas.

Land for farming was the great spur which prompted men and women to go West. (The cowboy on horseback might be a more romantic, attractive figure, but it was the pedestrian "sod-buster" who tamed the bulk of the West; agriculture was the new country's basic endeavour.) Sons of farmers, on finding the family claim too small to sustain division, left home and trekked west to find a place of their own. And then, in turn, their sons did the same. Southerners also found themselves driven westwards by soil exhaustion; their cash crops of tobacco and cotton took a heavy toll on the earth. The relative abundance of land did little to encourage good husbandry. There always seemed to be more land for the taking.

That is, for the taking from the continent's original inhabitants, the American Indian. For the land the settlers thirsted for was not unoccupied; the Indians had to be persuaded to part with it, or prised off it by force. If the frontier mentality had attractive features, it also had ugly aspects. It justified the cleansing of Indians from their lands in the name of Manifest Destiny, and encouraged the cult of the gun, the use of firearms to settle all matters, big or small. To "win" the West took the White man nearly three hundred years of warfare.

What befell the Indian was a tragedy, even a travesty. At times something like genocide was practised against the native people of America. But it is wrong to picture the American Indian as a noble but hapless victim. There are few innocents in war. The Indians did not see themselves as a homogenous entity, just as Europeans do not see themselves as alike, but as English, French, or German. Some Indian tribes, in conflict with their aboriginal neighbours, allied themselves with the White man as a means of winning local power struggles. The example of the Crow is only the most famous. And American Indian tribes could wage war as relentlessly and bloodily as the White man. The long enmity between the 7th Cavalry and the Sioux had as one of its fillips the killing and mutilation of Frederick Wyllyams by Sioux (and Arapaho and Cheyenne) braves at Fort Wallace, Kansas, in 1867. The 7th Cavalry never forgot or forgave what had been done to Sergeant Wyllyams.

The Indian wars had their ironies, as well as their brutalities. In the 1870s the Sioux fought bitterly to keep White settlers out of the Black Hills of Dakota, which they declared to be their ancestral and spiritual home. In truth, the Sioux were settlers too, and had only been in the Black Hills country for a century or so. The much cherished freedom of the Plains Indian to ride free like the wind over the prairie was a gift given him by the White man; the horse, after all, was introduced to America by the Spanish. And if the White man slaughtered the buffalo to near extinction, Indian hunters had long before wiped out the beast's giant prehistoric relative – along with the mammoth, the mastadon, and more than 70 other species of large game. (This ecological disaster seems to have caused the American Indians to rethink their attitude to American fauna; certainly they came to revere animals and to be zealous in their conservation, never killing more than were needed for the maintenance of the tribe.)

None of these culpabilities, however, excuse the treatment of America's native people by the White man. They are only given to illustrate the intricacy of the history of the West. The winning (or losing) of the American West is the greatest story ever told, bar one epic of biblical times, but it is not a simple tale of Good versus Bad, however these attributes are apportioned. Western history is infinitely shaded.

And it is even more wondrous and terrible than its fictional and mythic tellings. Few of the legends of the West, the Earps and the Jameses, have much substance when truth is applied, but even a dime novelist would blush to write a scenario where a lone gunfighter engaged 80 assailants and won – which is exactly what Elfego Baca did in 1884. Baca was no superhuman but a naive teenager who wanted to be a lawman and who had tired of local anti-Hispanic racism.

It could only happen in the West, that place of nobility and endless possibilities, cruel violence and depredation.

This book was born in the late 1960s when, sprawled on the floor in my grandparents' house in the country, I used to watch *The Virginian* on television. Afterwards, I would go to my bedroom and peep out at the darkening land.

With just a touch of childish imagination, the fields below the window would be transformed into open range, the gently lowing Herefords into wiry Texan Longhorns. And then, over the far horizon would come a whooping band of Sioux braves, or a party of rustlers, or a no-good gunfighter.

The Virginian not only hooked me on Westerns; it stimulated an interest in the real West which has never left me. That interest has been abetted by many people over the years and thanks are due to them, as well as to those who helped directly in the preparation of this book. I especially thank my grandfather, Joe Amos, who made me my first bow and arrow and my grandmother, Margaret Amos, who taught me to smell for rain on the wind. My gratitude is also extended to Eric and Joyce Lewis, Kathleen and Bill Ashman, Joan Stempel, Kathryn and Richard Cureton, the Jordan Gallery in Cody, Wyoming, Maria Lexton, Marge and Gene Ensor, Tony Williams and Kathleen Ensor Williams, Phil Lucas, Joe Turner and Michele Lowe, John Powell, Julian Alexander, Nick Robinson, Mark Crean, Jan Chamier, Dinah Glasier, and Eryl Humphrey Jones. Special thanks are due to copy-editor Margaret Aherne for her patience and skill. As ever, my biggest thanks go to my wife, Penny Stempel, who is beyond praise.

To mount a horse and gallop over prairies, completely losing one's self in vast and illimitable space, as silent as lonely, is to leave every petty care. In these grand wastes, one is truly alone with God. Oh, how I love the West!

Mrs Orsemus Boyd, Army wife

Part I

The Way West

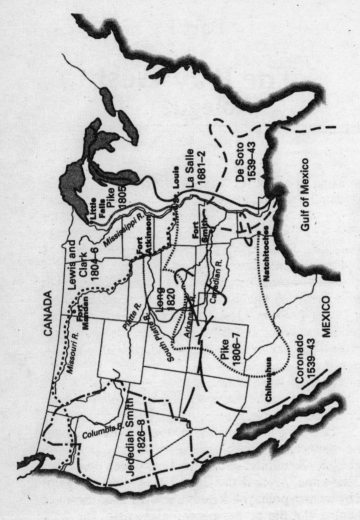

1. The Exploration of the West

Prologue

They came, the first inhabitants of the New World, in small family groups, pushing eastward over the land bridge from Siberian Asia. They sought neither God nor gold but game, in the vast archaic shapes of the mammoth and the mastodon. No one knows for certain when the feet of these nomadic hunters first touched the soil of what would become America; it was some time towards the end of the Ice Age, not before 30,000 BC but not later than 28,000 BC. From Alaska, they fanned out across the northern continent, and then down through the central isthmus to the south. They remained hunters until the mammoth and mastodons were all gone, after which they began to adopt ways of living suitable to the lands into which they had walked. Some who had reached the Southwest, turned to agriculture and built magnificent stone cities. The people of the plains continued to hunt smaller game, especially a sub-species of bison, *Bos bison americanus*, the million-strong herds of which blackened the landscape. Around the Great Lakes, wild rice gathered by women poling bark canoes was the main means of sustaining the life of the people. Geronimo, the wild Apache warrior, looking back on his homeland from exile, would express the Indians' beautiful adaptation to the land thus:

For each tribe of men Usen [God] created He also made a
home. In the land for any particular tribe He placed whatever would be best for the welfare of that tribe.

With the diversifying of lifestyle, came other changes,
of language, culture, even physique. Over time, the people no longer thought of themselves as a single entity but
as many differing tribes – Dakota, Mandan, Seminole,
Pequot, Pawnee, Kickapoo, Comanche and nearly 500
others, most of whose tongues were incomprehensible to
each other, and some of whom were incessantly warring
rivals. (The West never was Arcadia, despite its siren
beauty.) The original inhabitants of America, though, retained one common belief wherever they went, whom-
ever they became. They believed that the land belonged to
no one. Tribes might fight over hunting grounds, but they
had no concept of private property. The land was sacred,
to be handed on almost untouched. As an Omaha warri-
or's song expressed it:

> I shall vanish and be no more,
> But the land over which I now roam,
> Shall remain,
> And change not.

The great ceremonial song of the Navajo, "The Blessing
Way", contained a similar sentiment:

> All my surroundings are blessed as I found it,
> I found it.

And the aboriginal was bound to the earth by a mystical
union. It was part of his body. When it was cut, he wept.
The attitude of the European intruder was very different.
The first White to "discover" the New World is usually

held to be Christopher Columbus, who reached the Bahamas on 12 October AD 1492. Believing he had reached an outpost of India, he christened the people he found on the island of San Salvador *Indios*. "So tractable, so peaceable, are these people," Columbus wrote to his patrons, the King and Queen of Spain, "that I swear to your Majesties there is not in the world a better nation . . . and although it is true that they are naked, yet their manners are decorous and praiseworthy." Where Columbus had sailed, other Spanish subjects soon followed. Led by the conquistadors, merciless hard-fighting minor noblemen, the Spanish overran the Caribbean and moved remorselessly westwards, lured ever on by the prospect of gold. In 1513 Juan Ponce de Leon landed on the American mainland. He found no gold, only flora. His men duly named the place *Florida* ("full of flowers"). Another conquistador, Panfilo de Narvaez, decided that Florida, its lack of yellow metal notwithstanding, was ideal for colonization. The attempt proved disastrous. But it accidentally resulted in the first sighting by White eyes of the American West.

Fleeing Florida in the summer of 1528 for the sanctuary of recently settled Mexico, the makeshift craft of Narvaez's men was blown ashore on the Texas coast, near the mouth of the Sabine. Four Spaniards, led by Cabeza de Vaca and including the Black Moorish servant Estevan, survived shipwreck, disease, starvation, and enslavement by hostile Indians to reach Mexico on foot in 1536. Their saviour was Estevan. It was he who did the work, took the risks. As de Vaca later acknowledged, Estevan "talked to them [the Indians] . . . he inquired the road we should follow in the villages, in short, all the information we wished to know."

De Vaca's lost men could provide little cartographical information, but their tale prompted more purposeful

Spanish expeditions. In 1539 Don Francisco Vasquez de Coronado, the 31-year-old governor of New Spain, headed a great expedition which sought the fabled Seven Cities of Cibola, whose streets were reputedly paved with gold. From Mexico, Coronado marched northwards. Arriving in the land of the Zunis, who were astonished by the expedition's horses (a mammalian form absent from the Americas' indigenous fauna), Coronado demanded obedience to the rule of Spain. The ancient Zunis pelted him with stones, but then withered before the fire from modern Spanish arms. Disappointed at the Zunis' lack of precious metal, Coronado set off for another fabled golden land, Quivira. Eventually, he penetrated as far north as present-day Kansas. Meanwhile, a rival Spanish party under the leadership of Hernando de Soto landed in Florida and stumbled westwards, fighting repeated skirmishes with Indians, eventually reaching Arkansas. In 1542 de Soto "took to his pallet" and died. He was buried in the great river he had found: the Mississippi.

By now, there were White men from other European nations probing the new continent. John Cabot sailed from England along the Atlantic coast of the continent in 1497. Portugal's Gaspar Corte-Real reached Newfoundland and Labrador in 1500. Twenty-four years later the French-sponsored Florentine Giovanni da Verrazano entered New York harbour. In 1534 the intrepid Breton navigator Jacques Cartier explored the Gulf of Saint Lawrence. The response of the Spanish to this trespassing on their Forbidden Empire was to send a host of robed friars to America to establish missions and save the souls of the heathens (and surreptitiously pave the way for the later rule of Spain). In 1598 missionaries and settlers led by Juan de Onate founded the dried mud village of San Juan in the Rio Grande Valley, in what is now New Mexico. It was the first permanent European settlement in the American West.

More missions followed, in Arizona, Texas and California. Resistance by the aboriginals of the Pueblos (stone villages) to the word of God was met by military force and forced conversion. When the Acoma Indians of Sky City refused Spanish food requisitions, Onate sent an armed detachment which slaughtered 800 adult Acomans. Surviving males over the age of 25 had a foot severed, to make them living reminders of the folly of resistance. They were then herded into slavery.

Although the Spanish were the first to settle in the American West, ultimately its conquest lay with others. The great Pueblo uprising of 1680, which drove 2,500 Spanish from their homes and ranches, badly shook the Empire's frontiering will. And Spain was too riven by internal difficulties and too interested in skimming off the surface wealth of the Americas, gold, to develop a coherent colonization policy. France, too, tended to view the New World merely as a place to plunder, whether for gold, beaver furs or Newfoundland cod. As a result, the whole of the Eastern seaboard from Canada down to Florida – a temperate terrain highly suited to large-scale agricultural settlement – was left unclaimed.

It was the fortune and fate of Britain that when she came to build an empire, this rich land remained free. The first British expeditions failed, but in 1606 the London Company was granted the right by James I "to deduce a colony of sundry of our people" in America, north of the 34th parallel. Three ships made their way across the ocean in 1607. "The six and twentieth day of April about foure a clocke in the morning," wrote Master George Percy, "wee descried the Land of Virginia ... faire meddowes and goodly tall trees, with such Fresh-waters runninge through the woods as I was almost ravished at the first Sight thereof." After landing, the settlers built a village,

Jamestown, named in honour of the monarch. They were attacked by tidewater Indians and suffered a "Starving Time" (until the selfsame Indians brought them gifts of food), but they endured to become the first permanent British settlement in America. A timorous alliance with the Indian was even formed with the marriage of the Indian princess Pocahontas to the Englishman John Rolfe.

More British immigrants arrived; settlements and farms spread along the James River, and then to Maryland and the Carolinas. In 1620 a group of religious dissenters, the Pilgrims, landed in New England after their vessel *Mayflower* was blown off its course for Virginia. They decided to build their homes at Plymouth, where luck had washed them up. A decade later came the great 25,000-strong Puritan migration to Massachusetts. The European population of America grew inexorably – just as its native population declined inexorably. The White man's microbes (particularly smallpox) devastated up to 90 per cent of some of the Eastern Algonquin tribes. Some Indians tried to make a stand against the disease-carrying invader, with his insatiable hunger for land. The Wampanoags of Native American King Philip killed some 600 New Englanders in 1675. But still the Europeans came. The only result for the Wampanoags was slaughter and slavery.

Soon, stable British colonies stretched along the Atlantic seaboard from New Hampshire to Georgia (and included New York and New Jersey, seized from the Dutch). The coastal strip became used up, overcrowded. The colonialists needed more land. The Virginians needed it for their tobacco boom crop (for a while even the streets of Jamestown had been turned over to the cultivation of the "weed"), and the agriculturalists of New England needed it for their farms. There was only one way the territorial expansion of the British colonies could proceed – westwards, into the unmapped, unknown hinterland. It was now that the story of the West, of the frontier, really began.

Into the Wilderness

In the beginning the West was in the East. It was the unknown and magic forest land which lay beyond the cultivated fields of the tidewater colonialists and stretched away to the forbidding ridges of the Appalachians, which walled the coastal plain.

Not that it was unknown for long. There was no hill that land speculators or trappers, with profit before their eyes, could not climb or woods that farmers could not clear. In 1650, only 43 years after the founding of Jamestown, Captain Abraham Wood led a five-day expedition through the "wilderness" as far as the Roanoke Valley in search of real estate for future resale. Also of the mind to make money from land speculation was Virginia's governor, Sir William Berkeley, who organized an expedition in 1670 to discover a pass through the Appalachians themselves. The expedition was led by John Lederer, a German physician of courage and sensitivity. Lederer found himself overwhelmed by the beauty of the Blue Ridges. He did not find a way through. Thomas Batts and Robert Fallam did, in 1671, by following the Staunton River. They emerged into the Great Appalachian Valley, which runs from south of the Carolinas to northern New York, a place of almost Edenic character and fertility.

After the explorers came the settlers. By the turn of the

1700s pioneer hardscrabble farmers were streaming into the Valley, through the gaps in the mountain range carved by the Delaware and other rivers. Also entering the Great Appalachian Valley, but from the north, were German peasant immigrants displaced by war in the Rhinish Palatinate. Thousands settled in the Quaker province of William Penn, where the attraction was not religious pacifism – the Palatines were Lutheran or Reformed Church – but the rolling landscape which reminded them of home. The Germans, often misnamed the "Pennsylvania Dutch", brought with them a long agricultural heritage, and their huge stone barns, carefully tended land and hard-working women marked them out for the wonder and envy of other colonialists. Many of the Palatinate Germans arrived as indentured servants, who worked a seven-year contract with the farmer who had financed their sea passage, before purchasing a place of their own.

Another group of immigrants from a troubled land, the "Scotch-Irish", also found Pennsylvania to their liking. These were the descendants of the Scottish lowland Presbyterians who had moved to Ulster at the encouragement of James I as a means of subduing the Irish. Finding the best Pennsylvanian land already claimed by the Germans, the Scotch-Irish settled on the raw, westernmost frontier, an environment very similar to the Ireland their grandfathers had encountered. They began concentrating in the Cumberland valley of Pennsylvania west of Harrisburg during the 1720s. In the 1750s Pennsylvania was receiving as many as 10,000 Ulstermen a year. With each new wave, the Scotch-Irish pushed further on into the wilderness, built their rude log cabins and grubbed a few acres for corn and beans. By 1740 there were Scotch-Irish settlements in North Carolina; by 1760 they had reached South Carolina. They were incredibly fecund. "There is not a cabin but has ten or twelve children in it," wrote the

Anglican itinerant Charles Woodmason. "When the boys are 18 and the girls 14 they marry – so that in many cabins you will see children . . . and the mother looking as young as the daughter." A tenth of the population of America in 1776 was Scotch-Irish.

A rugged, determined people who feared only God, these Scotch-Irish were perhaps the first true Westerners. Years of clearing forests in Northern Ireland had taught them woodland lore even before they came to America. They also knew how to fight, for they had battled the Catholic tribes often enough. And they were possessed of a primitive democracy, for their church taught them that no man was great, only God.

Wherever the Scotch-Irish pioneers spread throughout the forest, the picture was the same. They chose the land they wanted, regardless of the forms of land patents or the claims of Indians, with whom they fought bloody running battles and whose scalps they hung in trophy from cabin walls. For the Scotch-Irish it was against "the law of God and nature that so much land be idle, while so many Christians wanted it to labor on, and to raise their bread." Above all, they were ever prepared, even eager, to pull up stakes and keep moving westwards. They were restless almost beyond belief.

In the isolation of the backcountry, the Scotch-Irish, and the Germans, the English, the Yankees [native New Englanders], the Welsh and the Scots, who mixed with them, began to evolve a new society. As they worked on the wilderness, cutting trees in the shadows of the Appalachians or by the bright water of the Juniata River, they became transformed themselves. They became less European. The mentality of the woodlanders was that of the future American: pragmatic, wary of government, inclined to optimism, and loving of religious and political freedom.

The woodlanders also brought frontiering to its maturity. To visitors they seemed indistinguishable from Indians. One visitor wrote: "The clothes of the people consist of deer skins, their food of Johnny cakes, deer and bear meat. A kind of white people are found here, who live like savages." Their tools were few, usually only the prerequisites of forest life: the long-handled axe and the rifle. With the axe they razed trees, built their log homes and carved the family utensils. With the rifle they fought Indians and shot game. Imported rifles were adapted by Pennsylvanian German gunsmiths for specific frontier needs. They lengthened the barrel to four feet for accuracy, reduced the bore size to half an inch (so saving on the lead for the projectile ball), and increased the size of the sights. An innovation was the "grease patch", which was wrapped around the ball, giving it a snug fit in the barrel yet allowing it to be rammed home easily by a light hickory ramrod. In time the rifle would be given a name deriving from its great popularity with the settlers of the bluegrass state, but the "Kentucky Rifle" was in fact born east of the Appalachian crest. A skilled marksman could put a bullet through the head of a deer at 300 yards with a fine Kentucky piece. A man's head could be drilled at 250 yards.

Such guns and the hardy souls needed to fire them were necessary if the British advance westwards was to continue.

Beyond the cloudy ridges of the Appalachians there were unfriendly Indians and equally unfriendly Europeans. For by the time the British were ready to move into the Ohio Valley in the mid-1700s the French had staked a claim to the continent from the Appalachians to the Rockies. They would be removed only by one hundred years of war.

The Clash of Empire

While the British had been laboriously hewing their way westwards, the French in Canada had swept towards the setting sun with awesome speed. Unlike the settled British frontier, however, that of New France consisted of isolated trading posts, thrust rapidly into the wilderness by the profit-hungry fur business. After establishing their base in Quebec in 1608, the French had reached west of Lake Michigan in the 1630s; in the 1670s they had entered the Ohio Valley. In 1681 Robert Cavalier, Sieur de La Salle, and a party of 23 Frenchmen descended the Illinois River. After entering the Mississippi they sailed down its entire length, reaching the Gulf of Mexico on Thursday, 9 April 1682. Disembarking onto the shore, the Cavalier ordered his personal Recollect friar, Zenobe Membre, to bless the cross and claim on behalf of the Sun King, Louis XIV, all the land the Mississippi drained.

The British colonialists, however, were not inclined to heed France's staked claim. Against the need for land, legal niceties mattered little. After a series of indecisive wilderness clashes – King William's War, Queen Anne's War and King George's War – the French and the British headed towards a final solution. The descent into war was inescapable. The French tightened their grip on the interior by building palisaded posts in the Illinois country. By the 1740s British colonialists were poised at the very peak of the Appalachians ready to descend and occupy the interior. Land companies were formed to locate suitable territories for settlement: the Ohio Land Company in 1747, the Loyal Land Company in 1749. Traders from the Pennsylvania backcountry infiltrated the Ohio Valley to trade with the Indians.

It was one such trader, a tough Irishman called George Croghan, who sparked off the last great war for empire between Britain and France. Croghan ordered a post to be built at the Miami Indian village of Pickawillany – in the very heart of French territory. For a while this prospered, but then in spring 1753 a new French Governor, Marquis Duquesne, ordered an attack on Croghan's post by French traders and Ottawa Indian allies. The post was destroyed and its defenders slain. A visiting Miami chief was unlucky enough to be killed, boiled and eaten. To prevent any future intrusions by Croghan and his trading ilk, Duquesne built a chain of four forts from Lake Erie to the Forks of the Ohio, sealing off the Ohio Valley from the trespassing Pennsylvanians. The last fort, on the Ohio Forks (the site of present-day Pittsburgh), Duquesne named after himself.

The French had thrown down the gauntlet. The British barely hesitated to pick it up. To lose the Ohio Valley would be to lose everything – the entire hinterland.

The Seven Years' War began almost as the final log was being hauled into place at Fort Duquesne. Virginia's Scots Governor Robert Dinwiddie had already sent the 21-year-old George Washington with a warning to the French to vacate it. When they refused, Washington returned with a small force. En route Washington's men met and defeated a French scouting party. Realizing that he had noisily lost his advantage of surprise, Washington reconsidered the wisdom of attacking the French fort, withdrawing to the

treeless valley of Great Meadows. There he ordered his
men to build an earth rampart. "The whole and the parts
were not a design of engineering art but of frontier necessity", he later wrote, "so I gave it the name, Fort Necessity." Sheltered behind a dirt bank, Washington waited
for the French to come to him. They did, on 3 July 1754.
The outnumbered British fought valiantly all day, before
surrendering honourably in the evening.

The next few years of the war were equally inglorious
for the British. General Edward Braddock, who arrived
from England to take command of the campaign, was
cocksure and incompetent. In June 1755 he grandly
marched his troops towards Fort Duquesne as though
on parade. In their van went 300 axemen cutting a
12-foot road through the virgin forest. ("Braddock's Road"
would later prove of inestimable value to those settling
the Ohio area.) Surprised by a smaller concealed force
of French and Indians, the British became trapped in a
valley clearing. They were mown down in their red-coated
hundreds. Braddock himself was mortally wounded.
George Washington, his aide, had a lucky escape with
"four bullets through my coat and two horses shot under
me."

Afterwards, the Indians began to raid British settlements. "It is incredible," wrote one French officer, "what a
quantity of scalps they bring us." The Indians may have
disliked the fur trade of the French, but most perceived
the populous British frontier as the greater threat.

Despite defeat upon defeat, the British managed to turn
the war around. Although they termed the conflict "The
French and Indian War", not all Native Americans were
allied to the cause of New France. Sir William Johnson, an
Anglo-Irish immigrant who became a Mohawk blood
brother, forged an alliance between Britain and the League
of Iroquois Indians. The League, which called itself "The

Longhouse", a reflection of the typical Iroquois dwelling, was composed of six tribes – the Mohawk, Oneida, Onondaga, Cayuga, Seneca and Tuscarara – and was versed in warfare, being frequent raiders of other tribes for the purpose of procuring prisoners for adoption or sacrificial torture. Armed with British guns the Iroquois successfully prevented the French resupplying their inland posts in the south and west.

Besides the Iroquois, the British had another irregular force which was expert at forest warfare, the rangers of Major Robert Rogers. A hard drinker of prodigious strength who had grown up on the border of New Hampshire, Rogers recruited to himself a band of frontiersmen of similar robust stock. They lived off the fruits of the land, travelled light and hit hard far inside New France. Their most famous exploit was the massacre of the St Francis Indians in 1759 at their village on the St Lawrence River. The village had long been a source of bloody raids, and New Englanders did not restrain their joy at its destruction.

Important though the Iroquois and Rogers's Rangers were to British victory, its main cause was a change of ministry in London. The new regime, led by the energetic and charismatic William Pitt the Elder, swept out the dusty relics who staffed Britain's army and replaced them with dynamic, brilliant unknowns. One of these, General James Wolfe, was dispatched to North America, which he dutifully won for king and country. The *coup de grâce* was administered on the Plains of Abraham beside the city of Quebec on 13 September 1759, when the French defenders were panicked into a bitter battle they could not win and which resulted in the Union Jack flying over France's New World capital. A year later Montreal fell. Although official peace was still two years away, the French military in North America could now only lose. Their Indian allies, seeing the way the war was heading, returned to their homes. Some even opportunistically changed to the British side, tempted by Rogers's promise that under British dominion their "Rivers would flow with rum – that Presents from the Great King would be unlimited – that all sorts of Goods would be in the utmost plenty and so cheap."

By the terms of the Treaty of Paris of 1763, the French lost all their possessions on the continent. Canada and all land east of the Mississippi went to Britain. With no use for its holdings beyond the Mississippi, France transferred the western half of the giant territory of Louisiana to its ally, Spain. But Spain herself also had to pay the victor a price. She ceded the long-held land of flowers, Florida, to Britain.

To the victor in the Seven Years' War went the spoils. So too all the difficulties of ruling a troublesome people, white and red. The ink on the Treaty of Paris was hardly dry before the tribes of the Ohio Valley and the Great Lakes were rising up in arms. Unhappy at being transferred to the rule of Britain, the tribes' unhappiness only increased when the British commander Jeffrey Amherst virtually abolished the annual gifts that were the staple of their economy. To Amherst the native peoples were "more nearly allied to the Brute than to the Human Creation" and he wanted to "extirpate them root and branch". (He would recommend that smallpox germs be somehow spread among the tribes.) With the threat of poverty and death before them, the natives of the region, led by Pontiac of the Ottawas, launched a revolt which captured all the western forts except Pitt (Duquesne), Niagara and Detroit. The frontier from New York to Virginia was ravaged by the torch and tomahawk.

Already wearied by the war with the French, the British decided to give the insurgents no further cause for discontent. On 7 October 1763, the British government issued a proclamation limiting White settlement to the east of the Appalachian crest.

The proclamation astounded America. With the removal of France, thousands of colonialists were expected to swarm into the fertile Ohio Valley. Many were volunteers who had served in the colonial militia with the lure of land as payment for service rendered. It now seemed that the interior would be barred to them forever. But when the shock died down, the colonialists realized that the proclamation was unenforceable. They simply ignored it and marched over the mountains. They had conquered one West, the wilderness up to the Appalachians. Now they would settle another, that between the Appalachians and the Mississippi.

Daniel Boone
and the Bluegrass

As early as 1750 Dr Thomas Walker of the Loyal Land Company had led a surveying party into Kentucky, after finding (or being shown by Indians) the massive gateway through the mountains which he named "Cumberland Gap", in honour of the Duke of Cumberland. This road to the interior would direct the course of Western settlement until after the Revolution.

But Walker himself, to his dismay, failed to locate the bluegrass country of Indian lore. Two years later, a Pennsylvanian trader by the name of John Finley did. Like many of the West's discoveries, it happened by accident. Finley was captured while canoeing down the Ohio with his wares by a party of Shawnees, who took him to their hunting encampment in the Kentucky lowlands. Finley escaped to tell his tale, but the Seven Years' War and Pontiac's Rebellion temporarily ended further exploration.

With the coming of peace, interest in bountiful Kentucky revived, especially among the backcountry's famous "long hunters", so-called because of the awesome distances they covered in pursuit of fur and flesh. For the coonskin-capped long hunters, the wild woods held no dangers, only adventure, wealth and nearly everything they needed to live: hides for their clothes, game and wild vegetables for their food, salt from natural brine licks, and even the "panes" for their cabin windows (made from doeskin membranes made translucent with bear oil). The furs of bear, beaver and other lush-coated animals were used to barter for the few items, such as gun and powder, that nature omitted to provide.

Long hunters began infiltrating Kentucky from the summer of 1766, men like Captain James Smith, Isaac Lindsay, James Harrod (the Latin reader who founded the stockade on the trail known as the Wilderness Road that became the state's first proper settlement) and Michael Stoner. But the most famous of them, and the one who would play the greatest role in the exploration of "Kentucke", was Daniel Boone.

Boone was born on 2 November 1734, to a Quaker family in Berks County, Pennsylvania. Boone's parents seem to have had problems with the Friends over a daughter's marriage outside the faith. This, and the rising fever over Western land settlement caused the Boones to move to the raw Yadkin Valley of North Carolina. There Daniel Boone learned to farm and, under the guidance of friendly Indians, the lore of the wild. For a period he fought in the Seven Years' War (where he met John Finley, a fellow waggoner on Braddock's ill-starred expedition), returning afterwards to the Yadkin. On 14 August 1756 he married a neighbourhood farm girl, Rebecca Bryan. Their marriage, however, was not the conventional frontier mating. Boone had the wanderlust. From spring to fall he farmed, but then took off for the winter on hunting trips, alone save for a packhorse to carry pelts.

Such was Daniel Boone's life until 1766. In that year he met up with his brother-in-law, John Stewart, who had just been into Kentucky with the expedition of Virginian

Ben Cutbird. Hearing Stewart recount the verdant wonders of the region, Boone resolved to go himself. He made his first trip to Kentucky in the winter of 1767, hoping to find the bluegrass country of Finley's captivity. Instead, he ending up wandering the hills south of the Big Sandy River. Boone made another try for the bluegrass land in May 1769 – he had now all but given up farming – this time accompanied by John Finley and two other long hunters. After passing through the Cumberland Gap the group followed the Warrior's Path across Kentucky as far as Station Camp Creek where they built a shelter to protect their furs. They then split up to explore the wilderness. Alone for most of the time, Boone spent months dodging Shawnee war parties (he was once captured, but escaped by diving into a giant canebrake) and living off the land. His great wander took him as far north as the Ohio, and over most of the great bluegrass region. When he met up with his brother, Squire Boone, on the Red River on 27 July 1770, he knew more about Kentucky than any other White man.

He had also fallen in love with it, with its level bluegrass fields and gentle cool streams. "I returned home to my family," he later recalled, "with a determination to bring them as soon as possible to live in Kentucke, which I esteemed a second paradise, at the risk of my life and fortune." A first attempt by the Boones to move to the new territory, in 1773, was beaten back by Indians, with the Boones losing their eldest son. Two years later, in January 1775, Boone led a party through the Cumberland Gap and with 30 axemen cleared a muddy trail, which came to be known as the Wilderness Road, to the Kentucky River. There, on the south bank, he founded the fort of Boonesborough.

Although this remote settlement took the backwoodsman's name, its real instigator was an old friend of Boone's,

Judge Richard Henderson. This Carolina land-jobber possessed, to use his own words, a "rapturous idea of property". Most rapturous of all was his dream to found a proprietary colony – Transylvania – beyond the mountains. The bluegrass region was ideal. It was lush almost beyond belief. More, the local Indians had been conveniently subdued.

The "Dark and Bloody Ground" had long been the hunting domain of both the Shawnees and Cherokees (although neither tribe lived there). But Chief Cornstalk's Shawnees had been defeated in battle by the Virginians at Point Pleasant on 9 October 1774. By the terms of the truce they signed, they agreed not to molest the White Kentuckians. Left as the undisputed owners of the region, the Cherokees decided on peaceable discretion. Having learned something of the White man's ways they were prepared to sell a great swathe of Kentucky. For £10,000 Henderson bought the land from the Kentucky River to the highland south of the Cumberland Gap. And he dispatched his friend Boone to blaze the emigrant trail to the Kentucky River.

Henderson's colony was destined to fail. Aside from a personal autocracy which made his Kentucky woodsmen "subjects" rise up against him, new immigrants settled where they chose, regardless of "Carolina Dick's" regulations. Henderson was powerless to stop them.

It was a problem the British Crown was dismally familiar with.

The Revolution in the West

The Fight for Paradise

The Kentuckians were not the only westering pioneers to ignore Britain's 1763 proclamation banning White expansion to the west of the Appalachians. Squatters had also filtered through into Tennessee and Pittsburgh. The law of Albion was no match for the lure of virgin land. There was money to be made, earth to be farmed. As George Washington observed: "Any person . . . who neglects the present opportunity of hunting out good lands and . . . marking . . . them for his own . . . will never regain it." Squatters visiting kin back in the land-hungry settlements, where farms were being divided over and over again to provide for maturing children, reported trans-Appalachia to be a "new Paradise".

Under the pressure of the speculators and settlers, who were pushing the frontier west from the mountains towards the Ohio at an average rate of 17 miles a year, Britain turned pragmatic and moved the proclamation line westward. If the Crown hoped to buy colonial goodwill it was mistaken. The vexed matters of taxation and the Navigation Acts (which imposed stiff duties on the export of American goods) irked her subjects beyond acquiescence. In 1775 America revolted.

The West played only a minor role in the War of Independence, which was largely fought out in a series of set-piece battles on the coastal strip. Of the 2.4 million colonialists in 1775, only a brave few hundred had moved from the safety of the east to scratch a dangerous living beyond the mountains. Most of these frontier dwellers cared little for taxation without representation, the Boston port troubles, or the theory of natural rights. They joined the American side in the war because they feared that the Indian-loving British would form an alliance with the native people which would devastate the precarious frontier of White settlement. The struggle for that thousand-mile-long line on the edge of the wilderness would produce some of the bloodiest moments of the revolt.

The war in the West was fought in three theatres. Fighting began in the southern backcountry when Cherokees – against the wishes of their ally, the regional British superintendent of Indian affairs, Colonel John Stuart – swooped on Eaton's Station in North Carolina on 20 July 1776. After a treasonous but humanitarian warning to the hamlet by Stuart, the Indians were rebuffed, and so moved on to Fort Watauga. Milkmaids in the fields outside just made the safety of the stockade, Kate Sherill being pulled over the wall by John Sevier, who shot her closest pursuer almost in the same motion. Again the Indians were rebuffed. Incensed by their double humiliation, Chief Dragging Canoe's warriors, along with Creeks, Choctaws, Tories and renegade trader Alexander Cameron, struck isolated farms and settlements all along the Watauga and Nolichucky rivers. The settlers struck back with equal savagery. South Carolina offered a bounty of £75 for Indian scalps. And in the fall some 5,000 militiamen from Virginia and the Carolinas swept down like an avenging storm on the Overhill, Middle and Lower Town Cherokee. By the treaty of DeWitt's Corner and

Long Island, the Cherokee were forced to surrender 5 million acres of tribal land, including most of the Tennessee basin. Settlers poured in, and in 1780 Nashville was founded.

In the northern theatre – New York's Mohawk Valley and Pennsylvania's Wyoming Valley – Iroquois braves and the loyalist Tory Rangers of John Butler battered the colonials almost into extinction. The Iroquois were led by the Mohawk chief Thayendanegea, better known to the Whites as Joseph Brant, a guerrilla leader of canny ability (and also a scholar of note: he would later translate St Mark's Gospel and the Book of Common Prayer into Mohawk). In November 1778 Brant virtually wiped out the settlement of Cherry Valley. The Revolutionary cause was only saved when, in 1779, General Washington felt he could spare enough troops to send to the northern frontier. He desired "the total destruction and devastation of [Iroquois] settlements." The means to this brutal end were Generals John Sullivan and John Clinton, whose retaliatory campaign in the Mohawk Valley removed 40 Iroquois towns from the face of the earth and burned 160,000 bushels of corn, plus apple, peach and pear orchards. They found a thriving country, and left a smoking ruin. By the end of the war, the once mighty Iroquois confederacy was broken for ever.

Between the northern and southern theatres lay the killing forests of Kentucky and western Pennsylvania. Shawnee and Delaware raids began in the summer of 1776, driving farmers and woodsmen into the posts at Harrodsburg, Boonesborough and St Asaph, which were hastily fortified with 10-foot-high stockades of pointed logs set vertically. The "forting up" of the Kentucky stations was no sooner finished in the spring of 1777, the infamous "year of the three sevens", than Chief Blackfish and 300 Shawnee invested Boonesborough. So thoroughly confined were the inhabitants that they were unable to plant crops. They might have starved if the siege had not been lifted by the arrival of Virginian troops.

Shortly after, Daniel Boone, who led the defence at the fort, took a party to get badly needed salt from the spring at Blue Licks. Shawnee captured the party and took them to the village of Chillicothe, north of the Ohio, where the bravery of the Kentuckians so impressed the Indians that they were adopted into the tribe. For the Kentuckians the brotherhood of convenience lasted until June 1778, when Boone discovered that another Shawnee raid on Boonesborough was imminent. He determined to warn the settlement. Waiting until the Shawnees were preoccupied with a turkey hunt, he dashed into the woods. Four days later, on 20 June 1778, he reached Boonesborough, after running 160 miles through pathless forest in a matchless feat of frontiersmanship. His warning was in time, and when Blackfish and his war party arrived the fort was able to resist them. After nine days of siege the frustrated Blackfish – who loudly berated Boone for deserting the Shawnee – departed, to cheers from the settlers. But Blackfish had only quit to pursue easier targets. Throughout the fall of 1778 bands of Indians roved Kentucky, picking off travellers and careless settlers, and for the second year in succession stopped the harvest.

It was becoming obvious to even the most cautious patriot that the defensive policy on the middle frontier was a disaster. The war needed to be taken to the enemy. The man to do it was the young red-haired George Rogers Clark, son of a Virginia planter, whose war exploits already included running a 400-mile gauntlet of ambushes to get gunpowder to the Kentucky settlements. Now, with the sanction of the Virginia authorities, Clark decided to mount a counter-thrust against the British in Illinois country. Accompanied by 175 seasoned Indian-fighters, Clark flat-boated down the Ohio in late June 1778, then marched to the town of Kaskaskia. Their arrival on 4 July was so complete a surprise that the first the British commander knew about it was when the Americans pushed open the gate of the palisade. By mid-August Clark and his men also held Cahokia and the key fort of Vincennes. In mid-winter Vincennes was recaptured by a British force under Captain Hamilton. Not to be outdone, Clark made an audacious march through freezing weather, took the fort again and sent Hamilton to Virginia as a prisoner-of-war exhibit. Clark's dazzling victories did much to ease pressure on the upper Ohio. But when he withdrew hostile Shawnee and Wyandot poured into the vacuum left behind. Neither tribe had originally been inclined to partake in the White man's war, until frontiersmen had massacred 90 friendly Christian Delawares – including women and children – as they sang hymns in their church at Gnadenhutten. In revenge, Indians scalped captured Americans and roasted them to death over beds of hot coals.

Despite the bloodiness of the war in the West it was ultimately inconclusive. Although American settlement west of the mountains had grown, British and Native American forces had the military edge in the wilderness at the war's end, including a stunning ambush of American militiamen at Blue Licks in August 1782.

Yet the British had already lost the War of Independence with Lord Cornwallis's surrender at Yorktown in the main, coastal theatre. It was a defeat from which the British were unable to recover, no matter what their triumphs elsewhere. The Revolution produced many American war heroes, among them Clark and Boone, but the West was won for America by her diplomats at the peace table.

The Selling of the West

By the Treaty of Paris of 1783, Britain granted the new nation its independence, plus sovereignty over a domain which stretched from the Great Lakes in the north to the 31st parallel in the south, and west to the Mississippi. It was a great chunk of land, but given entirely out of British self-interest. The grant lured the United States from the side of her allies, France and Spain; thus Britain weakened the diplomatic bloc against her. And not only that. By giving up such a generous domain, Britain was guaranteeing her former colony a host of troubles. And so it proved.

Even before Congress could ratify the Paris treaty, it was obliged to untangle the problem of competing claims by the various states to the land beyond the mountains. Virginia, for instance, claimed Kentucky (which had a population of 45,000 by 1780; not even war could halt the flood tide of settlement), and North Carolina claimed Tennessee. Other states also had western land claims. The problem was solved only when the states surrendered their claims to central government. New York took the lead in 1780. The rest followed reluctantly, Georgia quitting its claim only in 1802.

Having gained jurisdiction over trans-Appalachia, the national legislature then passed a series of ordinances, ending with the Northwest Ordinance of 1787, which were the most important laws in the history of westward expansion. Under the terms of the ordinances the Old Northwest, the area around Ohio, was divided into sections by a corps of surveyors, armed with compasses and 66-foot chains, and then grouped into townships six miles square. Surveyed land was to be auctioned off in eastern cities at a minimum of a dollar an acre.

Additionally, the ordinances set out a plan of government for the region, which was to be divided into five

districts and ruled initially by a Congressionally appointed
governor. Once 5,000 free males had settled in each district, a legislature would be elected. On reaching a population of 60,000, the territory could petition for statehood.
When admitted it would enjoy the same rights and privileges as original states of the Republic. The ordinance also
guaranteed civil liberties and the rights of common law,
and forbade slavery.

Underneath the legalistic prose, the ordinance hid a
revolutionary idea. The western regions were invited to
join the original 13 colonies as equal partners in shaping
national destiny. Eventually some 30 states would join the
Union on the basic principles laid down in the ordinances
(although not all would be required to outlaw slavery).

The ordinances also gave a great fillip to westward
expansion. For a man might now leave the old states
without fear of giving up his political and judicial rights.

Not that the ordinances were flawless. The minimum
price of $1 per acre was reasonable – but land had to be
bought in parcels of 640 acres. Few leather-clad pioneers
had $640. Consequently, the parcels were often bought by
unscrupulous eastern land companies, who then sold on
the land in small plots at hiked-up prices. The ordinance
was a speculator's charter. To lure the buyer the companies often published promotional pamphlets full of lavish
description of the acreage for sale, acreage which they had
never even seen. One such pamphlet read:

A climate wholesome and delightful . . . Noble forests,
consisting of trees that spontaneously produce sugar . . .
and a plant that yields ready made candles . . . Venison in
plenty, the pursuit of which is interrupted by wolves,
foxes, lions or tygers . . . A couple of swine will multiply
themselves a hundred fold in two or three years. (Prospec-
tus of the Scioto Company)

Many innocents fell victim to the speculators' scams, the most pitiful of all being the French citizens who read and believed the claims of the Scioto Company. Between 1787 and 1790 the Scioto Company sold, via its Paris office, 150,000 acres of land it did not own. Some 600 French arrived in America to be informed that they had been duped. The matter was a national scandal, not least because the head of the Scioto Company was Colonel William Duer – the official who handled government land sales. Eventually, a few tracts of land were given over to the French (including 24,000 acres by a pitying Congress), but it was no bountiful farmland Paradise. It was unbroken forested frontier, from which the French had to carve out smallholdings and vineyards. They passed their lives in poverty and squalor.

And attacks by Indians. The ordinances conveniently ignored the fact that the Northwest was already occupied. With tomahawk and burning torch, a coalition of the tribes tried to stem White settlement north of the Ohio. Fanning the flames was Britain, anxious to surreptitiously stymie American expansionism and still clinging – in violation of the Paris treaty – to her Northwest forts.

By the autumn of 1789 the United States was embroiled in its first Indian War. To crush the insurgent tribes the new president, George Washington, sent out two military expeditions. Both fared badly. The first, in 1790, under General Josiah Harmer, was mauled comprehensively by the warriors of Miami chief Little Turtle. The next year, General Arthur St Clair, governor of the Northwest territory, led his men one hundred miles north from Cincinnati – and into the waiting arms of Little Turtle. Inept and inexperienced, St Clair let his men sleep almost without guard. Throughout the night of 3 November 1791 Miami warriors infiltrated the sleeping Whites' camp south of the Maumee. At dawn, the war-whooping Miami rushed the Americans, killing almost at will. One hundred troops were killed. The rest fled in panic, reaching Fort Jefferson – a ten-day march under normal conditions – in under 24 hours. It was to be the worst defeat in the history of US Indian fighting.

A sobered Congress decided to seek a peace with the Indians of the upper Ohio. The Wabash and the Illinois were receptive, but the Miamis preferred the sound of a settler dying. A further operation of war was put in motion. To lead it, Washington called out of retirement General Anthony Wayne, a tanner turned dashing Revolutionary soldier. "Mad Anthony" patiently drilled his men and perfected their marksmanship and then led them to a decisive victory on 20 August 1794 in the tangled thickets of Fallen Timbers. Under cover of fire by riflemen, American infantry made a screaming mass charge into the thickets. The Indians broke and fled for the safety of Fort Miami, only to have the gate closed in their faces. The British commander was not prepared to openly violate Britain's neutrality. The rejection broke the Indians' morale and by the following year the Miamis were ready for peace. Under the Treaty of Greenville (1795), the Indians forfeited a slice of southeastern Indiana and nearly all of Ohio. White settlers flocked in. By 1803 Ohio was a state of the Union.

In the aftermath of Fallen Timbers, Britain also inclined to the negotiating table. Increasingly embroiled in Europe's wars, and her plotting in America undone by Wayne's revitalized hangdog army, Britain was keen to cut her losses. In Jay's Treaty of 1794, she agreed to evacuate her forts in exchange for trading rights amongst the Indians of the Old Northwest.

Britain, however, was not the only imperial menace on the continent. Spain owned the Louisiana Territory, and a whole swathe of the south. Yet Madrid, too, was becoming preoccupied with the affairs of Europe and tiring of her expensive intrigues with the Creeks, Choctaws, Cherokee and Chickasaw. It was a good time for prudence. In the 1795 Treaty of San Lorenzo (or Pinckney's Treaty), Spain ceded the so-called Yazoo Strip of Alabama to the United States, and opened up the Mississippi to American traders.

Spain was also desirous of ridding herself of Louisiana, a colony which cost the Spanish dear every year. Late in 1800 Madrid sold the entire land of Louisiana to a France whose imperial urge had been revived by Napoleon Bonaparte. The sale sent a shudder of apprehension throughout the United States. (It also ruined Daniel Boone, who had been given a large tract of Louisiana by an admiring Hispania; he died penniless at the age of 85, still wanting to wester.) France could be a powerful foe. Yet President Jefferson was her match. With considerable guile he convinced France that the United States was about to join a military alliance with Britain. This, plus the abject failure of Napoleon's troops to quell a slave revolt in Santa Domingo, made the French gratifyingly cooperative. On Easter Monday 1803 Napoleon announced his decision to sell to the US the whole of Louisiana. At around 800,000 square miles, it was an area larger than the United States at the time. The price agreed on was 80,000,000 francs – about $15 million (or 3 cents an acre). Thomas Jefferson had just struck the greatest real estate deal of all time. He had just bought most of the West beyond the Mississippi.

The Voyage of
Lewis and Clark

Discovery

What was in this land Jefferson had bought? Only a few
Europeans had ever been inside it, and then mostly along
the narrow ribbons of its major rivers. To unveil Louisiana's secrets Jefferson organized a "Voyage of Discovery". It would be the first and the longest of the United
States' journeys into the uncharted wilderness.

For Jefferson the Voyage was the realization of a com-
pulsive dream. He was an inveterate – if armchair –
Westerer. More, he was a scientist by hobby, and he had a
scientist's need to know what was in the unknown. He
also had a politician's need to know if a Northwest passage existed, which would connect shining sea to shining
sea. For 20 years Jefferson had tried to have someone
explore the lands west of the Mississippi. In 1786 he had
encouraged the Connecticut adventurer John Ledyard to
walk across Russia, boat the Bering Straits and then walk
eastward to St Louis (Ledyard never got further than
Irkutsk in Siberia). As Secretary of State, Jefferson had
again backed another frustrated trans-America exploration, that of the French botanist André Michaux in 1793.

(The idealistic Michaux became sidetracked by the French Revolution.) It was not until he became President that Jefferson could finally find the men and the money to journey the continent. The Voyage of Lewis and Clark was begun even before Jefferson had Louisiana in his pocket. Jefferson browbeat Congress into stumping up $2,500 for his enthusiasm in January 1803, two clear months before Napoleon agreed to sell.

With the Louisiana deal completed, Jefferson could move more openly. To lead the expedition he chose his personal secretary, Captain Meriwether Lewis, a 28-year-old Virginian. With the President's concurrence, Lewis invited his old friend, William Clark, to be co-leader. Clark accepted. The President gave the two men detailed and precise instructions on their task. By his charge they were to "explore the Missouri river, and such principal stream of it, as, by its course and communication with the waters of the Pacific Ocean . . . may offer the most direct and practicable water communication across this continent for the purpose of commerce." If the primary purpose of the expedition was imperial, it was also to observe and record the soil, topography, flora and fauna of the lands it passed through, and to note the languages and traditions of the peoples it encountered.

That the Voyage would accomplish so much of its grand brief was due to the quality of its commanders. Lewis had a talent for naturalistic observation. Clark, a 32-year-old Kentuckian, was a skilled map-maker. Both men were experienced soldiers, having fought in the Revolutionary War and under Wayne at Fallen Timbers. Such was their friendship that they co-led the Voyage, in defiance of military hierarchy, from first to last in complete harmony.

By July 1803 Lewis and Clark were ready to leave the East. They travelled overland to Pittsburgh, descending

the Ohio by keelboat, and then ascending the Mississippi
to St Louis, which was to be their jumping-off point into
the unknown. At winter camp by the banks of the river
they drilled the recruits to their "Corps of Discovery" in
the techniques of frontiering.

On 14 May 1804, Lewis and Clark began their historic
ascent of the Missouri. With them went 27 unmarried
members of the Corps. Two non-military personnel were
also in the party: George Drouillard, a half French-Cana-
dian interpreter, and York, an African-American slave
Clark had inherited from his father. Within a few days the
party, travelling in an iron keelboat and two pirogues,
had left all signs of civilization behind them, and the "Big
Muddy" had begun to reveal its watery dangers. Only ten
days into the journey, Clark recorded in the expedition's
red-morocco bound journals:

Set out early. passed a verry bad part of the River Called
the Deavels race ground, this is where the Current Sets
against some projecting rocks for half a Mile . . . The
Swiftness of the Current Wheeled the boat, Broke our Toe
rope, and was nearly over Setting the boat.

As they struggled upriver, they endured other problems of nature. Members of the party were frequently ill.
On 6 June Clark wrote: "I am Still verry unwell with a Sore
throat & head ache." Fifteen days later, he noted: "The
party is much afflicted with Boils, and Several have the
Deasentary, which I attribute to the water." There were
difficulties with discipline as well:

Camp New Island, July 12th. 1804

The Commanding officers, Capts. M. Lewis & W. Clark
constituted themselves a Court Martial for the trial of such

prisoners as are Guilty of Capital Crimes, and under the rules and articles of War punishable by DEATH.

Alexander Willard was brought forward Charged with "Lying down and Sleeping on his post" whilst a Sentinel, on the Night of the 11th. Instant" (by John Ordway Sergeant of the Guard).

To this charge the prisoner pleads Guilty of Lying Down, and Not Guilty, of Going to Sleep.

The Court after Duly Considering the evidence aduced, are of the opinion that the Prisoner Alexdr. Willard is guilty of every part of the Charge exhibited against him. it being a breach of the rules and articles of War (as well as tending to the probable distruction of the party) do Sentience him to receive One hundred lashes, on his bear back, at four different times in equal proportion, and Order that the punishment Commence this evening at Sunset, and Continue to be inflicted (by the Guard) every evening until Completed.

WM. CLARK
M. LEWIS

Such an object lesson was not lost on the rest of the party. There were few other breaches of discipline.

Slowly the party inched northward, Clark generally supervising the navigation, while Lewis hunted the riverbanks, making notes and collecting specimens. The men were constantly in wonderment at the beauty of the pristine Western landscape and the profusion of animals: "the whole face of the country," Lewis wrote on one occasion, "was so covered with herds of Buffaloe, Elk and Antelope . . . [they] are so Gentel that we near them while feeding . . ."

At the end of July the explorers passed the mouth of the Platte. On 3 August at Council Bluffs they held their first

parley with Indians, members of the Oto, Missouri and
Omaha tribes. In a scene which would be repeated many
times in the months to come, Lewis and Clark urged the
Indians to live in peace with the White man and gave
them medals bearing the likeness of Jefferson, the Great
Father who lived in Washington. Lewis also fired off a
few exhibition shots from an air-gun ("which astonished
those natives") he had brought along.

The Teton Sioux encountered at Bad River were considerably less tractable. On 25 September three Teton chiefs
were invited for a council aboard the keelboat. After much
drinking of whiskey, Clark escorted them to the bank,
whereupon he was suddenly surrounded by warriors
with bows drawn. "I felt My Self Compeled", Clark recorded later, "to Draw my Sword." He also signalled to
the men in the boat to raise their guns. There were several
minutes of stand-off, before one of the chiefs ordered the
warriors away.

The chill blasts of autumn found the expedition at the
Mandan villages in North Dakota, where they built a log
fort and went into winter quarters. During the long icy
months at "Fort Mandan", Lewis and Clark made copious
notes and maps, supervised the building of dug-out canoes, and held counsel with numerous Indian visitors,
from whom they learned much about the territory before
them. The Mandan Indians made life tolerable for the
party by regal hospitality, which included beaver tail, a
considerable delicacy. The Mandan were amused by the
White men's dancing, especially that of a Frenchman who
could spin on his head.

Not until the end of March 1805 did the ice on the
Missouri break up sufficiently for the explorers to recom-
mence travel. After watching the spectacle of Indians
killing buffalo floating past on ice floes, the Voyagers
moved out from the villages. The keelboat was sent back

to St Louis with expedition records and specimens. The remaining party – those most "zealously attached to the enterprise", according to Lewis – headed upriver to the Great Unknown. With them went three new recruits, a fur trapper named Toussaint Charbonneau, his Lemhi Shoshoni squaw, Sacajawea, and their baby. Sacajawea had been captured as a child by Hidatsa Indians, and knew the way back to the Rocky Mountains, where the Shoshonis lived.

A week later they reached the furthest point known to White traders, the mouth of the Yellowstone. The party pushed on, their light canoes skimming through the shallows. At the mouth of the Marias (named by Lewis in honour of a lover) they made a mistaken detour, before continuing their progress up the Missouri. The hills grew steeper, and on 13 June the expedition reached the Great Falls of the Missouri. To get around them required a back-breaking 25-day portage through rattlesnake-plagued land. By the time they were waterborne again they had reached the foothills of the Rockies. To make progress the canoes had to be dragged through the icy water. Lewis and Clark became anxious to find the Shoshoni, from whom they hoped to secure horses for the passage over the Rockies. At Three Forks they took the northernmost stream, the Jefferson, which Sacajawea informed them led to the Shoshoni villages. For days the party toiled on, but failed to spot a single Indian. Anxious that the Shoshoni might be scared off by the size of the expedition, Lewis went on ahead with a small advance party, following the Indian trail through the Beaverhead Range and crossing the Continental Divide at Lemhi Pass. Soon after, they captured two Shoshoni squaws who agreed to lead them to their village near the headwaters of the Salmon. As Lewis neared the camp, a band of 60 warriors rushed to intercept him. Their hostility abated when they saw that the women were unharmed:

. . . these men then advanced and embraced me very affectionately in their way which is by putting their left arm over you[r] wright sholder clasping your back, while they apply their left cheek to yourws and frequently vociferate the word *ah-hi-e*, *ah-hi-e* that is, I am much pleased, I am much rejoiced. bothe parties now advanced and wer all carresed and besmeared with their grease and paint till I was heartily tired of the national hug. I now had the pipe lit and gave them smoke; they seated themselves in a circle around us and pulled of[f] their mockersons before they would receive or smoke the pipe . . . after smoking a few pipes with them I distributed some trifles among them, with which they seemed much pleased particularly with the blue beads and vermillion.

After several days in the Shoshoni camp, Lewis asked the Indians to accompany him back to the main party of the explorers, who were still at the Jefferson. The Shoshoni became suspicious, and suggested that Lewis was in league with the Minataree and wanted to lead them into an ambush. Only after much haranguing from their chief, Cameahwait, would the Shoshoni warriors go with Lewis to the Jefferson. There, Shoshoni edginess turned to joy. Sacajawea was Cameahwait's long-lost sister.

Furnished with Shoshoni horses, the expedition began its arduous traverse of the Rockies, heading north over Lost Trail Pass, and then down Bitterroot Valley. At the mouth of Lolo Creek in Montana, they went west, struggling through the snow flurries and soaking rain. "I have been wet and cold in every part as I ever was in my life," wrote Lewis. After ten days of misery, they emerged into the open valley of the Clearwater River, where they gave their horses over to the Nez Perce Indians. Pausing only to build new dug-out canoes, the party took to the water on 7 October. For three days they ran rapids, before plunging into the Snake, and more whitewater. By now the explorers were exhausted and malnourished, Clark noting in the journal on 10 October: "Our diet . . . bad haveing nothing but roots and dried fish to eate, all the Party have greatly the advantage of me . . . as they all relish the flesh of the dogs." Soon after they emerged into the Columbia, the great river of the Far West, which poured them into the Pacific Ocean on 15 November 1805. "Men appear much Satisfied with their trip beholding with estonishment . . . this emence Ocian," wrote Clark in the journal.

Hastening Home

The Corps of Discovery wintered on the south bank of the Columbia, building a post which they named after the nearest Indian tribe, Fort Clatsop. After months made disagreeable by constant rain, pilfering Indians and a scarcity of game, on 23 March 1806 the explorers started for home. They retraced their route to the mouth of the Lolo Creek where, on 3 July, the party split. Clark, heading one group, explored the Yellowstone River and followed it to its confluence with the Missouri. Lewis, with nine men, went directly across country to the Falls of the Missouri. Before descending the Missouri he explored up the Marias as far as Cut Bank Creek in northern Montana. And there, on 27 July, the expedition's long good luck with the Indians finally ran out. A meeting with eight Piegan (Algonquian-speaking Blackfoot) turned quickly and confusingly sour. The Indians tried to steal the White men's guns, and in the ensuing argument a brave was stabbed. At this, the Piegans tried to make off with Lewis's horse. Lewis ran after them:

I called to them [Indians] as I had done several times before that i would shoot them if they did not give me my horse and raised my gun, one of them jumped behind a rock and spoke to the other who turned arround and stoped at the distance of 30 steps from me and I shot him through the belly, he fell to his knees and on his wright elbow from which position he partly raised himself up and fired at me, and turning himself about crawled in behind a rock which was a few feet from him. he overshot me, being bearheaded I felt the wind of the bullet very distinctly.

Fearful of Piegan revenge, the explorers immediately started east, riding their horses hard for a hundred miles before they dared rest. But the bodies behind them would not be forgotten. Henceforth the Blackfoot would always have a hatred for the White man.

Near the junction of the Yellowstone and the Missouri the two parties reunited and hastened for home. They reached the earth-lodges of the Mandan on 15 August, where they stopped long enough only to bid goodbye to one of the party, John Coulter, who wanted to go trapping, and to persuade the local Chief, Shaka, to return with them to the United States.

The small band of explorers was back in St Louis on 23 September 1806. They had been given up for dead by everyone except Jefferson.

Lewis and Clark had been gone for two years, four months and ten days. They were the first White men to cross the continent within the limits of the present-day USA. On that entire journey only one man, Sergeant Charles Floyd, had lost his life, and that probably due to a ruptured appendix (untreatable in those years, even in an Eastern hospital). Even Lewis's black Newfoundland dog, Seaman, made it home alive. While they did not find a Northwest Passage – for none existed – they did discover several routes through the Rockies, established friendly relations with half a dozen tribes, and vastly increased the knowledge of the West's topography, flora and fauna. The Voyage was a giant leap in the opening up of the trans-Mississippi West.

Spain provided a curious footnote. Between August 1804 and August 1806 no fewer than four Spanish expeditions were sent out to stop Lewis and Clark. All were forced to turn around, either by hostile Indians or through desertions in their own ranks. The last penetrated as far north as Nebraska, coming within 150 miles of the Americans without either party knowing it.

Pike's Progress,
Long's Labour

Seeking the Father of all Waters

Such was Jefferson's zeal for Western exploration that he
sent out other explorers into Louisiana even as Lewis and
Clark still trudged towards the setting sun. For Jefferson
the destiny of the United States lay beyond the Mississippi, in an easy portage to the Pacific, in prime earth for
farmers. Congress was less certain, and had to be tugged
and prodded into voting more funds for the President's
preoccupation. Two arduous expeditions up the Red River,
in 1804 and 1806, were halted by the Spanish, who resented US activity so close to their Texas border.

Frustrated by the Spanish in the South, Jefferson
decided to unleash his exploratory enthusiasm elsewhere, in the discovering of the source of the Mississippi.
This task was entrusted to a 26-year-old whose name
would become synonymous with the conquest of the West,
Lieutenant Zebulon Montgomery Pike. Born in Lamberton,
New Jersey, Pike had been a soldier since the age of 15,
and had served under General Wayne in the Old Northwest. His formal learning was meagre but his appetite for
learning was prodigious, and he had taught himself Span-

ish and French. Above all he desired to be famous. His chance came with the presidential order to reconnaissance the headwaters of the 'Father of all Waters'.

With a party of 20 soldiers to accompany him, Pike set off upriver from St Louis in a 70-foot keelboat on 9 August 1805. By September he had reached Minnesota, where he stopped to parley with the Sioux. Abandoning the keelboat at Prairie du Chien, the expedition continued in smaller craft. Although winter was pressing, Pike journeyed on until he reached Little Falls, where he built an encampment for some of the men. After the snow fell, he set out with a dog sled and the remainder of the men into the lake-dotted forests of Minnesota to find the Mississippi's source. The party was only saved from a frozen grave by a string of trading posts of the North West Company, all manned by Canadians flying the Union Jack. If the Canadians expected thanks for their rescue of Pike, they were to be disappointed. An undisclosed part of Pike's mission was to show the Indians and British in the area who was sovereign. Accordingly, Pike ordered his hosts to pay American duties and haul up the Stars and Stripes. When one commander refused, Pike ordered his men to shoot down the British flag.

Soon after this episode Pike stumbled upon Lake Leech, wrongly assuming its drainage system to be the true source of the river.

In the spring of 1806, Pike and his soldiers floated back down the Mississippi. By the last day of April they were in St Louis. The expedition had been only a moderate success. The Senate refused to ratify the treaty he had negotiated with the Sioux, and he was mistaken in the source of the Mississippi (which is Lake Itasca, on a branch of the river Pike did not take). He did, however, produce the first accurate cartographical knowledge of the Upper Mississippi.

No sooner had Pike written his report than he was dispatched as the escort to a party of Osage Indians who were returning to their home in the Southwest, after being freed by the US military from their captivity in the hands of the Pottawattamie tribe. Ascending the Osage River as far as it was navigable, Pike's expedition traded their barges for horses, and took off across country to the Pawnee villages on the Republican River. The Pawnee were hostile, having just been goaded into an anti-American fervour by a detachment of Spanish military sent out to stop the Americans in this region of debatable ownership. An angry Pike told the Pawnee that "the warriors of his Great American father were not women to be turned back by words." Impressed by Pike's determination, the Pawnee duly hoisted the American flag.

From the Pawnee villages, Pike headed south across the Great Plains to the Arkansas River, then along that stream towards the Rockies. To Pike the plains seemed a treeless wasteland, an opinion which would be instrumental in establishing the myth of the Great American Desert. By late November Pike's company was in mountainous Colorado. On Thanksgiving Day, he and three companions made an attempt in zero temperatures to scale the 14,147 ft peak that would ultimately bear his name.

Winter closed in, the winds cutting through the men's light cotton summer uniforms, for they had not expected cold weather in the Southwest. In Wet Mountain Valley the party holed up in improvised shelters. Nine men became crippled with frostbite and food stocks ran dangerously low. At the bleakest moment, Pike and party member Dr Robinson went hunting – and killed a lone buffalo.

Even before the snow had left the high country in the spring of 1807, Pike was on the move, crossing the Sangre de Cristo Mountains and down into the Rio Grande, which he believed to be the Red River. On the Conejus, a western affluent of the Rio Grande, he hurriedly built a fort. Shortly afterwards he was taken into custody by a Spanish patrol for trespass. After being conducted to Santa Fe, the Americans were then taken under guard to Chihuahua for questioning. Eventually, they were escorted to Natchitoches and deposited on the US side of the border.

It is certain that Pike was genuinely lost when he built the rude stockade on the Conejus. But it is equally certain that he wanted to be captured by the Spanish so that he could spy on Santa Fe, a town Americans had been banned from. Although Pike's maps and notes were confiscated by the Spanish, he remembered enough to write a report which did much to expand his countrymen's understanding of the Southwest.

The Great American Desert

For a decade after Pike's expedition to the Southwest, federal-sponsored exploration all but ceased. Government was too involved in disputes with America's old enemies, 'Perfidious Albion' and the Indians, which culminated in the War of 1812. While the US prevailed over the Creeks at Horseshoe Bend and the Shawnee of the Tecumseh at Thames River, the campaign against the British dragged on inconclusively. (It also claimed the life of Brigadier-General Zebulon Pike.) The Treaty of Ghent, signed on Christmas Eve 1814, was an admission of stalemate and surrender by both sides.

It was not until the 1820s that the nation felt revived enough to send out another official expedition into the West, a final effort to find the source of the Red River. On 6 June 1820, an engineer by the name of Major Stephen Harriman Long led a party of 19 soldiers (and two offi-

cially appointed artists, Samuel Seymour and Titian
Ramsay Peale) out of Fort Atkinson and up the Platte.
Under the shadows of the Rockies one of Long's party
succeeded in climbing Pike's Peak, before they headed
south to the Arkansas. There the expedition split, with
one party descending the Arkanksas, the other under
Long continuing the hunt for the Red River. Having crossed
the Purgatory and Cimarron Rivers, Long emerged at a
broad stream which he decided was the elusive Red River,
and turned the party eastward along its banks. To his
disgust, Long found that the watery course was the Canadian and only returned him to the Arkansas. By mid-
September, both parts of Long's expedition were back at
Fort Smith on the Arkansas, their numbers reduced by
disease and desertion.

The only result of Long's expedition was negative. Like
Pike before him, Long viewed the treeless plain between
the Mississippi and the Rocky Mountains unfavourably.
"I do not hesitate," wrote Long, "in giving the opinion
that it is almost wholly unfit for cultivation, and of course
uninhabitable by a people depending on agriculture for
their subsistence." The map of the expedition drawn up
by Dr Edwin James accordingly labelled the area east of
the Rockies the "Great American Desert". A psychologi-
cal barrier was set up which would retard White settlement of the plains for generations. Not until the 1860s
would the myth of the Great American Desert be exploded.

With the exception of Lewis and Clark's Voyage of
Discovery, the years of governmentally funded Western
exploration had accomplished little. Most of the far West
remained the Great Unknown.

Those who would do most to reveal its secrets would
do so unofficially, in the spirit of private enterprise, not
public duty. In their days of glory, between 1807 and 1830,

the mountain men or fur trappers would swarm all over trans-Mississippi America. They would leave hardly a stone unturned, a blade of buffalo grass untrodden.

Of Mountain Men and Furs

Castor Canadensis

Of the many animals which drew trappers into the wilderness, the most prized was an industrious, small-eyed rodent by the name of *Castor canadensis*. The beaver's lustrous fur was used for the coats and muffs of fashionable women, but it was the tendency of the animal's underfur to mat or "felt" which made it particularly valuable. Shaved from the animal's skin, vibrated by the hatter's bow (which caused the hairs to hook together), boiled, beaten and moulded, the underfur made suitable headwear for every gentleman in America and Europe. Such was the demand for beaver felt hats – whether in stovepipe, bicorn, tricorn or Paris beau styles – in the early nineteenth century that up to 100,000 beaver pelts were bought by the hattery industry each year.

The trade in beaver resulted in an animal slaughter of epic proportions. It caused wars between rival firms, and even between nations. And along the way it opened up the West, and produced some of its most remarkable frontiersmen.

The French were the first to exploit the peltry of the New World. As early as 1535 Jacques Cartier, on his first expedition to Canada, obtained some furs from the Indians in the St Lawrence region. With the founding of Quebec and Montreal, the French pursued the fur business with a vigour that led bands of her traders (*coureur de bois*) deep into the wilderness. In return for beads and blankets and metal tools, firearms and whiskey, Indians were persuaded to gather huge quantities of precious pelts. When enough furs had been obtained, they were tied into 90-pound bales which were ferried back to the settlements in the birchbark canoe of a *voyageur*. On the frequent and long portages, the *voyageur* carried the bale in slings on his back. A good *voyageur* could make 2,000 miles in a fortnight.

The French were not the only ones to find the furs of the New World lucrative. The British chartered the Hudson's Bay Company in 1670, in the hope that its profits could be diverted to the Treasury. After Britain's victory over France in 1763, she emerged with a monopoly of the trade in North America. A new British company, the North West, spread trading posts as far west as Vincennes, Kaskaskia and Kahoka. To the north lay the trading grounds of the Hudson's Bay Company. Increasingly the two fur companies clashed. Murder, arson, bribery and theft became common. Each side employed whiskey-plied Indian tribes to protect its domain. Eventually, the London government could ignore the bloody activities of the companies no more. In 1821 it forcibly merged them into an enlarged Hudson's Bay Company.

But by then another power had risen in the continental fur trade. America determined to enter the skin business in the years after the Revolution, her traders wilfully ignoring the regulation which forbade them to exchange liquor for pelts. Trade boomed. The demand for beaver was insatiable. American trappers ventured further and further into the interior in pursuit of the persecuted, disappearing beaver. Their interest in the West was only stimulated by the information brought back by the Lewis and Clark expedition: of lands which teemed with beaver, and a waterway in the Missouri which could take them right to their heart. Throughout the winter of 1806–7 fur traders poured into St Louis, ready to start upriver as soon as the ice broke. The most important of them was the Mexican entrepreneur Manuel Lisa. In the spring of 1807 Lisa worked his way west as far as the confluence of the Yellowstone and Bighorn rivers, where he built a fortified trading post, Fort Manuel. From here Lisa sent out his beaver-trappers, among them John Coulter, the Virginian who had served with Lewis and Clark's Corps of Discovery. In a long solitary hunt through 1807–8, Coulter became the first White man to gaze upon the wonders of what is now the Yellowstone National Park, the steaming geysers of Wyoming ("Coulter's Hell").

He was also captured by Blackfeet. Coulter escaped death only by uncanny grit. Stripped naked, he was told to run for his life while a band of braves chased him. He dashed for the river six miles away, with stones and cactus tearing his feet. When one brave gained on him, Coulter stopped abruptly and spread out his arms. The Indian tumbled – and Coulter killed him with his own spear. Finally, Coulter fell into the stream and hid under a mass of wood for hours. Under the cover of darkness he stole back to Fort Manuel. It took seven days of hard marching, with only roots and berries for food. A year later, having survived another encounter with the Blackfeet, John Coulter retired from the West saying he would "be damned if I ever come into it again." He died of jaundice in St Louis in 1813.

Even without the redoubtable John Coulter in his employ, Manuel Lisa and his Missouri Fur Company continued to make money out of furs. His partners included the explorer William Clark and two of the famous St Louis fur-trading Chouteau family, Auguste and Philippe. A ruthless and sharp competitor, Lisa knew his business well enough to cultivate good relations with the tribes of the upper Missouri. So prevailing did his influence become that he personally secured their allegiance to the United States during the War of 1812. But the company needed his firm personal hand at the helm. When Lisa died in 1820, the Missouri Fur Company sank into financial oblivion. Many other fur firms boomed (and bust) in the West, but only two others left a real mark behind them: the Rocky Mountain Fur Company, and the American Fur Company of John Astor.

The Astorians

A squat New York merchant of German birth, John Jacob Astor made his first fortune exporting furs to China. His next, he decided, would be by monopolizing the fur trade of Louisiana. To this grandiose end, Astor planned a chain of trading posts across the far West from the Great Lakes to the Pacific Ocean. With the encouragement of Thomas Jefferson, Astor founded the American Fur Company in 1808; in 1810 he created a subsidiary, the Pacific Fur Company, which was to have its headquarters at the mouth of the Columbia. Astor named the post after himself, Astoria. There only remained the matter of building it.

Astor sent out two expeditions to the Pacific, an overland party under Wilson Price Hunt and a maritime force in the sailing vessel, the *Tonquin*. Neither group fared well. The *Tonquin* was ruled by a petty tyrant, Jonathan Thorne, and barely escaped a mutiny en route. When the ship reached the Columbia, its leaking longboat foundered in heavy seas with the loss of eight lives. Only with luck did the *Tonquin* itself find a safe harbour, on 12

April 1811, and the workers staggered ashore to build
Astoria.

While the fort was being built, the *Tonquin* sailed north
along the coast to trade with the Indians and collect furs.
At Nootka Sound, on Vancouver Island, Captain Thorne
slapped an Indian chief in the face. The Indians' revenge
was to seize the ship and slaughter her crew. One sailor
survived by hiding, but when the Indians came back next
day for another round of looting, he fired the ship's magazine, blowing them and himself to pieces.

The "Overland Astorians", meanwhile, had set out from
St Louis along the route pioneered by Lewis and Clark.
But fearful of encountering the Blackfeet, they took numerous detours. When they reached the Snake they ignored the advice of the Indians and exchanged their horses
for canoes. After two days the Snake became unnavigable.
Four men drowned when their canoes capsized, and almost all the party's provisions and equipment were lost.
The Overland Astorians then separated into small groups
to make the best way they could to the fort on the Columbia. Intense cold and deep snow hindered progress through
the Cascades. Several men died of exposure; one went
mad. Not until January 1812 did the first survivors stagger into Astoria. Hunt's own group appeared in February;
the final group did not make it until May. A number had
been stripped naked by contemptuous Indians.

It was all in vain. In June 1812, Britain and the United
States went to war. Anticipating an attack from a British
warship, the Astorians had little choice but to accept an
offer for their holdings (at a fraction of their worth) from
the North West Company.

This inglorious saga did not prevent Astor from becoming one of the richest men in America. In 1822 he
established the Western Division of his American Fur
Company, which gobbled up competitors. At first "The

Company", as it became known, confined itself to the Missouri and its tributary streams, but then in 1831 turned towards the Wyoming beaver fields on the Green and Wind rivers. Here "The Company" fought a battle with its principal rival, the Rocky Mountain Fur Company, almost to the extinction of the beaver east of the Rockies.

The Rocky Mountain Fur Company

Founded in 1822 by two St Louis fur merchants, General H. Ashley and Andrew Henry, the Rocky Mountain Fur Company employed some of the far West's most famous trappers: the unlettered but supremely intelligent Jim "Old Gabe" Bridger, probably the first White man to see the Great Salt Lake; the Black trapper James P. Beckwourth and the half-Black half-Cherokee Edward Rose, an ex-river pirate; the Sublette brothers, William, Milton and Andrew, who all fought in the 1832 Battle of Pierre's Hole, when a group of mountain men were besieged by Gros Ventre Indians; and, most famous of all, Jedediah Strong Smith, the pious New Hampshire Methodist who was the first White man to travel overland from the Rocky Mountains to California, and the first White man to cross the Great Salt Lake Desert. The extraordinary Bible-toting Smith also held the probable record for beaver caught in a single season (668 pelts).

There was more to the Rocky Mountain Fur Company than the luminosity of its contract roll. Ashley and Henry revolutionized the skin trade. Instead of creating permanent posts, the Rocky Mountain Company organized annual rendezvous at predesignated spots, at which furs were collected and provisions doled out, and a Bacchanalia was had by all. Their innovation was born out of painful experience. In 1822, Ashley and Henry had organized a trading expedition to build a fort and trading post at the

mouth of the Yellowstone. Arikara Indians had molested
the boats, and Blackfeet the hunting parties. The next year
the Arikara had attacked again, and Ashley decided on a
new method of tapping the beaver country. Instead of
building trading posts – which the Indians hated as a
symbol of White occupation – he would send his trappers
overland singly or in small groups, and meet them at a
rendezvous at the end of the spring hunt.

The Life of a Mountain Man

Ashley and Henry were thus the first merchants to rely on
the free trapper or Mountain Man who, instead of trading
with Indians for pelts and receiving a fixed salary, set his
own traps, lived off the land, and could sell his furs to the
highest bidder.

George Frederick Ruxton, the chronicler of the far West,
recorded his impressions of these free men in his *Adventures in Mexico and the Rocky Mountains* (1849). The equipment of the trapper comprised, as the necessary minimum:

> ... two or three horses or mules – one for saddle, the
> others for packs – and six traps, which are carried in a bag
> of leather called a trap-sack. Ammunition, a few pounds
> of tobacco, dressed deer-skins for mocassins &c. are carried in a wallet of dressed buffalo-skin, called a possible-
> sack. [His dress consisted of] a hunting-shirt of dressed
> buckskin, ornamented with long fringes; pantaloons of
> the same material, and decorated with porcupine-quills
> and long fringes down the outside of the leg. A flexible felt
> hat and mocassins clothe his extremities. Over his left
> shoulder and under his right arm hang his powder-horn
> and bullet pouch, in which he carries his balls, flint and
> steel, and odds and ends of all kinds. Round the waist is a
> belt, in which is stuck a large butcher-knife in a sheath of

buffalo-hide, made fast to the belt by a chain or guard of steel; which also supports a little buckskin case containing a whetstone. A tomahawk is also often added, a long heavy rifle is part and parcel of his equipment.

Almost half of the American trappers bought an Indian wife to help them in their work (and ease the loneliness of the wild), paying as much as $2,000-worth of furs for a chief's daughter. Only the entrepreneurial mountain man could afford such a price; the "hired hand" or engaged trapper, who was attached to a company, had to find someone altogether cheaper. African-American trappers were readier than Whites to marry Indian women and maintain close relationships with the tribes. The eminent Bongas, slaves of the British commandant at Fort Michilimackinac before they became fur traders, inter-married with the Chippewa. Jim Beckwourth, born in 1798 of Black–White parentage, was adopted by the Crow and rose to tribal chieftainship. Called "Morning Star", he led them in many raids against their long-time adversary, the Blackfeet. "My faithful battle-axe was red with the blood of the enemy," he proudly remarked. The Crow agreed, and changed his name again, to "Bloody Arm". Having survived numerous wilderness adventures, Beckwourth died of food poisoning in 1866.

While the trapper set his $14 metal beaver traps in the water of nearby streams (to which the attractant was judiciously placed drops of oil from beaver castoreum glands) and collected the previous day's catch, the Indian wife prepared skins and cooked food. Roast or stewed buffalo was the trapper's delight, but his basic foodstuff was the pemmican prepared by his squaw, a mixture of buffalo meat, fat and berries which was pounded into cakes.

In 1830 Astor scored a major coup in the fur trade war

by reaching a deal with hostile Blackfeet by which they opened their pristine beaver country to him. Four years later, the Rocky Mountain Fur Company accepted the inevitable and sold out to Astor, who then astutely sold his shares in the American Fur Company and retired to enjoy his $20 million profit. As Astor had noticed, silk had begun to replace beaver on the fashionable heads of Europe and America. The price of beaver pelts dropped by 500 per cent in the 1830s. The trade was largely ended by 1840, when the American Fur Company announced it would not organize another rendezvous.

Probably the last great rendezvous was in June 1837, at Wyoming's Green River, which was attended by a motley crowd of fur company agents, over 1,500 Shoshoni, and more than a hundred trappers. Jim Bridger was there; so too were the independents, Joe Meek and Christopher Houston "Kit" Carson, who worked the Southern Rockies. Recording the scene was the Baltimore artist Alfred Jacob Miller, who penned a vivid eye-witness sketch of the major social date in the "Mountain Man" calendar:

At certain specified times . . . the American Fur Company appoint a "Rendezvous" . . . for . . . trading with Indian and Trappers, and here they congregate from all quarters. The first day is devoted to "High Jinks", in which feasting, drinking, and gambling form prominent parts. Sometimes an Indian becomes so excited with "Fire Water" that he commences "running a muck" – he is pursued . . . and secured . . . "Affairs of honour" are adjusted between rival Trappers – one . . . of course, receiving a complete drubbing; – all caused evidently from mixing too much Alcohol with water. Night closes this scene of revelry and confusion. The following days exhibit the strongest contrast . . . The Company's great tent is raised; the Indians erect their picturesque white lodges; – the accumulated

furs ... are brought forth, and the Company's tent is a
besieged and busy place. Now the women come in for
their share of ornaments and finery. (Alfred Jacob Miller,
The West of Alfred Jacob Miller)

With the decline of the beaver trade, most trappers
took up other occupations. Tom "Broken Hand" Fitzpatrick
and Kit Carson became wilderness scouts, both helping
the flamboyant government explorer John Charles Frémont
on his much fanfared journey through the far West in the
1840s. Jim Bridger scouted for the army, and would appear numerous times in the future history of the frontier.
Caleb Greenwood led the first wagon train through the
Sierras, at the age of 81. A number of beaver trappers
turned to hunting another fur-bearer doomed to wholesale butchery, the buffalo. Some trappers retired east, but
found their Indian wives aroused loathing.

Few mountain men, when they looked in their buckskin pouches, had made any money; the profits in the fur
trade were made by the John Jacob Astors, not the trappers. But no one had done more to open up the West.

Only one other group of men made even a comparable
contribution. These were the traders who blazed the trail
to Santa Fe and the Spanish-speaking Southwest. For years
American traders had tried to reach the thriving New
Mexico town of Santa Fe, but had been turned back – even
imprisoned – by isolationist Spanish officials. In 1820,
however, the Mexicans threw off Spanish rule and became eager for commercial contact with the US. The first
to benefit from this changed situation was a Missouri
Indian trader called William Becknell. In September 1821,
as Becknell laboured his way along the Arkansas River
towards the Rockies, he encountered in the rugged Raton
Pass a party of Mexican soldiers, who told him that he
would be welcome in Santa Fe. Hardly able to believe his

luck, Becknell hastened to the New Mexican capital, where the commodity-lacking citizenry gave him a warm – and profitable – welcome. Becknell, "The Father of the Santa Fe Trade," returned to Franklin, Missouri, his saddlebags heavy with silver.

The following spring, Becknell led another expedition to Santa Fe, this time with three heavily loaded wagons. To avoid the precipitous Raton Pass, Becknell pioneered a short cut through the searing Cimarron Desert, once becoming so low on water that he and his men were reduced to drinking the stomach contents of a buffalo they had shot. They were also dogged by Indian attacks. Yet they made it to Santa Fe, and their route would become the famed Santa Fe Trail.

By 1824 the Santa Fe trade was thoroughly established. That spring, for their better protection, traders travelled together in a mighty, lumbering caravan of 25 wagons. They took goods worth $35,000; they returned with $190,000 in gold, silver and furs.

The style of the Santa Fe trade was thus set. A decade later, up to a hundred caravans undertook the gruelling but lucrative annual journey to New Mexico, typically returning with profits of between 10 and 40 per cent.

The Santa Fe trade had notable spin-offs. It encouraged other entrepreneurs, such as brothers Charles and William Bent and their partner Ceran St Vrain, to begin trade with the Indians of New Mexico and its borders. In 1832, the Bents and St Vrain built a massive adobe trading post, with walls 14 feet high and four feet thick, on the upper Arkansas River. The Bents married into prominent Cheyenne families and this, plus the partners' industry and rare financial honesty, ensured that Bent's Fort dominated the commerce of the Colorado region for nearly 15 years.

The other consequence of the Santa Fe trade was more

notable, if less tangible. The Mexicans proved incapable
of enforcing their tariffs and their laws on the American
traders. Along its northern borders, Mexico was weak, its
land there for the taking.

"And Remember the Alamo"

No Land More Lovely

There were Americans in Texas from about 1803, intruders who settled around Nacogdoches, one of the fortified
outposts on the northern frontier of New Spain, which
spanned a 2,000-mile arc from Texas to California. These
Anglos were barely tolerated, but then in 1821 Mexico
won her independence from Spain, and the new republic
decided to swing open the doors of its Texas province to
American immigrants, mostly to strengthen the local population base against Indian attacks.

A sheet-lead manufacturer by the name of Moses Austin was among the first to consider settlement. Born in
1761 in Connecticut, Austin had drifted into Missouri
when it was still part of Spanish Louisiana, and begun
business. After a severe financial reverse, Austin decided
to move on to Texas, petitioning the governor to allow
him to build a colony there. His petition was granted,
mostly because he was a Spanish citizen by virtue of his
residency in Missouri.

Exhausted by the journey to Texas, Moses Austin fell ill
and died of pneumonia. His last request would be the
inheritance and destiny of his eldest son, Stephen Fuller
Austin, whom he asked "to go on with the business in the

same way." Although hardly in the classic mould of pioneer leader, the diminutive 27-year-old journalist and banker left at once for the far frontier.

Stephen Austin began his mission by exploring the central regions of Texas, eventually hitting on the deep, alluvial land between the Brazos and the Colorado rivers for the site of the American colony. Settlers proved easy to recruit; the hard times following the financial Great Panic of 1819 made many US citizens eager for free Texan land. Austin was able to pick and choose the founding members of his father's colony.

As with many new settlements, the colony suffered initial hunger and hardship, also drought and Indian attacks. Much the worst setback, though, was when Austin was informed by the Mexican government that the settlement needed the authorization of the republic's Congress. The almost destitute Austin was obliged to travel to Mexico City and plead his case. It took nearly a year to be heard, but his diplomacy eventually gained him the land grant he wanted. Under the terms of the Congressional approval, each family in the colony was allowed one *labor* (177 acres) of land for farming and 74 *labors* for stockraising. Austin was allowed to collect 12½ cents an acre for his services, and was promised a bonus of 65,000 acres on the arrival of the 200th family. There were a number of other clauses in the contract. The settlers had to accept the Roman Catholic faith; they had to be of good moral character; and they were allowed to bring in slaves, but not to buy or sell them within the state.

While Austin was absent in Mexico City, the colony was welcoming a steady trickle of newcomers. A town, St Felipe de Austin, began to take shape on the lower crossing of the Brazos. "It does not appear possible," one "Texian" pioneer wrote home, "that there can be a land more lovely." By 1823 the original 300 families (known to

Texas history as the Old 300) had arrived, and Austin was permitted to recruit another 500 .

The success of the Austin colony as a bulwark against both the tribes and unofficial American landgrabbers led the Mexican government to encourage further immigration. The 1824 National Colonization Law joined Texas to its neighbouring state of Coahuila (so ensuring a Spanish-speaking majority), while allowing land-contractors or empresarios in rivalry with Austin to settle another 2,400 families. The number of US-born Texans grew dramatically. In 1827 they numbered 10,000; three years later, 20,000.

Friction with the Mexican authorities also grew steadily. It was at its worst in the eastern part of the province, where hardscrabble farmers, squatters and fugitives from US justice were staking claims to land. Few had legal titles, fewer still were inclined to follow the laws of far-off Mexico City.

Official settlers also had complaints. Few, with free land before their eyes, had paused to muse on their loss of religious freedom, and the small say in their own affairs that a Mexican feudal system of government would allow.

For their part Mexicans found the newcomers ill-mannered and bent on taking Texas over. Their fear was only confirmed by the "Fredonia Revolt" of 1826, when an empresario named Haden Edwards tried to remove squatters from his land grant at Nacogdoches. The Mexican authorities upheld the rights of the squatters and expelled Edwards from the province. Angered at the "injustice" done to his brother, Benjamin Edwards led a small band of men into Nacogdoches, unfurled a flag, seized the old fort and proclaimed the birth of the Republic of Fredonia. Edwards called on Austin for help. The father of Texan colonization, however, called out his own militia and helped the Mexicans put the revolt down.

The Fredonia Revolt was a risible affair but, already fearful over the intentions of the Anglos, Mexico interpreted it as positive proof that America was determined to appropriate Texas. The noisy Anglo resentment over the 1819 Adams–Onis Treaty (the US–Mexico boundary settlement), and the offer of expansionist President Andrew Jackson to buy Texas for $10,000, provided additional evidence.

The Texan Revolution

Matters inched slowly but surely towards war. Mexican general Manuel de Miery y Teran, sent to report on the state of Texas in 1828, was appalled by the influence of the Anglo-Americans, and concluded: "Either the government occupies Texas now, or it is lost forever." Teran's gloomy prediction fitted well with the prejudices of the conservative, anti-American Centralist government which had just seized power in Mexico City. Customs duties were imposed, Mexican troops were garrisoned in Texas and a Colonization Law passed prohibiting American immigration. The result was the opposite of what its authors intended. The ban only kept out law-abiding Americans. Hot-headed squatters continued to cross the border, with the US population in the province leaping from 20,000 in 1830 to 30,000 in 1835. Among the illegals were frontiersmen Sam Houston and William B. Travis, both of whom would play major roles in days to come.

Then, in January 1835, Mexico installed a venal tax collector at the port of Anahuac. Anglo resentment grew into a local rebellion. The Centralist President Santa Anna led an army north to cow the Americans and put down risings by the Mexican opposition party, the Federalists. News of Santa Anna's march stirred those Texans intent on self-government to desperate action. On 29 June 1835, a band of 40 radicals under W. B. Travis marched on the garrison at Anahuac and obliged it to surrender.

Santa Anna's response was to order the arrest of Travis and his men, to reinforce the garrison at San Antonio, and threaten military rule in Texas. Even moderate Texans were outraged. Stephen Austin put his name to a proclamation which declared: "There is no other remedy but to defend our rights, ourselves, and our country by force of arms."

While Spanish reinforcements under General Cos marched to San Antonio, a Spanish cavalry detachment was sent meanwhile to the town of Gonzales to seize an aged brass six-pounder cannon loaned to the inhabitants to ward off Indians. The inhabitants, instead of handing the cannon over, hung a sign on it that read "Come and Take It!" Then, on 2 October, they fired a shot of scrap iron at the Mexicans, who retreated to San Antonio.

The Texan revolution had begun. The men of Gonzales, flushed with victory and with Stephen Austin at their head, assembled an "Army of the People" and marched on San Antonio, where they settled down for a lengthy siege of Cos's army. To oversee the war effort, the Texan settlers appointed a 12-man ruling council, with Sam Houston made commander-in-chief of the Texas forces. Houston, born in Virginia in 1793 but brought up in Tennessee as the adopted son of an Indian chief, had a lifetime's worth of experience under fire. His persistent gallantry during the war with England had seen him rise to the rank of lieutenant. After the war he had entered politics, becoming Governor of Tennessee. Difficulties with Indian agents he had accused of fraud had caused him to leave the United States for Texas.

As commander-in-chief Houston found himself constrained by Texas's cautious provisional government. His advertising campaign in US newspapers ("Let each man come with a good rifle, and come soon") brought a host of volunteers but the provisional government was loath even to let him have control over the settlers ringed around San Antonio.

Consequently, it was on the settlers' own initiative that they stormed the town on 5 December. After four days of close-quarters fighting, with the settlers moving from house to house, breaking through the adobe walls with crowbars and making a mad dash inside, Cos and 1,100 garrison surrendered.

Santa Anna determined to put an end to the Texan rebellion. Raising an army of 6,000 men and placing himself at its head, Santa Anna started for San Antonio. The town was nearly abandoned, with the exception of a skeleton force of 187 men holding the ancient mission station of San Antonio de Valero: the Alamo.

As Santa Anna neared, there was initially only confusion at the Alamo. The garrison demanded reinforcements, but Houston wanted them to abandon the station, so the Texan defence could be concentrated elsewhere. Then some of the men, objecting to the youth of the station commander, the studentish William Barrett Travis, staged a virtual mutiny. In democratic American fashion they were allowed to elect a leader. They chose the Tennessee Indian-fighter Jim Bowie, whose elder brother Rezin had invented the famed "Bowie Knife", a one-edged blade with a guarded hilt so perfectly balanced it could be thrown to killing purpose.

Jim Bowie was not a leader of men. He drank and cared nothing for discipline. When Bowie contracted pneumonia, Travis took over sole and unfettered command. For all their antagonism, Travis and Bowie were agreed that they would make a stand against the Mexicans when they arrived.

As a place to make a stand the Franciscan mission of the Alamo had drawbacks. Situated on three acres a little to the east of San Antonio, it had low scaleable outer walls, with no loopholes. Worst of all, there was a large 50-yard gap in its southeastern face which was secured only by a cedar-post stockade and an earth parapet. But the walled convent yard and the stone chapel, with its walls 22 feet high and 4 feet thick, offered good cover.

The first Mexicans arrived on 22 February 1836 along the Laredo road, the bells of the town clanging the alarm. The Mexican commander, Colonel Almonte, demanded the immediate surrender of the Texan post. As a reply, Travis shot a cannon ball at a group of waiting Mexican soldiers.

The siege operation that followed was conducted personally by Santa Anna, the self-styled "Napoleon of the West". He began by subjecting the post to a 24-hour artillery bombardment, which caused surprisingly few casualties inside the Alamo. During a lull afterwards, Travis drafted an appeal for help, which was sent out with a Mexican *vaquero* (cowboy) loyal to the Texan cause. The message read:

> Commandancy of the Alamo
> Bexar, Feby 24th 1836

Fellow citizens and compatriots,

I am besieged by a thousand or more of the Mexicans under Santa Anna – I have sustained a continual bombardment and cannonade for 24 hours and have not lost a man. The enemy has demanded a surrender at discretion, otherwise the garrison are to be put to the sword, if the fort is taken. I have answered the demand with a cannon shot, and our flag still waves proudly from the walls. I shall never surrender or retreat.

Then, I call on you in the name of liberty, of patriotism and everything dear to the American character to come to our aid, with all dispatch. The enemy is receiving reinforcements daily and will no doubt increase to three or four thousand in four or five days.

If this call is neglected, I am determined to sustain myself as long as possible and die like a soldier who never forgets what is due to his own honour or that of his country.

Victory or death.

WILLIAM BARRETT TRAVIS
Lt. Col. Comd.

P.S. The Lord is on our side. When the enemy appeared in sight we had not three bushels of corn. We have since found in deserted houses 80 or 90 bushels and got into the wall 20 or 30 head of beeves.

TRAVIS

The next day, the 25th, the Mexicans received reinforcements, and attempted to set up a battery south of the Alamo. This was prevented by accurate fire from the fort's ramparts, to the cheer of the men inside. But the respite was short-lived. On the 26th, two of Santa Anna's batteries were sheltered behind earthworks on the northeast side of the river. From then on they kept up a slow, resolute bombardment. Hardly an hour went past without a cannon ball falling on the fort, and men rushing out with picks and shovels to plug the breach. By now, also, Jim Bowie, fighting despite the grip of pneumonia, had fallen from scaffolding supporting a gun emplacement and broken his hip. He was placed in a cot in a building beside the south gate of the yard.

The lines of earthworks grew around the men of the

Alamo. Each dawn the sentries found new entrenchments, until it was ringed by an unbroken Mexican circle.

Despite the encirclement, on the night of 1 March, a small reinforcement of 32 men crept through the Mexican lines to join the defenders. They were from Gonzales, a settlement which numbered only 30 split-plank cabin homes. Their arrival crowned a good day for the defenders. Earlier, a lucky round from the 12-pounder on the roof of the chapel had struck Santa Anna's lodging in the town.

But already the end was in sight for the men of the Alamo. The enemy were simply too many. Understanding this, Travis rallied the men during the sunset of 3 March. According to a drifter named Louis Rose, who escaped the fort that evening, Travis paraded the men in single file and then stood before them, almost overcome with emotion. He declared that he was intent on staying and fighting it out to the end, but that every man must do what he thought best. Then Travis drew a line on the ground with his sword and said: "I now want every man who is determined to stay here and die with me to come across this line." Almost before he had finished, Tapley Howard bounded across saying "I am ready to die for my country." He was followed by every man except the bed-ridden sick and Rose. "Boys," called Bowie from his cot, "I wish some of you would . . . remove my cot over there." Four men lifted him over. Every other wounded man made the same request, and had his bunk moved over.

This left only Louis Rose. He wrote later in a memoir:

> I stood till every man had crossed the line. Then I sank to the ground, covered my face with my hands, and thought what best I might do. Suddenly an idea came. I spoke their [the Mexicans'] language, and could I once get safely out of the fort might easily pass for a Mexican and effect my

escape. I stole a glance at Colonel Bowie in his cot. Colonel Davy Crockett was leaning over talking to him. After a few seconds, Bowie looked at me and said, "You don't seem willing to die with us, Rose." "No," I said. "I am not prepared to die, and shall not do so if I can avoid it." Then Crockett looked at me, and said, "You might just as well, for escape is impossible." I made no reply but looked up at the top of the fortress wall. "I have often done worse things than climb that wall," I thought. Then I sprang up, seized my travelling bag and unwashed clothes and ascended it. Standing on top, I glanced down to take a last look at my friends. They were all now in motion, but what they were doing I heeded not. Overpowered by my feelings, I turned away.

In the darkness Louis Rose made it through the Mexican lines and out of San Antonio without incident.

Somebody else escaped the Alamo that night. A woman Mexican non-combatant deserted and told Santa Anna's commanders how small the garrison was. Emboldened, they ordered a mass storm of the fort on the morning of the thirteenth day of the siege, 6 March 1836.

In the pre-dawn darkness of the 6th, the Mexicans approached the barricade surrounding the fort, forming an armed ring through which none could escape.

As daylight broke, Santa Anna sent 1,800 men against the sides of the Alamo while his band blared out the "No Quarter" call of the Spanish battle march, the "El Deguello". Twice the Mexicans charged, and twice they were rebuffed. Then Santa Anna sent in his reserves, and these breached the walls of the fort on the west and northeast. Colonel Travis died in the latter place, slumped next to a cannon, a bullet through his forehead. The outer walls were now abandoned and the survivors, fighting hand to hand, fell back to the convent and the chapel. Davy

Crockett apparently fell outside the chapel, using his rifle as a club (although some evidence suggests that he, and six of his Tennesseans, were captured and tortured to death).

What is known of the last minutes of the men of the Alamo comes from the non-combatants in the fort whose lives were spared, particularly the wife of Lieutenant Dickinson, Ham, the Black servant of Jim Bowie, and Joe, the Black servant of Travis. The rooms of the stone buildings were fought for one by one. Armed with his knife and a brace of pistols, Jim Bowie fought from his sickbed in the baptistry. The chapel was the last place to be taken.

At around 7 a.m. with the din of battle dying down, Santa Anna judged it safe to approach the fort. One of the handful of Texans still alive in the chapel fired a last defiant volley, and the dictator retired to his adobe-walled command post. Only when the last Texan was dead did Santa Anna again venture forth to the Alamo, directing that the bodies of the fallen Texans should be burnt in two great funeral pyres.

To capture the Alamo cost General Antonio Lopez de Santa Anna over 1,000 of his men. He had also given the new Republic of Texas a battle cry which would bring it ultimate victory.

Victory for the Republic

The Republic of Texas had been declared on 2 March 1836, four days before the fall of the Alamo. Meeting in the village of Washington-on-the-Brazos, 59 delegates agreed a Declaration of Independence and a constitution borrowed from that of the United States. Slavery was legalized, and all Texans guaranteed an ample land grant. Almost as important as these acts, the delegates finally agreed to let Sam Houston lead the Texan army in meaningful fashion.

Taking command of his rag-bag army in mid-March 1836, Houston began an elaborate, zig-zagging eastward retreat, always just out of Santa Anna's impatient reach. Thinking "Old Sam" was scared to fight, many settlers panicked and raced for the US border – an affair known as the "runaway scrape". Some of Houston's army wept in shame, others became mutinous. Texas's new government bombarded him with missives: "Sir: The enemy are laughing you to scorn . . . You must retreat no farther. The country expects you to fight. The salvation of the country depends on you doing so."

None of this had any effect on Houston, who kept his men steadfastly marching east. Smelling victory, Santa Anna threw military caution to the wind. Dismayed by the slowness of his over-extended, poorly fed army, he pressed ahead with 900 picked troops.

This was the mistake Houston had hoped for. When Santa Anna turned aside to attack Harrisburg in the hope of seizing Texan officials, Houston fell in behind him. The hunter became the hunted. On 20 April 1836 Houston closed in on the Mexican force which was camped beside the junction of Buffalo Bayou and the San Jacinto River. Santa Anna, confident in his military knowledge, prepared his men for a dawn attack. Dawn came, but no Texan attack. In mid-morning 500 Mexican reinforcements arrived and Santa Anna, knowing his men were weary, ordered a hot noon meal and a rest. Only a small guard kept watch as the mass of the Mexican army enjoyed a siesta.

Houston pounced. His short speech to his troops contained just 16 words: "Victory is certain. Trust in God and fear not. And remember the Alamo – remember the Alamo!" The Texans slipped quietly through the tall prairie grass and reached within 200 yards of the Mexican lines before the alarm was raised. Then, yelling "Remember the Alamo!" the Texans charged. Within 18 minutes the battle was won, though killing of fleeing Mexicans continued until night-fall. The prairie was littered with 600 Mexican dead, and over 700 of Santa Anna's "Invincibles" were taken prisoner – including the General himself, who had tried to escape disguised as a private. He was given away by the cries of "El Presidente!" by the other prisoners.

To secure his release, Santa Anna pledged independence for Texas. He soon repudiated this, but Mexico was never able to conquer the new Republic. Most of the 2,000 Mexicans who were in the country at the time of the battle left for Mexico shortly afterwards.

Settling Texas

For ten years after the battle of San Jacinto Texas remained a free and sovereign republic. Settlement expanded rapidly, swelling the population of Texas to 140,000. Of these a significant number were Germans, who came to represent the largest foreign-born element in Texas. At places like New Braunfels, Fredericksburg and Sisterdale, this industrious people built homes which were exact replicas of those they had left behind in Europe. They were also startlingly different from the rough-and-ready log cabins and "picket huts" (made of staked walls and with roofs of grass, bound with rawhide) of the American Texans. The writer and landscape architect Frederick Law Olmstead described the incongruity of these German houses in his *A Journey Through Texas* (1857):

I never in my life, except, perhaps, in awakening from a dream, met with such a sudden and complete transfer of associations. Instead of loose boarded or hewn log walls, with crevices stuffed with rags or daubed with mortar, which we have been accustomed to see during the last month [elsewhere in Texas] ... we were in Germany. There was nothing wanting ... A long room, extending across the whole front of the cottage, the walls pink, with stenciled panels, and scroll ornaments in crimson, and with neatly-framed and glazed pretty lithographic prints hanging on all sides ...

Aside from Germans and a sizeable French colony at Castroville near the Medina River, most of those settling in Texas were American farmers, thrown off their land by the Great Panic of 1837. "G.T.T" ("Gone to Texas") was found scrawled across cabin doors the length of the frontier and the width of creditors' books. With its generous land grants, the Texan Republic provided a second chance.

The men and women who went there were determined to take it. They inclined to play hard and drink hard, and displayed a fondness for settling arguments with fists, knives and guns. The social rank of the opponent hardly mattered. Sam Houston was challenged to no fewer than 24 duels during his two terms as Texas president. Much of the future lawlessness of the West would ride north from Texas.

Yet if most Texans saw themselves as a breed apart, they also considered themselves Americans. Under Sam Houston several attempts were made to secure annexation by the United States, but these were thrown out by Congress at the instigation of abolitionists who charged that the Texan revolution had been a "slaveocracy conspiracy" by Southerners. But by 1845 the mood of Congress had relented. European states were urging Texas to a dangerous sovereignty, and President Polk had just been elected US President on an expansionist ticket. On 29 December of that year James K. Polk signed the proclamation making Texas the 21st state of the Union.

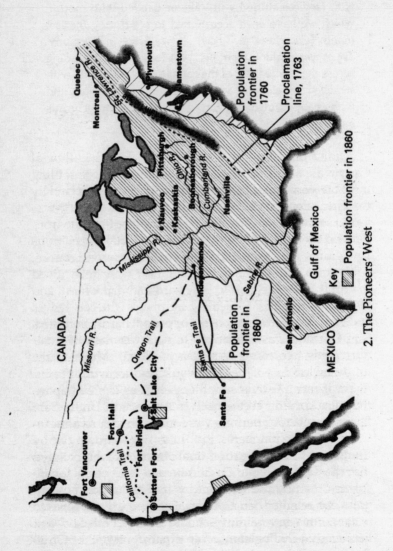

2. The Pioneers' West

Pioneers Across the Plains

"Millions are marching at once towards the same horizon.
Their language, their religion, their manners differ; their
object is the same. Fortune has been promised them somewhere in the West, and to the West they go to find it."
                    Alexis de Tocqueville, *Journey to America*

Reaching for the Pacific

In 1846 the frontier burst asunder as America sought to
fulfil its "Manifest Destiny" The flow of emigrants westward grew from a trickle to a flood. Within only a handful
of years, the number of White Americans living beyond
the Mississippi River would exceed the 350,000 Indians
who made the far West their home or their last refuge. The
most tumultuous period in American history had begun.

While some pioneers had been gazing longingly across
the Sabine River towards Texas, others had cast their eyes
further westwards, to California, and to Oregon, the delights of which had been discovered by Yankee sea captains, who had traded along the Pacific coast since the late
eighteenth century. But a home in either place would
have only been a gleam in the pioneer's eye if it had not
been for some myth-shattering by an intrepid – or perhaps foolhardy – few.

The Pacific was believed to be unreachable by land
for ordinary mortals. It was 2,000 gruelling miles from
the edge of settlement. There were treeless plains, scoured
by alkali dust, and guarded by Indians. And then there
were the Rockies, the prevailing opinion of which was
summed up in a Congressional report: "Nature has fixed
limits to our nation; she has kindly interposed as our
Western barrier, mountains almost inaccessible . . . This
barrier our population can never pass." A mountain man
might make it through to the shining sea, but not a mass of
people.

The people took no notice. They just went, prompted
by whips of information from traders and trappers.
In 1830 the fur company of Smith, Jackson and Sublette
showed that the plains could be crossed by wagons
when they took a train to a rendezvous in the Rocky
Mountains. Accompanying the 12-wagon train were
13 beeves. Water and grass proved easy to find. "The
wagons," the company noted, "could easily have crossed
the Rocky Mountains over the South Pass." Two years
later, in 1832, Hall Jackson Kelley, an acid-natured
New Englander who believed himself the American Moses, led a handful of followers to Oregon Country. The
journey, by an incomprehensibly roundabout route which
included New Orleans and Mexico City, took two years.
Along the way, all Kelley's disciples were dismissed.
Though the venture failed, it gave others hope. Among
them was the ice-manufacturer Nathaniel Wyeth, who
formed a joint stock company to exploit Oregon's bounty.
Departing from Independence, Missouri, in the spring of
1832 Wyeth and his companions travelled with the Rocky
Mountain Fur Company to its annual rendezvous at the
foot of the Shining Mountains. From there they were
guided to Fort Vancouver by trapper Milton Sublette,
brother of the more famous William. They were the first

party of White Americans to travel what would become the Oregon Trail.

More followed in Wyeth's still warm tracks, several Methodist missionaries among them. Once in the promised land of Oregon, it struck the reverend men that the place was replete with earthly delights. The climate was gentle, the soil tillable and good, the Willamette Valley a sort of farming heaven. Jason Lee, the nephew of Wyeth, was the most prominent of the Oregon proselytizers. To secure more American colonizers for Oregon – a region outside Louisiana and viewed proprietorially by the British – Lee retook the journey over the Rockies and the plains, but eastwards this time, to spread the good word about Oregon. Thomas Jefferson Farnham heard it in the farm town of Peoria, organized an emigration society, the "Oregon Dragoons", and had his wife sew them a flag with the legend OREGON OR THE GRAVE. Nineteen Dragoons set out for the Far West. None of them had adequate supplies or any real knowledge of wilderness frontiering. Yet some of them, including Farnham, made it to the Willamette. Afterwards, he wrote a no-truth-spared account of his westering experience, which did not fail to mention that he passed more than one night "more to the apparent satisfaction of vermin than for ourselves."

To those who doubted the wisdom of overland migration such words were a welcome confirmation. Despite the fact of successful land crossings they jibed and railed at the migrants. The editor of the New York *Tribune*, Horace Greeley, usually held to be an unrestrained enthusiast for westward migration, warned one party setting off for Oregon that the route "wore an aspect of insanity" and asserted that "we do not believe that nine-tenths of them will ever reach Columbia alive." Yet there was more and more evidence that the overlanders could make it across. In 1842 flamboyant explorer and Western expansionist John Charles Frémont, guided by scout Kit Carson, made an accurate map of the Oregon Trail, detailing such things as campsites and estimates of possible daily travel. Frémont then published the report of the expedition, done up as a colourful adventure story, which became an instant bestseller. With the path marked, more and more people came to believe that they could, God willing, make the Pacific coast overland.

And there was more and more need for poor men and women to do so. The Great Panic of 1837 had dispossessed and impoverished many farmers of the East and Mid-West. They were cheered on by the expansionist-minded so-called "boosters", who wished to see Oregon as part of the United States.

Then, in the spring of 1843, 1,000 pioneers stepped off into the wilderness at Independence, Missouri, bound for Oregon and California. Their vast train of wagons was guided by Marcus Whitman, a religious-minded physician who was one of Oregon's leading propagandists. The pioneers made it to the Pacific. With their wagons. The doubts were dispelled. Americans had come to the Pacific coast to stay.

By 1846 thousands of pioneers were surging westwards. On the move too, in "The Year of Decision" as historian Bernard De Voto termed it, were the Mormons, leaving their Illinois base at Nauvoo, heading towards the setting sun. The trails west were becoming so well trodden that, in places, they were highways a mile or more wide.

Not that it was ever an easy road to the promised land. Most emigrants followed a route that began at one of the towns on the Missouri River, such as Independence, Council Bluffs or St Joseph. From there they proceeded up the Platte to Fort Laramie and over the continental divide at South Pass. At Black's Fork of the Green River in southwest Wyoming, the trapper Jim Bridger had built, in an astute piece of entrepreneurship, a trading post where the emigrants could rest and buy supplies – at a dismayingly high price. Up to this point, the going was pretty easy, for the kids a glorious lark. After Fort Bridger the trail divided, the northern route going to Oregon, the southern to California. The terrain on both routes grew progressively rougher. The Oregon-bound travellers followed a tortuous track along the banks of the Snake, then headed across 150 miles of barren desert. To get the wagons up the Blue Mountains required ropes and pulleys.

The trail to California went south to the Humboldt River, and then along that disappearing waterway until it sank into the dry sands of the Nevada desert. Then it was 50 dry miles of alkaline waste, which sent up billowing clouds of ash, covering people, wagons and beasts. Men and women went mad, and animals died of heat and thirst. One chronicler counted the bodies of 350 horses, 280 oxen and 150 mules in a single 15-mile stretch of the wasteland. Animals would stampede when they smelled the saving water of the Carson River. After the Carson there came a final steep climb up the Sierra Nevada, and through the mountains it was downhill to journey's end in the Sacramento Valley.

The favoured means of travel was a canvas-covered wagon or Prairie Schooner, destined to become the enduring symbol of the Old West. Derived from the heavier Conestoga wagon of the Pennsylvania Germans, the schooner was superbly appropriate for the job of transporting pioneers' families. The heavy-duty canvas top kept off the elements, while the big wooden wheels (the rear pair were up to six feet in diameter) with their wide, iron-covered rims rolled easily over bumps and dips and soft ground or sand. The wagon's 10 by 3½ feet body could take a ton and a half in weight, though the prudent traveller would keep the load lighter.

Drawn by mules or oxen, lines of these wagons billowed across the west at the sedate pace of 15 to 20 miles a day. The journey to the Pacific took five months and began in May when the prairie was firm enough for the wagons and there was enough grass for the beasts of burden. Pioneering was a seasonal activity, only wise over the spring and summer. Late starts or slips in schedule due to misfortune could be calamitous. If the wagons failed to get across the Sierra Nevada before the snows, the settlers could become marooned. Such a fate befell the Donner Party in 1846.

For dirt-poor settlers a wagon was a luxury. Their lot was a handcart. Many simply walked to the Pacific. A number pushed wheelbarrows. At least one dog pulled his owner's chattels across the plains. But in general pioneers were not the very poor. The destitute were too poor to move.

The pathfinders often wrote letters to their kinfolk detailing the pitfalls and perils of the overland trips. Newspapers were full of sage advice, and publishers issued "Guides" by the score for the would-be emigrant. Sometimes the advice was sound:

Obtain Illinois or Missouri Oxen, as they are more adaptable to trail forage, and less likely to be objects of Indian desire.

Every male person should have at least one gun.

Of all the places in the world, travelling in the mountains is the most apt to breed contentions and quarrels. The only way out of it is to say but little, and mind your own business exclusively.

Despite the advice, the emigrants were not always well

prepared. Often the wagons were overloaded, and the non-essentials had to be thrown overboard en route. Among the more bizarre items found littering the prairie were a gothic bookcase and a diving bell. "Short-cuts" advertised by unscrupulous traders or ferryboat proprietors proved a frequent disaster for those who failed to heed the experience of others or thought they knew better.

Whatever the preparedness of the overlanders or their mode of travel, there were common hazards and fears. Deep rivers were always a tribulation. The oxen, mules and accompanying cattle had to swim for it. Wagons were converted into crude boats by a sheath of watertight rawhide or tarpaulin stretched around the body, or – if timber was plentiful – were floated across on rafts. Some rivers had to be crossed many times. The Mullan Road in Montana required that the St Regis be traversed 19 times in six miles. Accidents were common: between 1840 and 1860 around 300 overlanders died by drowning.

Water. In one way or another, it ruled the emigrants' lives. There was either too much of it, or too little. Kansas in a wet spring bogged down hundreds of wagons. The dry stretches of the High Plains under a blazing sun caused tormenting thirst. The cholera which struck down so many hundreds of pioneers at the crowded wells of the Platte was borne by water. So too were other infectious diseases. The trails were marked by graves their length long.

Helpers, Scalpers

But the biggest fear of the overlander was not disease – it was the Indian. Yet this was a fear more imagined than real.

Initially, at least, Indians were more helpers than scalpers along the trail. Marcus Whitman's Great Migration of 1843 was trailblazed in parts by an Indian guide. When the Stevens–Murphy party of 1844 pushed their wagons beyond the Humboldt Sink, they were following the directions of Truckee, a Paiute Chief, in whose honour the route became named. Indians were especially valued for river crossings; an 1846 guidebook penned by J. M. Shively even went as far as to state that "you must hire an Indian to pilot you at the crossings of the Snake River." Overlanders happily placed wagons, persons, beeves and beasts in the care of the Sioux at the Platte and Laramie Rivers.

The Indians were quick to learn the White man's pecuniary ways. And drove hard bargains. When crossing horses over the Columbia River, the Chinook were apt to stop in mid-stream to demand more payment to finish the job. The Native Americans were especially wily when it came to the selling of horseflesh. As one overlander, James Payne, put it in 1850: "Plenty of Indians and pretty ponies today; we tried to make a trade with them, but you can't cheat them in horses." By 1852 the Sioux were asking as much as $125 per horse. The trade was particularly profitable when the Indians had stolen the self-same horse from another overlander. Such sharp practice was common enough to merit cautions in more than one overland guide.

As payment for services rendered, Indians took money, but preferred the tangibly useful. Ammunition, guns, knives, blankets and clothes were popular. Whiskey was much sought after. One traveller, Alonzo Delano, reported that the first request of the Sioux near Ash Hollow was for "firewater". Delano believed that the Indians would trade anything for it, even horses. Overlanders, though, tended to avoid passing the bottle over. When they did, the result, complained one disapproving emigrant, was "brawling and such a noise!"

Yet White–Indian mutual aid soon gave way to hostility. The Native Americans were dismayed by the sheer numbers of Whites trekking through their lands, and felt heavily the threat posed to their way of life. The overlanders scared away or wantonly slaughtered game, especially buffalo, overgrazed the prairie, exhausted the water supply, fired grasslands by accident or design, and depleted the precious tree stocks. As compensation, from 1843 the Indians began to demand a tribute from the passing trains for safe travel through their lands. A number of tribes also erected toll bridges over streams. Most travellers viewed these Indian tributes and tolls with disgust. What irked them was not so much the money but the idea that the Red man had any rights over the White man. In such a circumstance, refusing payment and brandishing arms was a sore temptation. Violent confrontations became commonplace. The Pawnee toll at Shell Creek was a particular hotspot, with something like a battle occurring there in May 1852, after the Indians tore down their bridge in protest at toll refusals. One group of emigrants rebuilt the bridge and pushed on across, declining to make the due payment. The next day, the Pawnee demanded a toll from another party, who likewise refused to pay the 25 cents per wagon asked. The emigrants rushed the bridge in their wagons – only to find that the Pawnee had cut a hole in its centre, which they had camouflaged with brushwood. The lead wagon fell straight through to the water, and shooting started. The Pawnee had the worst of it with nine killed. They were back soon after, but with retaliation, not tolls, in mind. Subsequent overlanders paid the price in plunder for those who rushed the Pawnee bridge at Shell Creek.

Emigrants refused the toll, preferring to fight than to pay. Indians took revenge on later caravans, and indignant overlanders complained. Newspapermen scented a suitably shocking story of Indian depredations. When this was published White citizens requested military protection. The spiral of hostility was precise and unyielding in its rising. In such an atmosphere, relations between White Americans and the tribes could only become strained.

Even so, there was remarkably little White blood shed. Most of the fatalities occurred, contrary to myth, not on the plains but west of South Pass, with the Applegate route to Oregon being a particularly deadly stretch of trail. Indians hesitated to attack well-disciplined trains (especially when drawn up in a circle), so most engagements took the form of ambushes on individuals or running skirmishes. Sizeable slaughters did occur, though. An entire train of 23 or more overlanders was wiped out at Tule Lake in 1847. Five years later, 14 emigrants were killed and mutilated at Lost River, and 22 at "Bloody Point" near Tule Lake. At midday on 20 August 1854, approximately 30 Snake Indians attacked a small five-wagon train after a dispute over a horse. Only two (who feigned death) of the 20 persons in the train, most belonging to the family of Andrew Ward, escaped. Another group of emigrants stumbled into the massacre, and lost one of their number, before retreating. When volunteers from Fort Boise rode out late to bury the bodies, they found a nightmarish scene. The emigrant children had been burned alive, the women raped, one with a piece of hot iron. Much of the tomahawk mutilation of the women had apparently been done by Snake squaws.

The tragedy caused a chorus of White rage. The editor of Portland's *Weekly Oregonian* demanded that the authorities "either exterminate the race of Indians, or prevent further wholesale butcheries by these worthless races resembling human form." When Bannock and Shoshoni Indians attacked the Otter–Van Orman train on 9 September 1860 the rage reached a crescendo. Exactly what befell the eight-wagon Otter–Van Orman train is uncertain, but it was a rare instance of Indians engaging an encircled train. After withstanding the Indians for several days, the emigrants abandoned the train during a lull in the fighting. Four discharged soldiers travelling with the train took to their horses and galloped off, leaving the rest of the party to their fate. Around 18 were cut down by Indians, including Mrs Abigail Van Orman, four of whose children were abducted. Another 18 emigrants escaped, to wander starving and lost. Jacob and Joseph Keith reached the Umatila Indian Agency on 2 October. Twelve others were found near the Owyhee River – about 90 miles from the initial attack – where they had been subsisting in part on the flesh of dead companions.

As Abigail Van Orman and others discovered to their dread and to their cost, sometimes the Indian menace was real. Even so, such souls were unlucky to die by an Indian's hand. According to historian John Unruh only 362 overlanders were killed by Indians between 1840 and 1860, out of an overall death toll on the trail of 10,000. Where blood flowed, it tended to come from Native American bodies. (The settlers probably inflicted 426 violent deaths on the Indians.) The usual form of Indian retribution was not an arrow but a sneaky pilfering of horses, mules and just about anything else on four legs. Writing to his wife in 1849, Henry Page penned words which summed up the typical overlander's experience of Indians: "We are & shall not be, in any danger of our lives from Indians – the only trouble is to keep them from stealing . . . "

Going the Plains Across

Indian attack or no, it was a wonder and an achievement to have crossed overland to the Pacific. Many emigrants

understood that they were taking part in one of the great
happenings of history, and dutifully put quill to diary.
Nearly 800 such pioneers' diaries have been found and
preserved. William E. Taylor's is a classic, laconically
listing the suffering, awe, boredom, travail and excitement of going the "plains across". Taylor went overland
to California in 1846 with the Craig–Stanley party, one of
the first to take wagons over the Sierras:

Monday April the 20th 1846   We this day lef home for
Oregon and proceeded 5 [15?] miles to Elk horn whare we
got some work done on our waggon Our company consisting of Craig Shreve and myself

Tuesday, the 21. We Left at 10 O'clock and Standlly's
wagon Broak 2 miles from Elk horn whare we continued
all night

Wed. 22. Left at 12 O'clock after having finished all the
repares our waggon proceeded about 3 miles This day
one of our Crowd (Shreve) took his [illegible] Mr. Lad
Joined us

Th. 23. went 12 miles

Friday 24. passed plattsburg travailed 12 miles

Sat. 25 traveled 20 miles

Sund. 26. got to St. Josephs, traveled 3 miles

Monday 27 Tuesday 28   we remained at St. Josephs

Wen. 29 we Left St. Josephs went to parrots ferry 5
miles above town. Weather fair wind high

Th 30 Remained In Camp Wind prevents us from
Crossing

May 1 Crossed over the river which was very hig for
the season we find an abundance of grass for the oxen

2 Remained in camp

3. Struck our tents and proceeded to wolf River whare
we had some difficulty in getting over went 14 mils

    4. Started Early passed the Iowa Agency, distance 25 [miles]

    5. Left camp Early travled 15 miles

    6. We overtook 18 waggons at the Nemihaw River crossed over found 6 wagons encamped making 27 waggons and 50 men. A view from the prairie hills of this Little River is very sublime and beautiful it Surpasses any thing I have yet seen

    7 we traveled about 20 miles the road verry undulating and the Land of the Richest kind Scarcely any timber or Water Some symptoms of discord in camp owing to all not being present at the Election of officers

    8 we travel^d over Level wet prairie 18 ms

    9 we traveld 2½ miles Crossed one fork of the Blue. Staid all day found we were wrong

    10 Changed our course Crossed over the other fork of Blue came to Independence trail we are ahead of all distance 16 miles

    11 traveled 14 miles Camped in a small grove on a tributary of Blue

    12 Camped on Horse Creek 7 miles

    13 Travailed 7 miles Camped on Blue

    14 Camped on Sandy a tributary of the Blue after travling 20 miles

    15 Camped on the blue 16 miles verry warm The Mercury stands 76 at noon in the shade

    16 traveld up Blue 16 miles Stanley killed a deer Mercury Stood at 86 at noon in the shade

    17 traveled 4 miles

    18 we went But 2 miles owing to the indisposition of Mrs Munkerass who brough an increase in to the emigration

    19 travailed 8 miles

    20 traveled 16 up Blue

    21 Arrived at the Nebraska, travailed 17 miles

    22 to day we saw a party of pawnees some hunters

quite friendly distance 18 miles

23 traveld 8 miles

24 traveld 20 miles Saw and killed some Buffalo

25 traveled 18 miles thousands of Buffalo

26 Traveled 18 A sevier h[a]il storm in the Evning.

27 "   16 miles quite Cool Mercury at 57

28 "   23 another hail Storm Reached the South fork of platt

the 29 travaled 16 miles first used the excrement of the Buffalo for fuel

30 Crossed the South fork which is one mill wide with an average depth of 18 inches dis. 12 miles this evening we had the most sevier storm I ever saw

31 Lay by all day owing to incessant Rain and intense Cold with Some Snow Tem. 48 Fah[renheit]

June the first today there was quit a snow storm passed over to the Ash hollow distance 25 miles Tem. 38 deg. Fah.

2 Staid here all day

3 went 10 miles Camped out of the Rain Tem. 57 deg

4 travelled 20 miles Saw wild horses

5 travaled 20 miles. Came in sight of Castle Rock also the Chimney Rock Crossed Sandy

6 passed the Chimney Rock dist. 25 miles

7 passed Scotts Bluff Beautiful Scenry dist 18 miles

8 Company divided distance 19 miles

9 Travelled 15 miles Temp. 90 deg of Fah

10 Went 7 miles came to Laramie. Tem. 100 deg of Fah

11 Lay By. mercury at 100 Fah.

12 travelled 20 miles through the Black hills Camped on the Bitter Cotton Wood a Smal Stream

13 Came 20 miles camped on horse Shoe Creek

14 camped on Butte creek distance 20 miles

15 camped on Black Creek dist 20 miles Red Rock

16 travelled 18 miles camped on deer creek

17 traveled 16 miles Tem 90 deg of Fah.

18 Came to the Crossing of platt not fordable met some Return emigrants Tem. 81 deg. of Fah.

19 Remained trying to cross our Cattle

20 Do Do   16 more waggons Came up

21 got all over Rafted the waggons Swam the Cattle

22 passed the Red Butt[e]s dist 12 miles a good Spring

23 Came to the Willow Spring distance 20 miles

24 20 miles Braught us to the Rock Independence

25 Passed the Kenion on Sweet water saw mountain sheep travelled 16 miles

26 Went 18 miles, passed a party of men

27 traveled 25 miles Thousands of buffalo

28 Lay By all day

29 Traveled 20 miles a plain view of the wind River mountains Covered with snow Bad roads Some Sick

30 Came to the South Pass at 16 miles

July the 1   23 miles Braught us to Little Sandy extremely sterile country in sight of eternal snow on the Bear River mountan

2 Broak a waggon a man sick dist 10 miles Camped on Big Seany [Sandy] Mr L W Hastings visited our camp

3 travelled 18 miles Tem. 29 deg. of Fah.

4 crossed the colorado of the west a stream of 40 Rods wide 2 feet deep dis. 16 miles

5 traveled 15 miles camped on Blacks Fork near half the company confined by sickness

6 traveled 2 miles Lay By on account of the sick Tem 90 Deg. of Fah.

7 Lay By Sick get worse Mr. S Sublett & three others staid with us they ware from California Wrote home By them. Tem. 105

8 We Left the main croud with 7 waggons travelled 16 miles some Rain

9 16 miles Braught us to Bridger Shoshone in abundane

Mr Joseph Walker et al from California

    10 Lay By Indians visited us in great numbers

    11 traveled 18 miles Cam[p]ed on muddy a bad camp

    12 traveled 18 miles Camped at a good Spring

    13 Crossed the Bear River mountain Rain 25 miles

    14 16 miles Brought us to Smiths fork

    15 traveled 22 verr[y] Bad Roads hard Rain

    16 traveled 14 miles more Rain

    17 21 Braught us to the Soda Spring

    18 Lay By Rain thunder and Lightning

    19 Left our company with our 2 waggons alon never
shall I forget the deep Regret at a Leaving our friends
passed the old Crater travaled 12 miles

    20 our oxen sensable of the impropriety of Leaving
their as well as our friends Left camp and ware overtaken
3 miles from the Soda Spring so that we only got to
portneif River 7 miles

    21 traveled 22 miles Crossed divers streams

    22 traveled 21 to the Blue Spring 5 miles from fort Hall

    23 passed Ft hall traveled 14 miles to portneiffe River.

    24 traveled 18 mils passed the American falls of Snake
or Saptin River.

    25 travelled 18 miles to Casua Bad Road

    26 Left the Oregon Road traveled 22 miles up the casua
or Raft River good Road

    27 traveled up casua 18 miles Rain Lightning and
thunder

    28 20 miles Braught us to a good Spring Road Bad
Crossed over to goose creek [*deleted:* 10 miles]

    29 we came 10 miles

    30 travelled 15 miles

    31 we came 18 miles Tem. 30 deg. Fah morning

    August the 1 traveled 17 miles

    2 passed a verry hot Spring 20 miles Struck the head of
Marys River

3 met Black harriis and applegate who had Been to view a new Road to oregon and designed meeting the emigrants to turn them into it travelled 20 miles Tem 88 of Fah.

4 Traveled 17 miles down Marys Rive. Tem. 90

5 This day we came 20 miles sevral diggers [Indians]

6 passed sevral Remarkabley hot Springs 20 miles

7 Came 14 miles

8   "   17 miles hot Springs

9   "   16 miles

10 "   20 miles quit steril[e]

11 "   23 miles   "   "

12 "   18 miles Natural Soap

13   "   18 miles Salaeratus visited by Large party of Indians

14 Travelled 22 miles (Rain Lightning

15 "   20 miles. divergence of new oregon road

16 "   20 "   Extreme Sterility

17 "   25 "   to day we Suffered for water as the Road Left the River for 14 miles Rain

18 Lay By Joined By Col. Russell of Mo. & 8 others packing Tem. 42 morning 96 noon

19. 20 miles Braught us to the Sink of Marys Riv Vegetation entirely disappear water verry bad

20 traveled all day and all night passed some Boiling Springs quite salt distance 40 miles making 60 miles that 8 of us had 12 gallons of Water Extreme suffering Reached Trucky

21 Lay by all day Tem 100 of Fah.

22 Entered the Siera Nevada or Cascade mts up Trucky vally 15 miles Tem 87 deg of Fah.

23 Traveled 18 miles Bad Road

24   "   10 miles came to timber Tem 94 deg Fah

25 Crossed a spur of the mts 12 miles Tem 84.

26 travelled 12 miles good Road Tem 32.

27   "   8 miles Trucky Lake Tem 30

28 travelled 1 mile up the worst mountain that waggons ever crossed sevier frost Tem 28

29 got up the mts. Distance 2 miles

30 travelled 3 miles Lay by the Ballance of day

31   "   15 miles on top of the mt. Bad Road Tem 22
at day Light & 60 at Sun down

Sept 1 travelled 7 miles Bad Bad Road Bear sign Tem.
40 deg morn

2 traveled 7 miles of distressing Road

3rd   "   8 miles ove if possable worse Road

4 Lay by to Rest our oxen

5 travled 16 miles principally upon the top of a high
Spur of the mountain our Oxen are worn nearly out we
have but three that are able to Render service and we have
as steep a hill befor us as we have Left behind us Heaven
only knows how we are to get Along Our Oxen are almost
perishing for food and nothing grows in this hateful valley that will sustain life.

6 Lay by to day as yestardys Long drive has well nigh
done for the oxen. We cut down Oak Bushes and trees, for
them to Brows on, or such of them, as are able to Stand on
their feet.

7 the indians drove off two of Mr. Stanley's ablest
Oxen; tho' we succeeded in Recapturing one of them We
unloaded our waggons and packed the Load near a mile
on our horses We then took four of the best yoaks of Oxen
and put to the empty waggons with a man at each wheel
and by such exertions as I have seldom saw used we got
the wagons up one at a time and proceeded about 5 miles
grass verry Scarce and dry Our oxen are as near gone as I
ever saw oxen to be driven at all

8 This morning we found that the Indians had taken off
another one of Stanley's oxen, it was seen by following the
trail that they had taken him up a steep hill and carfully
Covered Evry track for the distance of a mile he was taken

probably whilst I was on guard. I do not know how he managed to affect this Roguery it must have been very Sly W[e] travelled 11 miles and Stoped at a Small patch of dry grass and no water for the Cattle or horses

9 we traveled 3 miles and Stoped for the day at a Little grass and a hole of water one of Mr. Craigs Best oxen has gave out; the hills have got much Smaller and the Rocks are not so much in the way as on any part of the Road Since we Struck the waters of Trucky River

10 Lay by all day our oxen are so near worn out and our provisions are getting scarce

11 Started on slow went about 6 miles today we had to Leave an ox on the Road

12 we traveled 7 miles and Stopt we are in five miles of the first settlement today we left another ox we have but two oxen to our waggon

13 We this morning got into the Valley and stoped at Cap. Wm. Johnsons Whare we ware Recieved in the most Kind and hospitable manner We made several trades Bought a beef swaped our broak down oxen for fresh ons this day our company Lay by and so for several days distance 5 miles

So Ends my Diary

The Donner Tragedy

"Never take no cut ofs and hury along as fast as you can."

This advice, penned in an 1847 letter from an overlander to his eastern kin, was based on terrible experience. The writer was one of the emigrant party led west by George Donner in the summer of 1846 with California their goal, but tragedy their eventual destination.

It started easily enough. Although the emigrant party took the name of George Donner, its captain, it was originated by James Reed, a businessman of Springfield, Illinois, who was descended from Polish nobility (his family surname was Reednoski). Reed had been a private in the same company as Abraham Lincoln during the Black Hawk War of 1832, when Illinois troops had driven Sauk Indians from their tribal lands and slaughtered them in the Bad Axe Massacre. Afterwards, Reed had become a manufacturer of cabinet furniture, a farmer and railroad speculator. His wife, Margaret, suffered from "sick headaches", and it was because of these that he decided to go west, hoping that the climate of California would improve her health. When Reed told his ageing Springfield neighbours the Donner brothers, George and Jacob, that he was heading west, they invited themselves along. So did Hiram

Miller and Gersham Keyes. Nine wagons in all left Springfield in early 1846, rolling to Independence, Missouri, their jumping-off point for the wilderness, without incident.

On 12 May 1846 the emigrants, with George Donner as their elected wagonmaster, left the frontier for the trail west. Chimney Rock, Red Buttes, Courthouse Rock and other landmarks came and went in carefree miles. More recruits were picked up along the way, and by the time the Donner party reached the Little Sandy River in Wyoming in late July it numbered some 60 wagons and 300 souls. Here the plans were laid for the remainder of the journey. The Donner brothers had read the *Emigrant's Guide to Oregon and California* by the land speculator Lansford W. Hastings, and wanted to take the author's advice: depart the regular California trail at Fort Bridger, "thence bearing west southwest, to the Salt lake; and thence continuing down to the Bay of St Francisco." Hastings modestly called this route – which he estimated would reduce the travelling time to California to 120 days – the "Hastings Cutoff". At the meeting on the Little Sandy, mountain men guides argued against the new trail. As a result, the train split in two. The majority took the usual route via Fort Hall in Idaho; 88 others, under George Donner, headed for Fort Bridger, where Hastings had promised to join the Donners and lead them along the Cutoff.

When the party reached Fort Bridger on 3 August 1846, they found that the adventurer was leading another group westward, but had left word that he had marked the trail for them. For good measure, George Donner hired a Fort Bridger guide named Juan Baptiste to pilot the emigrants around the southern end of the Great Salt Lake and to the head of Weber Canyon. There they found a note from Hastings stuck on a stick. It asked them to wait until he could lead them through the Wasatch Range.

So began the first of many fateful delays. After eight days, George Donner sent a messenger to find Hastings. The messenger returned without Hastings but with his instruction to proceed along a new trail. At this point, Juan Baptiste refused to accept any further responsibility and returned to Fort Bridger. After pushing past count-less, time-consuming boulders, the party emerged onto the blinding white alkali flats of the Great Salt Lake Desert.

According to Lansford W. Hastings, this parched waste-land would take two days to cross. It took the Donner party almost a week. Behind them in the sand they left most of their valuables, four wagons, and 300 head of oxen and cattle. Paiutes began to raid the stock and the wagons, making it dangerous to leave the train's vicinity. Hunting had to be abandoned. With food low, it was decided on 18 September to send two men on to Sutter's Fort in California for supplies. Charles Stanton and William McCrutchen volunteered, and left on fast horses. The rest of the party struggled onwards to the distant Sierras.

By now the emigrants were weak in body and morale. Old man Hardcoop was struck by illness and left to die by the side of the road. Arguments and bickering broke out constantly. A man named Wolfinger was murdered. James Reed quarrelled with the driver of another family, John Snyder, when their wagons became entangled on a grade. Snyder attacked Reed with his whip; Reed drew a blade in self-defence and killed him. Reed was banished to the desert alone, unarmed and on foot (although his family and friends secretly supplied him with a horse and rifle).

On 19 October Charles Stanton returned from Sutter's Fort. With him were two of Captain Sutter's Indian guides and a mule train of food. At Truckee Meadows they fed and rested. Not until 23 October did the pioneers' wagons begin snaking towards the jagged peaks of the Sierra

Nevada. The first snow of winter began to fall, a month early. The wagons ground upwards. At Alder Creek, George Donner's wagon broke an axle, the remaining 15 schooners going around the hapless family and on to the high water that is now Donner Lake. There, on the evening of 28 October, they camped in cabins abandoned by earlier overlanders. A final push and they would be through the mountains. That night a snowstorm struck. When the emigrants awoke in the morning, the ground was deep in snow and the Truckee Pass was blocked. The Donner Party was snowbound in the high sierras.

Panic set in. Some emigrants hurriedly fashioned tents out of their wagons' canvas tops, others holed up in the shanties. The Donners themselves failed to arrive. Eventually, Charles Stanton waded back to Alder Gulch, where he found George and Jacob Donner bedridden. Mrs Tamsen Donner was feeding them, her five children and their hired hands on strips of cowhide. They could not be moved to the main camp up at the lake. Blizzards continued to howl down from the mountains. The animals began to die in droves, of cold, or of suffocation in the drifts. Patrick Breen Sr, an Irish-born farmer and patriarch of the Breen clan amongst the emigrants, commenced writing a diary, his thoughts turned inwards by the ordeal. On December 1st he noted:

Still Snowing wind W about 5½ or 6 feet deep difficult to get wood. no going from the house Completely housed up looks as likely for snow as when it Commenced, our cattle all Killed but three of four of them, the horses & Stantons mules gone & Cattle suppose lost in the Snow no hopes of finding them alive.

The first emigrant died of starvation on 15 December. He was Bayliss Williams, a hired man of the Reeds. It was

clear that someone must go for help, or the whole party
would perish from hunger. Fifteen of the strongest survivors (eight men, five women and the two Indian guides)
volunteered to try to reach Sutter's Fort. Led by Charles
Stanton, the "Forlorn Hope", as the party of volunteers
was called, left on 19 December wearing improvised snow-
shoes and carrying six days' rations.

Shortly after the volunteers left, news came up to Donner
Lake from Alder Gulch of four deaths among the party
there. By now all the cattle had long since died, and for
most there were only hides left to eat. Patrick Breen shot
his dog Towser for food. The drifts reached the roofs of
the shanties. "We pray to the God of mercy to deliver us
from our present calamity," wrote Breen on the first day
of 1847, while he and the others huddled waiting for
rescue.

It was a long time in coming. The "Forlorn Hope" had
run into tribulations beyond comprehension. Stanton had
developed snow blindness and was left to freeze to death.
A violent storm on Christmas night caused the demise of
four of the party through hypothermia. The starving survivors stripped the flesh from the bones of the dead,
roasted it and ate it, their weeping eyes unable to look
each other in the face. The remaining flesh was carefully
packed and labelled, so that no one would eat their kin.
The band struggled on. Two more men died and were
eaten. When this obscene food ran out the Indians, who
had refused to eat human flesh, were shot and butchered.
Finally, the survivors stumbled into Johnson's Ranch on
18 January 1847. Of the 15 who had hazarded the journey
from Donner Lake, only seven – two men and five women
– came through alive.

A small rescue party, the first of four, was sent out and
reached the lake camp on 19 February to find many of the
emigrants dead, others half mad. Twenty-three of the

skeleton-like survivors decided that they were strong enough to be led out of the Sierra graveyard. The rest, too weak to walk, clustered around the stoves, and waited for a larger relief force, expected at any moment.

The second relief was delayed by snowstorms. The food at Donner Lake and Alder Gulch again ran out. Like the "Forlorn Hope", the emigrants in the camps turned to cannibalism. Patrick Breen wrote in his diary on 26 February, in his first mention of human flesh-eating:

> ... Mrs Murphy said here yesterday that thought she would Commence on Milt. [Milford Elliot, a teamster for James Reed] & eat him, I dont [think] that she has done so yet, it is distressing The Donnos [Donners] told the California folks [the first rescue party] that they [would] Commence to eat the dead people in 4 days, if they did not succeed that day or next in finding their cattle then under ten or twelve feet of snow & did not know the spot or near it I suppose They have done so ere this time.

Not until the very end of February did the main relief force, burdened with heavy food packs, manage to fight their way through the last of the winter storms. It was led by James Reed, who had managed to find his way to California alone. As he climbed towards the camp, he met his wife and two of their children coming down with an earlier relief. He pressed ahead, and in two days found his other two children alive, both well and in the care of Mr Glover, a fellow Freemason. (The Reeds and the Breens were the only families to survive the Donner tragedy without loss.) Reed's joy was tempered by the cannibalistic scenes he found as he moved through the cabins, where human "bones and skulls ... filled camp kettles." For most of the living at Donner Lake and Alder Gulch, the Reed relief meant survival. Some, though, were still unable to be moved. They included George Donner and his wife Tamsen, who refused to leave her husband's side.

For these last pitiful few another relief was organized. It was sent up in the April thaw under the command of Captain Fellun. To Fellun and his men fell the last and worst sights of the Donner tragedy. Fellun committed these to his journal "Entered the cabins," he wrote on 17 April 1847, "and a horrible scene presented itself – human bodies terribly mutilated, legs, arms, and sculls [sic] scattered in every direction. One body, supposed to be that of Mrs Eddy, lay near the entrance, the limbs severed off and a frightful gash in the skull. The flesh from the bones was nearly all consumed . . ."

Fellun then trudged over to Alder Gulch. "At the mouth of the tent stood a large iron kettle, filled with human flesh cut up, it was the body of Geo. Donner, the head had been split open, and the brains extracted therefrom . . ." Donner's wife, Tamsen, was also dead.

Although the Fellun party had expected to find several emigrants still alive, they found only one, Lewis Keseberg. He was in a lamentable condition, haggard and wild. His subsistence on human flesh had lasted so long that he refused anything in its place.

Of the 87 emigrants who had set out from Fort Bridger on the Hastings Cutoff, 39 died in the Sierras.

Westward With God

The emigrant families who went west over the trails were a God-fearing people. Something about the limitless sky and the vastness of the land inclined the mind to religion. Missionaries went into the wilderness to baptize the heathen Indians and to tend their remote and scattered settler flocks. Spiritual "awakenings" periodically gripped and fevered the frontier, giving birth to new sects: the Campbellites, the Shakers, the Millerites and the Oneida Colony. The most important of them, for the history of Western expansion, was Joseph Smith's "Church of Jesus Christ of the Latter-Day Saints".

In 1827, according to Joseph Smith's own account, he was visited by the angel Moroni, who revealed to him the whereabouts of the gold-leaved *The Book of Mormon*, which contained missing parts of the Bible and God's own purpose for Smith. Since Smith, a 21-year-old New York farmer's son, was near illiterate, a pair of magic glasses was attached to the book, enabling him to read and interpret it. What he learned from the golden tablets was that in ancient times two lost tribes of Israel had found their way to America. The savage Lamanites (from whom the American Indians were descended) had then slaughtered all the civilized Nephites, but not before their chief prophet, Mormon, had written their history in hieroglyphical

"Reformed Egyptian" on golden plates. Smith's sacred mission was to build a new, true, Christian Church.

Smith published *The Book of Mormon* in 1830 (the bill was paid by an enthusiastic local farmer) at the God-revealed price of $1.75 a copy, later reduced to $1.25. With five followers, Smith founded the Church of Jesus Christ of the Latter-Day Saints on 6 June 1830 at Fayette, southeast of Rochester, New York. Personable, energetic and with a flair for persuasive oratory, Smith recruited converts rapidly. He also aroused hatred and hostility from non-believers or "Gentiles". His house was assaulted by mobs, fellow "Saints" shot at in the street.

After prayers for guidance, Smith took his followers west, to Kirtland, Ohio. From this Stake of Zion proselytes were sent forth, and a thousand people converted, among them Brigham Young. A new Mormon colony was founded at Independence, Missouri. The industry of the Saints was boundless. At Kirtland they built their own mill, store, bank and printing press and started work on an inspiring temple.

Such prosperous, clannish success only attracted more of the hatred which had driven the Mormons out of New York. Smith was tarred and feathered in Kirtland. The governor of Missouri called out the militia against the Saints in 1838, asserting "that the Mormons must be treated as enemies and must be exterminated or driven from the State." Nineteen unresisting Mormon men and boys were killed at their village of Haun's Mill.

The Mormons backtracked east to Illinois, where a liberal law allowed them to establish a virtually independent state at Nauvoo. There, on the banks of the Mississippi, Smith and his congregation turned a malarial swamp into a shining and populous city. Under Smith's theocratic rule, thousands of Mormons tried to create an ideal society where no one went barefoot or hungry, and which was free from the sins of drink and smoking (although Smith himself continued to indulge in both).

Troubles, however, again descended on the Saints. Joseph Smith received a "call" from God to cast off monogamy. By 1844 Smith and many of his entourage had already done so. His bodyguard, John Scott, had five wives, Brigham Young more. (Nauvoo, unlike most pioneering settlements, had a surplus of women, many of them converts from Europe.) Some Mormons were outraged, and published a dissenting newspaper, the *Expositor*. Smith had it closed down, and the dissenters fled to the county seat at Carthage. Rumours of the Saints' new marital practice had already reached Carthage. The dissenters confirmed it.

Outraged Illinois newspaper editors denounced Smith, and anti-Mormon mobs formed. To assuage the angry protesters, the authorities issued warrants for the arrest of Joseph Smith and his brother Hyrum. Smith, in turn, placed Nauvoo under martial law and donned his uniform of lieutenant-general of the Nauvoo Legion. Then, choosing against confrontation, he surrendered himself to the authorities at Carthage on 24 June 1844.

As Smith entered the Carthage jail he was struck by a premonition of doom. He confided to an aide, "I am going like a lamb to the slaughter; but I am as calm as a summer morning." Three days later Joseph and Hyrum Smith were shot by a masked mob who stormed the jail. The bullets were fired at point-blank range. Hyrum died instantly. Joseph Smith, mortally wounded, shouted "O Lord, my God" and fell through a window to the ground below.

With Joseph Smith martyred, the leadership of the Mormon church was assumed by the senior apostle Brigham Young. The pragmatic Vermonter decided that the survival of the Mormons depended on their moving to a remote place beyond the malice and power of the Gentiles. They would have to go into the empty wilderness of the West.

Young had studied J. C. Frémont's report of his 1843-4 expedition surveying the Oregon Trail, also the infamous Lansford W. Hastings' guide to Oregon and California. From these he gleaned that the most isolated area in the West – and consequently that most unlikely to appeal to westering Gentiles – lay around the Great Salt Lake, nearly 1,400 miles away. This would be the Mormons' new Promised Land.

The first 600 Saints to leave Nauvoo crossed the icy Mississippi into Iowa on 4 February 1846. The rest followed in a regular series of parties, almost military in their order of march and discipline. Young was a genius of leadership and organization. Bugle calls awoke the faithful each morning at five o'clock, and thereafter the day was divided into rigid periods for prayers, food, travel and rest. At 8.30 each evening the train halted, and was wheeled into a protective circle. By 9 o'clock everyone was asleep. As the detachments crossed Iowa they occasionally stopped to plant crops, which could be harvested by later trains of the Saints. In this way, 16,000 Mormons worked their way over Iowa to a staging camp they called Winter Quarters on the bank of the Missouri near present-day Omaha. Here over the summer and fall they built a vast temporary city, described by Thomas Leiper Kane in his *The Mormons* (1850):

> This landing, and the large flat or bottom on the east side of the river, were crowded with covered carts and wagons; and each one of the Council Bluff hills opposite was crowned with its own great camp, gay with bright white canvas, and alive with the busy stir of swarming occu-

pants. In the clear blue morning air the smoke streamed up from more than a thousand cooking fires. Countless roads and by-paths checkered all manner of geometric figures on the hillsides. Herd boys were dozing upon slopes; sheep and horses, cows and oxen, were feeding around them, and other herds in the luxuriant meadow of the then swollen river. From a single point I counted four thousand head of cattle in view at one time. As I approached the camps, it seemed to me the children there were to prove still more numerous. Along a little creek I had to cross were women in greater force than *blanchisseuses* upon the Seine, washing and rinsing all manner of white muslins, red flannels and parti-colored calicoes, and hanging them to bleach upon a greater area of grass and bushes than we can display in all our Washington Square ...

It was Young's intention that the Mormons should wait out the winter on the bank of the Missouri in something like comfort. However, the winter of 1846-7 was terrible beyond his belief. Seven hundred Saints died of exposure, starvation and disease. But their faith held firm.

As soon as the first spring sun appeared, the Mormons were on the move. The first group out – the "Pioneer Band" – was led by Brigham Young, and consisted of 148 trailblazing volunteers in 73 wagons. To avoid clashes with Gentile pioneers, Young took a route along the north bank of the Platte instead of the Oregon Trail on the river's south bank. Rain made travel uncomfortable, but failed to dampen spirits or slow the steady progress. May found the Pioneer Band carefree and chasing buffalo, and so joyous did they become that Young had to remind them of their religious obligations: "Joking, nonsense, profane language, trifling conversation and loud laughter do not belong to us. Suppose the angels were witnessing the hoe-down the other

evening, and listening to the haw haws . . . would they not
be ashamed of it?"

The chastened Mormons pushed on past Fort Laramie.
At Casper they built two ferries to cross the river, leaving
a party behind to convey other emigrants. (Gentiles had to
pay; Saints travelled gratis.) On 27 June 1847 – the third
anniversary of Smith's martyrdom – Young's advance
party crossed South Pass.

In the foothills of the Rockies they encountered the
trapper Jim Bridger. He was discouraging, and informed
them that the Great Salt Lake region was too dry to support anything except cactus. He offered to give them
$1,000 for the first bushel of corn they grew there. Un-
daunted, Young pressed ahead.

On 22 July 1847, after a trip of three months across
plains and peaks, the Mormon wagon train rounded Big
Mountain. According to Mormon accounts Young, sick
with mountain fever, sat up, looked out over the Great
Salt Lake Valley and said: "It is enough. This is the right
place. Drive on."

The valley was as dry as Bridger had said. But the soil
was fertile. Young threw off the sickness and began organizing irrigation, and laying out a plan for the capital of
his new nation, where each adult male would have a town
house as well as a farm. "We propose," wrote Young, "to
have the temple lot contain 40 acres, that the streets will be
88 feet wide, sidewalks 20 feet, the lots to contain 1¼ acre,
eight lots a block." The Mormon state would be independent and sovereign. Its name would be Deseret, after the
Mormon word for honeybee.

With the coming of spring 1848, Mormon hands turned
to the sowing of wheat in a huge 5,000-acre field. The rains
were unseasonally good, and the wheat did well – until
May, when dark clouds of crickets descended and consumed the ripening corn. In their despair the Saints turned

to prayer. As if by miracle, flocks of seagulls appeared and fell on the crickets. Half the crop was saved, sufficient for the winter of 1848, even for a population swollen by migration to 4,000.

The next year Young's state-building dream received a setback when Congress refused to accept Deseret as part of the Union; instead, they created the Territory of Utah (included within it was present-day Nevada). To appease Young, he was declared Governor.

As a means of boosting the population of Deseret, Young dispatched missionaries to the United States, and to Britain and Europe. The response was overwhelming, partly because of the missionaries' zeal, partly because of the secular lure of a new life in the open spaces of the West. To aid matters, the Mormons offered prospective emigrants a repayable loan to get to Deseret. The response from Britain, in particular, was phenomenal. A deterioration in Albion's economy encouraged thousands from the Valleys of South Wales and other industrial centres to follow the Mormon call. Some 33,000 left Britain for the Mormon Zion in 1851 alone, transported across the Atlantic in special emigrant ships, and on by train to the Missouri. At Fort Leavenworth or Winter Quarters they were provided with teams and wagons and given instruction in plains travel. On reaching Utah they were provided with employment and a home.

When the Mormon Perpetual Emigration Fund ran low in 1855, Young displayed his usual ingenuity. An edict went out from his office: "The Lord through his Prophet, says of the poor 'Let them come on foot, with hand carts or wheel barrows, let them gird up their loins and walk through and nothing shall hinder them!' " Hundreds of simple two-wheeled hardwood handcarts were made, costing a fraction of the price of a Prairie Schooner. Between 1856 and 1860, some 2,962 Mormon converts from

Europe walked the 1,300 miles from Iowa to Salt Lake City, pushing or pulling their handcarts. As they went they sang:

> Some must push and some must pull,
> As we go marching up the hill,
> As merrily on the way we go,
> Until we reach the valley, OH!

They made as good time as wagon trains. It was one of the most remarkable experiments in overland travel.

Inevitably, the Saints were not allowed to build their Utopia undisturbed. When gold was discovered in California in 1848 thousands of prospectors passed through Mormon territory, and complained of the high prices the Mormons charged them. (The miners had a case; the Mormon price for a hundredweight of flour was $25, ten times the standard price.) Nor could the gold-hunters understand the Mormon attitude to American Indians, which was respect for them as one of the original races of the continent. The Mormons wanted to convert the Indians; most frontier folk wanted to eradicate them. President James Buchanan responded to the growing anti-Mormon feeling in 1857 by dismissing Young as Territorial Governor, and sending 2,500 federal troops to Utah. The threat of invasion caused Mormon tempers to rise and some tragedy came to be expected. It took the shape of the infamous Mountain Meadows Massacre of the "Gentile" emigrants travelling with the Fancher wagon train.

Most of the members of the Fancher party overlanding to California in the late summer of 1857 were peaceable Arkansas farmers. A number, however, were self-styled "Missouri Wildcats", who habitually insulted and attacked Mormons. Several even boasted of having had a hand in the killing of Joseph Smith. When refused supplies by the

Saints, the Wildcats vandalized Mormon property and threatened to return from California with a conquering Gentile army. Scared, yet also anxious for revenge, Mormons in south-west Utah stirred up the local Indians into attacking the train as it lay encamped at Mountain Meadows near Cedar City on 11 September 1857. Seven emigrants were killed, the rest obliged to fort up. After five days of siege, the train received word from the Mormons that the Indians had been pacified and that they could leave safely with an escort of Mormon militiamen. Relieved, the emigrants piled their weapons into a wagon. As the party marched out through a defile at the edge of the meadow, they were ruthlessly shot and hacked down by Mormons and their Indian allies. Within minutes 120 people lay dead. The only survivors were 17 children. The enormity of the slaughter quickly sobered the Mormon executioners. Frightened of punishment from the Church – the act was entirely unsanctioned – and the US authorities, the Mormons blamed the Indians for the massacre.

Few believed them, and rumours spread through the land that Mormons were arming Indians to fight the Gentiles. A full-scale "Mormon War" loomed as bands of Saints held off the invading federal army in the Wasatch Mountains. Yet the prospect of the hills and desert running with blood ultimately appealed to neither side. Young accepted a Gentile governor in his stead, while the army of the government made a purely symbolic march through Great Salt Lake City and then departed.

Thereafter, the Territory developed in peace. By 1860 more than 60,000 people lived in Utah, nearly all of them Saints, and a vast irrigation system of canals watered more than 100,000 acres. More hundreds of acres were added every year.

The ceaseless labour and steadfast vision of the Saints had made the desert bloom.

The Gold Rush

"Jane, i left you and them boys for no other reason than this to come here [California] to procure a littl property by the swet of my brow so that we could have a place of our own that i mite not be a dog for other people any long."

Californian gold prospector, letter to his wife

"Gold from the American River!"

It was the lure of gold rather than God which pulled most pioneers west in the mid-years of the nineteenth century. On 24 January 1848, a carpenter named James W. Marshall made a discovery which would produce one of the most astonishing population movements in history. Inspecting a sawmill on the Sierra Nevada ranch of John Sutter, Marshall noticed something glittering at the bottom of the stream. "Boys," he said, "I believe I've found a gold mine."

Marshall had. Tests quickly confirmed the nature of the metal. Ranch owner John Augustus Sutter was less than pleased. Since 1840 the Swiss-born immigrant had built up a vast baronial estate where his word was law. It had endured Mexican government, and the 1846 "Bear Flag" rebellion by which the American settlers in California had wrested the state from Mexico and joined it to the United

States. But as Sutter correctly guessed, his empire would not endure a gold rush – it would be literally trampled into the ground. He tried to suppress news of the strike, but too many workmen were involved and word got out to the small town of San Francisco.

A sharp-trading Mormon merchant by the name of Sam Brannan was the main messenger of the good news. In the spring of 1848 Brannan tramped up to Sutter's Mill to check whether the gold story was true. When he saw that it was Brannan, who would soon be excommunicated by Brigham Young for misappropriation of Church funds, astutely realized that the easiest and most assured way of getting gold from the strike was by selling miners the victuals and tools they needed – in exchange for the gold they dug with their hands. Brannan set up shop near the Coloma diggings and returned to San Francisco with a quinine bottle full of precious gold dust. Crying "Gold! Gold! Gold from the American River!" he pounded the streets, and talked up a gold rush. Within days every able-bodied man had left San Francisco (the male population of which dropped from 400 to 5) for the gold fields on the American, where they found Sam Brannan open for business.

From San Francisco the gold fever spread to Monterey and Los Angeles. By July most of the state was empty of men. The San Francisco schooner *Louisa* carried the contagion to Honolulu, and it spread from there around Cape Horn to the East Coast. On 5 December 1848, President James K. Polk confirmed the wild rumours exciting Washington. He told Congress: "The accounts of the abundance of gold . . . would scarcely command belief were they not corroborated by . . . officers in the public service." For good measure, 259 ounces of California gold dust (valued at $3,910.10) sent by the state's military governor, Colonel R. B. Mason, were placed on public display.

America went gold crazy. The epidemic spread to the rest of the world. It was said that Californian rivers and streams ran with gold, that an average miner made $1,000 a day, that one man had dug up $9,000 in an afternoon. The California Gold Rush was on. Thousands of men left their homes and jobs, bought picks and pans and headed off to California. The day of the "forty-niner" had arrived.

There were several routes to El Dorado. The most convenient was judged to be by ship, either around the Horn or via the Panamanian isthmus. However, the length of the trip, which could be as much as six months, and the high cost for passage charged by the shipping companies, obliged many gold-seekers to go overland. (Of the 89,000 who went to California in 1849, 41,000 went by sea and 43,000 went overland; the remainder were Mexicans from Sonora.) Most popular of the overland routes were the Mormon and Oregon Trails over the Rockies to the California Trail, which led through the Sierras directly to the gold fields around Sacramento. Overland, the Argonauts (as the gold-seekers came to be called, in reference to the Greek myth of the Golden Fleece) encountered all the problems of the earlier emigrants, and more. Most pioneers were of seasoned frontier stock and used to hardship; most Argonauts were town people with no experience of outdoor living. To make matters worse, the spring of 1849 was dismally wet. "It blew, rained, thundered & lightened tremendous heavy," recalled one overlanding Argonaut. Mud bogged down the wagons, and a cholera outbreak took the lives of 5,000 would-be prospectors. The rest, fearful of being snowbound in the Sierras, like the infamous Donners, jettisoned much of the load in their wagons. They overworked their oxen and mules, who collapsed under the strain. The plains became a junkyard and an abattoir.

Watching askance at the despoliation and endless stream of wagons rolling west were the Indians. Native Americans began to talk of emigrating eastwards. They could not believe that any Whites could be left living there. Between 1848 and 1852 the population of California leaped from 14,000 to a staggering 250,000. In 1851, California became the 31st state of the Union.

Hitting Pay Dirt

Some of the early prospectors did pan out fortunes of the treasure formed by nature 150 million years before. One Argonaut found $26,000 in gold dust in a single summer. Even the moderately lucky could hope to find an average $20 of gold a day, well above average pay for manual work. What made such success so possible for such inexperienced miners as the forty-niners was that all but a fraction of California's first gold came from placers and not veins. The difference was essential. To extract gold from its quartz bed needs hydraulic machinery and chemical processes and is all but impossible for the untutored and the poor. But if the veins are eroded by nature, the gold comes free and runs off into streams as nuggets, flakes or dust. And the golden particles can be won by the simple process of placer mining (pronounced *plah-sir*, and taken from the Spanish for gravel beds), where the prospector needs only to throw some dirt in a pan, swill it around with water to wash the gravel and dirt away, and collect the heavy grains of gold left at the bottom. If "pay dirt" was hit, miners might use a device such as a "long tom", a 12-foot stepped trough with a riddle at the bottom end, into which a stream was diverted while miners shovelled in earth. Unskilled work, but not easy labour. Placer mining was back-breaking, with men digging all day in temperatures over 100 degrees Fahrenheit or wading for

hours in icy mountain water. Scurvy, dysentery and pneumonia were occupational diseases. A great fist of what the
miner earned was handed over to the storekeepers in the
goldfields, Brannan at Coloma, Weber at French Camp on
the Yuba, and Syrec at Mokelumne Hill, all of whose
prices were fantastically high. Salt pork was $20 a barrel,
flour $2 a pound.

Few cared. The forty-niners were a notoriously reckless, big-spending lot. Mark Twain caught them well in
his classic frontier travelogue *Roughing It*:

> It was a splendid population – for all the slow, sleepy,
> sluggish-brained sloths stayed at home – you never find
> that sort of people among pioneers – you cannot build
> pioneers out of that sort of material. It was that population
> that gave to California a name for getting up astounding
> enterprises and rushing them through with a magnificent
> dash and daring and a recklessness of cost or consequences,
> which she bears unto this day . . . But they were rough in
> those times! They fairly reveled in gold, whiskey, fights
> and fandangoes, and were unspeakably happy. The hon-
> est miner raked from a hundred to a thousand dollars out
> of his claim a day, and what with the gambling dens and
> the other entertainments, he hadn't a cent the next morn-
> ing, if he had any sort of luck.

The miner without a cent always knew that tomorrow,
the day after at most, he would strike the Mother Lode. To
cater for the needs and appetites of the miners, fabulous
camps of tents and shacks sprang up: Poker Flat, Red Dog,
Rich Bar, Indian Bar, Eureka North and Hangtown. Gambling dens, bars and brothels abounded. San Francisco
boomed into a "Babylon-by-Sea", luring the miners down
with its glittering, fast pleasures. At the height of the Gold
Rush, in 1853, San Francisco boasted 537 drinking estab-

lishments. Prostitutes from as far away as Chile and China charged $16 for soothing words, $400 for a night. In a gold-crazy, all-male society few Christian sons remembered their commandments, or their mothers' sage advice.

The gleam of Californian gold attracted not only the Argonaut, the merchant, the gambler, the barkeep and the fancy lady. Professional criminals swarmed like flies. Gangs of cut-throats roamed San Francisco and the camps, led by the fearsome "Sydney Ducks", former convicts from the British penal colonies in Australia. Murder became a commonplace, while the agencies of the law were either non-existent or incompetent. Matters became so critical in San Francisco that a Committee of Vigilance was formed on 9 June 1851. In a ten-week period it tried and hanged four men, and forced other criminals to flee. They came back, however, and the Committee had to be revived. Not until the Gold Rush was over and gone did San Francisco, and the camps which struggled into permanent existence, enjoy something like peace and order.

Race was one factor which perpetually provoked violence in the camps' heyday. Upwards of 15 nations mixed together in the camps: White Americans, Black Americans (as slaves and free men), Indians, Mexicans, Turks, English, Welsh, Scots, French; Chinese, Germans, Chileans, Peruvians and Australians. Some White American camps barred all foreigners, others were selective. Mexicans were loathed as "greasers" and their claims ignored. There were attempts to ban Blacks from entering the state at the 1849 constitutional convention. Standardly, Whites refused to work alongside Blacks, although there were exceptions. When Daniel Rogers, a Black forty-niner, gave his Arkansas master a thousand dollars in gold dust for his freedom, the owner reneged on the deal and refused to release him. But other Arkansas Whites raised the money for the slave's liberty and presented it to the surprised Rogers with a certificate commending his "honesty, industry and integrity". Rogers joined the 2,000 free Blacks in the goldfields, eventually purchasing his entire family out of bondage. Slavery was abominated in the goldfields, for the independent prospectors feared that mass cheap labour would strip all the prime claims. When Thomas Green and several other Texas slaveholders arrived in California with their chattels in 1850, White miners at the Rose's Bar camp organized two protest meetings. The Texans were informed that, unless the slaves departed, they would be forcibly expelled. Outnumbered, the Texans left.

Undoubtedly, the greatest racial hate was reserved for the Chinese forty-niners. According to custom house figures 25,000 Chinese passed through San Francisco in 1852 alone. Alien and incomprehensible, the Chinese were despised even for their careful reworking of claims long since abandoned by Whites as unprofitable. They were routinely harassed and sometimes murdered, while cutting off their pigtails was considered fine sport in a drunken spree.

By the middle 1850s it was clear that the day of the independent Californian prospector was over. California's surface and near-surface gold had been taken, the region prospected from top to bottom. There was still gold, but it was locked in lodes of quartz or buried deep in the ground. To get it required tunnels, mills and machinery. Few independents had the necessary finance. The day of the eastern capitalist mining corporation had come.

Thousands and thousands of prospectors gazed on a dull and poor future. Few could conceive of any other life. Mining was an incurable disease; in the eye of the Argonaut every river was gold-bedded, every hill veined with precious yellow. Only mining would do.

In Pursuit of the Golden Fleece

The prospector was curiously blessed, for just as the last placer gold in California was drying up, gold was discovered in America's far western interior. With pack mule, pan and boundless hope the prospector headed to the Gila River in southern Arizona in 1853. The first Colorado gold rush, in the Pike's Peak area, came in 1859. Gold-seekers from the depressed Mid-West rolled Colorado way in wagons emblazoned with the slogan "Pike's Peak or Bust!" (later, failed Argonauts headed home with "Busted, by God!" scrawled on their tailboards). The same year saw the discovery of the famous Comstock Lode in the eastern Sierras of Nevada.

The Washoe field in Nevada had been prospected in a desultory fashion since 1848, but in June of 1859 Peter O'Riley and Patrick McLaughlin discovered the fabulous Ophir Vein at Six Mile Canyon. As they dug furiously the man whose name would eventually grace the strike rode up, the dubious, slothful Henry T. P. Comstock, who declared that he and his partners, James "Old Virginny" Finney and Manny Penrod, owned the claim. Although O'Riley and McLaughlin did not believe him, they took the three into partnership. Before the Lode gave out it yielded $300 million in precious metals, and helped finance the Union side in the Civil War.

Among the 10,000 Californians who rushed to the Washoe strike was George Hearst, father of the future newspaper magnate. Hearst bought out Patrick McLaughlin's share in the Ophir Mine for $3,500 – a sum Hearst got back countless times over. The other Ophir partners proved almost as gullible; O'Riley was bought out for $40,000 and "Old Pancake" Comstock for $10,000, he already having bought out the hapless, bibulous "Old Virginny" Finney for a blind horse and bottle of bourbon.

To Virginny's cold comfort, the shanty town which rose in the valley below the find was called after him: Virginia City.

After the Comstock rush, the mining boom moved north into Idaho and onwards to Montana, where rich placers were found between 1862 and 1864. The large discovery at Alder Gulch in 1863 was made by Henry Edgar, who kept a journal detailing his life as a miner, a classic account of the lows, dangers (which in Montana numbered Indians) and the occasional excitements of the independent prospector:

May 2nd: All went well through the night, but towards morning the horses became restless, and required a good deal of looking after. Just as morning came I took two of them where the boys were sleeping and woke them up. I put the saddles on and was just going out to Bill when the hills were alive with Indians. They were all around Bill and I got on the horse and started for him, but an Indian grabbed him by the head; I pulled my revolver, Simmons was along side of me and told me not to shoot. Well, I got off and gave the rope of the other horse to my Indian. Here they come with other horses and Bill mounted behind another Indian with hat in one hand and rifle in the other, digging his heels in the horse's flanks and yelling like the very devil he is. "How goes it boys?" he asked as he got off. Simmons was talking to the Indians and told us to keep quiet. Quiet, everything we had they had got, but our arms! A young buck took hold of Cover's gun and tried to take it from him. Bill stuck his revolver in the buck's ear, he looked in Bill's face and let go of the gun. We told Simmons to tell them that they had got everything but our guns and that they could not get them without killing us first. We were told to keep them. Everything we had was packed and off to the village. Such a hubbub when we got there. Our traps were put in a pile and a tent put over them. Simmons and the chiefs held a long pow wow. The women brought us some breakfast; good of the kind and plenty. Simmons told us we were prisoners, to keep still and not to be afraid. I went through the village and counted the lodges; there were 180 of them. We talk the matter over and agree to keep together and if it has to come to the worst to fight while life lasts. All the young ones are around us and the women. What fun! We get plenty to eat; Indians are putting up a great big lodge – medicine lodge at that. Night, what will tomorrow bring forth? I write this – will any one ever see it? Quite dark and such a noise, dogs and drums!

May 3rd: All is well. What will we get for breakfast, that is the first thing? Barney has got some flour. Bill asks "If we can get some coffee?" I go to the grub pile. Sugar and coffee all gone. An old woman is watching me. I take the coffee pot and show it to her. She knows what I want and hands me some coffee and sugar; buffalo meat in plenty, cut what we want; high living. The Medicine man made medicine all night. Wonder what the outcome will be? The village is on a large, low flat on the left bank of the river, with a large wooded hill back of it. Could we make that? Yes, the boys say when the time comes we will make it. Simmons tells us we are wanted at the medicine lodge; up we go. Bill says, "Ten o'clock, court now opens." We went in, the medicine man sat on the ground at the far end; both sides were lined with the head men Red Bear and Little Crow, the two chiefs of the village, sat beside the medicine man. We were taken in hand by an old buck; in the center of the lodge there was a bush planted, – the medicine bush – and around and around that bush we went. At last their curiosity was satisfied and we were led out to Red Bear's lodge and told to remain there. We had a good laugh over our cake walk. Bill says if they take us in again we will pull up that medicine bush and whack the medicine man with it. We tell him not to, but he says he will sure. An order comes again, and we go in and around the bush. At the third time Bill pulls up the bush and Mr. Medicine Man gets it on the head. What a time! Not a word spoken; what deep silence for a few minutes! Out we go and the Indians after us. We stand back to back, three facing each way; Red Bear and Little Crow driving the crowd back with their whips, and peace is proclaimed. Red Bear mounts his horse and started in on the longest talk I ever heard of; I don't know what he is talking about; Simmons says he is talking for us. He began the talk about noon and he was still talking when I fell asleep at midnight. We are all in Red Bear's lodge and a guard around it.

May 4th: All's well that ends well. We were told this morning what the verdict was. If we go on down the river they will kill us; if we go back they will give us horses to go with. A bunch of horses were driven up and given to us. I got a blind eyed black and another plug for my three; the rest of the boys in the same fix, except Bill, he got his three back. We got our saddles, a hundred pounds of flour, some coffee, sugar, one plug of tobacco and two robes each for our clothes and blankets; glad to get so much. It did not take us long to saddle up. Simmons asked us what was best for him to do, stop with the Indians or go with us. I spoke for the boys and told him he had better stay with the Indians, if he was afraid to risk his scalp with white men. He stayed. We got away at last. Harry Rodgers was riding by my side. I asked him what he thought would be the outcome. His answer was "God is good." The Indians told us to cross at the ford and go up the south side of the river. We met an old Indian woman and she told us not to cross the ford. She made us understand that if we did we would all be killed. When we came to the ford

we camped and got something to eat and when it was
dark saddled up and traveled all night; took to the hills in
the morning; we were about forty or forty-five miles from
our friends, the Indians. They told us Stuart was one day
ahead. What has become of them? . . .

May 26th: Off again; horse pretty lame and Bill leading
him out of the timber; fine grassy hills and lots of quartz;
some antelope in sight; down a long ridge to a creek and
camp; had dinner, and Rodgers, Sweeney, Barney and
Cover go up the creek to prospect. It was Bill's and my
turn to guard camp and look after the horses. We washed
and doctored the horse's leg. Bill went across to a bar to
see or look for a place to stake the horses. When he came
back to camp he said "There is a piece of rimrock sticking
out of the bar over there. Get the tools and we will go and
prospect it." Bill got the pick and shovel and the pan and
went over. Bill dug the dirt and filled the pan. "Now go"
he says, "and wash that pan and see if you can get enough
to buy some tobacco when we get to town." I had the pan
more than half panned down and had seen some gold as I
ran the sand around, when Bill sang out "I have found a
scad." I returned for answer, "If you have one I have a
hundred." He then came down to where I was with his
scad. It was a nice piece of gold. Well, I panned the pan of
dirt and it was a good prospect; weighed it and had two
dollars and forty cents; weighed Bill's scad and it weighed
the same. Four dollars and eighty cents! Pretty good for
tobacco money. We went and got another pan and Bill
panned that and got more than I had; I got the third one
and panned that – best of the three; that is good enough to
sleep on. We came to camp, dried and weighed our gold,
altogether there was twelve dollars and thirty cents. We
saw the boys coming to camp and no tools with them.
"Have you found anything?" "We have started a hole but
didn't get to bedrock." They began to growl about the

horses not being taken care of and to give Bill and me fits. When I pulled the pan around Sweeney got hold of it and the next minute sang out "Salted!" I told Sweeney that if he "would pipe Bill and me down and run us through a sluice box he couldn't get a color," and "the horses could go to the devil or the Indians." Well, we talked over the find and roasted venison till late; and sought the brush, and spread our robes; and a joyous lot of men never went more contentedly to bed than we.

May 27th: Up before the sun; horses all right; soon the frying pan was on the fire. Sweeney was off with the pan and Barney telling him "to take it aisy". He panned his pan and beat both Bill and me. He had five dollars and thirty cents. "Well, you have got it good, by Jove!" were his greeting words. When we got filled up with elk, Hughes and Cover went up the gulch, Sweeney and Rodgers down. Bill and I to the old place. We panned turn about ten pans at a time, all day long, and it was good dirt too. "A grub stake is what we are after" was our watchword all day, and it is one hundred and fifty dollars in good dust. "God is good" as Rodgers said when we left the Indian camp. Sweeney and Rodgers found a good prospect and have eighteen dollars of the gold to show for it. Barney and Tom brought in four dollars and a half. As we quit, Bill says "there's our supper,"a large band of antelope on the hillside. We had our guns with us. He took up one draw and I the other, it was getting dark, but light enough to shoot, got to a good place within about seventy five yards and shot; the one I shot at never moved; I thought it missed; I rolled over and loaded up my gun, then the antelope was gone. Bill had shot by this time; I went to where the one I shot at was standing, and found some blood, and the antelope dead not ten steps away; Bill got one too; ate our fill; off to bed.

May 28th: Staked the ground this morning; claims one

hundred feet. Sweeney wanted a water – a notice written
for a water right and asked me to write it for him. I wrote
it for him; then "What name shall we give the creek?" The
boys said "You name it." So I wrote "Alder." There was a
large fringe of Alder growing along the creek, looking nice
and green and the name was given. We staked twelve
claims for our friends and named the bars Cover,
Fairweather and Rodgers where the discoveries were made.
We agree to say nothing of the discovery when we get to
Bannack and come back and prospect the gulch thoroughly and get the best. It was midday when we left; we
came down the creek past the forks and to its mouth,
made marks so we could find the same again and on down
the valley (Ram's Horn Gulch) to a small creek; the same
we camped on as we went out and made camp for the
night; a more happy lot of boys would be hard to find,
though covered with seedy clothes.

May 29th: All well. Breakfast such as we have, bread
and antelope and cold water and good appetites. What
better fare could a prince wish! It might be worse and
without the good seasoning given by our find. Down and
over the Stinking Water along a high level bench twelve
miles or more to the Beaverhead River, then up about six
miles and camp. We have come about twenty-five miles.

May 30th: All well. Ate up the last of our meat for
breakfast; will have supper at Bannack, ham and eggs.
Away we go and have no cares. Crossed at the mouth of
the Rattlesnake and up to the Bannack trail, the last stage
over the hill and down to the town, the raggedest lot that
was ever seen but happy. Friends on every side. Bob
Dempsey grabbed our horses and cared for them. Frank
Ruff got us to his cabin. Salt Lake eggs, ham, potatoes,
everything. Such a supper! One has to be on short com-
mons and then he will know. Too tired and too glad.

May 31st: Such excitement! Everyone with a long story

about the "new find". After I got my store clothes on, I was
sitting in a saloon talking with some friends; there were
lots of men that were strangers to me; they were telling
that we brought in a horse load of gold and not one of the
party had told that we had found a color. Such is life in the
"Far West." Well we have been feasted and cared for like
princes.

After Montana the next rush was to the exact centre of
the North American continent, the Black Hills, where an
expedition led by George Armstrong Custer had discovered gold in 1874. Prospectors swarmed over what was
the Sioux's most hallowed ground. But not even war with
the most feared of the Plains Indians could stop a rush for
gold, and Deadwood boomed.

Four years later, silver was discovered at Tombstone in
Arizona. Like scores of other mining towns before it,
Tombstone grew from nothing into a gaudy, thriving
settlement. And when the metal was exhausted, after
years or sometimes decades, so was the world's use for
the town. Reputedly "too tough to die", Tombstone was
in its grave by the 1890s.

After Tombstone, there was only one further big strike
in the contiguous United States, at Cripple Creek in Colorado in 1890. Thereafter, the mining frontier went north,
to the Klondike River in Canada, and Nome and Fairbanks
in Alaska. The placer miners of the West had finally had
their time. Few had become rich, and one in five of the
latter-day Argonauts died in pursuit of the American
golden fleece. Their legacy, though, was enormous. They
took a rough form of frontier civilization to California,
and from there into the interior, across the mountains of
Colorado and Nevada, the deserts of Arizona, to the wilderness of Montana and the hallowed Black Hills. Not
every mining camp and region busted. When a rush was

over, a pinch of miners usually stayed, as did a pinch of the merchants, farmers and business and professional people who had trailed in their wake. San Francisco was built on gold, so too was Denver. And where there was a sizeable mining settlement there arose a demand for communication and transportation. The railway, the Pony Express, the telegraph, and the stagecoach were all driven across the continent by the power of gold.

Motive Power

The Liquid Highway

The buffalo made the first trails over the illimitable and rolling West. Indians followed the animals' paths from the earliest times, and learned to use the rivers for transport. When the White man arrived, he copied the ways of the Indian. In the north, the Indian canoe was used by the French *coureurs de bois* for the conveyance of furs from the Northwest to Montreal. A dug-out, usually made from the trunk of a cottonwood, would take four men four days to build, using a specially shaped round adze, or *tille ronde*. In a dug-out or birchbark, a *voyageur* could traverse the near 5,000 miles of waterways with five tons of goods in a hundred days. River traffic was dependable and inexpensive.

As trade grew, so did the size of vessels. "Flatboats" were rough 40-feet long shallow boxes (their draw was negligible), which floated sedately downriver. At Pittsburgh in the 1790s, emigrant westering families exchanged their jolting wagons for a $35 flatboat, loading on their cattle to the open deck, and taking shelter themselves behind a shedlike "broadhorn". Since they were unable to make headway against the stream, flatboats were one-way craft only. At their destination they were unloaded, then broken up and sold for lumber.

Flatboats gave way to keelboats, made manoeuvrable by a wooden keel and tapered prow. These crafts could make the journey back upstream, but only by Herculean human labour. Men stood on the stern of the boat with long poles which they plunged to the river bottom, and then walked forwards, thus propelling the vessel along. The alternative was to tow the boat from the bank by means of a line or "cordelle" or, in the gratefully received deepwater stretches, put up the sail. Keelboats could carry up to 50 tons of freight, and the keelboater became the proletarian king of the inland waters. At least one, Mike Fink, assumed the status of legend. "I'm a Salt River roarer, half horse and half alligator, suckled by a wild cat and a playmate of the snapping turtle," boasted Fink.

Born in about 1770 in Pittsburgh, Fink (he insisted on spelling his name Miche Phinck) served as a frontier scout in his teens. Even then he was an unbeatable marksman, being nicknamed "Bangall" by fellow militiamen. After scouting, he began as a hand on a keelboat that worked the Ohio–Mississippi run, soon becoming captain of his own boat. It is said that he never lost one of the bloody bare-knuckle fights ("rough and tumble") that were the keelboaters' main sport. Fink's reputation as a marksman was only increased by the shooting of a whiskey glass off a friend's head at 20 paces. The keelboater was also possessed of a streak of sadism; he shot off the protruding heel of a slave, claiming to a judge that he did it so that the man would be able to wear a fashionable boot. On another occasion, Fink set the clothes of a mistress alight, forcing her to jump overboard.

When the steamboat killed off the keelboat business, Fink took to the Rocky Mountains as a trapper. Accompanying him were two cronies, Carpenter and Talbot. In 1822, during a dreary winter at Fort Henry, Fink and

Carpenter vied for the affection of an Indian woman. The resolution of the quarrel came when, during a drinking bout, Fink proposed they take turns at shooting whiskey cups off each other's heads, a party trick they had performed in every port along the Mississippi. Carpenter walked out and placed the whiskey on his head. Fink shot, promptly blowing Carpenter's head off. "Carpenter," jested Fink, "you have spilled the whiskey." The outraged Talbot shot Fink through the heart.

The great age of Western steamboating began on 11 October 1811, the day Nicholas Roosevelt's *New Orleans* left Pittsburgh for her namesake, which she reached under two months later, having survived an earthquake and an attack by a canoeload of outraged Indians. By 1850, steamboats dominated transportation in the cotton-growing Old West and the farming West, carrying 3 million passengers a year on Westerner waters. Their design had become standardized into a long, narrow hull, with the engines on the main deck, and the passenger accommodation above. The big Mississippi boats usually had two paddle wheels, one on each side. On the smaller Western rivers, the more manoeuvrable single-paddle sternwheeler was standard.

Steamboats were fast and cheap. In 1853 the *Eclipse* made the journey from New Orleans to Louisville in four days and nine hours. The cabin fare was around 1 cent a mile. At 350 feet in length the *Eclipse* was a veritable "floating palace", gaudily decorated with luxurious first-class staterooms and a glittering saloon, complete with chandeliers and stained-glass skylights. To Westerners, such Queens of the River were the pinnacle of elegance. Yet underneath their beautiful skin steamboats were hastily, even dangerously, made. To reduce the draft (as low as two feet) and cut construction costs, they were light to the point of being flimsy. Sand banks and snags regularly

holed craft, causing them to sink. An entire fleet of steamboats was ground to kindling wood at St Louis during the
"Great Ice Gorge of 1856". The *Missouri Republican* reported that "the terrible sweep of waters with its burden
of ice, the mashing to pieces of boats and the hurrying on
shore of the excited crowd was one of the most awful and
imposing scenes we have ever witnessed."

A steamboat could be a deathtrap. Most feared of all
was an explosion in the wood-burning boilers. Not until
the 1850s did steamboats have pressure gauges, leaving it
to the crew to estimate or guess when boilers were running dry or building up too much steam. Technical knowledge among steamboat mechanics was virtually nil. "The
management of engines and boilers is entrusted," wrote
visiting British engineer David Stevenson in 1838, "to
men whose carelessness of human life is equalled only by
their want of civilisation." Disasters were inevitable. Fifty-
five German emigrants were scalded to death when the
boilers of the *Edna* blew up at Green Island in 1842. The
steamboat *Big Hatchie* killed 35 and wounded more when
she exploded at Hermann, Missouri, in 1845.

Unsurprisingly, the exigencies of the steamboat trade
engendered a certain fatalism among crews. Nor was
crewing aboard the boats the only dangerous occupation
associated with their running. The boat burned wood,
which had to be supplied by men who lived along the
banks of the Western rivers: the woodcutters known to
steamboatmen as "woodhawks".

The woodhawks lived out miserable and lonely lives.
And dangerous ones. Seven woodhawks were murdered
by Indians in the area between Fort Benton, Montana and
Bismarck, North Dakota during 1868 alone.

The diary of Peter Koch, a Danish youth who cut wood
at the mouth of the Musselshell River in 1869 and 1870,
cogently reflects the lot of the woodhawk:

Oct. 4. Commenced chopping. Blistered my hands and broke an ax handle.

8. Twenty five years old and poor as a rat. Cut down a tree on the cabin.

20. Cutting while Joe is on guard. Snow tonight.

24. Killed my first buffalo. He took 7 Spencer and 6 pistol balls before he died. River full of ice.

Nov. 7. A Gale of wind. Those Arapahoes who camped abt. 10 days at Jim Wells woodyard have moved down the river after shooting into his stockade.

15. Chopped hard all day. B.M. says 3 cords. Fred came back all wet. He had started in a skiff with Dick Harris, both drunk, and upset at Squaw Creek.

25. Fred and Olsen started out wolfing. We stopped chopping on account of shooting and shouting in the hills. Joe and I found 4 wolves at our baits.

Dec. 10. Sick. No meat.

11. Sick yet. Bill, Joe and Mills went to Musselshell, said Indians had attacked and stolen 3 horses and mule but lost one man.

24. Christmas eve. No wolves.

Jan 16. Awful cold. Froze my ears.

17. Too cold to work. Went up to Musselshell. Froze my nose.

24 Thawing heavily. Mills drunk.

Mar. 22. Saw three geese. (Spring has come, gentle Annie.) Martin sick.

Apr. 24. Sixty Crows went up the river after Sioux to avenge the killing of 29 Crows. They were all looking dreadful, had their hair cut off, their fingers and faces cut, with the blood left on their faces.

May 9. One hundred and seventy cords on the bank. We put fire to the brush piles. The fire spread and burnt up 50 cords. We were played out before we got it checked. Nothing to eat.

13. Wind turned and started the fire again. About 20 cords burned.

22. The "Nick Wall" passed about two o'clock in the morning without stopping.

23. 40–50 Indians showed themselves at Musselshell the 20th. The crazy Frenchman started toward them and was badly beaten but when firing started they turned and ran.

24. Raining. The "Ida Reese" passed about daybreak without our knowing it.

28. Sold "Deerlodge" about 10 cords of wood.

June 13. The "Sallie" passed after midnight and took on 15 cords of wood.

16. The "Ida Stockdale" passed without stopping. We threw 6 cords back from the bank to keep it from falling into the river.

July 4. Indians firing at us from nearest cottonwood trees and all through the sage brush. The balls whistled pretty lively but we returned the fire and drove them from their shelter. We went out and found one young warrior killed by a shot through the upper thigh. We got his gun, bow and arrows and two butcher knives and threw his body in the river. Waring scalped him.

One woodhawker on the Musselshell found a desperate remedy to keep Native Americans at bay. John Johnson was a burly, matted-haired ex-mountain man who pursued a personal war against the Crow tribe after they murdered his pregnant Flathead wife. He began killing and scalping Crow warriors, and eating – or pretending to eat – their livers. This practice gave him a remarkable immunity from Crow attack; for good measure, "Liver-Eating" Johnson decorated his landing-stage with the skulls of dead braves.

"A Glorious Triumph for Civilization"

As the steamboat had replaced the keelboat, so it too would be replaced as the West's most eminent form of travel. The steamboat had a drawback which sank it more surely than its safety record. The boats could only go where the water was, and the main liquid highway, the Mississippi, ran north to south. As the frontier moved further into the plains and mountains of trans-Mississippi America, so the steamboat became increasingly obsolete. Wagons, horses, and later the railroads, were the only way west for most freight and passengers.

It was the colonization of Oregon and the California Gold Rush which forced the roads and ribbons of steel across the land, tying coast to coast and region to region. Before the colonizing of the Pacific coast, pioneer communities had been sufficiently near settlement for their needs to be served. The Oregonians and the Californians were remote from civilization. The East feared for their spiritual welfare; the wants of the Far Westerners were more prosaic. They wanted mail and news from home, and sometimes a fast means of getting there.

As early as 1848, the federal government had been obliged to organize a mail service to the West Coast via Panama. The service, however, took 30 days, cost as much as 80 cents an ounce, and only stimulated California's desire for an overland transcontinental service. When 75,000 Californians signed an overland petition in 1856, Congress agreed to act. Almost immediately, the matter ran into sectional strife. Northerners favoured a direct route from St Joseph, Missouri to San Francisco via South Pass. Southerners wanted a route from St Louis crossing Texas, passing through El Paso and Fort Yuma into southern California. It was, they conceded, much longer, but less likely to be affected by heavy snow in winter.

Unable to agree the route, Congress handed the matter over to the post-master, Aaron V. Brown. As Brown was an ardent Southerner from Memphis, it came as small surprise that he awarded the $600,000 contract to veteran Eastern stagecoach operator – and his friend – John Butterfield, who would ply the "Ox-Bow" southern route. The North was disgusted. The Chicago *Tribune* called the award of the contract "one of the greatest swindles ever perpetrated upon the country by the slave holders." Many doubted that Butterfield could fulfil the terms of his agreement: Tipton, Missouri to San Francisco in 25 days.

Butterfield spent a million dollars preparing his 2,812-mile route west, building nearly 200 relay and home stations. The coaches he introduced transformed Western travel. Named after the town in New Hampshire where it was made by the firm of J. Stephens Abbott and Lewis Downing, the Concord had an iron-reinforced oval wooden body swung on 3½ inch oxhide thoroughbraces which absorbed some of the worst shocks. The coaches were often brightly coloured, with landscape pictures on the doors. Nine passengers could be accommodated inside, with another two on top behind the driver and conductor.

The first Butterfield Overland Mail coaches went into operation on 16 September 1858. That morning two coaches departed on a great journey, one westwards from Tipton, and one eastwards from San Francisco. For days they careered over dirt track, desert, and prairie – and both came in on time. President Buchanan was so pleased that he sent Butterfield a telegram which read: "I congratulate you on the result. It is a glorious triumph for civilisation and the Union." For the next three years Butterfield's coaches raced over the southern trail, two a week in each direction, through all weathers, with hardly a break in service. Marauding Apaches, Kiowas and Comanches were an occasional hazard, with one driver complaining to writer Mark Twain that "he became so leaky with bullet holes" that "he couldn't hold his vittels."

Since the southern route had effectively become the official overland road, it fell to private enterprise to develop a direct overland trail. In 1855 the firm of Russell, Majors and Waddell started a freight wagon service from the railhead at St Joseph to San Francisco. The enterprise grew with astonishing rapidity to become the unchallenged giant of western freighting; by 1858 it employed 4,000 men and operated 3,500 covered wagons.

A prime cause of the company's success was the efficient method that partner Alexander Majors devised for moving their massive cargoes overland. Each caravan of wagons sent out by Russell, Majors and Waddell contained 25 covered wagons, each carrying three tons of goods and pulled by mules or oxen. Alongside each wagon walked a teamster or "bullwhacker", who controlled the animals by use of a 12-foot long whip. Tipped with a rawhide popper, the bullwhip could crack the air with a pop-pop that could be heard two miles away. Most drivers were rough and tough frontier types, who signed and then conveniently ignored the company pledge the pious Majors made them sign, promising not to swear, "nor to get drunk, nor to gamble ... and not to do anything incompatible with the conduct of a gentleman."

Unfortunately for Majors, his flamboyant New Englander associate William H. Russell was an inveterate financial gambler. When the company lost money in the so-called Mormon War, after the army reneged on payment, Russell hit on two fantastic ventures to refill the vaults. The first was a stagecoach line to Denver to cash in on the Pike's Peak gold rush. Majors and Waddell, believing that such an enterprise was doomed without a government subsidy, refused to back it. Undeterred, Russell found a less cautious associate, John S. Jones, and began operating the Leavenworth & Pike's Peak Express Company in April 1859. The L&PP was admirably efficient. It was also, as Majors and Waddell had foreseen, completely unviable. The expenses were over $1,000 a day. Concerned that Russell's impending bankruptcy would bring the freight company down, his partners were obliged to take over the stagecoach venture. Reorganized as the Central Overland, California and Pike's Peak Express, the new company was soon known by all as "Clean Out of Cash and Poor Pay".

More desperate than ever, Russell dreamt up another fantastic money-making scheme: a relay of fast horsemen which would take the mail between Missouri and California in ten days. And so was born one of the West's most celebrated services – the Pony Express.

A chain of 190 waystations was built at ten-mile intervals on the most direct route between St Joseph and San Francisco. Five hundred fast horses were bought, and a team of dare-devil boy horsemen hired. Lightweight saddles, stirrups and a special leather-pocketed mail bag, a "mochila", slung over the horn and cantle of the saddle, were devised. At each relay station the rider would dismount, throw the mochila on a fresh pony, jump up and be away.

To cheering crowds, the first relay rider of the Pony Express streaked west out of St Joseph, 49 letters in his mochila, on 3 April 1860. Only 19 months later, the last rider delivered the mail in San Francisco and was looking for gainful employment. The Pony Express had been instantly rendered obsolete by technology. The Pacific Telegraph Company and the Overland Telegraph Company of Hiram Sibley completed its transcontinental line on 24 October 1861. The Express's record time for the trip was for the delivery of Lincoln's inaugural address in March 1861: an astounding seven days and 17 hours. Yet the telegraph took mere seconds to get a message from East to West and West to East.

If the Express was short-lived it was also glorious. Among those who rode for it was the 14-year-old Buffalo Bill Cody. When Cody later toured his Wild West show around the world, the Express regularly featured as one of the acts. There was much to dramatize. One Express rider, "Pony Bob" Haslam, was once attacked by Paiutes in Nevada, wounded in the face and arm, then escaped the attack to travel 120 miles in eight hours and 10 minutes, using 13 horses. Then he rested a few hours, and did the return trip.

The telegraph not only finished the Pony Express; it finally drove Russell, Majors and Waddell into bankruptcy. For some years, the firm had been taking infusions of capital from the stagecoach entrepreneur Ben Holladay. In 1862 he foreclosed and took over the assets of Russell, Majors and Waddell. Energetic and ruthless, Holladay then built a huge freight and coach operation out of the ruins, becoming the "stagecoach king" of the West and controlling 5,000 miles of stage routes. For "The Overland Stage Line", Holladay bought new Concord coaches and fine animals. His staff were alternately bludgeoned and bribed (his general manager was paid an astonishing $10,000 per annum salary) into loyalty and efficiency. To travel on the Overland, however, was no more a pleasurable or comfortable experience than on any other line. The coaches were cramped, dusty, stiflingly hot in summer, bitterly cold in winter. Hold-ups became an increasing nuisance, with one company alone recording 313 robberies of its stages on the California line between 1870 and 1884, 27 of them by the notorious Black Bart. More irksome to passengers, however, were the poor meals they received at the waystations. The suffering traveller Mark Twain recorded the experience in *Roughing It*:

The station buildings were long, low huts, made of sun-dried, mud-colored bricks, laid up without mortar (*adobes*, the Spaniards call these bricks, and Americans shorten it to '*dobies*). The roofs, which had no slant to them worth speaking of, were thatched and then sodded or covered with a thick layer of earth, and from this sprung a pretty rank growth of weeds and grass. It was the first time we had ever seen a man's front yard on top of his house. The buildings consisted of barns, stable-room for twelve or fifteen horses, and a hut for an eating-room for passengers. This latter had bunks in it for the station-keeper and a hostler or two. You could rest your elbow on its eaves, and you had to bend in order to get in at the door. In place of a window there was a square hole about large enough for a man to crawl through, but this had no glass in it. There was no flooring, but the ground was packed hard. There was no stove, but the fireplace served all needful purposes. There were no shelves, no cupboards, no closets. In a corner stood an open sack of flour, and nestling against its base were a couple of black and venerable tin coffee-pots, a tin teapot, a little bag of salt, and a side of bacon.

By the door of the station-keeper's den, outside, was a tin wash-basin, on the ground. Near it was a pail of water and a piece of yellow bar-soap, and from the eaves hung a hoary blue woolen shirt, significantly – but this latter was the station-keeper's private towel, and only two persons in all the party might venture to use it – the stage-driver and the conductor. The latter would not, from a sense of decency; the former would not, because he did not choose to encourage the advances of a station-keeper. We had towels – in the valise; they might as well have been in Sodom and Gomorrah. We (and the conductor) used our handkerchiefs, and the driver his pantaloons and sleeves.

By the door, inside, was fastened a small old-fashioned looking-glass frame, with two little fragments of the original mirror lodged down in one corner of it. This arrangement afforded a pleasant double-barreled portrait of you when you looked into it, with one half of your head set up a couple of inches above the other half. From the glass frame hung the half of a comb by a string – but if I had to describe that patriarch or die, I believe I would order some sample coffins. It had come down from Esau and Samson, and had been accumulating hair ever since – along with certain impurities. In one corner of the room stood three or four rifles and muskets, together with horns and pouches of ammunition. The station-men wore pantaloons of coarse, country-woven stuff, and into the seat and the inside of the legs were sewed ample additions of buckskin, to do duty in place of leggings, when the man rode horseback – so the pants were half dull blue and half yellow and unspeakably picturesque. The pants were stuffed into the tops of high boots, the heels whereof were armed with great Spanish spurs, whose little iron clogs and chains jingled with every step. The man wore a huge beard and mustachios, an old slouch hat, a blue woolen shirt, no suspenders, no vest, no coat – in a leathern sheath in his belt, a great long "navy" revolver (slung on right side, hammer to the front), and projecting from his boot a horn-handled bowie-knife. The furniture of the hut was neither gorgeous nor much in the way. The rocking-chairs and sofas were not present, and never had been, but they were represented by two three-legged stools, a pine-board bench four feet long, and two empty candle-boxes. The table was a greasy board on stilts, and the table-cloth and napkins had not come – and they were not looking for them, either. A battered tin platter, a knife and fork, and a tin pint cup, were at each man's place, and the driver had a queens-ware saucer that had seen better days. Of course, this duke sat at the head of the table. There was one isolated piece of table furniture that bore about it a touching air of grandeur in misfortune. This was the caster. It was German silver, and crippled and rusty, but it was so preposterously out of place there that it was suggestive of a tattered exiled king among barbarians, and the majesty of its native position compelled respect even in its degradation. There was only one cruet left, and that was a stopperless, fly-specked, broken-necked thing, with two inches of vinegar in it, and a dozen preserved flies with their heels up and looking sorry they had invested there.

The station-keeper up-ended a disk of last week's bread, of the shape and size of an old-time cheese, and carved some slabs from it which were as good as Nicholson pavement, and tenderer.

He sliced off a piece of bacon for each man, but only the experienced old hands made out to eat it, for it was condemned army bacon which the United States would not feed to its soldiers in the forts, and the stage company had bought it cheap for the sustenance of their passengers and employees. We may have found this condemned army bacon further out on the Plains than the section I am locating it in, but we *found* it – there is no gainsaying that.

Then he poured for us a beverage which he called *"Slumgullion,"* and it is hard to think he was not inspired when he named it. It really pretended to be tea, but there was too much dish-rag, and sand, and old bacon-rind in it to deceive the intelligent traveler. He had no sugar and no milk – not even a spoon to stir the ingredients with.

We could not eat the bread or the meat, nor drink the "Slumgullion." And when I looked at that melancholy vinegar-cruet, I thought of the anecdote (a very, very old one, even at that day) of the traveler who sat down to a table which had nothing on it but a mackerel and a pot of mustard. He asked the landlord if this was all. The landlord said:

"*All!* Why, thunder and lightning, I should think there was mackerel enough there for six."

"But I don't like mackerel."

"Oh – then help yourself to the mustard."

In other days I had considered it a good, a very good, anecdote, but there was a dismal plausibility about it, here, that took all the humor out of it.

Our breakfast was before us, but our teeth were idle.

I tasted and smelt, and said I would take coffee, I believed. The station-boss stopped dead still, and glared at me speechless. At last, when he came to, he turned away and said, as one who communes with himself upon a matter too vast to grasp:

"*Coffee!* Well, if that don't go clean ahead of me, I'm d—d!"

The Ribbon of Steel

The poor facilities Holladay provided for his customers hardly mattered: he had a near monopoly on the lines in the West. But Ben Holladay was astute as well as arrogant. From the resolute spread of railroad tracks across the nation, he realized that the era of animal power was at its close, and in 1866 he sold out to the New York enterprise Wells, Fargo and Company for $1.8 million. He acted none too soon. Wells Fargo itself only survived the next decade by restructuring, running "feeder" coaches to railheads and concentrating on its express and bullion interests.

The dream of a transcontinental railroad had excited the imagination of the nation ever since the discovery of gold in California. A railroad could haul gold east by the truckload. In 1861 the vision started to become reality, when four California-based merchants, Collis P. Huntington, Charles Crocker, Leland Stanford and Mark Hopkins, sank eight and a half million dollars into founding the Central Pacific Railroad. A year later Congress granted them a charter. At the same time, the legislature approved federal funds for the Union Pacific in the East. The financial practices of both companies were dubious in the extreme, but they got the job done. By 1866 the Union Pacific was advancing through Nebraska at a remarkable mile a day.

Men flooded in to work on the iron road. Ten thousand Chinese "coolies" employed by Central Pacific (on the suggestion of Charles Crocker's Chinese manservant, Ah Ling) struggled against the terrible geology and weather of the Sierra Nevada. They hung in baskets against sheer rock faces, drilling holes for dynamite; they died of heat exhaustion in mountain tunnels from which they did not emerge for months. When hundreds of coolies and miles of track were swept away by blizzards, the company was forced to build 40 miles of snow sheds. The Chinese endured, and got the Central Pacific over the hump of the Sierra Nevada and on the downgrade.

As the Chinese gangs drove eastwards, the gangs of the Union Pacific – who were predominantly Irish – rushed to meet them, a trail of steel behind. The recreational needs of the Chinese, save for gambling, were almost non-existent; those of the Irish were many and predominantly sinful. At "end of track" on the Union line was a temporary tented city, where a navvy could throw away his money in saloons and brothels. When the tracks had been laid out for another stretch, the claptrap canvas town was dismantled and moved along to the new "end of track". A number of Western towns grew up this way, such as Cheyenne in Wyoming. More usually, the "hell on wheels" became extinct as the line moved on, or rotted and was blown away by the winds of the high plains.

In the early spring of 1869, six years after the first spikes had been driven, the two lines were fast approaching each other. When they did meet in northern Utah – they passed each other. Congress had inadvertently set no junction point. Moreover, the more track each company laid the more money and land – which could later be sold off – it received. They had no incentive to stop. The farce was only halted when Congress ordered the rails to be joined at Promontory Point, Utah. On 10 May 1869, workers and officials observed the laying of the last tie, laurelwood bound in silver, and the driving of the last spike, made of gold, by the sledgehammer swings of President Stanford of the Central Pacific and Vice-President Durant of the Union. The crowd groaned when Stanford missed, but then the spike pierced the laurel and the tracks were joined. Two locomotives, the CP's *Jupiter* and the UP's *No. 110*, gently chugged forward and touched cowcatchers. A telegraph operator tapped out to a waiting nation, so recently divided by Civil War, a single word: "Done".

America celebrated that night, from coast to coast, North to South. Only one people felt no joy. The American Indians gazed down on the iron road and could only see how dire their future was.

For American cowboys, however, the railroad was a godsend, the means by which their poor and tattered beef economy was rescued from despair.

Part II

The Trampling Herd

I RIDE AN OLD PAINT

I ride an old paint, I lead an old dam,
I'm goin' to Montana to throw the hoolihan.
They feed in the coulees, they water in the draw,
Their tails are all matted, their backs are all raw.

Refrain

Ride around, little dogies,
Ride around them slow
For the fiery and snuffy
Are rarin' to go.

Old Bill Jones had two daughters and a song,
One went to Denver and the other went wrong,
His wife she died in a poolroom fight,
Still he sings from morning till night.

Refrain

Oh, when I die, take my saddle from the wall
Put it on my pony, and lead him from his stall.
Tie my bones to his back, turn our faces to the West
And we'll ride the prairie that we love the best.

Refrain

(Old cowboy song)

3. The Trampling Herd: the Cattle Industry Frontier

Prologue

The cattle came to the New World with Columbus. On 2 January 1494 the explorer, making his second voyage, unloaded 24 stallions, ten mares and an unknown number of beeves onto the island of Hispaniola. The animals proliferated, and ranching became established throughout the Caribbean. From there the cattle spread to the mainland, with Gregorio de Villalobos shipping the first herd across in 1521. Used to the swamps of Santa Domingo, the cattle thrived on the rich coastal grasslands of Mexico. Richard Thomson, a visiting Englishman, wrote home in 1555: "There is in New Spain a marvelous increase of cattell which dayly do increase and they are of greater growth than ours. You may have a great steer that hath a hundred weight of tallow for sixteen shillings and some one man hath 20,000 head of cattell of his own."

Explorers and missionaries took the cattle north. The first stock-raising in what would become the United States was done in Florida in the 1560s. Wherever the Spanish went, so went their cattle. Organized ranching first appeared in the American Southwest in 1598, with the *estancia* of Juan de Onate at San Juan.

The British colonies in America also developed a cattle culture. Jamestown imported cattle as early as 1611. Herders tended beeves in colonial Carolina and Virginia, and a cattle industry had spread as far southwest as Georgia by the eighteenth century. Much of the labour of tending the stock, which was penned, was done by Black slaves. It was the British who imported the term "cowboy", the first recorded use of which was in AD 1000 in Ireland. Yet, aside from this piece of nomenclature, the British contribution to the development of the United States cattle culture was negligible. Overwhelmingly, it would be the Spanish who would shape that seemingly most American of enterprises, the ranching of cattle. The American cowboy would be indebted to the Spanish-Mexican *vaquero* for everything from his equipment to his language. Almost inevitably, then, the cradle of the American cattle industry was a sometime Spanish province: Texas.

The Cradle of the Cattle Kingdom

That Texas was the cradle of the American cattle industry was no accident. The great diamond-shaped area formed by the Nueces and Rio Grande Valleys is God's own cattle country, with plentiful open grass, a temperate climate, and stalls of trees for protection and shade. Jose de Escandon drove the first stock there in 1748, wiry Andalusian cattle with sharp-pointed horns. More Spaniards brought more cattle. Within a generation, there were major Spanish livestock enterprises around Nacogdoches, the Rio Grande Valley and San Antonio.

To prevent the Indians running the beeves off, the Spanish let them roam semi-wild, with the *vaquero* keeping a trailing watchful eye. Over time the *vaquero* would evolve a distinct set of tools and prejudices concerning his labour. Machismo prevented him from riding a mare, while his vanity required an ornate and expensive saddle. To protect his legs from cacti and thorns he wore leather *chaparreras*, and *la reata* was his universal implement. Much of the dress code, technique and language of the *vaquero* would be passed down to the American cowboy. *Stampida* would become stampede, *la reata* the cowboy's lariat, and *chaparreras* his chaps. Even the *vaquero* himself would be corrupted into buckaroo.

Anglo-Americans did not originate the Texas cattle industry; when Stephen Austin and his followers arrived in the province in the 1820s they found a beef economy already in place. In 1836 they took it over. During the Texan Revolution, Mexican ranchers headed south in droves, and those who remained found their stock plundered. Together with genuinely feral cattle, these abandoned and stolen beeves were the seed herd for many Anglo-American ranchers. Probably the one major innovation of the Anglo settlers was in stock quality: they crossed the scrawny Retino cattle of the Spanish (which was immune to tick fever) with fleshier descendants of the English Longhorn breed they brought with them. The result was the storied Texas Longhorn, which would come in time to dominate the western livestock industry.

By the end of the 1830s, cattle outnumbered Texans in Texas by a ratio of six to one. Mostly the cattle were slaughtered for their hides and tallow, and the carcasses left to rot. As early as 1842, however, Texans were driving small herds into New Orleans and Shreveport, and in 1846 Edward Piper made the first northwards drive when he moved a herd up to Kansas. The California Gold Rush, with its meat-hungry miners, also provided an outlet. The drive overland to California was perilous and time-consuming; it was also financially rewarding. Texas Ranger Jack Cureton drove 1,100 brawling Longhorns through the Apache country of New Mexico and Arizona. At sale in San Francisco the herd fetched $20,000, a small fortune.

But the big market for beef lay in the industrial, populous North and East. A trial attempt to supply the North with Texan beef was made by two young Illinoisans, Washington Malone and Tom Candy Ponting. Late in 1852, Malone and Candy left Christian County, Illinois, for Texas, where they bought 700 head of cattle. The next spring they drove the beeves all the way back to Illinois, reaching Christian County again on 26 July 1853. Here the Longhorns were rested for winter, but in the spring of 1854 Malone and Candy selected the best 130 steers and shipped them by train to New Jersey, then ferried them to New York's Hundred Street Market. These much travelled steers were the first Texas Longhorns to reach New York. The city's *Tribune* commented:

> This drove started in April, 1853, and drove four months to Illinois, where they were watered, and then drove to Marius, Indiana, and thence by cars to Cleveland, Erie, Dunkirk and by way of the Erie road. This made about 1,500 miles on foot and 600 miles on the railroad. The expense from Texas to Illinois was about $2 a head, the owners camping out all the way. From Illinois here the expense is about $17 a head. The drove came 5,000 miles through the Indian country ... part of the route was through the Kansas Territory.
>
> The top of the drove are good quality of beef, and all are fair. These cattle are generally 5, 6, and 7 years old, rather long-legged, though fine-horned, with long tapir horns, and something of a wild look.

With the example of Malone and Candy before them, other cattlemen began driving Texas herds north, following the so-called Shawnee Road. Outbreaks of tick fever in Missouri and Kansas, however, caused farmers there to turn back Texas herds by force of arms. Although Longhorns had immunity to the disease, they carried the ticks that transmitted it. The farmers did not know how the disease was communicated, only that when their cattle came into contact with Texas stock, their cattle died. Northern cattle could die merely from crossing the trail of a Texan herd. Many states passed quarantine laws to keep Texas cattle out. When the Civil War broke out, the drives north stopped entirely.

Texas was overwhelmingly for the Confederacy. The young went off to fight in Virginia and Tennessee, and the herds ran wild. The price of beef plummeted. Some herds were driven over the Mississippi to supply the Southern armies, and were paid for in Confederate money that was worthless long before the final surrender. When the Texan war veterans returned home, they found their ranches in ruin and their families living in poverty. Their only asset was cattle: five million of them, with possibly a quarter of them untended and unbranded. In Texas, the animals were almost without value, selling for $3 per head. They needed to find a paying market.

During the Civil War, the Northern economy had expanded to a gigantic degree. Millions of Americans had flocked to the mills and factories. And these industrial workers wanted beef on their tables. Beef was the symbol of the American good life. When immigrants arrived from Europe, they too adopted the preference for beef. The markets of the East paid over $40 per head of cattle.

The cowmen of Texas determined to share in this bonanza. Throughout the winter of 1865–6 they spontaneously began rounding up their herds for the "Long Drive" to the nearest railhead, Sedalia in Missouri, from where the beeves could be shipped east. In the spring and early summer of 1866, about a quarter of a million cattle crossed the Red River and headed into Indian Territory.

The drives were nothing but trouble. Abnormally heavy rains turned the prairie to a mass of mud. The Indians were peaceable, but charged 10 cents a head for the grass the cattle consumed on their lands. Farmers, remembering the pre-War outbreaks of Texas fever, rode out with rifles. Worse, Kansas swarmed with Jayhawkers, settler-outlaws who had fought on the Union side. As their price for letting the Texan herds be, the Jayhawkers demanded money. Inevitably, violence sometimes ensued, as was shown by the experience of James M. Daugherty, a young Texan traildriver:

> Some twenty miles south of Fort Scott, Kansas, and about four o'clock one afternoon, a bunch of fifteen or twenty Jayhawkers came upon us. One of my cowboys, John Dobbins by name, was leading the herd, and I was riding close to the leader. Upon approach of the Jayhawkers John attempted to draw his gun and the Jayhawkers shot him dead in the saddle. This caused the cattle to stampede and at the same time they covered me with their guns and I was forced to surrender. The rest of the cowboys stayed with the herd, losing part of them in the stampede. The Jayhawkers took me to Cow Creek which was near by, and there tried me for driving cattle into their country, which [the cattle] they claimed were infested with ticks which would kill their cattle. I was found guilty without any evidence, they not even having one of my cattle for evidence.
>
> They began to argue among themselves what to do with me. Some wanted to hang me while others wanted to whip me to death. I, being a young man in my teens, and my sympathetic talk about being ignorant of tickey cattle of the south diseasing any of the cattle of their country, caused one of the big Jayhawkers to take my part. The balance was strong for hanging me on the spot, but through his arguments they finally let me go. After I was freed and had joined the herd, two of my cowboys and I slipped back and buried John Dobbins where he fell.

Jayhawker harassment caused some herds to turn back,

and bottled up others around Baxter Springs. As the summer wore into fall, frost killed the grass and the cattle died of starvation. Only 35,000 Texas cattle reached the railheads. The Long Drive of 1866, which had begun with such hopes, was a disaster.

A people less determined than the Texans might have given up in defeat. Instead, after a winter of recuperation, they began driving their Longhorns north again. And this time, thanks to an enterprising Yankee stockman called Joseph McCoy, the Texans would find a convenient railhead waiting for them.

On the Trail

"A Very Small, Dead Place . . ."

Late starters up the Sedalia Trail in 1867 were intercepted by William Sugg, agent of the cattle buyer, Joseph G. McCoy. Sugg informed the drovers of an easier and cheaper route to market. At the Kansas hamlet of Abilene, on the route of the Kansas Pacific Railroad, McCoy had built vast pens to receive Texas cattle. He would take all that they could deliver. So began the great Kansas cattle trade.

Born in 1837, the youngest of nine children, Joe McCoy had gone into the cattle-buying business at the end of the Civil War. When he heard of the 1866 Baxter Springs blockade, he saw immediately that the beef industry needed an open trail from Texas to an easy shipping point on a railroad: in McCoy's own words, "a market whereat the Southern drover and Northern buyer would meet upon an equal footing, and both be undisturbed by mobs or swindling thieves."

Establishment of such a cattle-shipping centre became for McCoy an obsession, "a waking thought, a sleeping dream." Early in 1867 McCoy visited Junction City, where local businessmen refused to sell him land for a stockyard. After being similarly turned down in Solomon City

and Salina, he settled on Abilene, almost at the end of the
Kansas Pacific rail line. "Abilene in 1867," wrote McCoy,
"was a very small, dead place, consisting of about one
dozen log huts, low, small, rude affairs, four fifths of
which were covered in dirt for roofing . . . The business of
the burg was conducted in two small rooms, mere log
huts, and of course, the inevitable saloon, also a log hut,
was to be found."

The hamlet, however, had everything necessary for a
cattle-shipping centre. All around were the grassy, well-
watered acres of Smoky Hill Valley, where cattle could
be fattened up at the end of a long drive. Nearby was
Fort Riley, which offered protection from Indian raids.
Moreover, Abilene was outside Kansas farming country.
And most importantly of all, it was on a railroad. The
cattle could be shipped eastward in open pens to Kansas
and thence to Chicago, and from there to the East for
butchering. Later, when Gustavus Swift created a fleet of
refrigerated railroad cars, the beeves would be slaughtered in Chicago and sent east as dressed corpses.

Having bought the 250 acres of land he needed, McCoy
set about building the required facilities. By now it was
July, and the herds were on their way north. Within two
months McCoy constructed a stockyard big enough to
take 3,000 surging Texas Longhorns. For the convenience
of the cattlemen, he erected a three-storey hotel, the Drover's Hotel. Meanwhile, McCoy sent William Sugg south to
intercept the Texas herds, and persuade them to Abilene.

The first herd to arrive at McCoy's stockyard was driven
by a Texan named Thompson. More herds followed. Despite its late start, Abilene shipped out 35,000 Texan steers
in 1867. The next year 75,000 cattle reached Abilene. In
1870 the figure was 300,000; in 1871, it was an astounding
700,000.

Nearly all these cattle came to Abilene up the famous

Chisholm Trail, which lay 150 miles west of the Sedalia Trail Shawnee road. It was named after Jesse Chisholm, a half-Cherokee trader. In 1864–5 Chisholm used an ancient buffalo route between Kansas and Texas to haul his goods wagons. When a herder later heading north from Texas crossed into Indian Territory, he found Chisholm's wagon ruts and followed them into Kansas. And so was born the greatest cattle road in the West. Years after it became defunct its course could still be seen, a depression 200–400 yards wide beaten into the earth by the tramp of over three million cattle.

Abilene boomed on the profits of the cow trade. By 1870, the town's Texas Street boasted ten false-fronted boarding-houses, ten saloons, five general stores, and four hotels.

The prosperity was short-lived. Abilene had no law. Celebrating cowboys drank and quarrelled, and several gunfights occurred. Some leading citizens posted notices forbidding the carrying of firearms within the city limits. The cowboys read them, and then shot them to pieces. To install order, the town employed a marshal, Thomas J. Smith, who had served on the New York City police force. For a brief summer "Bear River Tom" gave Abilene a taste of law, punching down rowdy cowboys and forcibly disarming them. He was killed in the fall by a settler in a dispute over land.

Abilene's next marshal was the noted frontier scout and Indian fighter, the fashionably dressed, long-haired James Butler "Wild Bill" Hickok, who was hired at $150 a month, plus a percentage of fines. At the behest of citizens Hickok ordered Texas gamblers Phil Coe and Ben Thompson to alter an offensive, pornographic sign outside their Bull's Head Saloon. Coe resented this interference, and trouble between Coe and Hickok grew, culminating in a gunfight on 5 October 1871. At around 9 p.m. Hickok heard a shot on the street and went to investigate. He found Phil Coe at the centre of a crowd of drunken Texan revellers, with a revolver in his hand. "Who fired that shot?" demanded Hickok. Coe replied that he had fired it – at a dog. Hickok told Coe to disarm. Instead Coe pointed his gun at the marshal. "As quick as thought", reported a newspaper, Hickok drew his Navy Colt pistols and fired at Coe, the bullet tearing through Coe's stomach and out his back. But in the confusion of bullets Hickok accidentally slew his own deputy, Mike Williams, who had run into the firing line. Afterwards, the grief-stricken Hickok took to patrolling the streets with a sawn-off shotgun.

When Hickok's contract expired at the end of 1871, it was not renewed. Instead, the town decided to stop cowboy lawlessness by the simple expedient of ending Abilene's cattle shipments. Many townsfolk, anyway, were farmers who had recently settled on the prime prairie around the town, and had no love for the Longhorns, who knocked down their fences and trampled their crops. In February 1872 a notice appeared in the Abilene *Chronicle* to the effect:

> We, the undersigned, members of the Farmers' Protective Association, most respectfully request all who have contemplated driving Texas cattle to Abilene the coming season, to seek some other point of shipment, as the inhabitants of Dickinson [the local county] will no longer submit to the evils of that trade.

On the Western Trail

The citizens of Abilene need hardly have bothered to prohibit the cattle trade. As the railroad extended west, new towns sprang up as shipping points, all easier and quicker for the Texans to reach: Ellsworth in 1871, Wichita in 1872, and Dodge in 1876, the last and longest lived of the Kansas cowtowns. Dodge was a ready-made trail town. Two buffalo hunters, Ed Jones and Joe Plummer, had earlier brought hides north from Texas, and their route was turned into a road for cattle. It was known variously as the Jones and Plummer Trail, then the Dodge City Trail, and eventually the Western Trail.

There were more reasons to trail a herd north than to meet a train. At the peak of its glory, the Western Trail would stretch from Texas to the Sioux reservations in Dakota, where Texas beeves fed surrendered Indians. Also using the Trail were drivers stocking the Great Plains, for in the 1860s the cattle frontier had pushed far beyond the Red River. To their astonishment, cattlemen had discovered that steers could overwinter on the plains with little care.

Amongst the first to realize this was J. W. Iliff, a failed gold miner in the 1859 rush to Pike's Peak. Determined to make something out of his misfortune, the Ohio-born Iliff opened a store, bartering with passing migrants for their lame and emaciated cattle and oxen. These he turned loose on the plains and found that they thrived. To most eyes, the bunchgrass of the plains looked scanty fare, but Nature had made it a storehouse of proteins, a form of hay on the stem. This natural hay was also accessible in winter, for the snows of the plains did not usually crust, so the hay could be reached by pawing cattle.

Bunchgrass and a ready market of hungry miners made Iliff the first of the cattle kings of Colorado. Eventually, his herd expanded to 35,000 head, built in the main from cattle driven north from Texas. Among those who supplied Iliff were the restless Charles Goodnight and his partner Oliver Loving.

In 1866, while most Texans had their hopes pegged on the Missouri railheads, Goodnight and Loving had trailed their herds from Fort Belknap to the Apache–Navajo reservations in New Mexico. After receiving $12,000 in gold for a proportion of their beeves, the rest were driven north into Colorado, some being sold to the miners and some to Iliff. The routes used by Goodnight and Loving soon became the principal cattle routes to New Mexico and Colorado, and were known as the Horsehead Route and the Goodnight–Loving Trail. Oliver Loving, however, did not live to enjoy the prestige or money the route derived; in 1867 he and cowboy One-Armed Bill Wilson were attacked by a Comanche war party. Although both men escaped alive from three days of Comanche siege and days of wandering starvation, Loving had been wounded by a Comanche arrow. His arm turned gangrenous and he died at Fort Sumner, after extracting a promise from Goodnight to bury him in the Lone Star state. Goodnight kept his word, and ordered his cowboys to make a coffin from oil drums. In this metal casket, Goodnight towed Loving's body home to Texas, along the trail they had blazed together. Till he died, Goodnight kept Loving's photograph on the wall of his home. (The story of Goodnight and Loving is celebrated in Larry McMurtry's novel, *Lonesome Dove*.)

After his partner's death, Goodnight went on to build up an immense ranch on the wide open Colorado range and to lavish money on the erection of an opera house in the town of Pueblo. Inspired by Goodnight's example, Texas cattlemen flocked north to the free range country of Colorado. And then to Wyoming, and Montana, and Nebraska, the whole plains across. They went up the Western Trail and they went up the Goodnight–Loving Trail. Somewhere between six and nine million cattle were driven out of Texas to the railheads and the plains between 1867 and

1886, with around 25,000 cowboys making the trip north. Around 2,000 of these cowboys were Mexican and 5,000 were Black Americans, who had started cowpunching as slaves or had come west after their emancipation.

Life on the Trail

First-hand accounts of life on the trail, such as Andy Adams's memoir *The Log of a Cowboy*, make it clear that there was little glamour, much labour and some danger. The drive began with the spring round-up, with the recalcitrant Longhorns pulled from the brush and chaparral. When the herd was collected, immature animals were "cut out" and returned to the range. Any unbranded animals were dragged to the bonfire where the branding irons were heated until orange-red hot and then stamped onto the steer's hide.

When the work of round-up and branding was done, preparations for the drive started in earnest. A cowboy selected his mounts – he would need between six and ten for the drive – and invariably chose geldings and horses of solid colour. (Native Americans, by contrast, preferred "paints", horses with broken white and black/brown markings, for their war ponies.) Then he gathered up the small amount of personal belongings he would take with him: a pair of blankets, a change of clothing, his hat, a "slicker" coat to keep off the rain, and his gun.

Occasionally the rancher himself would make the drive; more often he would entrust his foreman or sell his cattle to a professional driver like the famed Ike Pryor. For the driving of a herd of 3,000 head, a crew consisted of a trail boss, 15 to 20 cowhands, together with a horse wrangler to handle the herd of spare horses, the remuda or "cavvy". A cook or "Old Lady" was also essential, and was expected to be skilled in more than cuisine. He had to sustain morale and be an expert "bullwhacker", driving the chuckwagon over every terrain. Invented by Charles Goodnight, the chuckwagon was an adapted Conestoga, made from Osage orange, the toughest wood Goodnight knew of, the wood Indians used for their bows. A chuckwagon carried (in an allotted place) everything the cook needed, from tins of Arbuckle coffee to a Dutch oven. Many cooks were of Portuguese or Mexican descent.

At the start of the drive, the cattle were always jittery and it was necessary to proceed slowly. The beeves disliked leaving their home range, and had to be broken to the road. An astute trail boss singled out a dominating animal and made it the lead steer. Some animals were used year after year in this way, like Charles Goodnight's "Old Blue". After several days on the drive, the animals would take up a natural order of march. The cowboys, likewise, proceeded according to a set pattern. The trail boss rode out in front, surveying the route and seeking water or grazing. At the point of the herd rode the most experienced cowboys, and along its sides were the swing and flank riders. The tail or drag riders brought up the rear. They had the dirtiest, least desirable job, pushing along the lame or cussedest steers in the clouds of choking dust thrown up by thousands of hooves. Well behind the dust proceeded the remuda and the chuckwagon, which would be driven ahead of the herd in the afternoon for the cook to fix supper. Meals seldom varied beyond black coffee, drunk by the gallon, sourdough biscuits, pinto beans, meat, gravy and "SOB stew" (stewed entrails).

In a day's march, a herd would expect to cover an average of 15 miles, before being bedded down for the night. During the hours of darkness the cattle had to be constantly watched, with the men usually working two-hour shifts. Describing night duty, Andy Adams wrote: "The guards ride in a circle about four rods outside the sleeping cattle; and by riding in opposite directions make it impossible for any animal to make its escape without being noticed by the riders. The guards usually sing or whistle continuously, so that the sleeping herd may know that a friend and not an enemy is keeping vigil over their dreams."

Among the songs the cowboys crooned were "Cotton-Eye Joe", "Dinah Had a Wooden Leg", "Saddle Ole Spike", and "Sally Gooden". One of the most beautiful was "The Night Herding Song":

Oh, slow up dogies, quit moving around,
You have wandered and trampled all over the ground;
Oh, graze along dogies and feed kinda slow,
And don't forever be on the go.
Move slow, little dogies, move slow,
Hi-o, hi-o, hi-o.

Oh say, little dogies, when you goin' to lay down,
And give up this driftin' and rovin' around?
My horse is leg-weary and I'm awfully tired,
But if you get away, I'm sure to be fired.
Lay down, little dogies, lay down,
Hi-o, hi-o, hi-o.

Oh, lay still, dogies, since you have laid down,
Stretch away out on the big open ground;
Snore loud, little dogies, and drown the wild sounds,
That'll go away when the day rolls around.
Lay still, little dogies, lay still,
Hi-o, hi-o, hi-o.

The crooning was not always successful. At night the

steers, their vision limited by darkness, were easily "boogered". Stampedes were an ever-present menace. Thunder and lightning were amongst the most common causes. The only way to stop "running beeves" was for the riders to gallop alongside the front and side of the herd and turn the leading animals into the centre, creating a circular mill. At night this was a dangerous, terrifying task made strangely eerie by the blue flames which flickered at the tips of the steers' horns – the result of friction from their jostling bodies. (The same friction also generated a heat that could blister the skin on the face of a cowboy who got too close.) Often it was impossible to turn a stampeding herd. A witness to a stampede in Idaho in 1889 reported the grisly – and typical – result. The stampede killed 341 cattle, two horses, and one cowboy, the latter "literally mangled to sausage meat". Steers and men were scattered over a huge area by such runs. Reassembling the herd and crew was a laborious and costly business, made worse by the knowledge that a herd which had stampeded once was likely to be "spoiled" and do it again. The depressing and ruinous effect of constant stampedes was caught by George Duffield in his diary of a drive to Iowa in 1866.

May 1. Big Stampede. Lost 200 head of Cattle.

May 2. Spent the day hunting & found but 25 Head. It has been Raining for three days. These are dark days for me.

May 3. Day spent in hunting Cattle. Found 23. Hard rain and wind. Lots of trouble.

After five more days rounding up the scattered beeves, Duffield started on the trail once more. After only a week of progress, the herd scattered again:

May 15 . . . Cattle all left us & in morning not one Beef to be seen.

May 16. Hunt Beeves is the word – all Hands discouraged & are determined to go. 200 Beeves out & nothing to eat.

May 17. No breakfast. Pack & off is the order. All hands gave the Brazos one good harty damn & started for Buchanan.

Eventually, Duffield reached the Red River at the end of May. But no sooner was he out of Texas than the herd "spooked":

June 1: Stampede last night among 6 droves & a general mix up and loss of Beeves. Hunt Cattle again. Men all tired & want to leave.

June 2. Hard rain and wind Storm. Beeves ran & I had to be on Horse back all Night. Awful night. Men still lost. Quit the Beeves & go to Hunting men is the word – 4 P.M. Found our men with Indian guide & 195 Beeves 14 Miles from camp. Almost starved not having had a bite to eat for 60 hours. Got to camp about 12M. *Tired*.

And so Duffield's drive continued, with one stampede after another, all the way to Fort Gibson in Indian Territory (Oklahoma). By the time he arrived he had only 500 of the thousand steers with which he had started off.

He had also lost a man to the waters of the Brazos. After stampedes, the most feared hazard of a trail drive was crossing rivers. The Brazos, Red, Trinity, Washita, Canadian, Cimarron and Arkansas all flowed east across the path of the herd. If there was no ford, and the water was deep, the cattle had to be swum over. In spring, or after heavy rain, the rivers roiled and spat. It was considered good practice to approach the water at a brisk pace, "crowding" the cattle, letting them build up a momentum which would carry them into the water. One seasoned drover, Colonel Andy Syder, had two "swimming steers" which were more or less trained to take the plunge, the herd instinct causing the rest to follow.

Even when the cattle started in the water, many things could go wrong. The steers were as easily "spooked" in the water as they were on land. An unusual wave, a floating branch, or a whirlpool could make the leaders stop swimming to the opposite bank and attempt to turn back. Hundreds of animals would then mill around, become exhausted and drift downstream to their deaths. To save the cattle, the cowboys had to swim their horses into the mêlée, and with blows and kicks get the Longhorns swimming straight. Many cowboys drowned in such situations. Their fear of river crossings was all the greater in that few of them could swim.

Stampedes and river crossings did not exhaust the dangers of a drive. Horses could step into gopher holes and throw their riders. A foot caught in a stirrup could mean a fatal drag across the ground. Lightning on the open prairie was a perennial peril. A Texan cowboy by the name of A. B. Withers was riding with his brother and a rancher called Gus Johnson when lightning struck: "It set Johnson's undershirt on fire and his gold shirt stud, which was set with a diamond, was melted and the diamond never found. His hat was torn to pieces . . ." The bolt killed Johnson, and also blinded Withers' brother in one eye. In camp, cowboys took off their spurs, pistol and any other metal objects, put them in a pile, and slept well away from them.

Although drives were rarely attacked by Indians, lone outriders were sometimes assaulted or the herd stampeded. The "Indian menace" faced by the drives tended to be either the toll the Indians demanded for passage over their grounds or their begging for food. Andy Adams was witness to one such encounter:

> We were following the regular trail, which had been slightly used for a year or two, though none of our outfit had ever been over it, when late on the third afternoon, about forty miles out from Doan's about a hundred mounted bucks and squaws sighted our herd and crossed the North Fork from their encampment. They did not ride direct to the herd, but came into the trail nearly a mile above the cattle, so it was some little time from our first sighting them before we met. We did not check the herd or turn out of the trail, but when the lead came within a few hundred yards of the Indians, one buck, evidently the chief of the band, rode forward a few rods and held up one hand, as if commanding a halt. At the sight of this gaudily bedecked apparition, the cattle turned out of the trail, and Flood and I rode up to the chief, extending our hands in friendly greeting. The chief could not speak a word of English, but made signs with his hands; when I turned loose on him in Spanish, however, he instantly turned his horse and signed back to his band. Two young bucks rode forward and greeted Flood and myself in good Spanish.
>
> On thus opening up an intelligible conversation, I called Fox Quarternight, who spoke Spanish, and he rode up from his position of third man in the swing and joined in the council. The two young Indians through whom we carried on the conversation were Apaches, no doubt renegades of that tribe, and while we understood each other in Spanish, they spoke in a heavy guttural peculiar to the Indian. Flood opened the powwow by demanding to know the meaning of this visit. When the question had been properly interpreted to the chief, the latter dropped his blanket from his shoulders and dismounted from his horse. He was a fine specimen of the Plains Indian, fully six feet

in height, perfectly proportioned, and in years well past middle life. He looked every inch a chief, and was a natural born orator. There was a certain easy grace to his gestures, only to be seen in people who use the sign language, and often when he was speaking to the Apache interpreters, I could anticipate his requests before they were translated to us, although I did not know a word of Comanche.

Before the powwow had progressed far it was evident that begging was its object. In his prelude, the chief laid claim to all the country in sight as the hunting grounds of the Comanche tribe, – an intimation that we were intruders. He spoke of the great slaughter of the buffalo by the white hide-hunters, and the consequent hunger and poverty amongst his people. He dwelt on the fact that he had ever counseled peace with the whites, until now his band numbered but a few squaws and papooses, the younger men having deserted him for other chiefs of the tribe who advocated war on the palefaces. When he had fully stated his position, he offered to allow us to pass through his country in consideration of ten beeves. On receiving this proposition, all of us dismounted, including the two Apaches, the latter seating themselves in their own fashion, while we whites lounged on the ground in truly American laziness, rolling cigarettes. In dealing with people who know not the value of time, the civilized man is taken at a disadvantage, and unless he can show an equal composure in wasting time, results will be against him. Flood had had years of experience in dealing with Mexicans in the land of *mañana,* where all maxims regarding the value of time are religiously discarded. So in dealing with this Indian chief he showed no desire to hasten matters, and carefully avoided all reference to the demand for beeves.

His first question, instead, was to know the distance to

Fort Sill and Fort Elliot. The next was how many days it would take for cavalry to reach him. He then had us narrate the fact that when the first herd of cattle passed through the country less than a month before some bad Indians had shown a very unfriendly spirit. They had taken many of the cattle and had killed and eaten them, and now the great white man's chief at Washington was very much displeased. If another single ox were taken and killed by bad Indians, he would send his soldiers from the forts to protect the cattle, even though the owners drove the herds through the reservation of the Indians – over the grass where their ponies grazed. He had us inform the chief that our entire herd was intended by the great white man's chief at Washington as a present to the Blackfeet Indians who lived in Montana, because they were good Indians, and welcomed priests and teachers amongst them to teach them the ways of the white man. At our foreman's request we then informed the chief that he was under no obligation to give him even a single beef for any privilege of passing through his country, but as the squaws and little papooses were hungry, he would give him two beeves.

The old chief seemed not the least disconcerted, but begged for five beeves, as many of the squaws were in the encampment across the North Fork, those present being not quite half of his village. It was now getting late in the day and the band seemed to be getting tired of the parleying, a number of squaws having already set out on their return to the village. After some further talk, Flood agreed to add another beef, on condition they be taken to the encampment before being killed. This was accepted, and at once the entire band set up a chattering in view of the coming feast. The cattle had in the mean time grazed off nearly a mile, the outfit, however, holding them under a close herd during the powwowing. All the bucks in the band, numbering about forty, now joined us, and we rode away to the herd. I noticed, by the way, that quite a number of the younger braves had arms, and no doubt they would have made a display of force had Flood's diplomacy been of a more warlike character.

The drive to the Kansas railheads took three months, the drive to Montana or Dakota six months. Most of the men, horses and cattle endured. And then, after all the Indians, stampedes, rain, choking alkali dust, heat, 14-hour days in the saddle, mosquitoes, rustlers and short rations, it was the end of the drive. And time to go to town.

Babylons of the Plains

"EVERYTHING GOES IN WICHITA"

Notice posted on town approaches

Helling Around

When a drive reached its destination, the cowboys were customarily given their wages. With money jingling in their pockets they mounted their ponies and galloped to the excitements of the trail town, desperate to forget the back-breaking monotony and dangers of the drive. They wanted to eat, drink, gamble and dance with painted women – to "hell around".

The names of the towns into which they rode were Abilene, Ellsworth, Caldwell, Wichita, Newton, Hays, Dodge, Miles City, Cheyenne, and Ogallala. What they were called or where they were hardly mattered. To the cowboy rushing in on his pony, firing his pistol in the air – "just to raise a little excitement and let people know he is in town," as the Dodge City *Times* put it – cow towns were virtually identical to each other: a collection of shabby false-fronted buildings strung out along a long dirt street. They milled with people and dinned with the noise of cattle, carousing cowboys, and the constant sound of gunshots. "The firing of guns in and around town," re-

called one resident of Newton, "was so continuous it
reminded me of a Fourth of July celebration from daylight
to midnight. There was shooting when I got up and when
I went to bed."

Although the citizens of cattle towns made their money
out of cowpunchers, they tended not to like them or their
ways. The Topeka *Daily Commonwealth* editorialized in
1871 that: "The Texas cattle herder is a character, the like
of which can be found nowhere else on earth ... He
generally wears a revolver on each side of his person,
which he will use with as little hesitation on a man as a
wild animal. Such a character is dangerous and desperate,
and each one had generally killed his man." The fears of
the townsfolk had some justification. Ellsworth, Kansas,
had eight homicides during its first year as a cowtown;
Dodge City had ten. Attempted homicides with guns
were probably around three times these figures.

They may have been disorderly and dangerous, but
Texas cowboys were also very good business. During the
cattle season, 300–400 cowpunchers could ride into town
daily to spend their wages. A town could take as much as
$40,000 in its tills each day. Much of the money would go
to saloons and "soiled doves" (prostitutes), but a good
chunk would also go to the bootmakers, grocers and other
citizens of substance. The difficulty for the towns was
finding a way of containing the cowboys' violence without implementing a law-and-order regime which was so
puritanically iron-clad it put them off visiting. The solution hit upon was to allow the rowdy "dens of sin" the
cowboys demanded but to either restrict their number or
congregate them in a particular area of town. To enforce
law and order a small police force was hired. Astutely,
their costs were often met by charging the brothels, saloons and gambling houses a licence fee and implementing a system of fines for such offences as carrying a

concealed weapon. According to the Topeka *Daily Commonwealth*, the rival town of Ellsworth

> ... realizes $300 per month from prostitution fines alone
> ... The city authorities consider that as long as mankind is
> depraved and Texan cattle herders exist, there will be a
> demand and necessity for prostitutes, and that as long as
> prostitutes are bound to dwell in Ellsworth it is better
> for the respectable portion of society to hold prostitutes
> under restraint of law.

When the cowboy fresh off the trail arrived in town, however, sin was not his immediate preoccupation. After hitching his horse he usually headed for the nearest barber shop, for a haircut and a proper shaping, blacking and waxing of his long moustache. His head spruced, he then went to the dry-goods store to buy a new set of clothes. Preferably these were gaudy and expensive. The outfit chosen by Teddy Blue Abbott, who rode the Texas trails in the 1870s, was by no means untypical:

> I had a new white Stetson hat that I paid ten dollars for
> and new pants that cost twelve dollars, and a good shirt
> and fancy boots. They had colored tops, red and blue,
> with a half-moon and star on them. Lord, I was proud of
> those clothes! They were the kind of clothes top hands
> wore, and I thought I was dressed right for the first time in
> my life.

Decked out in his new finery, the cowboy completed his ritual of preparation by walking to the best hotel in town, and ordering a meal of eggs, ice cream and fresh oysters. The elite establishment in Abilene was the Drover's Cottage, where J. W. and Lou Gore served drinks with ice cut from the Republican the previous winter and stored in a cellar. With the demise of Abilene, the Gores hauled over part of the hotel building to Ellsworth to establish a Drover's Cottage there.

His stomach full, the cowboy was ready for entertainment. The cowtowns' saloons and dance-halls were often bunched together outside town limits, usually a short walk across the railroad tracks. In Abilene, the vice district was known as the Devil's Addition, in Ellsworth it was Nauchville, and in Newton Hide Park. The sinning area of Dodge City, "Queen of the cowtowns", was the Red Light district, named after the Red Light House, a two-storey frame brothel with red glass in the front door, through which light shone in lurid welcome. From Dodge, the name would go all over the globe. Another term Dodge would bequeath the world was "Boot Hill", because so many of its citizens were buried in the town cemetery with their boots on after gunfights. The first to occupy the Dodge cemetery was an African-American cowboy called Texas, who was shot by a gambler called Denver.

Cowboys were congenital gamblers. They played cards in the bunkhouse, and around the camp fire on the trail, but it only became meaningful in a saloon, where they could pit their wits and money against a professional. The saloons of the trail towns boasted names which were promisingly colourful – the Crystal Palace, the Alhambra, Old Fruit – or consciously designed to appeal to Texans, like the Lone Star and the Alamo. Some were gaudy to the rafters. The Alamo in Abilene had three sets of double glass doors, and giant murals of nudes in imitation Italian Renaissance style. Music blared incessantly from piano and bull fiddle. Wild Bill Hickok was an almost constant fixture in the Alamo during his period as marshal. In 1871 a reporter from the *Daily Kansas State Record* described the scene inside the saloon: "A bartender, with a countenance like a youthful divinity student, fabricates wonderful drinks, while the music of a piano and a violin from a raised recess, enlivens the scene, and 'soothes the savage breasts' of those who retire torn and lacerated from an unfortunate combat with the tiger."

The card games cowboys liked were faro, monte, and poker. They distrusted fancy games and any sort of gambling machinery. Many lost their wages to the gamblers and sharps. As the cowboys played, so they drank. They favoured whiskey – bourbon, rye, or corn – or "Kansas sheep-dip" as they called it. (Very strong whiskey was a "Brigham Young cocktail", since it made a man a "confirmed polygamist".) The combination of alcohol and cards could have fatal results, as with the cowboy Texas buried in Dodge's Boot Hill. A verse from the old song "The Cowboy's Lament" warned wisely:

It was once in the saddle I used to go dashing,
Once in the saddle I used to go gay;
First to the dram house, then to the card house,
Got shot in the breast, I am dying today.

There were other ways to die in a saloon than by calling "cheat". Saloons bred drunken rowdiness, horse-play that spilled easily from camaraderie to the hasty pulling of a knife or gun. To refuse a drink was to breach bar-room etiquette, and led to the deaths of numerous men. Some saloons just seemed to spawn violence, like Shorty Young's Bucket of Blood Saloon in Le Harve, Montana, which caused cowboys to apply the name to any tough frontier whiskey-mill. Cowboy violence almost always took the form of knives or "manstoppers" (guns). Fisticuffs was unmanly. "If the Lord had intended me to fight like a dog," as one cowboy put it, "He'd a-give me longer teeth and claws."

The Calico Queens

After some hands of monte and "Kansas sheep-dip", the mind of many a cowboy turned ineluctably to female companionship. There were few "respectable" women in a cowtown; the only women a poor cowboy associated with were prostitutes and dance-hall girls, who careered around the floor with the cowboy for a price. Joe McCoy drew a vivid picture of the cowtown dance-hall in his 1874 memoir, *Historic Sketches of the Cattle Trade in the West and Southwest*.

> Few more wild, reckless scenes of abandoned debauchery can be seen on the civilised earth, than a dance hall in full blast in one of the many frontier towns. To say they dance wildly or in an abandoned manner is putting it mildly . . . The cowboy enters the dance with a particular zest, not stopping to divest himself of his sombrero, spurs or pistols, but just as he dismounts off his cow-pony, so he goes into the dance. A more odd, not to say comical sight is not often seen than the dancing cowboy: with the front of his sombrero lifted at an angle of 45 degrees, his huge spurs jangling at every step or motion, his revolvers flapping up and down like a retreating sheep's tail, his eyes lit up with excitement, liquor and lust, he plunges into it and "hoes it down" at a terrible rate in the most approved yet awkward country style, often swinging his partner clear off the floor for an entire circle; then "balance all" with an occasional demonic yell near akin to the war whoop of the savage Indian. All this he does entirely oblivious to the whole world and the rest of mankind.

Although civic-minded reformers tried to ban them, prostitutes graced most cowtowns, entering the periodic census under such euphemisms as "horizontally employed" or "night worker". The occupation of Ettie

Baldwin in the 1870 Ellsworth census was written in red ink as "squirms in the dark". The prostitutes came from all over America, the fortunate ones working out of brothels under a madam, where there was some comfort and hygiene. Most "soiled doves" or "calico queens", however, worked above saloons or dance-halls, or in rough wooden shacks known as "cribs".

There was little stigma attached to a visit to a "crib" or "sporting house" (although Black cowboys were not allowed to visit White houses of prostitution). Not infrequently the cowboys formed strong attachments to the girls. Teddy Blue Abbott, in his autobiography, was unapologetic about the relationship between cowpunchers and prostitutes:

I suppose those things would shock a lot of respectable people. But we wasn't respectable and we didn't pretend to be, which was the only way we was different from some others. I've heard a lot about the double standard, and seen a lot of it, too, and it don't make any sense for the man to get off so easily. If I'd been a woman and done what I done I'd have ended up in a sporting house.

I used to talk to those girls, and they would tell me a lot of stuff, about how they got started, and how in Chicago and those eastern cities they wasn't allowed on the streets, how their clothes would be taken away from them, only what they needed in the house, so it was like being in prison.

They could do as they pleased out here. And they were human, too. They always had money and they would lend it to fellows that were broke. The wagon bosses would come around looking for men in the spring, and when a fellow was hired he would go to his girl and say: "I've got a job, but my bed's in soak." Or his saddle or his six-shooter or his horse. And she would lend him the money to get it back and he would pay her at the end of the month.

The Newton Massacre

For every woman in a trail town there were eight men
wanting companionship. Disputes over affections were
inevitable. None, however, had such a bloody consequence
as that between Mike McCluskie and the gambler Bill
Bailey, the so-called Newton "General Massacre".

Newton's reign as the "Cowboy Capital" lasted for the
single frenzied year of 1871, before the lines of the Santa
Fe railroad pushed ineluctably on to Wichita. Among
those charged with the keeping of Newton's order was
Mike McCluskie, a night policeman, who formed an at-
tachment to a prostitute who worked the red light district
of Hide Park. Texan gambler Bill Bailey, alias William
Wilson, was a rival for her favours. On the evening of
Friday 11 August, the two men had a drunken argument
over the woman in the bar of the Red Front saloon. Bailey
ran out of the saloon into the street, McCluskie following
with his pistol drawn. As Bailey crouched in the dark,
McCluskie shot him. The gambler was taken to the Santa
Fe hotel, where he later died.

Many of the people of the town considered the shooting justified, but Bailey had numerous friends among the
Texan cowboys who had just come up the Chisholm Trail.
One of these, the young and unstable Hugh Anderson,
decided on revenge. Past midnight on Saturday 19 August, Anderson, accompanied by several friends, walked
into the bright lights of Perry Tuttle's dance-hall, and over
to the gaming table where McCluskie was sitting. Drawing his pistol, Anderson screamed at McCluskie: "You
cowardly dog! I'm going to blow the top of your head
off!" Anderson fired twice. One bullet entered McCluskie's
neck, but he managed to stagger up and pull the trigger of
his revolver. The hammer failed to detonate the cap,
McCluskie collapsed onto the floor, and Anderson shot
him again, this time in the back.

The matter might have ended there, except that a youthful watching stranger pulled a gun and began blazing away at the Texans. (The gunfighter would never be positively identified, although a contemporary poem by Theodore F. Price would name him as a consumptive friend of McCluskie's called Riley.) A pitched battle ensued. Bystanders screamed and dived for the floor. Someone hurled a chair at the lights, and orange flashes of gunshot glowed in the darkness.

The shooting lasted for a bare minute, petering out in the uncertainty of the dark and the cries of the wounded. When the lights were turned on they revealed a scene of carnage.

Hugh Anderson was writhing and moaning in a pool of his own blood. Three of his trail crew – Jim Martin, Billy Garrett, Henry Kearns – were dead. Another hand, Jim Wilkerson, was badly wounded. A railwayman, Pat Lee, was mortally shot through the stomach. The "Avenging Nemesis" had disappeared.

On his arrival the marshal, Tom Carson, moved to arrest the surviving members of Anderson's crew, but the Texans gathered in an armed knot. Something like a street riot threatened to break out, and the marshal withdrew.

At eight o'clock the next morning Hugh Anderson was found guilty of murder of Mike McCluskie by a Newton coroner's jury. But before he could be arrested the wounded man was hidden by friends in the washroom of a train and taken away. He survived his injuries but would be killed three years later in a fight at Medicine Lodge, Kansas, by a man said to be Mike McCluskie's brother.

The "General Massacre" did not end Newton's summer of violence. The dance-hall owner Rowdy Joe Lowe killed Jim Sweet in a street fight. Buffalo hunter Cherokee Dan Hicks fell to a bullet from the revolver of Harry Lovett, after Hicks had shot up the nude frieze in Lovett's saloon. At this the marshal, Tom Carson, a nephew of the trapper Kit Carson, resigned his post. Newton was getting too hot. Captain King took over, until he was killed by a man whose name has only come down to us as Edwards.

Something of the violence which plagued Newton, and the other Kansas cattle towns, had its bitter roots in the Civil War. The Texan cowboys came north with resentment in their hearts. Some still wore items of their distinctive Rebel grey uniforms. As Teddy Blue Abbott explained it:

> Most of them that came up with the trail herds, being from Texas and southerners to start with, was on the side of the South, and oh, but they were bitter. That was how a lot of them got killed, because they wouldn't let an abolitionist arrest them. The marshals in these cow towns were usually northern men, and the Southerns wouldn't go back to Texas and hear people say: "He's a hell of a fellow. He let a Yankee lock him up." Down home one Texas Ranger could arrest the lot of them, but up North, you'd have to kill them first.

As Abbott observed, many of the lawmen who would ply their trade in the tough Kansas cattle towns were Northerners: Bat Masterson, Wild Bill Hickok, Captain King, and Tom Smith, among them. The unfinished business of the Civil War would be finished by these men and the towns who employed them, the means by which the wild, unreconstructed Rebels would be incorporated into the civilizing Union. A dividing line of blood would run between Southern outlaws and Northern peacekeepers throughout the history of the Wild West.

"Oh, To Be a Cowboy"

We deem it hardly necessary to say . . . that the cowboy is a fearless animal. A man wanting in courage would be as much out of place in a cow-camp, as a fish on dry land. Indeed the life he is daily compelled to lead calls for the existence of the highest degree of cool calculating courage.

Texas Live Stock Journal, 1882

The life of the cowpuncher consisted of more than driving cattle to market and "hellin' round" in town. There were all the chores of ranch work to be done, which were never ending. Working cattle was some of the hardest work under the West's sky. There were horses to be broken, steers to be doctored for screwworm, stuck cattle to be pulled out of bogs, and rustlers to be watched for. Sometimes the work was perilous, usually it was unglamorous, and it was always poorly paid. Above all it was a job for the young. The typical cow waddy was aged between 17 and 28.

The Round-Up

In the cycle of ranch work, the round-up (in Spanish, *rodeo*) was the central event. It was the time when the stock was inventoried, branded and sorted. The main

round-up – which might take upwards of three months –
was held in the late spring, just as the grass was turning
green, with a smaller "gather" in the fall. Whenever it was
held, the round-up proceeded in a standard fashion.

The first duty of the cowboy was to ride over a given
area of range and flush the cattle out of chaparral, draws
and other hiding places, and drive them bawling back to
the round-up site. The area of the round-up might cover as
much as 4,000 square miles, and involve 10,000 cattle. It
was the cowboy's job to sweep the range clean.

When the cattle were finally gathered in the main corrals,
the tasks of "cutting out" and branding began. Cattle
were "cut out" or sorted for several purposes: to brand
unmarked calves, to select the best stock for market, or
because they belonged to another ranch. When the animal
to be separated had been identified, the cowboy would
chase the dodging calf or steer and finally rope it, either
by looping the lariat over the animal's head or by "heel
roping" it. Cutting out required considerable horseman-
ship, together with a special pony, one which almost
instinctively understood what was demanded of it. It
made for a great spectacle. The artist Frederic Remington
vividly described cutting out at a round-up in the 1880s,
which was held in Mexico but could have been anywhere
on the North American continent:

> You see a figure dash about at full speed through an
> apparently impenetrable mass of cattle; the stock becomes
> uneasy and moves about, gradually beginning the milling
> process, but the men select the cattle bearing their brand,
> and course them through the herd; all becomes confusion,
> and the cattle seek to escape from the ever-recurring horse-
> men. Here one sees the matchless horsemanship of the
> punchers. Their little ponies, trained to the business, re-
> spond to the slightest pressure.

Roping had its dangers, as well as its satisfactions. A
steer which suddenly pulled on a rope could topple rider
and horse. Fingers misplaced on a saddle horn could be
cut off by a tightening lariat. The rope tricks of the show
cowboys were merely by-products of the skilful efforts of
real punchers to avoid injury.

When a calf was roped it was dragged towards the
branding irons, which were heated in a long pit. In a
number of states, Texas among them, the branding was
done in a corral, a legal requirement to prevent the quick,
illegal branding by rustlers on the open range. At the fire,
one "flanker" grabbed the calf by the head, another by its
tail, and the calf was thrown down. The brander then
stamped the animal's flank with the sizzling iron. A tally
sheet kept a record of the work done.

Branding, the heraldry of the range, was another cow
country convention which came from the Spanish. When
Hernando Cortes the conquistador settled down to become a Mexican *ranchero* he branded his cattle with three
Christian crosses. The first brands in America tended to
be initials of the owner, Richard H. Chisholm (HC) of
Gonzales, Texas, entering his brand before the Alamo
siege of 1836. Such simple brands, however, were easily
changed by the rustler's "running iron" (or, better still, his
heated wire). In only seconds, an artistic cattle thief could
change a "C" to an "O", a "V" to a "W". To forestall this,
brand designs became more exotic. Rancher Burk Bennett
had "Four Sixes", W. E. Jackson a "Too Hot" (2HOT), and
Cabler & Mathis a "Keno" (a NO with a key on top). The
famous XIT brand stood for "Ten in Texas", so called
because the huge ranch took in parts of ten Texas counties. Some of the bigger ranches did not bother with complicated brands, relying instead on their size and reputation
to keep away rustlers. The giant ranch of Captain Richard
King – who once tried to develop a method of meat

preservation based on injecting cows with brine – relied on a minimalist "Running W", the Matador company a "Flying V". John Chisum, who would figure peripherally in the story of Billy the Kid, had a "Long Rail" (a dash), although he also cut his steer's ears in a "jingle-bob" for additional identification.

Unbranded cattle were known as "mavericks" after the absentee Texas owner, Colonel Samuel A. Maverick. In 1847 Maverick had taken 400 Longhorn cattle as payment for a debt, and driven them to his ranch on the Matagorda Peninsula. His duties as an attorney kept him in San Antonio, and the cattle ran free and multiplied. Many of these wild, unbranded cows strayed onto the mainland. When their ownership was inquired of, people would answer "They're Maverick's". Since they were stray and unmarked, other cattlemen rounded them up and branded them. Henceforth, any adult unbranded range cow became known as a maverick.

If the calf the flankers were holding down for branding was male, the cowboy took the opportunity of castrating it with a knife. Castration or "steering" added weight to the animal and made it more docile. The wound caused, however, often became infected by blowfly, the worms of which would eventually cause the animal to die. Branding was also the time when the wounds of previously castrated cattle might be treated with some crude ointment. Another job most conveniently done at round-up time was dehorning, whereby cattle whose horns had become so sharp or long that they were a danger to man and cow were reduced to a stump.

After the big spring round-up, around two thirds of the hands would be laid off. A favoured few would be retained and assigned jobs around the ranch, or detailed to drive the beeves to market. The work of the cowboy was sharply seasonal. Unemployed hands "rode the grub line", drifting from ranch to ranch in the hope of a free meal. Some hunted wild game to survive, others took odd jobs. The average cowboy probably worked only five months a year at his chosen occupation.

As well as the season for round-up, spring was also the time for the breaking of wild horses to the saddle. Much of the breaking was done by professional "bronc peelers", who would work around six to eight horses a day. The expertise of the peelers earned them higher wages than the cow waddy. Typically, a peeler would earn $5 for each bronc "busted". Every peeler would have his individual technique, but the standard method of breaking a wild horse was to corral it and rope it. A blindfold would be attached, since a blinded horse would usually stand still while the single cinch saddle and a rawhide hackamore were put on. The hackamore (from the Spanish *jaquima*) had an adjustable nosepiece; when pulled it would smother the horse, making it possible to be controlled. After the peeler mounted the horse, twisting its ear to distract it, the animal would buck and roll. To bring it under man's dominion, the peeler would pull on the hackamore, and whip it with his quirt. A yellow slicker (coat) would be waved around the horse's face to accustom it to flapping objects.

Eventually, the animal, exhausted and fearful, would quit bucking. If necessary, these steps would be repeated for several days, either by the peeler or by an ordinary cowboy. All cow hands tried their luck at broncbusting, for the law of the range had it that "There ain't no hoss that can't be rode; there ain't no man that can't be throwed."

Broncbusting took a hard toll of the rider as well as the horse. It strained the neck, spine and abdomen, and the constant jarring could make the cowboy bleed from his ears and mouth. A "sun-fisher", a high-bucking horse, could throw him, breaking his bones. A horse which rolled could crush him. More than one peeler died breaking a horse.

Life on the Range

With the excitements of spring over, the cowboy's life settled down for months of hard, routine chores. Fences had to be mended, and hands had to "ride bog" – free animals trapped in the bogs created by spring rains. Bulls were taken to the ranges for mating, and in Texas cowboys checked cattle for screwworm. From the 1880s ranchers began growing hay, and cowboys – although they had a prejudice against any labour which smacked of farming – were obliged to spend weeks in summer haying. As fall chilled the air, there was another round-up, and on the northern ranges beeves were driven to market. More hands lost their paychecks, with the rancher keeping only a skeleton crew for winter. One Texan cowboy, who worked the Nebraska range, remembered that those kept on during winter "chopped and hauled logs, corral poles, posts; they built barns, houses, ice-houses, corrals or anything the foreman ordered done. The Texas Puncher was always sighing for spring." Some cowboys took on the loneliest job of all, line-riding. Either alone or with a partner, the line-rider patrolled the boundary of spreads too large to be overseen from the main ranch. Every day he ventured out from a line camp (a primitive hut) to round up stray cattle, kill predators, and to do any other job necessary to protect the cattle and land.

Range life was harsh. The cowboy lived in the saddle for days on end, rode in blizzard and heatwave, and was lucky to eat one good meal a day. The ranch bunkhouse he bedded down in was often a sod hut sunk into a hillside, sometimes a log cabin, its walls covered in newspaper to keep out winter winds. In summer the bunkhouse would crawl with lice and bedbugs, and snakes and rats would be attracted inside by the shade. To while away the boredom of the evenings, the cowhands would read, compose ditties, play practical jokes, and tell tall tales. The cowboy's evening, like the rest of his day, was often hedged by the petty restrictions of the ranch owner. Charles Goodnight even forbade the game of mumblety-peg on his spread, while many banned liquor, gambling and swearing. R. G. Head, of the Prairie Cattle Company, occasionally sent circulars to his hands reminding them of their moral responsibilities.

For all this the cowboy was paid between $25 and $50 a month. Most cowboys accumulated nothing beyond the clothes on their back and their saddles; they did not even own the horse they rode. Occasionally the exploited cowboy banded together with his fellow cow workers to improve his lot. In March 1883 Panhandle cowboys from the LX, LIT and LS ranches went on strike. They drew up a charter which declared: "We, the undersigned cowboys of the Canadian River, do by these presents, agree to bind ourselves into the following obligation, viz: First, that we will not work for less than $50 a month . . ." The strike failed, and most went back at their old pay rate of $25 per month. Three years later, 80 cowboys formed the Northern New Mexico Small Cattlemen and Cowboys' Union, resolving that "the working season of the average cowboy is only about five months, and we think it nothing but justice that the cowmen should give us wages the year around." Many cowboys joined the Knights of Labor union.

These and other attempts at unionization failed. Stockmen's associations blacklisted union cowboys, while striking hands were easily replaced. And cowboys generally worked lonesome, scattered lives, which made meetings and communication difficult. There was some truth, too, in the hallowed independence of the cowboy, a vein of self-reliance which cut against the collective ethos.

Yet, despite the poverty, the bone-breaking toil, the patronizing attitude of ranchers, for thousands of young men there was something yearningly attractive about a life in the saddle. Those who had fought for the Confederacy wanted a fresh beginning in the West, as did many Union veterans. Farmboys and city boys hoped to escape their humdrum lives, and a surprising number of cowboys were Englishmen and Scotsmen from noble families – known as "remittance men", after the money they received from home – desiring romance. Filling out the ranks were Mexicans and Blacks. Racial barriers tended to prevent African–Americans and Hispanics rising to positions of authority on the ranch, although there were exceptions. When Bose Ikard, Charles Goodnight's African-American top hand died, Goodnight erected a marker: "BOSE IKARD: Served with me for years on the Goodnight–Loving Trail, never shirked a duty, or disobeyed an order, rode with me in many stampedes, participated in three engagements with the Comanche, splendid behaviour. Charles Goodnight." Another legendary Black cowboy was Bob Lemmons, who was known for his ability to "walk down" wild horses by pretending that he was one of them. Bill Pickett and Nat Love both found fame as rodeo stars. Prevented from becoming foremen or trail bosses, a number of Black cowboys managed to save their wages and set up as independents, even becoming prosperous, like Texans Daniel "80 John" Wallace, and Jess Pickett.

As it was with African-Americans, so it was with Hispanics – but worse. *Vaqueros* made up something like 10 per cent of the West's cowboys, but despite their reputation as superior horsemen they were seldom foremen. Even the King Ranch of Texas, which employed a high proportion of *vaqueros*, hired only caucasian foremen. Unlike Blacks, *vaqueros* were paid a lower wage than Anglo cowboys, typically receiving half the latter's pay packet.

Women cowpunchers were a rare sight, since frontier society did not consider ranch work to be "ladylike". To ride astride was considered scandalous. Those women who did work the range were female relatives of the ranch owner, helping out on the family spread. A few, on the death of their husbands, took over the ranch themselves, the most extraordinary of them being Mrs E. J. Guerin ("Mountain Charlie"), who passed as a man for 13 years in order to support her child after her husband died, and once drove a herd of cattle to California.

Probably the only salaried cowgirl in the nineteenth-century West was Middy Morgan, an Irish immigrant who wandered to Montana. There her cattle expertise impressed a local rancher who hired her as a hand, then admitted her to partnership on the ranch. In the "bonanza years" of the early 1880s, Middy Morgan advised several British-financed ranches. She caught the eye of *The North British Agriculturalist*, who described her in detail in its June 1880 issue:

> At every fair or market may she be seen, with broad-brimmed hat tied down beneath her chin by a bandanna handkerchief, a thick frieze coat with many capes, short skirt, ingeniously gathered into high leather boots, something like knicker-bocker costume. With a long cowhide whip in hand, wending her way with skill between the droves, now stooping low to examine the hoofs, now standing on tiptoe to examine the head of the beast brought to her for valuation; and so great is the reliance placed by farmers on her judgement in these matters, that none would ever seek to cheapen the animal after Middy Morgan has pronounced her verdict.

If cowgirls were few, cowboys were many. Running away from home to become a cowpoke was almost a national disease amongst juvenile males in the 1870s and 1880s. In words which might speak for many, one retired cow waddy remembered his boyish infatuation with cowboying:

> I always wanted to be a cowpuncher. When I was a little kid on the farm in East Texas I couldn't think of nothin' else . . . Once in a while someone would drive a bunch of cattle by our place. I couldn't have been more'n eight years old when I followed one bunch off . . . I had an uncle livin' down the road about four miles. He happened to see me goin' by his place.
> "Whatcha doin', kid?"
> "A-working stock", says I.
> He finally talked me into goin' on back home with him – I stuck it out until I got to be about fifteen. Then I pulled out for good.

Few questions were asked of a prospective cowboy. His life was nobody's business but his own. This privacy was part of the cowboy's code. As Teddy Blue Abbott explained it:

> A man might tell as much or as little about himself as he saw fit, or nothing at all. Nobody cared. All that was required of him was to do his work faithfully, and not disturb the peace and harmony of the outfit by ill-temper or viciousness. These men might live together and work together season after season, year after year, without knowing anything about each other personally other than the names they went by.

There were many like Jim Culver, who arrived at the Lang ranchhouse more dead than alive after an adventure

in the icy waters of the Little Missouri. Lang liked him and
hired him. He was a young man of about twenty, fearless,
of good morals, and with an unusual amount of energy
and initiative. When a mean horse side-flopped and killed
him two years later, all that was known about him was –
"He said his name was Jim Culver".

Dressing the Cowboy

Part of the allure of the cowboy was his distinctive dress,
which set him apart from mere pedestrian farm hands. "I
see by your outfit that you are a cowboy," runs the line
from the song "The Cowboy's Lament". Although cowboy clothing sometimes tended towards the fancy, it was
mainly designed as a practical work uniform for ranch
labour in western climes.

The essential items of cowboy dress were hat and boots.
At first, Anglo cowboys wore the sombrero of the Mexican *vaquero*, the enormous brim of which gave the rider
shade under the southern sun. When cowboys drifted
north to work the plains of Montana and Wyoming, they
cut or rolled the brim back so that the hat would catch less
wind. Headgear was generally homemade – the favourite
material being straw – and of poor quality until the 1860s,
when New Jersey hatter John Batterson Stetson went west
for his health. Recognizing that a market existed for practical cowboy hats, in 1865 Stetson set up a shop and
factory in Philadelphia (which had skilled workers aplenty
and good rail links to the West) specializing in headwear
for the range. Within only a matter of years, "Stetson" and
cowboy hat were synonymous. By the turn of the century
Stetson employed a workforce of thousands and turned
out two million hats a year. These were in a variety of
styles, but the "Carlsbad" was the most popular. The "ten

gallon" hat enjoyed a brief vogue among drugstore cowboys and movie stars, but such extravagant styles were
rarely worn by genuine ranch hands. For a cow waddy, a
hat was an implement that kept him cool or dry, and
which could be used to scoop water for himself and his
horse if necessary. It could even be used to slap a bucking
bronc.

The cowboy boot was always made of top grade leather.
Even the most impecunious cowhand would somehow
find the $20–$30 for a fine pair of handmade boots, preferably from the shop of Joe Austin in Texas. Even more than
his hat, a cowboy's boots were his badge of office. Their
high heels kept his feet from shifting in the stirrups (and
served as brakes if he was roping on foot), while the high
tops protected his calves from chafing the fender of the
saddle. Initially boots were plain and straight, but gradually they became more ornate. The first fancy top was a
"Lone Star" motif set in a wide red band. Since boots were
difficult to don, pull straps were stitched on the inside or
outside ("mules' ears"). Until the 1890s most westerners
stuffed their pants legs inside their boots.

Spurs were a necessary accessory, their name deriving
from the Spanish *espuela*, meaning "grappling iron". Many
had vicious-looking rowels (serrated spinners) but the
first thing a cowpuncher would do with new spurs would
be to blunt them down. Spurs were for the control of a
horse, never for its punishment.

A bandanna, chaps and slicker were also common cowboy issue. The bandanna, usually blue or red, was a multi-
purpose tool; it could be tied over the mouth to keep out
dust, dipped in water to become a flannel, or used as a
tourniquet. Chaps were seatless leg-coverings that protected against ropes, brush and bad weather. Straight-
legged leather or "Shotgun" chaps were the familiar style,
but loose Bat-wings or Texas legs also had their adher-

ents. In winter, cowboys wore woolly chaps of Angora or sheepskin. Flamboyant cow waddies even made chaps out of mountain lion, ponyskin and buffalo hide. A yellow slicker saddle coat or "Fish" (after the brand name) was standardly tied behind the saddle, ready to be unrolled in inclement weather. The mail order advertisement for the Fish slicker – cowboys were regular catalogue shoppers – described it thus:

> This coat is gotten up especially for horseback riders; made from yellow slicker, very heavy cloth, and makes the most perfect rain coat ever manufactured for the use of the horseman. This coat covers the entire saddle, as well as rider, thus insuring a dry seat, while the lower part is wide enough to cover the length of the rider. It is a combination coat, which can be made from a riding to a walking coat by simply adjusting one of the buttons. The best coat obtainable; has patent eyelet fasteners, non-corrosive zinc buttons; all of the latest improvement. Guaranteed to be strictly waterproof, and the best coat of its kind ever put on the market.

The cost was $2.65.

If these were the characteristic items of a cowboy's wardrobe, the manner in which he dressed and undressed was no less distinctive. As William Timmons remembered it from his cowpunching days:

> A cowboy undresses upward: boots off, then socks, pants and shirt . . . He never goes deeper than that. After he has removed the top layer he takes his hat off and lays his boots on the brim, so the hat won't blow away during the night. Spurs are never taken off boots. In the morning a cowboy begins dressing downward. First he puts on his hat, then his shirt, and takes out of his shirt pocket his Bull

Durham and cigarette paper and rolls one to start the day. He finishes dressing by putting on his pants, socks, and boots. This is a habit that usually stays with a cowboy long after his days in the saddle are over.

More than hat, boots or any item of clothing, the saddle was the cowboy's most valuable possession. A stock saddle took many uncomfortable hours to wear in, and might cost more than a horse. One cowboy song went: "Oh a ten dollar hoss and a forty dollar saddle, / And I'm riding out to punch in Texas cattle." The sturdy stock saddle of the American West weighed around 40–50 pounds and came in a variety of models, but common to them all was a prominent front horn and a high cantle. With a rope looped or "dallied" around it the horn, usually fashioned from iron with a leather cover, was required to withstand the pull of a 2,000-pound bull. Outside of the horn and cantle, there were substantial regional differences in saddle-making. A Cheyenne saddle had a flatter seat than the popular "Brazos tree", while Texas, Montana and Wyoming saddles were all two-cinch or "rimfire" rigs. "Single-fire" rigs, on the other hand, were common in California and Oregon.

Bridle and bit likewise differed from region to region. Horsemen of the southern plains used the half-breed bit, which was gentle on the horse's mouth but required the cowboy to tug firmly. His compatriot on the northern plains, influenced by migrating Californian *vaqueros*, preferred a spade bit, the sharp point of which lay across the horse's tongue. When pulled back, the bit made the horse stop dead. Used roughly, the spade bit would cut the mouth, but in practised hands it could control the horse with the lightest touch. On winter mornings, Montana cowboys would warm the horse's bit by dipping it in coffee.

Such care for the horse was not occasioned by sentiment. Contrary to myth, cowboys tended to view horses as mere instruments, and changed them several times a day, much as a carpenter might move from saw to chisel to plane. A horse which was comfortable with its bit was a more efficient, less troublesome horse. This is not to say that cowpunchers never felt affection for their horses. Andy Adams, at the end of the long drive to Montana, found he had come to like and admire his mounts:

At no time in my life, before or since, have I felt so keenly the parting between man and horse as I did that September evening in Montana. For on the trail an affection springs up between a man and his mount which is almost human. Every privation which he endures, his horse endures with him – carrying him through falling weather, swimming rivers by day and riding in the lead of stampedes by night, always faithful, always willing, and always patiently enduring every hardship, from exhausting hours under saddle to the sufferings of a dry drive.

Now, when the trail is a lost occupation and reverie, and reminiscences carry the mind back to that day, there are friends and faces that may be forgotten, but there are horses that will never be. There were emergencies in which the horse was everything, his rider merely the accessory. But together, man and horse, they were the force that made it possible to move millions of cattle which passed up and over the various trails of the west.

Bonanzaland

The Taking of the Northern Plains

The American cattle business enjoyed a gilded age in the late 1870s and early 1880s. Slaughter by hunters had reduced the buffalo that competed with their cattle for grazing to a few scattered herds. The power of the Plains Indians was being challenged by the cavalry. The tables of the East were desperate for beef, and there was a growing demand for American beef in Europe. By the end of 1881, 110 million pounds of frozen beef were being shipped to Great Britain alone. And best of all, there were thousands of acres of free grass on the northern plains, there for the taking for those who could claim it or hold it with a gun. The profits that could be made from raising livestock on the grasslands of the West seemed almost unlimited.

Investment in the ranching business became a mania in America and Europe. Men and women begged and borrowed money to invest in steers and spreads. The finance-drumming letter of Connecticut's Judge Sherwood was typical. "The profits are enormous," wrote Sherwood to potential backers. "There is no business like it in the world, and the whole secret of it is, it costs nothing to feed the cattle. They grow without eating your money. They literally raise themselves."

Even responsible stockbreeding journals caught the delirium. The *Breeder's Gazette* enthused: "A thousand of these animals [cattle] are kept nearly as cheaply as a single one, so with a thousand as a starter and an investment of but $5,000 in the start, in four years the stock raiser has made from $40,000 to $45,000."

Probably the man who was most responsible for promoting the beef boom was James S. Brisbin. A Pennsylvania schoolmaster who joined the Union army in 1861, Brisbin had stayed on after the Civil War to fight the Indians. Impressed, however, by the way cattlemen drove a herd into a reservation and left with a bag of money, Brisbin appointed himself the proselyte of ranching. He wrote glowing reports for the sporting paper *Wilke's Spirit of the Times*, and eventually wrote a book, *The Beef Bonanza, or How to Get Rich on the Plains*, published in 1881. Urban readers were fascinated by his purple, rousing prose, one paragraph of which read:

The West! The mighty West! That land where the buffalo still roams and the wild savage dwells: where the broad rivers flow and the boundless prairie stretches away for thousands of miles; where new States are every year carved out and myriads of people find homes and wealth . . . where there are lands for the landless, money for the moneyless . . .

The would-be rich who pored over Brisbin's book were equally hypnotized by his examples of those who struck it rich in the cow business:

Mr R. C. Keith of the North Platte, Nebraska, began raising cows in the fall of 1867 with 5 American cows. Each year he and his partner bought more cows. The total cost of the cattle from 1867 to 1873 inclusive, was under $50,000.

This did not include expenses of ranch, herding, etc. . . .
which, however, were small, as they had no land or timber
to buy. They had several employees; their men cost $50
per month plus board . . . They have sold and butchered
cattle which brought them $12,000 profit. They have, re-
maining on hand, cattle worth $93,000. Thus they have
made an enormous profit.

Brisbin's book sold well in the East. In Britain it did a
phenomenal trade. English boardrooms and gentlemen's
clubs talked of little else except the beef bonanza. Aristocratic British families packed "black sheep" sons off to the
West to make easy money. Thousands of acres of Montana, Texas and Wyoming were bought up by cattle companies based in London and Edinburgh.

There seemed to be no end to British money. Wyoming
stockman Alexander Hamilton Swan managed to persuade a group of Scottish financiers to buy out five-sixths
of his holdings for $2.4 million, while he and a partner
retained the remaining stock and Swan stayed on as manager of the new enterprise, the Swan Land & Cattle Company Ltd. On the southern plains, the King Ranch, the
largest in the country, was financed by an English syndi-
cate. The Prairie Cattle Company purchased the Quarter
Circle T ranch of Thomas and Molly Bugbee in the Panhandle for the fantastic sum of $350,000. The same com-
pany also bought George Littlefield's "squatter" LIT ranch
– which had no legal claim to the land it grazed – for
$125,000. Spread after spread was swallowed by the Prai-
rie Cattle Company. Texas ranchers said of it that it "owned
all the outdoors". In a little under three years, the Prairie
Cattle Company had purchased a range which stretched
unbroken from the Arkansas to the Canadian rivers.

Some of the English and Scots financiers and cattlemen
cut a curious spectacle on the range. In 1883 the Rocking

Chair Ranche Company was formed, with the Earl of Aberdeen and Baron Tweedmouth as its principal shareholders. To oversee the Ranche's operation in the Panhandle, the company sent out a relative of Tweedmouth's, Archibald John Marjoribanks. The young Marjoribanks called his employees "cow servants", and antagonized them by insisting that they address him as Sir Archibald. When Marjoribanks rode the range, dressed in his elegant black scissor-tailed hunting jacket, his employees would bushwhack him, yipping like Indians and firing off their pistols.

Moreton Frewen, the son of a Sussex gentleman, arrived in the West and promptly had himself photographed in a tasselled and embroidered outfit. For the headquarters of his Powder River Company he built a rambling wooden house, "Frewen's Castle", which featured a 40-feet square room, where guests could dine while musicians played on the adjoining mezzanine. However, although the house boasted the luxury of a telephone, Frewen could not persuade his wife, Eastern heiress Clara Jerome, to endure frontier life, and she returned to her New York home. (Clara's sister, Jennie, was the mother of Winston Churchill, later to become British prime minister.) Though energetic and ambitious, Frewen had no luck in corporate ranching. He was constantly in time-consuming difficulties with his London board of directors, and after several years of bubble prosperity the Powder River Company went into liquidation. Afterwards, Moreton Frewen became nicknamed "Mortal Ruin".

Other cattlemen from Albion did better. In the late 1880s, the British-financed XIT Ranch added 15,000 square miles of Montana to its considerable Texas holdings. To move cattle to the northern spread, the company forged a route which ran through seven states, the 1,200-mile-long Montana Trail. Equally impressive was the Scotsman

Murdo Mackenzie, manager of the immense Matador Ranch. Mackenzie, vigilant and frugal, ensured that the Matador paid a steady 15 per cent to investors for three decades.

There seemed to be almost as many British capitalists as cowboys chasing cows in the West. Between 1880 and 1885, English and Scots investors poured $40 million into Western ranching. But the British were not the only pursuers of the beef bonanza. There were German barons, titled Frenchmen (including the Marquis de More, who arrived in the Dakota Badlands with no fewer than 20 servants), Ivy League graduates, and farm boys from Illinois. Anyone who was footloose and who could scrape together enough for a seed herd seemed to be heading West. Above all, there were East coast financiers from Boston and New York, who outspent even the British.

For them all, mecca was the free grass of Wyoming, Dakota and Montana. The small independents began with sod huts, heavily fortified because the Plains Indians had not been entirely subdued. A gentleman's agreement gave grazing rights to all land stretching back from a claimed stream. Some, through hard work, luck and guile, did become successful ranchers, even "cattle barons": men like Granville Stuart, a Virginian gold prospector turned rancher, who started with a spread in the Yellowstone in 1879.

The social centre for the cattle barons of the northwest plains was the famous Cheyenne Club. Established in 1880 by wealthy ranchers and stock managers in the frontier town of Cheyenne, Wyoming, the Club – originally called the Cactus Club – was a Great Plains facsimile of a London establishment for gentlemen. In the summer, stockmen sat on its broad verandah sipping cool drinks and reading the London *Times*. There were rooms for reading, playing billiards and cards, and its baths were much sought after. The management was especially proud to be the first club in America to install electric lighting. Rules of behaviour were strict. Members could be disciplined for profanity and drunkenness, and expelled for an act "so dishonorable in social life as to unfit the guilty party for the society of gentlemen." The colourful Charles M. Oelrichs, one of the Club's founders, was suspended for 30 days for hitting a bartender. When he refused to accept his punishment, the board of governors terminated his membership. Another member, John Coble, was suspended for shooting an oil painting of a pastoral scene, which he declared to be a travesty on purebred stock.

John Clay, a Scotsman who managed several Wyoming ranches, described the ambience of the Cheyenne Club in his memoir, *My Life on the Range*:

It was a cosmopolitan place. Under its roof reticent Britisher, cautious Scot, exuberant Irishman, careful Yankee, confident Bostonian, worldly New Yorker, chivalrous Southerner and delightful Canadian, all found a welcome home . . . a motley group full of ginger and snap, with more energy than business sense.

There at the club they met and they fashioned it after eastern and foreign methods. The foreigner was caught up by the ease and luxury of its café and dining room. There was an atmosphere of success among its members. They spent money freely, for all along the line there was a swelling song of victory.

Fencing off Texas

The northern plains were not the only great range to be opened up for cattle in the bonanza years. There was also the *Llanos Estacados*, the Staked Plains of the Texas Panhandle, long the domain of the buffalo and the Comanche.

The man who opened up the Panhandle for ranching was the ubiquitous Charles Goodnight. The financial panic of 1873 had wiped his Colorado cattle enterprise "off the face of the earth," obliging him to sell his property and most of his stock. From the wreckage of his empire he managed to salvage 1,800 head of cattle, and with veritable grit decided that he would start up a new cattle venture in a new land.

Thus in the fall of 1875 Goodnight began driving his remaining Longhorns south towards the unbroken grassland of the Panhandle, an area he knew from youthful service fighting Indians with the Texas Rangers. A volunteer assistant on the drive was Englishman James T. Hughes, the son of the author of *Tom Brown's Schooldays*. Another was the Scot J. C. Johnston, later director of Murdo Mackenzie's Matador Ranch. Both men had money, and invested it in Goodnight, buying a third of his herd.

As Goodnight's outfit trailed their way southwards they found the army everywhere before them, fighting their final campaign against the Comanche of the Staked Plains. Wintering on the Canadian, Goodnight began to search for the exact place where he would build his new ranch. By chance a Mexican trader, Nicholas Martinez, drifted into Goodnight's camp and told him of the Palo Duro Canyon, a fabulous grassy valley where Chief Lone Wolf had fought Mackenzie's cavalry. Goodnight employed Martinez to lead him to the canyon. They wandered for days, Martinez seemingly lost, until Martinez gestured Goodnight to the brink of an enormous gash in the earth.

One glimpse over the edge was enough to convince the rancher he had found the place he sought. Buffalo grass carpeted the bottom of the Palo Duro, while its towering walls made it a natural enclosure. A creek – the headwaters of the Red River – ran through it, giving it a plentiful supply of water. Only a few feet wide in parts, in other places the canyon bulged out to form miles of broad range. To get the cattle in, Goodnight had to drive them in single file down an old buffalo trail. His beloved chuckwagon was taken apart and lowered down the cliffs by lariat.

In the valley, Goodnight and his men discovered thousands of buffalo, which they "choused" out by firing bullets near their feet. To prevent the buffalo returning a guard had to be mounted at the mouth of the canyon. Then, on a choice piece of green level ground near the creek, Goodnight built the log house of what he called the "Old Home Ranch".

With the ranch house completed, Goodnight returned to Colorado to collect his wife, Mary Ann. On the journey he met the Irish financier John G. Adair, who proposed he back the cattleman in his venture. So was established the 1.25 million-acre "JA Ranch", after Adair's initials, which realized a profit of more than $500,000 in five years. Astutely, Goodnight upgraded his cattle by crossbreeding them. An experiment with shorthorned Durham bulls was a failure, but when in 1882 Goodnight tried white-faced Herefords he was immediately successful. The Hereford, as it developed, was the answer to the western livestock problem. It was hardy enough to survive the range, but produced plentiful, fatty meat.

Adair himself stayed in the East and left the ranching to Goodnight. When the Irishman died in 1885, however, his wife took to descending on the Palo Duro to check over the investment. A prominent Eastern socialite, Cornelia Wadsworth Adair always brought with her a vast train of maids, butlers and baggage.

Despite her customary scandalously late hour of rising, Cornelia Wadsworth Adair proved a canny rancher and by 1890 the JA Ranch grazed 100,000 cattle, many of them Herefords, which were given their own special JJ brand. But, ever restless, Goodnight decided to withdraw from the JA. Once again, he started up a new ranch, this time along the Fort Worth & Denver Railroad. Fuelled by a diet of black coffee, meat and a box of cigars a day, Goodnight also found time to develop a safe sidesaddle for women, and breed a cross between cows and buffalo which he called cattaloes.

He also spent many hours on the affairs of the Panhandle Stock Association of Texas, of which he was a prominent member. Although the cattlemen liked to surround themselves with an aura of individualism, the bonanza years saw them band together in powerful oligarchical association. The Cheyenne Club, behind its façade of carefree opulence, was the headquarters of the hardnosed Wyoming Stock Growers Association, who would achieve infamy with their range war in Johnson County in 1892.

The livestock associations offered many advantages to the established rancher: they supervised round-ups, registered brands and ran down rustlers. Above all, they sought to protect the wealth and advantage of the big cattle raiser by denying latecomer ranchers – pejoratively termed "range pirates" – and farmers access to the free grass.

Barbed wire was one means of doing this. Invented in 1873 by Illinois farmer Joseph F. Glidden, the coiled barb had initially been looked on with suspicion by the beef barons, who feared it would cut their cattle. When Glidden demonstrated to them that it would not, they bought roll upon roll of it, fencing off huge areas of grassland, even public highways. The XIT spread in Texas employed so much barbed wire that the staples needed to attach it to posts had to be shipped in by the freight-car load.

As more and more of the open range was closed to

small stockmen and farmers, they began to take counter-measures. Letters of protest were sent to Washington. They formed masked, night-riding groups which cut the ranchers' wire. The barons responded in kind, trampling down farmers' crops and cutting their wire. Violence and murder were the result. To stop the bloodshed, Congress enacted a law in 1885 which forbade fencing on the public domain.

This brought a sort of peace to range country, but only the peace which precedes the storm. Overstocking, range wars and blizzards were about to bring the beef bonanza crashing down.

Billy the Kid

Before the cattle kingdom fell, a curtain-raiser was played out on the vast plains of New Mexico. The Lincoln County War of 1878 was the first of the great range wars. It also created a legend in one of its dramatis personae, Billy the Kid.

Trouble began with the attempt of ex-Californian army officer Lawrence G. Murphy and his business associate James J. Dolan to turn Lincoln County into their private economic empire, based on the mercantile store and bank they operated in the county seat, also known as Lincoln. This empire – known to all as "the House", after Murphy and Dolan's imposing store building – was thoroughly corrupt, had much of the local political-legal machine in its pocket, and derived a principal source of its income from rustling the Long Rail cattle of John Simpson Chisum, which were then sold by government contract to the Mescalero Apache Reservation and Fort Stanton. Chisum, the so-called "cattle king of New Mexico," had been the pioneer rancher on the Pecos Plains; by the mid-1870s he had carved out a range of grama grass 200 miles long, and lived in palatial splendour in his adobe ranch set within irrigated orchards and shady cottonwoods.

By 1876 local discontent with the House's monopoly and high prices was rising, but found no practical expression until the arrival of patrician, tweed-wearing Englishman John Henry Tunstall in Lincoln County. Tunstall bought a small ranch on the Rio Feliz – and also opened a new store in Lincoln. His partners in this enterprise were the town's only lawyer, Alexander McSween, and John Chisum who opened a bank in the rear of the store. Patrons flocked to the Tunstall–McSween store, to the considerable irritation of the House. Matters were exacerbated when Murphy accused McSween of embezzling the estate of a former partner. As a precautionary measure against any sequestering, the lawyer transferred his property to Tunstall.

Such was the simmering country into which William H. Bonney, Billy the Kid, rode in September 1877.

The Kid

Born Henry McCarty in the immigrant Irish slums of New York in 1859, the Kid moved west to Kansas during the Civil War. After the Kid's father died in Coffeyville, his tubercular laundress mother moved on to the healthier, drier climes of Colorado. The first time the Kid entered the official records was on 1 March 1873. On that day Henry McCarty stood in Santa Fe's First Presbyterian Church with his brother Joseph, as witnesses to the marriage of their mother, Catherine McCarty, to one William Henry Harrison Antrim, a sometime prospector and barkeep.

In the raw mining settlement of Silver City the Antrims built themselves a log cabin home near the bridge which spanned Big Ditch. The Kid had an ordinary boyhood. His teacher, Miss Mary Richards, remembered him as being "no more a problem in school than any other boy." Among his favourite pastimes were singing and dancing, and with other boys he formed a minstrel troupe which

played to appreciative audiences at Morrill's Opera House.
His other passion was reading. In the few years left to
him, the Kid would read voraciously.

On 16 September 1874 Catherine Antrim succumbed
finally to the tuberculosis mining into her. Henry was 14.
With the removal of parental discipline, the Kid began to
err towards petty crime. One dark night, the Kid accompanied a local thief, Sombrero Jack, on a raid on the local
Chinese laundry. The duo absconded with a bundle of
washing. Henry's part in the deed was soon discovered
and Sheriff Harvey W. Whitehill locked the Kid up. Displaying the cunning that would distinguish his later career, the Kid persuaded the sheriff to let him have use of
the corridor outside his cell. Left unguarded for half an
hour, the Kid squeezed up a chimney and out of gaol. In
what would be the first of the Kid's many press notices,
the escape was related by the local newspaper, *Grant
County Herald,* with some sarcasm:

> Henry McCarty, who was arrested on Thursday and committed to jail to await the action of the grand jury, upon
> charge of stealing clothes from Charley Sun and Sam
> Chung, celestials, sans cue, sans Joss sticks, escaped from
> prison yesterday through the chimney. It's believed that
> Henry was simply the tool of "Sombrero Jack", who done
> the stealing whilst Henry done the hiding. Jack has skinned
> out.

The Kid also "skinned out". At 15 he was now officially
a fugitive from the law. Alone, he struck a course towards
Mount Graham, Arizona, where he worked as a teamster
and cowboy. These occupations equipped him with the
necessary lore for life on the violent frontier, including the
handling of a pistol and rifle. The Kid's tender years,
though, did not properly allow him to do a man's work on

a ranch. So, on being discharged as a cowpoke, he drifted into cattle rustling and horse theft. On 17 November 1876 the Kid stole a horse too many, the mount of a cavalry sergeant. He was tracked down and placed in Camp Grant's guardhouse. The army, like Sheriff Whitehill before it, discovered that the Kid was hard to imprison. He escaped on the same day he was confined, 25 March 1877.

By high summer the Kid was back in the Camp Grant area. According to a ranch acquaintance who saw him arrive, the Kid was "dressed like a 'country jake', with 'store pants' on and shoes instead of boots. He wore a six gun stuffed in his trousers."

If the Kid had the air of a strutting youth looking for trouble, he soon found it. Frank P. Cahill was a civilian blacksmith attached to Camp Grant, who was nicknamed "Windy" because of his overbearing manner. Windy Cahill used to delight in tormenting the Kid, ruffling his hair, and slapping his face. After a card game on 17 August 1877, the Kid and Windy became involved in a quarrel, with Windy calling the Kid "a pimp" and the Kid replying that Windy was "a sonofabitch". Cahill wrestled the Kid down, whereupon the Kid pulled Cahill's gun and shot him through the stomach. Windy Cahill died the next day.

A coroner's inquest decided that the killing of Frank P. Cahill "was criminal and unjustifiable, and that Henry Antrim, alias Kid, is guilty thereof."

The Kid was arrested as he ate breakfast at his hotel. Before he could be brought for trial, he escaped.

The Kid returned to the New Mexico he had fled two years previously as a juvenile thief. By the time of his return the Kid, now 17, had taken on the physique and personality that he would retain until the end of his short life. Wiry and lithe, he weighed 135 pounds and stood 5 feet 7 inches tall. Everyone noticed his blue eyes and wavy brown hair, while most found his buck-teeth attractive rather than ugly. From the hands of the ranches around Camp Grant he had learned the Code of the West, how to use a firearm, the carousing lifestyle of the cowboy (the Kid, although only a modest imbiber of tobacco and drink, was an inveterate card player, singer and girl-chaser), and gunmanship. He was an accomplished rustler, and somewhere along the line had picked up fluent Spanish.

When the Kid first entered Lincoln County, he hired himself out to whichever side in the growing conflict was willing to pay him. Usually he rode with "The Boys", a gang led by ex-Chisum hand Jesse Evans, the speciality of which was raiding Chisum's scattered herds on behalf of Lawrence Murphy. Tiring of "The Boys", the Kid – who now used the alias "William H. Bonney" – left their ranks and took a job working on Frank Coe's small ranch on the Ruidoso. Frank Coe noted his easy charm and his preoccupation with guns. "He spent all his spare time cleaning his six-shooter and practising shooting," recalled Coe years later. "He could take two six-shooters, loaded and cocked, one in each hand ... and twirl one in one direction and the other in the other direction, at the same time."

Among the Coes' neighbours on the Ruidoso was Dick Brewer. As well as managing his own spread, Brewer acted as ranch foreman to John Tunstall. It was probably through Brewer that the Kid was introduced to Tunstall, and hired by him as one of his cowboys-cum-gunslingers. Although Tunstall personally abhorred violence he was realistic enough to see that gunplay might be necessary in the feud with the House. Employing cowboy-gunfighters proved expensive. "It has cost a lot of money," Tunstall wrote in a letter to his munificent London parents, "for men expect to be well-paid for going on the war path."

The Kid was recruited to the Tunstall war party in late January 1878, and formed a deep liking for the cultured

Englishman. "He was the only man," said the Kid of
Tunstall, "that ever treated me like I was free-born and
white." The Kid's idolization of Tunstall would be a key
factor in the blood-spilling that led to the Lincoln County
War.

The Lincoln County War

The War was initiated at first light on the morning of 18
February 1878, when a posse led by pro-Murphy sheriff
William Brady swept into Tunstall's ranch. Brady had an
order to retrieve in cattle what Murphy considered was
owed him in the embezzlement case. The posse included
several bandits specially recruited for the occasion, one of
whom was Jesse Evans.

Finding Tunstall absent, the posse decided to hunt him
down. That evening, as dusk was falling, the posse caught
up with Tunstall and several of his men on the Lincoln
road. Tunstall's party were ambushed as they breached a
hill on the road. The Englishman was killed by a rifle
round to the chest in some scrub just off the trail.

The official version of the killing, as reported by Sheriff
Brady, was that the Englishman had been shot resisting
arrest. Billy the Kid, along with the other Tunstall men,
watching from the side of the trail, saw the killing as
murder.

The Kid was deeply affected by Tunstall's death, telling
Frank Coe: "I never expect to let up until I kill the last man
who helped kill Tunstall, or die in the act myself."

McSween, to whom leadership of the Tunstall faction
now fell, had little appetite for an armed fight with
Murphy. Initially, therefore, McSween tried to have
Tunstall's murderers dealt with by legal means. Little
cooperation could be expected from Sheriff Brady, so
McSween persuaded a Lincoln justice of the peace, John B.

Wilson, to issue warrants for the arrest of the killers. On 20 February Atancio Martinez, the town constable, accompanied by a conspicuously pistolled Billy Bonney and another Tunstall hand, Fred Waite, went to the Murphy store to serve warrants on Billy Morton and Jesse Evans for the murder of the Englishman. Sheriff Brady, by chance in the store, refused to let Martinez serve the warrants. Instead Brady arbitrarily and arrogantly arrested the Kid and Waite ("Because I had the power," he told complainants). After several days the prisoners were released, but the Kid would never forgive or forget the humiliation he received at Brady's hands.

McSween, meanwhile, departed town. Sheriff Brady's action had shown the futility of the lawyer's approach. Almost all the law enforcement machinery in Lincoln and its environs was in the pay of the Murphy faction.

With McSween's departure, a number of Tunstall men, led by Dick Brewer and Billy Bonney, declared themselves the "Regulators". Bound together by a loyalty oath they called the "iron-clad", the Regulators were a voluntary vigilante organization determined to serve the warrants – forcibly, if necessary – against Tunstall's killers.

Top of the Regulators' wanted list was posse member Billy Morton, believed by them to be the actual slayer of Tunstall. The Regulators captured Morton, along with Frank Baker, a henchman of Jesse Evans's, after a chase along the Pecos. The Kid wanted to dispense immediate justice. "Dick," said the Kid, "we've got two of them and they are the worst of the lot. Let's avenge John Tunstall by killing them right now."

Brewer persuaded the Kid that the two men should go to trial, and the party started back to Lincoln with the prisoners. They stopped at John Chisum's South Spring River ranch on 8 March, where Billy went fishing with Chisum's 14-year-old nephew, Will.

While Billy was fishing, news reached the Regulators that the House had sent out a posse to apprehend them. The next day the Regulators resumed their journey to Lincoln, but took a back trail up Blackwater Creek. There, at a site later called Dead Man's Draw, Morton and Baker were shot. Believing that the posse would free Morton and Baker, the Regulators chose to kill them instead. The victims received eleven bullets apiece, one for each Regulator present, suggesting ritual execution. A Tunstall hand who was adjudged too friendly with Murphy's men was shot as a spy.

More killing followed on the broiling morning of Fool's Day, 1 April. The Kid and five other Regulators hid behind an adobe wall next to Tunstall's corral in Lincoln. As Sheriff Brady and four deputies came into sight, the Regulators suddenly rose and fired their Winchesters, sending a fusillade of bullets down the street. Brady died instantly. A deputy, Hindman, was also killed. The other lawmen managed to scramble to safety. A wild round caught Justice Wilson in the buttocks as he hoed onions in his garden.

Three days later at Blazer's Mill, the Regulators cornered Andrew L. "Buckshot" Roberts, a Murphy gunman and a member of the posse which had killed Tunstall. The Kid's homicidal reputation was obviously growing, for when Roberts was called upon to surrender he laughed, "Surrender? Never, while I'm alive. Kid Antrim is with you and he would kill me on sight."

Roberts proved to be a one-man army. Though shot through the gut he made a stand in a doorway which wounded Regulators Charlie Bowdre, George Coe and John Middleton. Calculating that Roberts had run out of ammunition, the Kid impetuously rushed him, only to be repulsed by a Winchester butt to the stomach. Roberts forced a way into the room behind, found a Springfield

and ammunition and carried on the battle. At this, Dick
Brewer decided to take a sniping shot at Roberts from
behind a woodpile, only to have the top of his head blown
away. The Regulators, knowing that Roberts must die
from his stomach wound (as he did), chose discretion, and
retreated. With Brewer's demise, the Kid became the sole
leader of the Regulators.

The War carried on throughout the summer of 1878,
Murphy cowboys and Regulators meeting in running skirmishes across the range country. The Kid, however, also
found the time to woo Chisum's niece, Sallie, giving her
gifts of candy hearts and an Indian tobacco sack.

The relationship, however, had little chance to develop.
Alexander McSween, tiring of the War's indecisive course,
determined on a final, climactic battle. Accompanied by
nearly 50 Regulators, McSween slipped into Lincoln on
the night of 14 July and deployed his forces – many of
them Hispanic friends of the Kid's – at strategic points
around town. McSween himself, his wife Sue, the Kid and
14 other Regulators barricaded themselves in McSween's
house on Lincoln's lone street.

The so-called Battle of Lincoln began the next day.
Murphy's force, strengthened by cowboys from the Seven
Rivers country and hired guns of outlaw John McKinney,
surrounded Regulator positions and began blasting away.
For three days the fighting continued, with neither side
gaining an advantage, but on the morning of 19 July the
rattle of gunfire in Lincoln was interrupted by the sound of
bugles. Lieutenant-Colonel Nathan A. M. Dudley, four of
his officers and 35 enlisted men drew up outside McSween's
door. With them was a Gatling gun and a mountain howit-
zer, which Dudley aimed at Regulator strongpoints.

Certain defeat before him, McSween sent out a letter
offering to surrender to the cavalry. Dudley refused, insisting that McSween's men enter the custody of the le-

gally appointed sheriff, George "Dad" Peppin. Since Peppin, a Murphy supporter, was leading the attack on them, the Regulators balked at this.

While the parlaying was taking place, some Murphy men crept to the rear of the McSween house and set the kitchen afire. Although the fire burned slowly, eating a room at a time, it defeated every attempt of those inside to extinguish it.

The mood of the Regulators sank, with the exception of the Kid. Recalled Sue McSween later: "The Kid was lively and McSween was sad. McSween sat with his head down, and the Kid shook him and told him to get up, that they were going to make a break." The Kid suggested to Mrs McSween that she surrender, saying "A dress ain't very good to run in." Not wishing to impede the others, she agreed.

The breakout came shortly after 9 p.m., as the flames from the house lit up the hills on both sides of town. Out the front door, drawing the fire of the Murphy men, went the Kid, Tom O'Folliard, Jim French and Harvey Morris. All, except Morris, made it to the security of the bank of the Rio Bonito.

McSween, who was meant to use the Kid's break to effect the exodus of himself and the remaining Regulators, dithered and finally hid behind a woodpile. When Murphy's men approached McSween he tried to surrender. They shot him on sight.

The Lincoln County War was over. McSween was dead. So was Major Murphy, having died of natural causes in a Santa Fe hospital just before the five-day battle began. With Murphy gone, Chisum lost interest in sponsoring the conflict, and angered Billy by denying him the combat pay Billy considered due for his service in the War. Thrown on their own, the Kid and the surviving Regulators drifted into cattle rustling (including, as punishment, the beeves of John

Chisum), selling them in the stock markets of the Texas Panhandle. The Regulators officially became outlaws.

Amnesty

This aimless, dangerous existence soon grated, however, and the Kid tried to find a way back into lawful society. An opportunity seemed to present itself with President Hayes's appointment of a new territorial governor to New Mexico in August 1878. This was Lew Wallace, Civil War general and future author of the best-selling novel *Ben-Hur*.

Wallace's first action on arriving in New Mexico was to offer an amnesty to those who had taken part in what he termed the "Lincoln County Insurrection". The amnesty was not quite broad enough to take in the Kid, under indictment for the murder of Sheriff Brady. However, the Kid got his opportunity to ingratiate himself with Wallace in February 1879. On a midnight excursion into Lincoln, the Kid chanced to see two Murphy men kill Huston I. Chapman, the one-armed lawyer called into town by Sue McSween to help settle her husband's estate.

The killing of Chapman particularly irked Wallace, coming as it did after the amnesty proclamation. Restoration of public confidence in the law seemed to demand the capture and conviction of Chapman's murderers. Billy's sharp mind instantly saw Wallace's need. On 13 March he wrote a letter to the Governor:

I was present when Mr. Chapman was Murdered and know who did it and if it were not for those indictments [issued against the Kid for the murder of Brady] I would have made it clear by now. If it is in your power to Annully those indictments I hope you will do so as to give me a chance to explain.

The Kid concluded: "I have no Wish to fight any more."
It was signed "W. H. Bonney".

Governor Wallace was not above bargaining with a 19-year-old outlaw and invited him to come alone to a meeting in Lincoln a few nights later. Wallace related in a memoir:

> Billy the Kid kept the appointment punctually, . . . his Winchester in his right hand, his revolver in his left.
>
> "I was sent for to meet the governor here at 9 o'clock", said the Kid. "Is he here?" I rose to my feet, saying, "I am Governor Wallace", and held out my hand.
>
> "Your note gave promise of absolute protection", said the young outlaw warily. "Yes", I replied, "and I have been true to my promise . . ."

The Kid put down his weapons and shook hands. The men talked for a few minutes and agreed a deal. Billy would submit to an arrest for the Brady killing: while imprisoned he would testify in the Chapman case. For this, the Governor would grant him a pardon for all his misdeeds, including the murder of Brady. Billy would go scot free.

Although the Kid played his part, he did not get his amnesty. District Attorney Ryerson, a Murphy supporter, refused to grant it. Against such implacable legal hostility, Governor Wallace proved powerless, possibly faithless. The Kid escaped to Fort Sumner, the former Navajo reservation now owned by the local Maxwell family, where he passed his days rustling and his evenings playing monte. His grace at the Mexicans' *bailes* (dances) won him the attention of a number of local beauties, including Celsa Gutierrez, whose sister was married to a Texan former buffalo hunter named Pat Garrett.

Manhunt

It was at Fort Sumner that the Kid claimed his next killing. On 10 January 1880 a drunken Texas hardcase called Joe Grant drew a gun on the Kid in Bob Hargrove's earth-floor saloon. Hearing the challenge, Billy whirled around and shot Grant in the head, three times. The holes were so close together, said one bystander, that "you could cover all of them with half a dollar."

This was one lawless act too many for the area's incipient business community. Under Roswell's Joseph C. Lea a coalition of entrepreneurs and cattlemen formed to silence the Kid's guns. Prominent in the coalition was John Chisum, who organized the election of the tall, drawling Patrick F. Garrett – an erstwhile cardplaying friend of the Kid's – as sheriff of Lincoln. Almost as Garrett pinned the tin star to his chest, the Kid killed again, a blacksmith named Jimmy Carlyle, on 1 December 1880.

Selecting a posse of the best deputies in the Southwest, Garrett set off on the Kid's trail. On the night of 19 December the posse laid an ambush for the Kid at Fort Sumner. Hearing horses approaching through the snow, Garrett guessed correctly that it was the Kid and his gang of young guns, and the posse opened fire. The Kid's lieutenant, Tom O'Folliard, was mortally wounded, but the Kid and the rest managed to get away.

Yet the snow made their tracks easy to follow. The posse caught up with the outlaws at an abandoned rock house near Stinking Springs in the early morning of 23 December. All five outlaws – the Kid, Charlie Bowdre, Billie Wilson, Tom Pickett and Dave Rudabaugh – were asleep, their snores audible to the lawmen. Garrett surrounded the house and waited. At daybreak a lone figure came out of the rock house to feed the horses. The posse opened fire, hitting – not, as they thought, the Kid – but another Lincoln County War veteran, Charlie Bowdre. The hapless Bowdre fell back inside the hut, only to be pushed outside by the Kid. "They have murdered you, Charlie," the posse heard Billy say, "but you can get revenge. Kill some of the sons of bitches before you go." Bowdre staggered forward and fell dead at Garrett's feet. After some hours of stand-off, the Regulators surrendered. They were taken in shackles to Mesilla to stand trial.

The spectators who packed the courtroom were shocked to see that the infamous "Billy the Kid" – a nickname invented by newspapers; to those who knew him he was always "the Kid" – was a youth with down still glistening his chin. The judgement was a foregone conclusion. "You are sentenced to be hanged by the neck until you are dead, dead, dead," intoned the judge.

The Kid grinned, and replied in his shrill voice: "And you can go to hell, hell, hell."

Under heavy guard, Billy was taken to Lincoln and locked in Murphy's old store.

The Kid made his escape on the evening of 28 April 1881. He asked Deputy J. W. Bell to take him to the privy behind the courthouse. On the way back up the stairs Billy slipped his thin wrists out of his handcuffs and seized Bell's holstered revolver. The deputy was shot as he ran for help. Hobbling to the window in his leg-irons, the Kid saw the other guard, Bob Olinger, running across the street towards him. The Kid grabbed a shotgun.

A bystander called out, "Bob, the Kid has killed Bell." Olinger looked up and exclaimed, "Yes, and he's killed me too."

After shooting Olinger, the Kid managed to sever the chain connecting his leg shackles. With a leisurely air, he then borrowed a horse, which he would later send back to

Lincoln, said goodbye to a number of citizens and moseyed out of town.

The exploit, so bold and clever, made news across the entire country. Governor Wallace offered a $500 reward for the Kid's capture. Garrett began a second manhunt for the Kid.

For nearly three months, Garrett could discover no trace of the Kid. Then a whisper – almost certainly from Pete Maxwell, who disapproved of his sister Paulita's love affair with the Kid – led Garrett to Fort Sumner. Accompanied by deputy Tip McKinney and the cattle-range detective John W. Poe, Garrett reached the Maxwell place in the evening of 14 July 1881.

At around midnight, the Kid appeared on Pete Maxwell's porch, where he had gone to cut some meat from a butchered steer hanging there. Surprised to see a strange figure on the porch, the Kid called out *"Quien es? Quien es?"* ("Who is it? Who is it?").

Receiving no reply, he ducked into Pete Maxwell's bedroom. In the darkness, Billy failed to see the man sitting at the head of the bed talking to Maxwell.

Garrett shot twice. The first bullet hit the Kid just above the heart, killing him instantly. The second went wild. The Kid was unarmed, save for a meat knife.

A crowd gathered on the porch, drawn by the noise of gunshot. Finding that the Kid was dead, many vented their anger and grief. Celsa Gutierrez, Garrett's sister-in-law, cursed the sheriff as "a piss-pot". Expecting to be attacked by the Kid's friends, the lawmen spent the re-mainder of the night on guard, their guns drawn.

Just six weeks later *The True Life of Billy the Kid* was selling on the streets of Eastern cities. The legend had begun. Those fuelling it included Pat F. Garrett, who promoted the mythic nature of his nemesis with his 1882 *An Authentic Life of Billy the Kid* (ghosted by itinerant newspaperman Ash Upson). Among Garrett's wilder claims was that the Kid had killed 21 men, "not counting Indians and Mexicans". In fact the Kid's total of solo kills was a rather more modest four – Windy Cahill, Joe Grant, J. W. Bell and Bob Olinger – although he had a hand in the deaths of more. As a gunfighter, the Kid only ranks in the middle of the West's ratings, well behind such less glorified – and perhaps less charismatic – killers as Jim "Deacon" Miller and Wes Hardin.

Snow, Sheep and Blood

Waiting in Vain for a Chinook

Throughout the long summer of 1886, a wreath of smoke from burning grass fires hung over the range country. Streams shrivelled in the sun's unceasing heat.

Experienced stockmen became panicky. The bad winter of 1885 had already depleted and weakened their herds. There was not enough good grass on the burning, overstocked, drought-ridden ranges to build them back up again. Many ranchers dumped their beeves on the market. Prices went tumbling. Beeves worth $30 a year before scarcely fetched $10 a head.

Those who sold, at whatever price, were the wise and fortunate ones. The winter of 1886–7 would be the worst in the annals of the west.

All the signs were there, for those who cared to look for them. Herman Hagedorn, who ranched near Theodore Roosevelt's Dakota spread, recalled the omens of wintry doom in his *Roosevelt in the Badlands*:

Nature was busier than she had ever been in the memory of the oldest hunters in that region in "fixin' up her folks for hard times." The muskrats along the creeks were building their houses to twice their customary height; the walls were thicker than usual and the muskrats' fur was longer and heavier than any old-timer had ever known it to be. The beavers were working by day as well as by night cutting the willow brush, and observant eyes noted that they were storing twice their usual winter's supply. The birds were acting strangely. The ducks and geese, which ordinarily flew south in October, that autumn had a month earlier already departed. The snowbirds and the cedar birds were bunched in the thickets, fluttering around by the thousands in the cane breaks, obviously restless and uneasy. The Arctic owls, who came only in hard winters, were about.

On 16 November the thermometer fell below zero and a blizzard blanketed the northern plains with snow so deep that the cattle could not paw down through it. Another blizzard howled across Wyoming three weeks later, halting stagecoach travel. A warm "chinook" wind in late December brought ranchers Christmas hope, but a blizzard on 9 January 1887 deposited snow at the rate of an inch an hour. The thermometer touched 46F below zero.

The Great Blizzard had not finished its work. It returned on 28 January with a fury beyond anything in the memory of cattle country. In the past cattle had withstood snowy tempests by drifting before the wind; now they piled helpless into the barbed wire fences the ranchers had greedily thrown around their acres. Thousands upon thousands of cattle died on the fences, frozen and starving, or were suffocated in drifts as they tried to find shelter in gulches.

Despite a cold that reached 60 below, the cowboys went out to help the cattle, wrapped up in layers of clothing and their faces darkened with lamp-black or burnt matches to stop snowblindness. Some wore their neckerchiefs over their faces, with eye-holes cut out, bandit fashion. To keep their feet warm they stood their boots in water till ice formed, creating an airtight layer. Teddy Blue Abbott was working in Montana at the time:

> The cattle drifted down on all the rivers, and untold thousands went down the airholes. On the Missouri we lost I don't know how many that way. They would walk out on the ice and the ones behind would push the front ones in. The cowpunchers worked like slaves to move them back in the hills, but as all the outfits cut their forces down every winter, they were shorthanded. No one knows how they worked but themselves. They saved thousands of cattle. Think of riding all day in a blinding snow storm, the temperature fifty and sixty below zero, and no dinner. You'd get one bunch of cattle up the hill and another one would be coming down behind you, and it was all so slow, plunging after them through deep snow that way! You'd have to fight every step of the road. The horses' feet were cut and bleeding from the heavy crust, and the cattle had the hair and hide worn off their legs to the knees and hooks. It was surely hell to see big four-year-old steers just able to stagger along. It was the same all over Wyoming, Montana and Colorado, western Nebraska and western Kansas.

Maddened, ice-encrusted cattle staggered into Western towns, desperate for warmth and food. Five hundred brawling beeves invaded Great Falls, Montana, and ate the trees the civic-minded townsfolk had recently planted. In Dakota, cattle were reported as eating the tar paper off shacks.

It was not only the cattle that died. So did many cowboys, their frozen bodies stored in drifts near ranch houses because the ground was too hard for graves. The Bis-

marck *County Settler* reported "an appalling loss of life".
Whole families were found perished from hypothermia.

At last the spring sun shone, thawing the frozen land.
The Little Missouri burst its banks, huge ice-cakes grind-
ing over and over each other. Countless carcasses of cattle
rolled and tumbled down the raging river.

As the ice and snow melted, the extent of the tragedy
became clear. Coulées were piled deep with dead cows,
and the few that survived were gaunt and barely able to
walk. The cowboy artist and rancher Charles M. Russell,
who was managing a herd in the Judith Basin, was asked
by the absentee owner for a report on the situation. Unable to find words, Russell painted a picture of a skeletal,
dying cow, "The Last of Five Thousand" (also known as
"Waiting for a Chinook").

Russell scarcely exaggerated. Losses were fantastic.
Some ranchers, the worst hit, lost 90 per cent of their
herds.

The suffering of the livestock affected even hardened
cattlemen. Confronted with a landscape littered with dead
and dying cattle, the Montana rancher Granville Stuart
suddenly found the industry distasteful. "I wanted no
more of it. I never wanted to own again an animal that I
could not feed and shelter." (This was only to come into
line with public opinion; the American Humane Society
had obtained legislation governing the treatment of cattle
as early as 1873.)

The blizzards dealt the industry a reeling blow. With
creditors clamouring at the ranch house door, those who
had cattle left loaded them on the market. Prices fell
through the floor. In the Chicago markets, grass-fed steers
worth $9.35 a hundredweight in 1882 were worth $1.00 in
the fall of 1887. Ranch after ranch slid into insolvency.
"From southern Colorado to the Canadian line, from the
100th Meridian almost to the Pacific slope it was a catas-

trophe," wrote Wyoming ranch manager John Clay. "The cowmen of the west and northwest were flat broke. Many of them never recovered. Most of the eastern men and the Britishers said 'enough' and went away. The big guns toppled over; the small ones had as much chance as a fly in molasses." Among the firms that went under were the giant Swan and Land Company of Wyoming, and the Niobara Cattle Company of Nebraska. The once mighty Cheyenne Club defaulted on its bonds and sold out for 20 cents on the dollar.

All over the plains, a shuffling, straggling army of bone-pickers appeared. Before, they had come for the skeletons of the buffalo. Now they came for the remains of the once mighty cattle herds.

The beef bonanza had come to an end. Some ranches – generally the better-run sort – hung on and revived. When the Western Ranche Ltd (registered in Edinburgh, Scotland) wound up in 1919 it was still paying shareholders £9.00 for every £5.00 invested. But never again would cattle carpet the open ranges of the West, and never again would a stockman assume his cattle could survive a plains winter unaided. In the aftermath of the Great Blizzard the industry underwent immense change. Ranchers fenced all the land they dared, but restricted the size of their herds and grew hay, alfalfa or sorghum for winter feed. The West became a land of enclosed pastures, stocked by carefully selected and sheltered beeves. (To their surprise, ranchers discovered that a relatively small herd of improved stock sold at a young, plum age yielded more beef and profit than the large scrawny herds of the open range system.) Cowboys, the knights of the saddle, spent much of their time doing farm chores, digging irrigation ditches and cutting hay. "I remember," reminisced one regretful, ageing cowboy to the *Independent* of Sidney, Texas, when we sat around the fire the winter through and didn't do a lick of work for five or six months of the year, except to chop a little wood to build a fire to keep warm by. Now we go on the general roundup, then the calf roundup, then comes haying – something the old-time cowboy never dreamed of – then the beef roundup and the fall calf roundup and gathering bulls and weak cows, and after all this a winter of feeding hay. I tell you times have changed. You didn't hear the sound of a mowing machine in this country ten years ago.

New work for the cowboy brought with it new rules governing his employment and lifestyle. Less and less was he a free spirit; more and more was he a company man, a rural proletarian. The XIT outfit in the Panhandle issued 23 new regulations for employees in 1888. Notably, employees at the XIT could not "own any cattle or stock horses on the ranch", thus preventing them from getting a start in ranching themselves.

Old-time cowboys who regretted such changes had other causes for alarm in the late 1880s. Farmers and sheepherders were pressing hard into the shrinking domain of the Cattle Kingdom.

The Rising White Tide

Sheep raising in the West began with the Spanish missions, Juan de Onate and his colonizers driving a flock of a thousand ewes and rams into New Mexico in 1598. For two and a half centuries the industry was concentrated in the Southwest, with itinerant Hispanic and Indian (mainly Navajo) herders tending flocks of the sturdy *churros*. In the nineteenth century, new strains of sheep were introduced – the American Merino from Kentucky, the French Rambouillet, the English Cotswold, Shropshire and Lincoln – which increased the wool yield for their unromantic keepers to four or five pounds per animal per year, at the same time producing an animal tender enough to eat. Eastern mills were prepared to pay a good price for the wool, while the gold miners who flocked to California were prepared to pay a good price for the meat. In the decade after 1849, nearly a half a million sheep were driven from New Mexico to California. Those delivering the sheep included Kit Carson, the noted fur trapper, scout and Indian fighter.

Under the incentives of California gold and Eastern banknotes, sheep ranching grew rapidly. By the early 1880s there were four million sheep pasturing in New Mexico alone. Inevitably, flocks spilled out of their traditional ranges into terrain that cattle raisers saw as their own.

Some ranchers turned sheepfarmer. "Woolies" made twice the profit of steers for relatively little effort. A man with two dogs could control up to 3,000 sheep. More, wool was a commodity which could be stored indefinitely, was protected by tariff from foreign competition (until 1894), and was harvested annually with little harm to the animal. Even the American cattle industry propagandist, James Brisbin, was forced to admit that sheep made a better investment than cows.

The majority of ranchers, however, fought back. They complained that the sheep close-cropped grass they needed for their horses and cattle, and that cattle hated the pervasive smell of sheep and would not prosper where they ran. Exacerbating this competition was the matter of race. Shepherds were often non-White and immigrant; they were Mexican Americans, Basques, and Scots. Mormons, too, often owned sheep, and in the West all Mormons – many of whom were anyway immigrants – were regarded as unAmerican. To the Anglo-American cattleman, sheep were an inferior animal tended by inferior men.

The ranchers were prepared to resist the rising white tide of sheep with violence. Something like open warfare existed on the western edge of cattle country for years. Cowboys slaughtered 600,000 sheep – mostly by driving them over the edges of cliffs – on the Wyoming–Colorado range alone. There were hundreds of injuries to humans. And not a few deaths.

Tonto Basin, Arizona, witnessed the worst of the West's cattle versus sheep feuds. Pleasant Valley, in the early 1880s, was as attractive as its name suggested, and among those drawn to settle it were the family of John D. Tewksbury, an old man with three half-breed sons, and the families of brothers Thomas and John Graham. At first, the Tewksburys and the Grahams were friends, and rode together as cowboys for neighbouring ranches. They also did some petty rustling and "mavericking". Then, in 1884, they had a dispute over cattle, probably because the Grahams were appropriating more than their fair share of stolen steers. The families became fierce enemies.

Matters might have rested there, except for the intrusion of history. The Grahams, with their increased stock, moved into a closer relationship with the region's cattle barons. Meanwhile, the Tewksburys, denied the profits of their illicit labours, grew increasingly bitter. When, in 1886, Ed Tewksbury was accused of horse theft by the foreman of a local ranch, Tewksbury shot him. But the real trouble began when the Tewksburys broke the cardinal rule of Pleasant Valley. The Tonto Basin was cow country, and sheep were specifically prohibited. In the fall of 1886, John D. Tewksbury made a deal with prominent sheepmen from Flagstaff to graze sheep in Pleasant Valley. The cattlemen responded with violent fury. Sheep were slaughtered by the hundred and in February 1887 a Navajo shepherd was cold-bloodedly murdered.

By the summer, all the sheep were gone. The animosities, however, remained, and the families were impelled deeper and deeper into bloodshed by associates who stood to gain more than either of them. On 10 August 1887, Hampton Blevins, a friend of the Grahams, together with several riders from the powerful Aztec Land and Cattle Company (the Hash Knife brand), stopped by the Tewksbury ranch. According to the cowboys, it was an innocent visit and Tewksbury shot at them from his doorway unprovoked. The Tewksburys claimed that the men drew revolvers as they turned away. Whatever, Jim Tewksbury killed Hamp Blevins and John Paine. When a Graham associate tried to ambush Tewksbury, his marksmanship claimed a third victim.

Up to this point, Tom Graham had tried to restrain the violence. When, however, his youngest son was murdered he personally led a raid on the Tewksbury ranch, on 2 September 1887. John Tewksbury and William Jacobs were shot down in the front yard as they tried to find cover. For hours, the Grahams directed a hail of bullets at the ranch house. Suddenly, the front door opened and John Tewksbury's wife stepped outside. The firing stopped. (The code of the West absolutely prohibited the shooting of a woman.) Mrs Tewksbury shooed away the hogs that were rooting at the body of her husband and his friend, and buried their bodies. When she returned indoors, the shooting started up again. It only finished when a posse arrived and drove off the attackers.

Two days later the long-haired Commodore Perry Owens, the new sheriff of Apache County, attempted to arrest Andy Blevins for the murder of two sheepmen in the feud. In the fight that followed, Owens, using a Winchester rifle, shot dead Andy Blevins, his brother and his brother-in-law. Another brother, John Blevins, was wounded in the shoulder. Despite the steady loss of personnel, the feud continued. Determined to end it, the sheriff of Yavapai County, Willam Mulvenson, moved to arrest the leaders of both factions. John Graham and Charles Blevins were killed when they resisted arrest. The Tewksburys surrendered without a fight. When they were brought for trial for the murder of Hamp Blevins no one would testify against them. Fear was more powerful than conscience.

Pleasant Valley continued to echo with gunfire. By December 1888 only Ed Tewksbury and Tom Graham survived from their respective families (Jim Tewksbury had died of tuberculosis). In an effort to avoid further trouble, Tom Graham moved out of the valley. But the hatreds and issues had grown far beyond two families by then. The killings continued.

It was not until August 1892 that the Graham–Tewksbury feud finally came to an end. In that month Tom Graham, returning to Tonto Basin to settle his business affairs, was assassinated. His killer was Ed Tewksbury. With the demise of Tom Graham, the five-year conflict had claimed its twenty-first life. Pleasant Valley had become Arizona's "dark and bloody ground". Ed Tewksbury – the charges against him eventually dropped because of a technicality – became a lawman in Globe, Arizona.

Pleasant Valley was one of the cattlemen's few victories. Elsewhere they were less able to hold back the trampling flocks of sheep.

By 1890 sheep on the Columbia plateau outnumbered cows four to one. The sullen, lowly sheepherder had triumphed over his mounted, romantic cowboy counterpart.

Time and defeat did little to alter the attitude of cowman to sheepherder. In his 1930 memoir of his life as a cowpuncher, *Lone Cowboy*, Will James (born Ernest Dufault) still felt moved to write:

What turned the cowman against the sheepman from the first is that the sheepman came in their country after the cowman had found it, claimed his part and made the range safe against the Indian. The cowman had fought for it for all he was worth and soon as he had the Indian tamed down and raids was getting far apart, why here comes the sheepman to tramp down the grass the cowman had fought for. The blatting woolies and the herders had no respect for the cowman's territory and not only trampled down his grass, but brought in a lot of loco and other poison weeds.

Contrary to James's claim, it was actually overstocking by cattle which opened up the range to non-grasslike plants and herbs, since the cattle overgrazed the bunchgrass. Cattle could not thrive on the resultant weedy growth; sheep could. The great irony of the Cattle Kingdom is that the grandees' own beeves were a fifth column working against them, literally preparing the ground for sheep.

Homesteaders

More dangerous even than the "woolies" were the invaders from the East. Since the Civil War, settlers had been establishing themselves on range country, fencing off plots and filing claims under the Homestead Act of 1862, passed to promote settlement in the West. Under the Act, any citizen over 21 years could claim up to 160 acres of the public domain. If he lived on the land for five years, thus proving good faith, and built a house, put up fences and so on, then the land became his.

The homesteaders were all kinds of people: pioneer farmers who had worked their way westwards over the generations, war veterans, immigrants and cowboys who had lost their jobs during hard times on the range. A few were horse thieves, like those driven from the Montana range in 1882–3 by Granville Stuart and a group of cowboy vigilantes who became known as "Stuart's Stranglers". Their campaign was devastating, the most violent vigilante movement in Western history. Over a hundred bandits were killed after being marked for death on a list provided by Stuart. Some taste of the Stranglers' activities is provided by Granville Stuart's own candid autobiography, *Forty Years on the Frontier*:

Billy Downs was located at one of the wood yards on the Missouri at the mouth of the Musselshell, ostensibly to trap wolves, but in reality to sell whiskey to the Indians. His place soon came to be headquarters for tough characters, and it was but a short time until Downs himself was stealing horses and killing cattle. Downs was a married man and his wife was at the wood yard with him. Because of sympathy for the woman, he was warned that he was being watched and that if he did not change his tactics he was sure to get into trouble. He paid not the least attention to the warning, but continued to surround himself with the worst characters on the river and kept on stealing horses and killing cattle.

On the night of July 4, a committee of vigilantes arrived at the Downs' place and called on him to come out. This at first he refused to do but after a short parley he did come out, accompanied by a notorious character known as California Ed. Both men plead guilty to stealing ponies from the Indians but denied that they had stolen from white men, but they failed to account for the twenty-six horses in the corral, all bearing well-known brands. They claimed that the quantity of dried meat found in the house was dried buffalo meat, notwithstanding the fact that there had not been a buffalo on the range for more than two years. In the stable was a stack of fresh hides folded and salted ready to be shipped down the river, all bearing the brand of the Fergus Stock Co. The two men were taken out to a little grove of trees and hanged.

At the time the vigilante committee started for the mouth of Musselshell, another party left for the vicinity of Rocky Point where two notorious horse thieves, known as Red Mike and Brocky Gallagher, were making their head- quarters. They had stolen about thirty head of horses from Smith river, changed the brands and were holding them in the bad lands. They had also been operating over on the Moccasin range and stolen horses from J. H. Ming's ranch and from J. L. Stuart.

When the vigilantes arrived at Rocky Point the men were not there but had crossed over on the north side of the river. The party followed after, and captured them and recovered some of the horses. Both men plead guilty to horse stealing and told their captors that there were six head of the stolen horses at Dutch Louie's ranch on Crooked creek.

Fifteen miles below the mouth of the Musselshell, at an old abandoned wood yard, lived old man James, his two sons, and a nephew. Here also was the favorite haunt of Jack Stringer. There was a log cabin and a stable with a large corral built of logs, connecting the two buildings. One hundred yards from the cabin in a wooded bottom was a tent constructed of poles and covered with three wagon sheets. At the cabin were old man James, his two sons, Frank Hanson and Bill Williams. Occupying the tent were Jack Stringer, Paddy Rose, Swift Bill, Dixie Burr, Orvil Edwards and Silas Nickerson.

On the morning of July 8, the vigilantes arrived at Bates Point. The men were divided into three parties. Three guarded the tent, five surrounded the cabin and one was left behind with the saddle horses. They then waited for daylight. Old man James was the first to appear. He was ordered to open the corral and drive out the horses. This he did but refused to surrender, backed into the cabin and fired a shot from his rifle through a small port hole at the side of the door. This was followed by a volley from port holes all around the cabin and in an instant the whole party was in action.

Two of the vigilantes crawled up and set fire to the hay stack and the cabin. The men inside stationed themselves at port holes and kept up the fight until they were all killed or burned up: The cabin burned to the ground. The tent was near the river bank and almost surrounded by thick brush and it was easier to escape from it than to get out of the cabin. Stringer Jack crawled under the tent and reached a dense clump of willows from which he made his last stand. Dixie Burr had his arm shattered with a rifle ball but jumped into an old dry well and remained until dark. Paddy Rose ran out of the tent, passed back of the men engaged at the cabin and concealed himself in a small washout and after dark made his escape. Nickerson, Edwards, and Swift Bill reached the river bank and crawling along through the brush and under the bank, succeeded in passing above the men at the cabin and hid in some brush and drift wood. Orvil Edwards and Silas Nickerson were the only ones that escaped without wounds. After the fight at the cabin the men went down the river and spent the day looking for the men who had escaped but failed to find them.

On the afternoon of the ninth, the fugitives rolled some dry logs into the river, constructed a raft and started down stream. At Poplar creek agency they were discovered by some soldiers stationed there, ordered to come on shore and were arrested.

Notice of their arrest was sent to Fort Maginnis and
Samuel Fischel, deputy U.S. marshall, started at once to
get the prisoners and take them to White Sulphur Springs.
At the mouth of the Musselshell a posse met Fischel and
took the prisoners from him. Nearby stood two log cabins
close together. A log was placed between the cabins, the
prisoners tied to this and shot.

By the time the Stranglers were disbanded in 1884,
rustling in the Montana–Dakota range country had been
all but wiped out. This was far from true in Wyoming's
Johnson County, where grandee cattlemen were losing
steers by the hundred to a motley crew of thieves which
included hardened criminals but were mostly homesteaders and disenchanted cowpunchers wanting to establish
their own spread. Through the agency of the powerful
Wyoming Stock Growers' Association, the cattlemen determined to protect their property and keep the range
open – or, more accurately, under their exclusive control.

Initially, the stockmen employed legal methods, hiring
former peace-officers and gunmen to act as "stock detectives". Posing as genuine cowboys, the detectives spied
on the homesteaders and reported evidence of rustling to
the barons. To prove brand alterations, the detectives
often skinned the hide from stolen beeves; the inner side
would reveal the original brand, which the rustler had
altered on the outside with a running iron. Suspects were
hauled to court, but juries failed to convict. Local people
had little sympathy for the big stockmen, who were often
wealthy absentees.

The grandee stockmen tried another way. They secured the passing of an extraordinary piece of legislation,
the Maverick Act, which made the branding of any
unbranded calf by anyone who was not a member of the
Stock Growers' Association a felony. Small ranchers and

settlers were thus unable to round up and brand their own calves without being charged with a crime.

To oversee the efficiency of the Maverick Act, the Stock Growers' Association hired Frank Canton as their chief range inspector. Previously the sheriff of Johnson County, Canton – whose real name was Joe Horner – had a long history of hired gunfighting and outlawry, including the robbery of a bank in Comanche, Texas. Under Canton's zealous leadership, Association inspectors at markets and shipping points seized 16,000 cattle not bearing approved brands.

While the seizing of the cattle outraged their homestead owners, the impounded cows' lack of suitable brands only proved to the grandees that rustling was still a major problem. With the inspiring example of Granville Stuart's Montana campaign before them, the local stockmen decided that Wyoming – especially Johnson County – required a dose of lynch-law medicine.

Among the first victims was the 170-pound Ella Watson (also known as Kate Maxwell), who ran a saloon in Sweetwater County. Her business partner was Jim Averill, a justice of the peace who liked to scribe letters to the Casper *Weekly Mail* denouncing cattle barons as landgrabbers. By most accounts, the Canadian-born Watson was a prostitute, with mavericked cattle the medium of exchange. These she used to stock a small ranch near the saloon.

Watson and Averill were both warned to leave the area, but refused. One night in July 1889 they were seized in their saloon and taken to Spring Creek Gulch, and hanged. A reporter described the scene when people from Casper found the bodies:

Hanging from the limb of a stunted pine growing on the summit of a cliff fronting the Sweetwater River were the

bodies of James Averill and Ella Watson. Side by side they
swung, their faces swollen and discolored almost beyond
recognition. Common cowboys' lariats had been used and
both had died by strangulation, neither having fallen over
two feet. Judging from signs too plain to be mistaken, a
desperate struggle had taken place on the cliff, and both
man and woman had fought for their lives until the last.

A local rancher called Albert J. Bothwell was widely
believed to be behind the lynching. No indictments, however, were ever returned in the case. Bothwell later appro-
priated Watson's cabin and turned it into an ice-house. To
justify the murder, subtle propaganda turned Watson
into the notorious rustler queen "Cattle Kate", who "had
to die for the good of the county."

After the execution of Watson and Averill, death spread
across the land. A horse-raiser named Waggoner was
lured from his home and hanged at "Dead Man's Canyon". In November 1891 four vigilantes, including Frank
Canton, made a dawn visit to a cabin on Powder River,
intending to kill two cowboys turned homesteaders, Ross
Gilbertson and a Texan called Nathan D. Champion. The
intruders burst in, one of them shouting "Give up, we
have got you this time." The assailant fired and missed.
Champion grabbed his gun and put all four vigilantes to
flight.

The vigilantes were more successful a month later,
shooting two homesteaders as they drove out of Buffalo,
the only town in Johnson County.

Such assassinations, however, only stirred up more
animosity towards the big cattlemen. They did nothing to
curb rustling. When, in spring 1892, the Wyoming Stock
Growers' Association heard that the homesteaders were
planning an unlawful pool round-up, they determined on
nothing less than a full-scale invasion of Johnson County.

Members of the Association formed themselves into a secret society they called the "Regulators", electing as their leader former US Army Major Frank Wolcott. The portly, pompous Wolcott owned a large ranch on Deer Creek. At Wolcott's instigation Tom Smith, a range detective with the Association, was sent south to hire an army of gunmen. The pay offered was $5 a day and expenses, plus a $50 bonus for every homesteader killed. Smith hired 22 gunfighters, one from Idaho, the rest from Texas. Wolcott, meanwhile, journeyed to Denver and hired a special train from Union Pacific – an engine, three freight cars and three passenger cars. When the train reached the state capital, Cheyenne, on 5 April, horses, guns, dynamite, ammunition and tents were loaded aboard. Just after nightfall, the gunfighters entrained, accompanied by five Association detectives and 19 cattlemen, including Frank Wolcott. A doctor Penrose signed on as official surgeon. Two pro-Association newspapermen, Sam T. Clover of the *Chicago Herald* and Ed Towse of the Cheyenne *Sun*, went along as war reporters.

The Johnson County War

At three o'clock in the morning of 6 April 1892, Wolcott's army arrived at Casper, end of the line. Here they cut the telegraph wire to Buffalo and set off on horseback for Johnson County. In Wolcott's pocket was a list of 70 homesteaders and rustlers who were to be executed by the Regulators. During a restover at the Tisdale Ranch, Wolcott learned that Nathan Champion and another homesteader, Nick Ray, were wintering at an old line camp, the KC. Wolcott consulted his list, and found that both Champion and Ray were on it. Wolcott's original intention had been to ride directly to Buffalo, but now he decided to swing over to the KC and eradicate Champion and Ray first.

The expedition reached the line camp in the bitterly cold morning of 9 April. Inside were Champion – who had already driven off one gang of Stockmen assailants – and Ray, together with two fur trappers to whom they were playing host, Bill Walker and Ben Jones. The cabin was surrounded, and when the two trappers came out they were silently captured. A few minutes afterwards Nick Ray walked out the front door and was wounded by a volley from Regulator guns. He began to crawl back to the cabin, and Champion rushed out into the gunfire, grabbed his collar and hauled him into the cabin.

Besieged on all sides, Champion began returning fire so dense and accurate that he kept his attackers at bay for hours. In amidst the action, Champion somehow managed to write an account of his ordeal in a little pocket book:

Me and Nick were getting breakfast when the attack took place. Two men here with us – Bill Jones and another man. The old man went out after water and did not come back. His friend went out to see what was the matter and he did not come back. Nick started out and I told him to look out, that I thought there was someone in the stable and would not let them come back. Nick is shot, but not dead yet. He is awfully sick. I must go and wait on him.

It is now about two hours since the first shot. Nick is still alive . . .

They are still shooting and are all around the house. Boys, there is bullets coming in like hail. The fellows is in such shape I can't get at them. They are shooting from stable and river and back of the house.

Nick is dead. He died about 9 o'clock. I see smoke down at the stable. I think they have fired it. I don't think they intend to let me get away this time.

It is now about noon. There is someone at the stable yet;

they are throwing a rope out at the door and drawing it back. I guess it is to draw me out. I wish that duck would get out further so I could get a shot at him.

During the early afternoon Black Jack Flagg, homesteader, rode by on horseback, trailing his stepson who was driving a wagon. Flagg saw the men around the cabin and guessed what was occurring. When the Regulators fired on him, he yelled to his stepson to jump on one of the team horses and cut the rest loose. Flagg and his stepson then galloped away to Buffalo to raise the alarm.

Realizing that he was losing precious time, Wolcott decided to fire Champion's cabin. An old wagon was dragged up, piled high with brush and lit. Burning, it was pushed by four men to the side of the cabin.

Champion stayed inside as long as he could. With the flames roaring around him, he wrote a final entry in his diary:

> Well, they have just got through shelling the house like hell. I heard them splitting wood. I guess they are going to fire the house tonight. I think I will make a break for it when night comes, if alive. It's not night yet. The house is all fired. Goodbye, boys, if I never see you again.
>
> NATHAN D. CHAMPION

Putting the book in his vest pocket and holding his Winchester in his hand, Champion rushed out the back of the cabin. The final moments of Nathan Champion were described by Sam Clover, one of the war correspondents with the Regulators:

> The roof of the cabin was the first to catch on fire, spreading rapidly downward until the north wall was a sheet of

flames. Volumes of smoke poured in at the open window from the burning wagon, and in a short time through the plastered cracks of the log house puffs of smoke worked outwards. Still the doomed man remained doggedly concealed . . . "Reckon the cuss has shot himself", remarked one of the waiting marksmen. "No fellow could stay in that hole a minute and be alive."

These words were barely spoken when there was a shout, "There he goes!" and a man clad in his stocking feet, bearing a Winchester in his hands and a revolver in his belt, emerged from a volume of black smoke that issued from the rear door of the house and started off across the open space surrounding the cabin into a ravine, fifty yards south of the house. But the poor devil jumped square into the arms of two of the best shots in the outfit, who stood with levelled Winchesters around the bend waiting for his appearance.

Champion saw them too late, for he overshot his mark just as a bullet struck his rifle arm, causing the gun to fall from his nerveless grasp. Before he could draw his revolver a second shot struck him in the breast and a third and fourth found their way to his heart.

Nate Champion, the king of cattle thieves, and the bravest man in Johnson County, was dead.

The Regulators stood around their fallen foe, more in awe than in triumph. Wolcott, looking at the lifeless Nate Champion, was moved to exclaim, "By God, if I had fifty men like you, I could whip the whole state of Wyoming!"

Champion's pocket diary was found and read. The dead homesteader had recognized some of his besiegers, including Frank Canton, and these names were removed with a sharp knife. The diary was thrown back on the corpse, to be picked up by Sam Clover and later published on the front page of the *Chicago Herald*.

After pinning a card saying "CATTLE THIEVES BEWARE" to Champion's vest, the Regulators lined up behind Wolcott and moved out towards Buffalo, 50 miles to the north.

In Buffalo, at that same moment, a citizens' army was being raised to resist the Regulators. Wild rumours of invasion had been flying into the office of Sheriff "Red" Angus all day, which had finally been substantiated on the arrival of Black Jack Flagg and his stepson. A leading merchant of the town, the venerable white-haired Robert Foote, rode up and down the street on a stallion exhorting the men to arms. "If you have no arms," Foote shouted, "come to my store and get them free of charge." Meanwhile, Sheriff Angus dispatched two deputies, E. U. Snider and Arapaho Brown, to summon outlying homesteaders.

At dawn on 10 April, Sheriff Angus rode out of Buffalo at the head of a 300-strong posse, whose ranks of volunteer citizens even numbered armed clergy. As it marched south, the giant posse was soon noticed by an advance Regulator scout who galloped back to warn Wolcott, now only 14 miles from town. Wolcott ordered a rapid retreat to the TA Ranch on Crazy Woman Creek, where the Regulators hurriedly built a barricade and prepared for a siege.

The battle lasted two days. Towards the evening of the second day, the homesteaders built an ark of safety or "go-devil", a moveable breastwork of logs six feet high attached to the front of a wagon. The plan was to push the ark close enough to the TA ranch house for men sheltered behind it to throw dynamite bombs. On the morning of 13 April, as the ark was being pushed into effective range, a bugle suddenly sounded over the hill.

On the very brink of annihilation, the Regulators were saved by the timely appearance of Troops C, D and E of the Black Sixth Cavalry Regiment under Colonel J. J. Van

Horn. During the previous night, Wolcott had succeeded in sending a messenger through the homesteaders' lines and the Wyoming Stock Growers' Association had then called on the sympathetic Republican Acting Governor Amos W. Barber for help. Barber, in turn, had sent telegram after telegram to Washington D.C. urging President Harrison to send Federal troops to the relief of the Regulators at the TA Ranch.

Colonel Van Horn gave Wolcott and his men protective custody and escorted them to safety at Fort D.A. Russell. Sheriff Angus was left to fume, "I had them [the Regulators] in my grasp, and they were taken from me."

None of the Regulators was ever brought to court, and the killings of Nate Champion and Nick Ray went unpunished. Farcically, all expenses (amounting to some $18,000) for the imprisonment of the Regulators while they awaited trial was charged against Johnson County, leading to the county treasury running dry. The county could not afford to prosecute. Moreover, the two trappers who witnessed the murders were spirited out of the state by friends of the Regulators and bribed into silence. With no money and no witnesses, the prosecution had no option but to move for dismissal of the case. In January 1893 the Regulators went free, and the Johnson County War was over.

Almost. Traces of fallout from the invasion continued to descend for years. The cattle barons and their dominant Republican machine lost much of their influence, especially when a former ally, Asa Shinn Mercer, publisher of the *Northwestern Livestock Journal*, left their camp. In 1894 Mercer published a little book with a long title, *The Banditti of the Plains, or the Cattlemen's Invasion of Wyoming in 1892*, which did much to expose the machinations of the "Cheyenne ring".

And, while it was clear to all that the era of open range had come to an end, the stock growers did not simply drop their campaign against rustlers. They only changed tactics. Instead of promulgating openly violent vigilantism, they paid bounty hunter Tom Horn to murder cattle thieves with stealth. Not cut short until 1903, Horn's homicidal career marked a last throe of wildness on the Wyoming range.

The Johnson County War was the starkest encounter between big ranchers and small farmers in the history of the West. Many of its events passed into popular stories and songs, among them "The Ballad of Nate Champion". Inspired by Champion's diary, the ballad became a favourite of settlers and cowboys everywhere, and ensured his status as one of the frontier's greatest folk heroes.

It was a little blood-stained book which a bullet had torn
   in twain.
It told the fate of Nick and Nate, which is known to all of
   you;
He had the nerve to write it down while the bullets fell like
   rain.
At your request, I'll do my best to read those lines again.

"Two men stayed with us here last night, Bill Jones and
   another man,
Went to the river, took a pail, will come back if they can.
I told old Nick not to look out, there might be someone
   near,
He opened the door; shot to the floor, he'll never live, I
   fear.

Two hours since the shots began, the bullets, thick as hail!
Must wait on Nick, he's awful sick, he's still alive but pale.
At stable, river and back of me, men are sending lead.
I cannot get a shot to hit, it's nine and Nick is dead.

Down at the stable I see a smoke, I guess they'll burn the
    hay.
From what I've seen they do not mean for me to get away.
It's now about noon, I see a rope thrown in and out the
    door.
I wish that duck would show his pluck, he'd use a gun no
    more.

I don't know what has become of the boys that stayed with
    us last night.
Just two more boys with me and we would guard the
    cabin right.
I'm lonesome, boys, it's two o'clock, two men just come in
    view,
And riding fast, as they went past, were shot at by the
    crew.

I shot a man down in the barn, don't know if I hit or not.
Must look again, I see someone, it look like there's a blot.
I hope they did not get those men that across the bridge
    did run.
If I had a pair of glasses here, I think I'd know someone.

They're just through shelling the house, I hear the splitting
    wood;
And I guess they'll light the house tonight, and burn me
    out for good.
I'll have to leave when night comes on, they'll burn me if I
    stay;
I guess I'll make a running break and try to get away.

They've shot another volley in, but to burn me is their
    game,
And as I write, it's not yet night, and the house is all
    aflame.

So good-bye boys, if I get shot, I got to make a run,
So on this leaf I'll sign my name, Nathan D. Champion."

The light is out, the curtain drawn, the last sad act is
    played.
You know the fate that met poor Nate, and of the run he
    made.
And now across the Big Divide, and at the Home Ranch
    door
I know he'll meet and warmly greet the boys that went
    before.

Part III

The Lawless Land

"There is no Sunday west of Newton, and no God west of Pueblo."

Charles M. Hager, 1880

CANADA

WASHINGTON TERRITORY
Centralia
Coeur D'Alenes
MONTANA
Helena
Butte
Virginia City

MINNESOTA

OREGON

IDAHO TERRITORY

NORTH DAKOTA

Deadwood
SOUTH DAKOTA

IOWA

WYOMING
Johnson County

NEBRASKA

Virginia City
San Francisco
NEVADA
Aurora
Bodie
Mussel Slough
CALIFORNIA

UTAH

Pleasant Valley

ARIZONA

COLORADO
Leadville   Denver
Cripple Creek

Hays City   Ellsworth   Abilene
KANSAS
Dodge City   Newton   Wichita

Clay Cou

MISSOURI

Colfax County
NEW MEXICO

Oklahoma City

OKLAHOMA (Indian Territory)

Little Rock

ARKANSAS

Tombstone
Bisbee
El Paso

Lincoln
Lincoln County

TEXAS

Fort Griffin

Williamson County
Austin

LOUISIA

Rio Grande R.

MEXICO

Gulf of Mex

Hispanic out
activity in Te

4. The Lawless Land

Prologue

The Code of the West

There were many things which conspired to make the West wild, a violent arena where the law of the gun was paramount. As settlement moved west, frontiersmen used firearms for ousting the Indians, becoming brutalized in the process. Settlements were often ahead of regular courts of law, beyond the reach of peace officers, leaving pioneers to settle disputes themselves, sometimes bloodily. Then there was the Civil War, which lit hatred along the Kansas–Missouri border, and generated bands of outlaws, among them the James–Younger gang, the Logan brothers and the McCarty brothers, the latter giving Butch Cassidy of the Wild Bunch his apprenticeship in crime. Civil War frustrations also burned bright in Texas, leading afterwards to a spate of White–Black killings (a forgotten amount of Western violence was inter-ethnic). When Texan cowboys went up the great cattle trails, they often took the "lost cause" with them and baited cowtown lawmen, who were predominantly Northerners. Economics, too, played its part. Big ranchers in Wyoming hired gunmen to kill homesteaders in the Johnson County War. When the Southern Pacific Railroad wished to evict farmers from Mussel Slough Valley in California they purchased the services of a gunfighter called Walter J. Crow, a man with seven kills already notched on his tally stick; the ensuing, little-known "Mussel Slough Shootout' on 11 May 1880 saw Crow kill five men, a record for a single-incident gunfight unsurpassed in the west, save for that of a Captain Jonathan R. Davis who was attacked by eleven robbers on a mountain trail near Placerville, California, in 1854. Davis shot down seven of his assailants and, for good measure, knifed to death another three. The last bandit escaped, pitifully wounded.

Underpinning violence, and even making it socially acceptable, was a set of mental beliefs which comprised the Code of the West. By the Code a man was required to personally redress wrongs done to him, to stand his ground in any conflict situation (in the words of the folk song, "I ain't no hand for trouble / But I'll die before I run") and violently avenge any insult. A classic example of how allegiance to the Code – particularly the latter clause – could produce a gunfight was witnessed by cowboy Andy Adams, when his trail crew visited Dodge City:

Quince Forrest was spending his winnings as well as drinking freely, and at the end of a quadrille gave vent to his hilarity in an old-fashioned Comanche yell. The bouncer of the dance hall of course had his eye on our crowd, and at the end of a change, took Quince to task. He was a surly brute, and instead of couching his request in appropriate language, threatened to throw him out of the house. Forrest stood like one absent-minded and took the abuse, for physically he was no match for the bouncer, who was armed, moreover, and wore an officer's star. I was dancing in the same set with a redheaded, freckle-faced girl, who clutched my arm and wished to know if my friend was armed. I assured her that he was not, or we would have had notice of it before the bouncer's invective was ended. At the conclusion of the dance, Quince and The Rebel passed out, giving the rest of us the word to remain as though nothing was wrong. In the course of half an hour, Priest returned and asked us to take our leave one at a time without attracting any attention, and meet at the stable. I remained until the last, and noticed The Rebel and the bouncer taking a drink together at the bar, – the former apparently in a most amiable mood. We passed out together shortly afterward, and found the other boys mounted and awaiting our return, it being now about midnight. It took but a moment to secure our guns, and once in the saddle, we rode through the town in the direction of the herd. On the outskirts of the town, we halted. "I'm going back to that dance hall," said Forrest, "and have one round at least with that whore-herder. No man who walks this old earth can insult me, as he did, not if he has a hundred stars on him. If any of you don't want to go along, ride right on to camp, but I'd like to have you all go. And when I take his measure, it will be the signal to the rest of you to put out the lights. All that's going, come on."

There were no dissenters to the programme. I saw at a glance that my bunkie was heart and soul in the play, and took my cue and kept my mouth shut. We circled round the town to a vacant lot within a block of the rear of the dance hall. Honeyman was left to hold the horses; then, taking off our belts and hanging them on the pommels of our saddles, we secreted our six-shooters inside the waist-bands of our trousers. The hall was still crowded with the revelers when we entered, a few at a time, Forrest and Priest being the last to arrive. Forrest had changed hats with The Rebel, who always wore a black one, and as the bouncer circulated around, Quince stepped squarely in front of him. There was no waste of words, but a gun-barrel flashed in the lamplight, and the bouncer, struck with the six-shooter, fell like a beef. Before the bewildered spectators could raise a hand, five six-shooters were turned into the ceiling. The lights went out at the first fire, and amidst the rush of men and the screaming of women, we reached the outside, and within a minute were in our saddles. All would have gone well had we returned by the same route and avoided the town; but after crossing the railroad track, anger and pride having not been properly satisfied, we must ride through the town.

On entering the main street, leading north and opposite the bridge on the river, somebody of our party in the rear turned his gun loose into the air. The Rebel and I were riding in the lead, and at the clattering of hoofs and shooting behind us, our horses started on the run, the shooting by this time having become general. At the second street crossing, I noticed a rope of fire belching from a Winchester in the doorway of a store building. There was no doubt in my mind but we were the object of the manipulator of that carbine, and as we reached the next cross street, a man kneeling in the shadow of a building opened fire on us with a six-shooter. Priest reined in his horse, and not having wasted cartridges in the open-air shooting, returned the compliment until he emptied his gun. By this time every officer in the town was throwing lead after us, some of which cried a little too close for comfort. When there was no longer any shooting on our flanks, we turned into a cross street and soon left the lead behind us.

It is noteworthy how close Forrest was to his man when he opened fire. Only in cinema and novels – such as Owen Wister's incomparably influential masterpiece, *The Virginian* (1902) – did the Code of the West require a formal "walkdown" on a dusty street. In reality gunfights happened at near point-blank range, anywhere, and without any formal challenge to draw. A rare, true example of a walkdown – which Wister may have known about when writing *The Virginian* – occurred on 21 July 1865, when "Prince of Pistoleers" Wild Bill Hickok met Dave Tutt on the Market Square of Springfield, Missouri.

James Butler Hickok, born in Illinois in 1837, had participated in his first gunfight in 1861, notoriously shooting unarmed Nebraska rancher Dave McCanles, who had taunted him for being a "hermaphrodite". During the Civil War Hickok served in the Union army as a wagonmaster, spy, and General Philip H. Sheridan's scout. His striking looks caught the attention of many, including George Custer's wife, Libby: "Physically, he was a delight to look on. Tall, lithe, and free in every motion, he rode and walked as if every muscle was perfection, and the careless swing of his body as he moved seemed perfectly in keeping with the man, the country, the time in which he lived."

Like Hickok, Tutt had fought in the Civil War, although on the Confederate side. The two had argued over cards, and Tutt had taken Hickok's watch in lieu of a debt, antagonizing Hickok by declaring he would wear the watch publicly in the town square. This was an unacceptable slight to Hickok's pride, and confrontation followed.

In front of an eager crowd, the two men approached each other from opposite sides of the square. When they were 50 yards apart, Tutt drew, fired – and missed. Hickok, drawing at almost the same time, shot Tutt through the heart, swiftly turning around to where Tutt's friends stood, in case they had any idea of instant revenge. "Aren't you satisfied, gentlemen?", he is reputed to have said. "Put up your shootin'-irons, or there'll be more dead men here." The men obeyed and dispersed.

After this moment of glory, Hickok became marshal of Hays City, Kansas, and Abilene in its last season as a cattle town, then wandered the West as a gambler and drinker, and spent some time with Buffalo Bill's play "The Scouts

of the Plains". He was sacked for shooting too close to the
other actors, causing them to have powder burns. Although Hickok once declared "I would be willing to take
my oath on the Bible tomorrow that I have killed over a
hundred [men]," his substantiated slayings total seven,
possibly less. The accidental killing of his Abilene deputy,
Mike Williams, together with failing eyesight due to gon-
orrhoea, inclined Hickok against gunplay in his latter
years. He was shot in the back by drifter (and possible
hired assassin) Jack McCall in a Deadwood saloon on 2
August 1876.

In his gunfighting days, Hickok's weapon of choice
was the Navy Colt revolver, two of which he stuck in his
belt, butts forward. Firearms were unquestionably the
pre-eminent means of inflicting violent death on the frontier, for the Code decreed that fists and knives were unmanly. (Conversely criminals, being men and women
unworthy of honour, were invariably executed by the
dishonourable method of hanging.) The gun was also
more lethally efficient than other weapons. To bloody
extent, the development of frontier violence can be traced
in the history of American weapons technology.

Fire and Lead

The first truly American firearm was the Kentucky rifle of
the eighteenth-century pioneers, its long barrel and relatively small bore designed to meet specific wilderness
needs. An acute shortage of artisans forced America to
mechanize and by the end of the same century Eli Whitney,
inventor of the cotton gin, began to demonstrate the virtues of mass production when his company started to
manufacture muskets from standardized, interchangeable
parts.

In the 1840s the Whitney Armory at Whitneyville,

Connecticut, produced under licence Samuel Colt's perfected revolving handgun, which had been successfully
tested by Captain Samuel Walker and the Texas Rangers
against the Comanche in 1834. About 1,100 of the Colt
"Walker" were manufactured, and Colt used the profits
to set up a factory of his own at Hartford, Connecticut.
Men going West for the Gold Rush and settlement gave
Colt a ready market, and his revolver became the staple
handgun of the West, eclipsing the manufactures of
Remington, Smith & Wesson, Savage, and Merwin &
Hulbert amongst others. "God created man, but it was
Sam Colt's revolver that made him equal" was the prov-
erb of the frontier. There were numerous models, and
Wild Bill Hickok was far from alone in finding the 1851
Navy in .36 calibre to his taste. Other prominent Colts
were the Model 1860 Army and, most famous of all,
the 1873 Peacemaker (also known as the Single Action
Army and the Frontier). The Peacemaker was the
first Colt to make use of an 1860 invention of rival firm
Smith & Wesson, the "fixed" or metallic cartridge, which
contained cap, ball and powder in a brass or copper
case. Before this, Colts were fired by percussion caps,
with paper cartridges or the powder and ball loose. The
tendency of the old-style guns to jam, and their slowness
in loading, created the custom – as with Hickok – of
carrying two guns. The second was a reserve. Generally,
guns were worn hip-high, either on a belt, or tucked in
pants tops.

   Those for whom gunfighting was a career, either inside
or outside the law, tended to view accuracy and calmness
as greater virtues than speed in the wielding of guns.
William B. ("Bat") Masterson, the dapper lawman of Dodge
and Trinidad, Colorado, summed up the successful
gunfighter thus:

Any man who does not possess courage, proficiency in the use of firearms, and deliberation had better make up his mind at the beginning to settle his differences in some other manner than by appeal to the pistol. I have known men in the West whose courage could not be questioned and whose expertness with the pistol was simply marvellous, who fell easy victims before men who added deliberation to the other two qualities.

Masterson's judgement was based more on observation than on personal experience. Although he cultivated a reputation as a gunfighter, Masterson took part in but three gunfights during a long career on the frontier, and there is no evidence that he killed anyone in the line of duty, although he is alleged to have shot Sergeant King, a member of the Fourth Cavalry based in Mobeetie, Texas, in an argument over a woman, Molly Brennan.

The advice of a gunfighter who had killed his man, Wild Bill Hickok, was notably prosaic: "If you have to shoot a man, shoot him in the guts near the navel. You may not get a fatal shot, but he will get a shock that will paralyse his brain and arm so much that the fight is over."

As the name Colt became synonymous with handgun, so did Winchester with shoulder arm. The 1873 Winchester 15-shot repeating rifle is famed as "the gun that won the West." At least one eminent Westerner was moved to write to the firm in praise of the new rifle's many glories:

Fort McPherson, Neb.

I have been using and have thoroughly tested your latest improved rifle. Allow me to say that I have tried and used nearly every kind of gun made in the United States, and for general hunting, or Indian fighting, I pronounce your improved Winchester the boss.

An Indian will give more for one of your guns than any other gun he can get.

While in the Black Hills this last summer I crippled a bear, and Mr Bear made for me, and I am certain had I not been armed with one of your repeating rifles I would now be in the happy hunting grounds. The bear was not thirty feet from me when he charged, but before he could reach me I had eleven bullets in him, which was a little more lead than he could comfortably digest.

Believe me, that you have the most complete rifle now made.

W.F. Cody
"Buffalo Bill"

The Winchester '73 became so popular that in 1878 Colt rechambered the Peacemaker revolver to hold its .44-calibre shell. This meant that a man only had to carry one kind of ammunition for both guns. Cowboys also found that the Winchester's iron-shod butt was indispensable for crushing beans when they wanted to boil up a cup of coffee.

All these weapons and others played a part in making the West a dark and bloody ground. Between 1866 and 1900 around 20,000 people died on the frontier of what was euphemistically called "lead poisoning".

The "Taming" of the West

Yet, ultimately, the story of White Western settlement is not one of lawlessness and violence, but of the triumph of law and order: the "taming" of the West. Even the Code, while stimulating violence, paradoxically contained tenets which installed a semblance of social order: shooting women and unarmed men was contemptible (therefore many men went unarmed); a man's word was his bond, and a bargain sealed with a handshake was as good as a lawyer's agreement. One observer of the cattle trade remarked: "I've seen many a transaction in steers, involving more than $100,000, closed and carried out to the letter with no semblance of a written contract." Other rules decreed that horse-stealing was an unforgivable evil (for without a horse a man could not negotiate the dangerous expanses of the West), and that strangers were to be treated with hospitality.

Sometimes settlers coming into a wilderness region devised their own systems of law and order, like the Mayflower Compact and the Watauga Association of trans-Appalachian Presbyterians, but in general they imitated the forms of government of the place they had come from. In essence, therefore, westering settlers traced back their legal system to two ancient British institutions: the sheriff, who had powers to deputize citizens, form a posse and collect taxes; and the justice court, headed by a justice of the peace.

Most justices on the American frontier had no legal training and little knowledge of the law. They included such colourful figures as Judge Roy Bean, saloon-keeper and the self-styled "law west of the Pecos" for over 20 years. Bean's mildest eccentricity was an obsession with the English actress Lillie Langtry, after whom he named the village (Langtry) from where he dispensed his verdicts. These were sometimes bizarre. They famously included fining the corpse of a railroad worker $40 for carrying a concealed weapon. He also once dismissed the Irish murderer of a Chinaman because the *Revised Statutes of Texas*, 1879 edition – the only legal work he knew or cared for – said nothing about killing "heathen Chinee". Bearded, his stomach hanging over his belt, Bean liked to have a cold beer at the end of a court session. Fortunately, the courthouse was also Bean's saloon. Despite his eccentricity, Bean's law was also effective, and was tolerated by the Texas Rangers because it gave peace of a kind.

As a region became more organized, responsibility for law enforcement increasingly came to rest on federal and territorial/state officials. Federal judges tended to be more learned and less prone to local influence than justices of the peace. Most famed of the federal judges was Isaac C. Parker, who became known as the Hanging Judge because of the 168 men he sent to the gallows (of whom 89 were reprieved). Yet Parker was not a sadistic man. A devout Methodist, he was appointed by President Grant in 1875 to clean up the US Western District centred on Fort Smith, which also had jurisdiction over Indian Territory (now Oklahoma). Aside from some 50,000 official Indian inhabitants, the Territory was infested with White outlaws – who used it as a sanctuary – and frontier "riff-raff" who followed the few legal White enterprises allowed there. Parker worked six days a week to round up and try lawbreakers. In a period of 21 years he tried 28,000 suspects. When a man, according to the rule of law, had to be hanged, he wept openly. The Indians, in particular, found in him a friend. When he died in 1896, a Creek chief brought wild flowers to put on his grave.

Also at the business end of federal law enforcement was the United States marshal and deputy marshal. Unlike the sheriff, who was elected (usually for two years) and parochial in his interests, the US marshal was appointed by the president, worked under the jurisdiction of a federal court, and tended to be concerned with the violation of federal laws such as mail robbery.

The US marshal was also less prone to political corruption than the sheriff. For his election, the sheriff depended on those with the money and the organization – invariably the local business community – to mobilize votes. The paymasters, in turn, expected their sheriff, when elected, to protect and serve their interests. Thus it was that Sheriff Henry C. Wheeler, an ex-Arizona Ranger, led the deportation of striking miners from Bisbee, Arizona, in 1917, an act openly undertaken on behalf of local mine owners.

The offices of sheriffs and US marshals frequently conflicted, especially in the lucrative matter of the arrest of criminals with a price on their heads. To make matters worse, many settlements also had another tier of law enforcement, the town marshal. Sometimes the post was elected, often the incumbent was appointed by the mayor and the aldermen. Contrary to the popular image of the Western lawman as sporting a frock coat and stetson, these policemen were often dressed like their Eastern urban counterparts. "They wear," recorded *Social Statistics of the Cities* in its 1880 report on the marshals of Leadville, Colorado, "navy-blue uniforms with brass buttons, and each [man] produces his own." The report went on to note that the officers carried "clubs and navy revolvers". (To police Leadville's 14,820 citizens the mining town's officials founded a constabulary which consisted of a city marshal, a captain of police, two sergeants, and 18 patrolmen.)

Some territories and states also created special bodies to assist in law enforcement. Texas, famously, had its Rangers. In 1853 California raised a force of mounted police to deal with gangs of Mexican highwaymen, while Arizona and New Mexico also created ranger-type forces at various times.

Indian reservations too had their own police forces. John P. Clum, the Indian agent at the San Carlos Apache reservation in Arizona, and later the editor of the Tombstone *Epitaph*, set up an Indian constabulary in 1874 to keep order. The idea took root, and gradually other reservations adopted Indian police, whose job included not only enforcement of law within reservations but the capture of renegades and holdouts who had "jumped" their confines. Shortly after becoming Indian agent at Pine Ridge, Dakota, in 1878, Valentine McGillycuddy appointed noted warrior Man-Who-Carries-the-Sword as captain of the Indian police. He became Captain George Sword, and proved his worth when Spotted Wolf and 25 Cheyenne slipped away to join the still hostile Sitting Bull. Fearing that the Cheyenne might attack Whites – which would cause the army to be brought in for a crackdown on all Indians – McGillycuddy ordered Captain Sword to bring back Spotted Wolf. He and his men did so 11 days later. Spotted Wolf was dead, having resisted arrest.

In addition to legal police agencies, the West proliferated with extra-legal ones. Mine owners, bankers, bullion-shippers, railroad and stage companies founded their own guards and detectives, or hired the services of the Pinkerton Detective Agency. Cattlemen in Texas and Wyoming, meanwhile, employed inspectors to spot stolen cattle at railheads and stock detectives to catch rustlers. As in the Johnson County War, the actions of these private police forces fostered trouble as well as solving it.

And then there was the curse and blessing of vigilantism. The taking of the law into one's own hands through some form of extra-legal committee was part of the experience of the frontier from the time it pushed over the Appalachians. Some 300 vigilante movements have been recorded in the trans-Appalachian and trans-Mississippi Wests.

At core, vigilante committees came together to establish order where there was disorder, where law was weak or non-existent. They particularly come into view in the mineral rushes to Montana and California, with the San Francisco Committee of Vigilance of 1856 the largest vigilante movement in American history, numbering around 6,000 to 8,000 members. They hung their victims from a custom-built scaffold on Market Street. Vigilantes believed their rude justice an effective and quick means of dealing with outlaw activity. Thus vigilantes brought to an end the terror-reign of Montana's Henry Plummer, who ran a small army of highwaymen known locally as "road agents". Plummer – who succeeded in getting himself elected Sheriff of Bannack – was finally suspected in 1864 and duly given a "suspended sentence."

The year 1864 was a busy one for Montana vigilantes, for hanged two months after Plummer was the notorious Jack Slade, a sometime stagecoach superintendent who was deadly violent when drunk. When sober, he had been the epitome of pleasantness, as traveller Mark Twain had found to his surprise on encountering him at an Overland station:

> In due time we rattled up to a stage-station, and sat down to breakfast with a half-savage, half-civilized company of armed and bearded mountaineers, ranchmen and station employees. The most gentlemanly-appearing, quiet, and affable officer we had yet found along the road in the Overland Company's service was the person who sat at the head of the table, at my elbow. Never youth stared and shivered as I did when I heard them call him SLADE!
>
> Here was romance, and I sitting face to face with it – looking upon it – touching it – hobnobbing with it, as it were! Here, right by my side, was the actual ogre, who, in fights and brawls and various ways, *had taken the lives of twenty-six human beings*, or all men lied about him! I suppose I was the proudest stripling that ever traveled to see strange lands and wonderful people.
>
> He was so friendly and so gentle-spoken that I warmed to him in spite of his awful history. It was hardly possible to realize that this pleasant person was the pitiless scourge of the outlaws, the raw-head-and-bloody-bones the nurs-

ing mothers of the mountains terrified their children with. And to this day I can remember nothing remarkable about Slade except that his face was rather broad across the cheek-bones, and that the cheek-bones were low and the lips peculiarly thin and straight. But that was enough to leave something of an effect upon me, for since then I seldom see a face possessing those characteristics without fancying that the owner of it is a dangerous man.

The coffee ran out. At least it was reduced to one tin cupful, and Slade was about to take it when he saw that my cup was empty. He politely offered to fill it, but although I wanted it, I politely declined. I was afraid he had not killed anybody that morning and might be needing diversion. But still with firm politeness he insisted on filling my cup, and said I had traveled all night and better deserved it than he – and while he talked he placidly poured the fluid, to the last drop. I thanked him and drank it, but it gave me no comfort, for I could not feel sure that he would not be sorry, presently, that he had given it away, and proceed to kill me to distract his thoughts from the loss. But nothing of the kind occurred. We left him with only twenty-six dead people to account for, and I felt a tranquil satisfaction in the thought that in so judiciously taking care of No. 1 at that breakfast-table I had pleasantly escaped being No. 27. Slade came out to the coach and saw us off, first ordering certain rearrangements of the mail-bags for our comfort, and then we took leave of him, satisfied that we should hear of him again, some day, and wondering in what connection.

Sometimes, vigilantism took the form of rebellion against corruption or unpopular laws. An extensive citizens' movement, for example, arose in Shelby County, East Texas, in the early 1840s to target corrupt officials, horse thieves and counterfeiters. New Mexico's Gorras

Blancas ("White Caps") were poor Hispanics who resisted the expropriation of communal village land by
Anglos and rich Hispanics, burning their barns and cutting their fences. Fugitive slaves in Meigs County, Ohio,
in the 1820s were protected by organized groups of abolitionists.

As a primitive system of *ad hoc* justice, vigilantism was
surprisingly effective, especially in the mining camps. Yet
its drawbacks are manifest. Many vigilante committees
were mere "lynch mobs", fired up on liquor and prejudice. The journalist Edward Buffum witnessed a miners'
court in California where five men were tried and found
guilty (rightly) of robbery. However, three of the men
were also accused and convicted of a murder that had
occurred months before. The 200 "jurors" accordingly
sentenced them to death. But the trio had been unable to
put their case because none of them could speak English,
one being Chilean and the other two French. "Vainly they
called for an interpreter," recorded Buffum, "for their
cries were drowned by the yells of the now infuriated
mob . . . the wagon was drawn from under them, and they
were launched into eternity." Buffum himself was nearly
hanged for speaking up for the trio.

Men also, once given a taste of dispensing vigilantism,
showed a marked reluctance to give it up, even when
regular judicial processes were established. They vaunted
it for its quickness – even its cheapness. An 1879 vigilante
hanging was praised by a Denver newspaper as "a positive gain to the county, saving it at least five or six thousand dollars."

Equally damning was the tendency of vigilante movements to become tools of men of wealth – tools which they
wielded for their narrow self-interest. As if to set a future
pattern, this was the fate of the Regulators of South Carolina, the first American vigilante organization. Set up in

1767, the Regulators punished not only horse thieves and outlaws, but settlers that local men of standing deemed to have insufficient respect for property and authority. Anyone judged shiftless or immoral was also punished. The list of such pro-establishment, pro-banker, pro-rancher, pro-railroad owner organizations is long, and is headed by the 1877 San Francisco "Pick Handle Brigade" (which attacked blue-collar protesters), the Johnson County War, and the deportation of nearly 2,000 striking miners and sympathizers from Bisbee, Arizona, in 1917.

Sometimes the depredations of biased vigilante committees were opposed and countered. If there was no law to do it, it was done by the might of the gun.

And so did the whirligig of Western violence spin around and around, until the law was strong and uncorrupt enough to stop it.

The Outlaw Breed

The "Cast-Iron" Breed

Out in the West, the land dictated the nature of crime, as it did much else. It had wide open spaces into which a wanted man might disappear beyond the reach of the law, and a wide open atmosphere which encouraged the illicit and the daring. More than these, it had long trails through remote wilderness where travellers and freight could be robbed with near impunity. Several types of crime would be closely associated with the West, such as cattle rustling and bank robbery, but the real larceny of the West was highway robbery.

No sooner had the frontier began pushing inland from the British colonies, than settlers were obliged to enact a Body of Laws to deal with "road agents". A first offence was punished by the branding of a "B" on the culprit's forehead. The third offence was the last. Still, road agents proliferated. By the early nineteenth century, the Natchez Trace, linking Natchez and Nashville, became their favourite hunting ground, 500 miles of swamp and dim-lit path. Land pirates John A. Murrel, Sam Mason and Joseph T. Hare became infamous the nation over, their deeds glorified in the *Police Gazette*. Time did little to diminish the road agents' activity. In

1877 the state adjutant of Texas posted descriptions of 5,000 outlaws in the Rio Grande district alone. The bulk were men who had held up travellers and stagecoaches. California's Black Bart was one of the few highwaymen who was a solo operator; most worked in gangs. Usually stagecoach robberies happened at night, and the targets were unguarded coaches; highwaymen rarely had the desire to tangle with the shotgun messengers who rode on the bullion stages. Surprise was the highwayman's best weapon. Commented one robbed Californian stagecoach driver: "I have seen four aces beaten by a royal flush; but I was never really surprised [in my life] until I looked down the muzzle of a double-barrelled shotgun in the hands of a road agent. Why, my friend, the mouth of the Sutro tunnel is like a nailhole in the Palace Hotel compared to a shotgun."

Outlawry on the frontier, however, was more than a matter of geography. History provided a continual source of likely human material. A significant proportion of immigrants to the New World were criminals fleeing justice elsewhere. Wars with the Indians, wars with the British and the war between the states divided and brutalized men, orphaned children (who became destitute) and spewed out listless, homeless veterans. Even the terrible Harpe brothers, Micajah and Wiley, were a product of their times, and not just of Evil. Pro-British sympathizers from North Carolina, they were hounded from their homes after the British surrender at Yorktown in 1781 and wandered into a life of robbery. Eventually their crimes on Wilderness Road became so degraded that the outlaw community is reputed to have expelled them.

More curious, perhaps, than the existence of outlawry on the frontier is the sympathy that ordinary, law-abiding Westerners had for the desperado. Even such a zealous lawman as Evett Dumas Nix, US marshal of Oklahoma in

the 1890s, had a high regard for those he pursued. Writing
in his 1929 autobiography, *Oklahombres*, he remarked:

> As for the old time Oklahoma outlaw, I am reluctant to
> compare him with the highjacker and gunman of today.
> As one who fought him to extinction, I must admit that
> I admire his sportsmanship . . . when they fought they
> stood up to it and took defeat like the cast-iron breed
> they were.

Something of the allure of the outlaw was to be found in
his manly virtues. He was a strong man – "cast-iron" – who
stood outside society, took his fate by the scruff of its neck
and did what he had to do. But more than this, outlaws were
often seen as "Robin Hoods" because they robbed banks,
mines and the railroads – institutions that settlers hated
and saw as predatory towards themselves. Hence the ven-
eration extended to the James–Younger gang, Oklahoma's
Doolin gang, Wyoming's Wild Bunch and the Californians
Chris Evans and John Sontag, who stuck up a score of
Southern Pacific trains between 1889 and 1892 to popular
acclaim. Jesse James, in particular, played the anti-rich
theme, even claiming falsely that wealthy enemies had
hounded him into a life of crime.

Nor did a fall into outlawry seem inexplicable or contemptible to Westerners. Pioneers and settlers lived poor,
precarious lives with ruin an ever-present possibility. A bad
break, with the weather, with illness, the loss of a family
member (and indispensable labourer), and they might slip
into a penury where stealing was an attractive option. To a
boy stuck on the infinite boredom of a farm, the excitement
of the outlaw life was a magnet that some could not resist.
And farm boys, with their long hours spent taking pot shots
at targets, tended to make excellent gunslingers.

A handful of outlaws became more than Robin Hoods;

they became symbols of – even fighters for – underdog causes. Notorious club-footed gunfighter Clay Allison, almost certainly mentally deranged by a blow to his head while serving with the Tennessee Light Infantry, became a central figure in the resistance of the residents of Colfax County, New Mexico, to a real-estate grab by the powerful Maxwell Land Grant Company. Apparently charming when sober but deadly when drunk, Allison killed four men in his gunfighting career, as well as leading a lynch mob against a man called Kennedy who had committed infanticide. Allison cut off the dead man's head and rode to the saloon with it. For a man who lived by his gun, Allison suffered an ignominious death. In 1878, probably drunk, he toppled from a wagon while trying to retrieve a grain sack and one of the wheels went over his neck. Meanwhile, the mysterious Mexican–Californian bandit Joaquin Murieta, who robbed Anglo "forty-niners", was a hero to Hispanics ill-treated by Whites in the goldfields. (See also postscript on p 279.)

At least at the beginning of his career John Wesley Hardin was an outlaw with a cause, even if it was an ignoble one. Less well known than Jesse James, Billy the Kid, or Butch Cassidy and the Sundance Kid, the "Terror from Texas" was perhaps the greatest killer in the history of the West, challenged only in homicides by professional gunfighters Jim Miller and Walter Crow. Hardin's victims are estimated to number anywhere from 11 to 44. The son of a Methodist circuit preacher (hence his middle name), born in 1853, Hardin grew up in a locale and time amongst the most violent in the Wild West – central Texas during the post-Civil War period. According to his family, he was deeply traumatized by the massacre of his uncle's family by a Union mob. While the miscreants did not include any Blacks, Southern sympathies and racial prejudice caused the 15-year-old Hardin to kill his first man, Mage, an ex-slave. "To be tried at that time," wrote Hardin in his autobiography, *The Life of John Wesley Hardin* (1896), "for the killing of a negro meant certain death at the hands of a court backed by Northern bayonets . . . thus, unwillingly, I became a fugitive not from justice, be it known, but from the injustice and misrule of the people who had subjugated the South."

By his own account, Hardin then killed three soldiers (one a Negro) who pursued him. For these actions, Hardin was applauded ecstatically by the White racist, anti-Reconstruction bloc in Texas politics, who elevated him to the status of a hero. If not hired directly by the anti-Reconstructionists, Hardin certainly used his gun for their ends. More deaths of Blacks followed.

By 1871 the fugitive Hardin had taken to the life of a cowboy, driving the cattle of Columbus Carol up the trail to Abilene. There the youthful, lithe gunslinger encountered Wild Bill Hickok and reputedly faced him down. Others declare that Hardin shot a man in the American Hotel because his snoring disturbed him. Hickok moved to arrest the gunfighter, but Hardin escaped out of the window dressed only in his undershirt.

Returning to Texas, Hardin took a hand in the Sutton–Taylor feud which had long troubled DeWitt County. The origin of the feud is obscure, but latterly it had taken a political turn; the Sutton faction was generally pro-Reconstruction, the Taylors anti-Reconstruction. Naturally, Hardin sided with the latter and on 17 May 1873, in front of the blacksmith's shop in Albuquerque, Texas, slew a prominent Sutton supporter, Captain Jack Helm. Although the shooting took place in front of a crowd of Helm's friends, none felt brave enough to retaliate. Hardin wrote later: "The news soon spread that I had killed Jack Helms [*sic*] and I received many letters of thanks from the widows of the men whom he had cruelly put to death.

Many of the best citizens of Gonzales and DeWitt counties patted me on the back and told me that it was the best act of my life."

The most dramatic gunfighting exploit in Hardin's life came a year later, in May 1874, in the wild Texas town of Comanche. After a day at the races, Hardin and deputy sheriff Charles Webb walked along the street to a saloon, Webb falsely procaliming friendship. When Hardin's attention was momentarily distracted, Webb drew his gun and began pulling back the trigger. At speed almost beyond belief, Hardin jumped aside, drew, and put a bullet in Webb's head, the latter's shot only wounding the outlaw.

But the killing of Webb forced Hardin to flee Texas and take up a refugee life in Florida and Alabama. Captured by the Rangers at Pensacola Junction, Florida, Hardin was taken back to Texas and incarcerated at Huntsville. While in prison his adored wife died.

By the time of his release in 1892, Hardin was a changed, dispirited man. He had taught himself law in prison and opened a legal firm in El Paso, Texas, but clients (unsurprisingly) were few. Much of his time was spent in heavy drinking in local bars. It was in such an establishment, the Acme Saloon, that he was shot in the back of the head on the night of 19 August 1895. His assailant was John Selman, a local policeman and old-style Texas gunslinger, who probably shot Hardin for the fame of it.

Hardin was not the only outlaw-hero in the pantheon of Texan anti-Reconstructionists. There was also William P. Longley, who killed his first Black in 1866, when Longley was 15. Longley was not prosecuted, and after killing three more Blacks, he left his home at Evergreen and worked the West as a cowboy, gambler and teamster. He returned home in 1875 and murdered Wilson Anderson, who was suspected of killing his cousin. Although Longley fled to Louisiana, Texas lawmen crossed the border and brought him back to stand trial for the Anderson murder. He went to the gallows on 11 October 1878. Before putting his head in the noose, he looked at the 4,000-strong crowd and remarked, "I see a good many enemies and mighty few friends." He had to be hung twice, for the first time he dropped his feet touched the ground.

Black Outlaws

But Blacks were not only on the receiving end of outlaw guns, they gave death and crime as well as taking it. Born into slavery in Arkansas in 1849, Isom Dart began his life in crime pilfering for Confederate officers during the Civil War. After the war he joined a young Mexican stealing cattle south of the border to sell in Texas, then transferred his rustling activity to rugged Brown's Park, Colorado, a haven for cattle thieves. Periodically, Dart tried to "go straight" and earned a local reputation as bronc-buster, but always ended up back in the rustler's saddle. On one notable occasion he was arrested by a Wyoming deputy sheriff who was then injured when his buckboard left the road. The uninjured Dart gathered up the horses, lifted the buckboard onto its wheels, loaded on the deputy and drove to the hospital at Rock Springs. There, Dart turned himself in at the town jail. The impressed officials immediately let him go. Local cattle barons were less impressed. Dart was assassinated in 1900, probably by the cattlemen's hired killer, Tom Horn.

Cherokee Bill was a Black Billy the Kid, sharing with the latter a youthful impulsiveness, a love of guns, and a life cut short at the age of 21. Cherokee Bill was born Cranford Goldsby on the military reservation of Fort Concho, Texas, where his father was a buffalo soldier (as Black servicemen became known, on account of their wiry hair, which Indians said reminded them of the bison) in the famed 10th Cavalry.

When the family split up and his mother remarried, the teenage Cranford was pushed out on his own and fell in with bad company. At 18 he had his first gunfight, wounding a middle-aged Black man who had beaten him with his fists. Afterwards, he roamed the Cherokee, Seminole and Creek Nations and joined the outlaw gang of Jim and Bill Cook. Unlike White outlaws, the Black Cherokee Bill (who also had Indian blood, hence the nickname) could travel Oklahoma's Indian lands without interference, something which gave him a distinct advantage over the posses who pursued him for his persistent armed robberies of stores and railroads. Finally, at the age of 20 Cherokee Bill was caught and sentenced to die for murder (it was claimed that he had managed to kill 13 men in his two-year run, and Judge Parker called him an "inhuman monster"). On a fine day in 1896 Cherokee Bill was taken into the courtyard at Fort Smith to be hanged. Looking up at the sky he remarked, "This is about as good a day as any to die." At the instruction of the guard he stood over the trap. Asked if he had any last words, Cherokee came out with one of the West's best epitaphs: "I came here to die, not make a speech."

Unlike Dart and Cherokee Bill, Dodge City Black outlaw Ben Hodges died of old age, expiring in 1929. Photographs show Hodges toting a shotgun, but he tended to rely on his wits and tongue above firearms. Arriving in the Kansas cowtown with a trail crew he heard a story about an unclaimed Spanish land grant, and promptly pretended to be from an old aristocratic Spanish family, the tract's rightful owner. Residents of Dodge, and even total strangers, supported his claim. When this failed, he successfully swindled Dodge City National Bank and made the railroads believe he was a VIP, at which they gave him an annual free pass. Later charged with rustling a herd of cattle, he pleaded his own case. His two-hour summary was a masterpiece of theatre:

What me, the descendant of old grandees of Spain, the owner of a land grant embracing millions of acres, the owner of gold mines and villages and towns situated on that grant of which I am sole owner, to steal a miserable, miserly lot of old cows? Why, the idea is absurd. No gentlemen, I think too much of the race of men from which I sprang, to disgrace their memory.

On another occasion, Hodges – protesting profound Republican sympathies – asked the governor to appoint him to a job as a livestock inspector. As one rancher put it, this was "like a wolf asking to guard the sheep pen." Needless to say, Hodges's application was turned down. A few years later, vigilantes caught Hodges and charged him with rustling. Unable to find definite proof, they satisfied themselves with a precautionary severing of the tendons in both Hodges's ankles, thus crippling him.

Only rarely did American Indians turn outlaw. A number so classed – like the Apache Kid – were more accurately renegades, men too full of independent spirit to submit to the confines of reservation life. But a few were unmistakably criminal, and several became lovers of "bandit queen" Myra Belle Shirley. These were Blue Duck, Sam Starr – whose name Belle took – and Jim July. All were horse thieves and robbers.

Another Indian outlaw, Ned Christie, served with the Cherokee tribal legislature, before a seven-year spree as an outlaw in the Oklahoma Territory. In 1892 Judge Parker's deputies finally cornered him and two accomplices in a log fort in Tahlequah. To assail the fortress, marshals Heck Thomas and Paden Tolbert used an army cannon. Thirty rounds of artillery fire bounced off the log walls, as did 2,000 rounds from rifles. The exasperated lawmen were reduced to blowing off the side of the cabin with dynamite. Christie came out fighting and was shot dead. A victory photograph was taken of the dead Indian, propped up on a photographer's board, with his rifle cradled in his arms.

For 13 days in 1895, the Creek gang of Rufus Buck went wild in Indian Territory, setting a criminal record exceeding that of more famous, White outlaws. The five teenagers began by shooting a Black deputy marshal, John Barrett, near Okmulgee, then raped two women, held up a stockman, killing the Black boy accompanying him, stole horses and committed several more hold-ups.

Their reign of terror ended on 10 August, when they were surrounded by marshals and a posse of Creek Light Horse (Creek police) in a grove outside of Muskogee. At the end of their trial before Judge Parker, the gang's despondent state-appointed attorney entered the shortest defence on record: "May it please the court and gentlemen of the jury, you have heard the evidence. I have nothing to say." The five – Rufus Buck, Maomi July, Sam Sampson, Luckey Davis and Lewis Davis – were hanged together on 1 July 1896.

When the hangman had finished, guards cleaning Buck's cell found a picture of his mother with a poem written on the back:

> I dreamt I was in Heaven
> Among the Angels fair;
> I'd ne'er seen none so handsome
> That twine in golden hair.
> They looked so neat and sang so sweet
> And played the Golden Harp.
> I was about to pick an angel out
> And take her to my heart:
> But the moment I began to plea,
> I thought of you, my love.
> There was none I'd seen so beautiful
> On earth, or Heaven above.

Good by, my dear wife and Mother
Also my sister.

Yours truly
RUFUS BUCK

No explanation was ever advanced as to why Buck and his confederates went on their spree.

Buck was not the only poet outlaw. Stagecoach robber Charles E. Bole, alias "Black Bart", liked to leave poems at the scene of his crimes, one of which read:

I've labored long and hard for bread,
For honor and for riches
But on my corns too long you've tred,
You fine-haired sons of bitches.

Another:

Here I lay me down to sleep
To wait the coming morrow,
Perhaps success, perhaps defeat
And everlasting sorrow;
Yet come what will, I'll try it once,
My condition can't be worse,
And if there's money in that box,
'Tis munney in my purse.

Bole was captured in 1882 after he left a handkerchief at a scene of a crime, Wells Fargo agent James Bunyan Hume tracking its tell-tale laundry mark, "F.O.X. 7", back to Bole through 91 laundries. However, he served only a moderate term in penitentiary because he had used an empty shotgun on his hold-ups. Released in 1888, Bole disappeared from view for ever.

By the time of Bole's release Western-style outlawry was on the decline. The badmen were hung, shot, in prison, or had been deterred by the increasing effectiveness of law enforcement. There would be a later flowering of female outlawry, and the Wild Bunch were still to have their prime, as were Bill Doolin's "Oklahombres". The Doolin gang were dangerous men, for they were the offspring of a criminal dynasty on the middle-Border which had 30 years of gunfights and larceny behind it: the dynasty of Jesse Woodson James, the most celebrated bank and train robber in American history.

Postscript

Much the most potent Mexican–American resister to Anglo racism was Juan Cortina in Texas. A well-to-do rancher, Cortina witnessed an Anglo marshal pistol-whipping a Mexican in Brownsville on 13 July 1859. When the marshal refused to stop the abuse, Cortina shot the lawman in the shoulder, scooped up the Mexican on his horse and lit out for safety. Two months later Cortina returned to Brownsville with an armed force. He released Mexican prisoners from gaol and summarily executed four Whites who had killed Mexicans but escaped punishment. Cortina then announced the founding of the "Republic of the Rio Grande" and issued a "Proclamation to Texans" which began:

> "There is no need of fear. Orderly people and honest citizens are inviolable to us in their persons and interests. Our object, as you have seen, has been to chastise the villainy of our enemies, which heretofore has gone unpunished. These have connived with each other, and form, so to speak, a perfidious inquisitorial lodge to persecute and rob us, without any cause, and for no other crime on our part than that of being of Mexican origin . . ."

For six months "Cortina's War" spilled along the south Rio Grande Valley ending only when the minority Anglos called in the US Army. Juan Nepomuceno Cortina himself escaped across the border to Mexico, where he continued his new military career and became a general in the Mexican Army.

Jesse James and His Men

The man who held up a train, a gold-laden stagecoach, or a bank, was seen as a Robin Hood, even though he forgot to share the loot.

Robert Elman, Badmen of the West

We are rough men, and used to rough ways.

Bob Younger

On the winter's afternoon of Tuesday 13 February 1866, twelve horsemen rode into the small town of Liberty, Missouri, and robbed the Clay County Saving Association Bank of $70,000 in bonds, currency and gold. Few, save for the stunned cashiers, saw the deed, for most of the townspeople were in the warm of the courthouse enjoying a local case. One who did witness it was a local youth, George "Jolly" Wymore, who watched the thieves uncertainly from the other side of the street. As the robbers rode out of town, one of them stopped and shot Wymore four times.

The citizens of Liberty were less shocked by the brutal shooting – murder in the Border County was a commonplace – than they were by the armed raid on the bank. Only once before had such a thing happened in the whole of the United States; in 1864 Confederate officer Lieutenant Bennett H. Young had raided three banks in St Albans, Vermont. Young's robbery had been patriotic: the raid on Liberty had no such noble excuse. It was for private gain.

It was also the beginning of the criminal careers of two men who would become pre-eminent in the folklore of Western outlawry: Jesse Woodson James and his elder brother, Alexander Franklin ("Frank") James.

The Rise of the James–Younger Gang

Sons of a farmer and Baptist minister, the James brothers were born (Jesse in 1847, Frank in 1843) into a Missouri torn by violence and sectional strife between pro- and anti-slavery forces. When the Civil War came, the family aligned with the Confederate cause, not least because they were slave holders. In 1863 Frank joined the Confederate Raiders of William Clarke Quantrill, a notorious plunderer and murderer. A year later, the slim, boyish Jesse – "Dingus" to his friends – joined a guerrilla band led by one of Quantrill's lieutenants, "Bloody Bill" Anderson, whose habits included the tying of victims' scalps to his horse's bridle. At Anderson's side James received an introduction into wholesale atrocity. At Centralia, Missouri, he participated in the massacre of 24 unarmed Union soldiers. With the end of the war in sight, Jesse attempted to surrender at Lexington under a white flag. However, since he was a guerrilla, Union forces shot him on sight. Seriously wounded in the right lung, he came close to death. Those nursing him included his first cousin, Zerelda Mimms, later to be his wife.

In the years following the surrender of the South at Appomattox in April 1865, Missouri was awash with embitterment and listless veterans steeped in killing. Many settled down, but some did not. Among the latter were ex-

guerrilla leader Arch Clements, whose war crimes had
been so extensive that he was one of the few Confederates
not to receive a parole. Almost certainly it was Clements,
not the James brothers, who put together the gang who
robbed the bank at Liberty. Those recruited by Clements
included, in addition to Jesse and Frank James, a former
Missouri bushwhacker, Thomas Coleman "Cole" Younger.
Thus did Jesse James and Cole Younger meet. It was the
beginning of a fateful relationship.

Cole Younger was the son of a well-to-do family from
Lee's Summit, Missouri, and had distinguished himself in
both depredation and honour during the Civil War. While
he had participated in Quantrill's infamous raid on Lawrence, Kansas, he had also intervened to save the lives of
his former teacher, Stephen B. Elkins, and a captured
Union officer. In one of the war's more tranquil moments,
he had also met Myra Belle Shirley, later to become infamous bandit queen Belle Starr. The relationship would
continue for several years, and Shirley would bear his
daughter, Pearl.

Younger's taste of bank robbery at Liberty was obviously to his liking, for over the next few years he gradually introduced his three brothers, John, James and Robert
("Bob"), into the outlaw fraternity.

After Liberty, the Clements gang robbed a bank at
nearby Lexington, but had to settle for $2,000 because the
vault could not be opened. The gang's next ventures were
disastrous. Clements himself was shot in an ambuscade
on a follow-up visit to Lexington, a job at Savannah brought
no booty, and a hold-up at Richmond turned into a
bloodbath in which three citizens were killed. Enraged
townsfolk then lynched several actual or alleged members of the gang. A fifth raid, on Independence in northwest Missouri, by contrast, was a notable success.

Although Jesse James helped plan the gang's hold-up

of the Norton-Long bank in the quiet town of Russelville, Kentucky, on 20 March 1868, he was not among the seven who showed up. The raid turned into a minor gun battle when Cole Younger, after trying to cash a counterfeit note, put a gun to the head of the bank's elderly president, Nimrod Young. The old man made a run for the door and reached the street, a bullet creasing his scalp as he did so. The robbers departed the bank with $14,000 but had to fight their way out through aroused and armed citizens. One of the gang, "Big George" Shepherd, shouted to a bystander, "You needn't be particular about seeing my face so well you'd remember it again."

This bravado resulted in Shepherd receiving a three-year term in penitentiary, when the Russelville bank hired a private detective from Louisville, D. G. Bligh, who traced Shepherd back to his Missouri home.

On 7 December 1869, the James brothers raided the Davies County Bank at Gallatin, Missouri. This was the first robbery in which they were positively identified. When the local press branded them outlaws, a still free Jesse James wrote to the *Kansas City Times* complaining that not only was he guiltless in the Gallatin affair, but since the war he had "lived as a peaceable citizen, and obeyed the laws of the United States to the best of my knowledge." The editor was Southern in sympathy, and regularly proclaimed that the James boys were innocent Confederate war veterans unfairly persecuted by (Yankee) authorities.

After Gallatin, the James brothers, in close cooperation with the Youngers ("the James–Younger gang"), undertook bank jobs from Alabama to Iowa. They also extended their operations to include hold-ups of stores, stagecoaches and trains. Although train robbery had been pioneered in America – and possibly the world – by the Reno brothers, when they flagged down and boarded a train in Indiana

in 1866, the James–Younger gang made it their speciality.
Their attack on the Chicago, Rock Island and Pacific Railroad train at Adair, Iowa, was typical. In preference to
holding up the train, they posed as passengers and at a
chosen point in the journey, whipped out guns and
"busted" the train from within. The driver was shot, and
the legitimate passengers so cowed that they dared not
resist. On this occasion, the gang got a moderate haul of
$3,000 in cash, plus such valuables as they found on the
passengers.

If the James–Younger gang were ruthless, they were
also impudent and audacious, daring in a manner which
caught public imagination. The examples were legion.
After robbing the bank at Corydon, Iowa, the gang rode
up to the local church, where a political meeting was in
progress. Jesse interrupted proceedings, to announce:
"We've just been down to the bank and taken every dollar
in the till." Then he and his confederates, raised their hats,
let out a yell, and galloped away. He once gave a dollar to
the driver of a train he had robbed so that the driver could
drink to James's health. On another occasion, in 1872, the
Jameses visited the Kansas State Fair and left with the
contents of the box office. Around the same time, they
dropped by to see a journalist whose sympathetic accounts of their activities had delighted them. The James
boys gratefully presented him with a gold watch. Somewhat startled, he refused, thinking it might be stolen.
"Heck no," said a wounded Jesse James. "This 'un we
bought with our own money."

The year 1874 was the peak of activity for the James–
Younger gang, their crimes over the 12 months compris-
ing: three robberies of stagecoaches; two train robberies; a
raid on the bank at Corinth, Mississippi; hold-up of a store
at Bentonville, Arkansas; and the robbery of two omni-
buses at Lexington, Missouri. In a somewhat novel turn,

they also robbed a steamboat at Point Jefferson, Louisiana.

Such a catalogue of efficient crime had its price for the gang, as well as those robbed. Early in March 1874 John Younger was killed by Pinkerton detectives hired by the banks and railway companies to track the gang down. (A Pinkerton and a deputy sheriff died in the same gunfight.) Ten months later, on 5 January 1875, a Pinkerton undercover agent spotted the James brothers at the Clay County house of their mother, Zerelda Samuel, she having married Dr Reuben Samuel after the death of the boys' father in 1850. The agent, Jack Ladd, managed to get a message out, and by night-time the house was surrounded by a posse of Pinkerton men. They tossed into the house a metal object, which they later claimed was a flare to let them see their target. The James family always insisted that it was a grenade.

The device exploded, blowing Zerelda Samuel's arm off. Her nine-year-old son by her second marriage, Archie Samuel, was killed by a fragment of metal casing.

The tragedy only increased public sympathy for the James–Younger gang, whose popularity was already considerable in areas which had sided with the South and which viewed railroads and banks as oppressive monopolies. So great was public anger that the state legislature came very close to voting an amnesty for the entire James–Younger gang.

Jesse James himself, in fact, was fast turning into an American Robin Hood; as the "Ballad of Jesse James" would later have it:

Jesse James was a lad who killed many a man
He robbed the Glendale train.
He took from the rich and he gave to the poor,
He'd a hand and a heart and a brain.

Typical of the stories to circulate about Jesse James was
the one in which he helped a poor widow whose mort-
gage was about to be foreclosed. James lent her the money
to pay the banker – and then robbed the banker as he rode
away, so taking his money back. In truth, the recorded
noble generosity of Jesse James, American Robin Hood,
amounts to the dollar given the robbed train driver and a
share in a gold watch given to an admiring pressman.

A Career Ends, a Legend Begins

Despite the public backlash caused by their attack on the
James house, the Pinkertons embarked on a campaign of
overt harassment against the gang in their heartland of
Clay County. This availed the detectives little, but it did
indirectly lead to the downfall of the James–Younger robber band. With Missouri uncomfortably full of Pinkertons
and lawmen wanting the generous bounty on the gang –
$5,000 for any known member, $15,000 for Frank James
and $25,000 for Jesse James – the outlaws decided to
venture further afield. The place they chose was Northfield,
Minnesota, on 7 September 1876.

Northfield was a death trap. Eight of the gang rode in,
wearing linen duster coats to hide their weapons. While
the rest kept guard, Jesse James, Bob Younger and another
gang member, Samuel Wells ("Charlie Pitts"), rushed into
the First National Bank and delivered the standard order:
"Throw up your hands!" However, a teller, Joseph L.
Heywood, ignored the injunction and tried to slam the
door on Pitts as he entered the vault. James then demanded that Heywood unlock the safe. When Heywood
told him that it had a time lock and could not be opened,
Pitts pistol-whipped the teller and slashed him across the
throat. Meanwhile another teller, A. E. Bunker, had got to
the back door of the bank unobserved and broke into the

street. Spotting him, Pitts put a bullet through his shoulder, but the teller managed to scramble to safety. The three bandits then tried to rejoin their cohorts outside. As they left the bank, one of them turned and shot the unconscious Heywood dead.

Outside, Cole Younger, hearing a shot from inside the bank (Pitts's attempt to shoot the teller Bunker), had panicked and shot an innocent bystander. Within seconds angry townspeople had grabbed guns and opened fire on the outlaws. Clell Miller was peppered in the face with buckshot, then shot off his horse by a medical student with a carbine crouched at a second-floor window. Another of the gang's riders, William Stiles, was also killed. For 20 furious minutes, the gang had to fight their way out of town, with Frank James, Cole, Jim, and Bob Younger all sustaining wounds. When Bob Younger's horse was felled, Cole picked him up under fire and, with the rest of the gang, managed to gallop through the last ring of the townspeople's fire.

There was to be no rest. A posse of Minnesota farmers was soon pressing the shattered band. Jesse James urged Cole Younger to abandon the badly wounded Bob Younger because he was slowing the escape. When Cole refused, he and Jesse James argued violently and the James brothers abandoned the Youngers. Jesse and Frank eluded capture and made it back to Missouri.

They were the only ones who did. The three Youngers, together with Pitts, skirmished several times with the manhunters before being cornered in a thicket at Hanska Slough. A wild gunbattle ensued in which a posse member claimed the life of Charlie Pitts. In the end only Bob Younger could stand. He struggled to his feet, held up his hands and shouted out: "The boys are all shot to pieces. For God's sake don't kill me!"

Another shot rang out, nicking Bob Younger's cheek,

but then the firing stopped and the posse took the Youngers prisoner. They were, indeed, "shot to pieces". Bob Younger's elbow was shattered and he was holed in the chest; Jim had five wounds, including a bullet which had smashed his jaw and lodged just below his brain; Cole Younger had 11 wounds. Despite these, he managed to make a bow to lady bystanders when he was hauled into the Madelia jailhouse.

At their trial, the Youngers pleaded guilty to robbery and murder and were sentenced to life imprisonment in the Minnesota State Penitentiary.

For three years after Northfield, the James brothers and their wives lived quietly under assumed names in Texas, Tennessee (where Jesse James's two children were born) and Kansas City. But in 1879, the James gang went back into business, collecting $6,000 from the Chicago & Alton Railroad train at Glendale Station, Missouri. Two years later, the James gang murdered two men in the course of a train hold-up at Winston, Missouri. These were two deaths too many, and Governor Thomas T. Crittenden easily persuaded the railroads to underwrite a reward of $10,000 for Jesse and Frank James.

The reward proved too great a temptation for two members of the James gang, brothers Bob and Charlie Ford. "I saw the Governor [Crittenden]," recalled Charlie later, "and he said $10,000 had been offered for Jesse's death. I went right back and told Bob and he said if I was willing to go, all right."

In the morning of Monday 3 April 1882, the Ford brothers rode up to the white timber house on the hill in St Joseph, Missouri, where Jesse James was living under the assumed name of J. D. Howard. Shortly after eight o'clock, Bob Ford fired his famous shot, killing Jesse James as he stood on a chair to straighten a picture on the wall. According to what Bob Ford ("the dirty little coward who shot Mr Howard") told Crittenden, the bullet hit James just behind the ear and he "fell like a log, dead."

Jesse James's career as a robber outlaw was over. But the legend was only beginning. "GOOD BYE, JESSE!" heralded the front page of the Kansas City *Daily Journal*. The *St Joseph Gazette* cried "JESSE BY JEHOVAH". The killing even made the front of the New York newspapers.

Six months later Frank James, who had tired of the outlaw life, surrendered to Crittenden in person. He was tried on several charges, but public sympathy – and fear – was such that the law could not get a conviction. Frank James went free, to spend his days firing starting pistols at country fairs, charging visitors 50 cents to visit the "Home of the James" and to dabble in showbusiness, notably the running of a Wild West show. In this enterprise he was joined by Cole Younger, who had been granted a pardon for his crimes. Fittingly, perhaps, this was due to the unceasing work of Warren C. Bronnaugh – the Union officer whose life Cole Younger had saved during the Civil War. Also pardoned, for good measure, was Jim Younger, Bob Younger having died in prison of tuberculosis in 1889.

Cole, in addition to working with Frank James in showbusiness, took a job as a salesman of tombstones. Jim Younger committed suicide not long after his release, but Cole Younger lived until 1916, a year longer than his old cohort, Frank James.

Violence Begets Violence

But the story of the James–Younger gang does not end with their deaths. As Paul Wellman has pointed out in *A Dynasty of Western Outlaws*, the James–Younger gang founded an outlaw dynasty, one perpetuated "by a long and crooked train of unbroken personal connections, and a continuing criminal heritage and tradition handed down from generation to generation." The James–Younger tradition of armed gang robbery was carried on by Belle Starr – Cole Younger's common-law wife – in the 1880s, and then by the Dalton brothers in the 1890s. The Daltons were kindred of the Youngers. After an elder brother Frank was killed while serving as a peace officer in Indian Territory, Grattan, Robert and Emmett Dalton also became lawmen. But blood or boredom got the better of them and they turned to horse-stealing. Then they graduated to train robbery. And then, possibly hoping to outshine the James–Younger gang, the Daltons decided to rob two banks in their home town of Coffeyville, Kansas – simultaneously.

Wearing false whiskers, Grat, Bob and Emmett, plus two henchmen, Bill Powers and Dick Broadwell, rode into Coffeyville on the morning of 5 October 1892. Unbeknown to the gang, the street between the banks was under repair, so they were forced to leave their horses a block away. The tragi-comedy continued with Grat Dalton, Broadwell and Powers being recognized (despite the fake facial hair) by a local man, who ran into the plaza shouting "The Daltons! The Daltons!" When the gang emerged from the two banks, they did so into a blast of gunfire. After the smoke cleared, it was found that four citizens had died – as had all the gang except Emmett, who was taken prisoner. On the following day, a local paper reported drily: "One of our banking institutions was visited yesterday by the firm of Dalton Brothers for the purpose of closing large accounts. When the transaction was completed they had been paid in full with interest compounded."

Emmett Dalton was sentenced to a life term in the Kansas State Penitentiary at Lansing, and served 15 years before being pardoned. On release, Emmett headed for

Hollywood and made several pictures which, he declared, gave a realistic portrayal of the West. They numbered a 1912 feature entitled *The Last Stand of the Dalton Boys*.

One of the Dalton gang was lucky, or wise, enough to miss the Coffeyville disaster. This was Bill Doolin, whose horse allegedly pulled up lame on the approach to Coffeyville, thus enabling him to escape the outraged bullets of the citizens. After the débâcle, Doolin (born in 1858) organized his own gang in Oklahoma Territory, thus carrying on the James–Younger–Starr–Dalton tradition of spectacular gunfight-bracketed robberies. A jovial, former Arkansas farmhand who married a Methodist preacher's daughter, Doolin led his "Oklahombres" on four years of armed raids, which were successful enough to persuade the railways and banks to underwrite a reward of $5,000 for his capture "dead or alive". (The wanted poster described Doolin as a "NOTORIOUS ROBBER OF TRAINS AND BANKS, about 6 foot 2 inches tall, lt brown hair, dangerous, always heavily armed.") Occasionally, Doolin was accompanied on his forays by Bill Dalton, who had aided but not ridden with his luckless brothers.

Among those chasing Doolin were the celebrated Oklahoma lawmen Bill Tilghman, Heck Thomas and Chris Madsen. On an icy, windy day in January 1895 Tilghman accidentally wandered into the gang's hideout, a ranch on the Cimarron River. As Tilghman warmed himself by the fire, he heard a faint rustle behind the curtains and saw the tips of several Winchesters pointing out. Tilghman made his excuses to the rancher and left. One of Doolin's gang, George "Red Buck" Weightman, started after him declaring that he was going to kill that "damn lousy marshal".

The fabled version of this incident has Doolin telling Red Buck: "Bill Tilghman is too good a man to shoot in the back." A more probable explanation, as suggested by Oklahoma Territory Marshal E. D. Nix in his memoir

Oklahombres, is that Buck was told that if he shot Tilghman a hundred men would be upon them by morning.

Whatever the truth, this brush with Tilghman was the beginning of the end for the Doolin gang. They would not be so lucky in their other meetings with Oklahoma lawmen in the remainder of 1895. Little Bill Raidler survived a gunfight with Bill Tilghman, only to be sentenced to the Ohio Penitentiary for ten years (where Raidler became a friend of fellow inmate, author O. Henry). Bill Dalton and Red Weightman both died resisting arrest. In December 1895 "Old Bill" Tilghman finally caught up with Doolin himself, arresting him in a bathhouse in Eureka Springs, Arkansas, where Doolin was receiving treatment for his rheumatism. Taken to Guthrie, Oklahoma, Doolin stepped off the train to a hero's welcome from a crowd of five thousand which had gathered to see him.

Doolin pleaded not guilty and was held over for trial at the Guthrie federal jail. He escaped in July 1896, freeing 37 others as he did so. Within a month, however, Doolin was cornered by a posse at a farmhouse near Lawson. This time he resisted arrest, and was killed by a blast from the shotgun of Heck Thomas. The "King of the Oklahoma Outlaws" fell near a wagon on which he had packed the possessions of his wife and baby son. Almost certainly, Doolin had been intending to leave the territory and quit outlawry.

Thus passed into history one of the last great Western outlaws. But not yet the dynasty of which he came. Little Dick West, a surviving member of the Doolin gang, would join Al Jennings for his 109 days in 1896 as an Oklahoma road agent. Al Jennings and his brother Frank – both attorneys – were unlikely and inept bandits, and their record in crime consisted of two abandoned attempts to hold up trains and one actual hold-up in which the five-strong gang got 60 dollars apiece. Four of the gang, including Al and Frank Jennings, were arrested single-handedly by deputy marshal Bud Ledbetter. Little Dick West had already quit the comedic Jennings gang. He would be shot down in the winter of 1897 in a gunfight with Bill Tilghman in Kingfisher County, Oklahoma.

A more serious perpetrator of the James–Younger bandit tradition was Belle Starr's nephew, Henry Starr ("The Bearcat"), who gained his schooling in guns in the Starr family's feud with neighbouring Cherokee clan, the Wests. According to Evett Nix, who knew him, Henry Starr was a "man of magnetic personality". He was also an inveterate criminal, serving his first jail term for the murder of deputy Floyd Wilson. After disarming fellow inmate Cherokee Bill, however, Starr was released. He stuck up banks in Oklahoma, Arkansas and Colorado, punctuating these with terms in prison. On 27 March 1915, he rode with his gang into the small town of Stroud and, like the Daltons before him, attempted to rob two banks on the same visit. He was wounded making his getaway and arrested. Released from prison a year later, he was killed by a shotgun blast in the face, courtesy of cashier William J. Myers, while trying to hold up the People's National Bank at Harrison, Arkansas.

When Starr began bank robbing he did so on a horse; for his last hold-up he went by car. Thus in Henry Starr was personalized the link between nineteenth-century brigandry and "1920s Mid-West gangsterism." Among his associates was Al Spencer, whose own lieutenant was Frank "Jelly" Nash. In 1933 Nash was captured by the FBI and accidentally killed during an ensuing attempt to free him by the pomaded gangster Charles Arthur ("Pretty Boy") Floyd at Kansas City railroad station. Only with the extermination of the Mid-West Dillinger-type gangs by the FBI in the 1930s did the outlaw dynasty founded by the James–Younger gang finally die.

Frontier Lawmen

Lawmen, Badmen

The frontier lawman spent as much time sitting in his office chair as he did in the saddle leading posses. Peacekeeping in the West was a job of many paper chores and administrative duties. There were records to be kept, court notices to be posted, reports to be written, wanted notices to be read, written and filed. When the lawman left his office, there were dogs to be shot (for a fee), fines to be collected, streets to be repaired, and stray steers to be moved.

Pay was low, although supplementary fees for duties performed could be high. Even in sparsely populated Cochise County, Arizona, Sheriff John Behan garnered an estimated $40,000 a year undertaking such common lawkeeping tasks as serving summonses, attending court, and advertising property for sale. But if the job of lawman was mundane, it also carried the sudden, chill risk of danger. Many towns had an ordinance against the carrying of firearms within town limits. Along with arrest of fugitives, enforcement of the firearms ordinance probably constituted the most dangerous part of a sheriff's job. Many Westerners regarded the taking of their "shooting irons" as an infringement on their manhood and their rights as freeborn Americans. Marshal Joe Carson lost his life in just this way in January 1880, trying to disarm the Henry gang in the Close and Patterson Saloon in Las Vegas, New Mexico. Accompanying Carson was his deputy Dave Mather, who avenged his boss by killing one gang member and wounding another.

If disarming frontiersmen was dangerous in Las Vegas, it was doubly so in a Kansas cowtown, where Texas cowboys whooping it up were drunk and unpredictable, as well as proud, and not inclined to take orders from Northern peace officers. A famous such incident involved Dodge City marshal Edward J. Masterson, older brother of the more famous Bat Masterson. At 10 p.m. on the evening of 9 April 1878 Ed Masterson and his deputy, Nat Haywood, quietly disarmed drunken cowboy Jack Wagner at the Lady Gay Saloon. Masterson gave the pistol to Wagner's trail boss, A. M. Walker. As Masterson and Haywood went outside, Walker returned the pistol to Wagner and both dashed outside after the lawmen. Masterson began grappling with Wagner for the gun, and when Haywood stepped forward to help, Walker prevented him doing so at gunpoint. Suddenly, Wagner's gun went off, the bullet entering Masterson's stomach. Mortally wounded and his clothes on fire from the gun flash, Masterson managed to shoot Wagner in the bowels and Walker in the arm and lungs. Wagner died the next day. Walker, however, eventually recovered.

Ed Masterson was a genuinely popular lawman, and something of a standard above previous policemen in the city, two of whom – William "Buffalo Bill" Brooks and Jack Allen – had backed down in fights. "A PUBLIC CALAMITY" said the Ford County *Globe* of Masterson's death, eulogizing: "Everyone in the city knew Ed Masterson and liked him. They liked him as a boy, they

liked him as a man, and they liked him as their marshal.
The marshal died nobly in the discharge of duty; we shed
a tear upon his grave . . ."

Few other lawmen would receive such a fulsome
tribute.

Harried town officials frequently appointed hardcase
gunfighters to keep order, men who were little or no
better than the rowdies they were intended to control.
Thus did Ellsworth add the drunken loudmouth
gunfighter known as John "Happy Jack" Morco to its
police force. Morco, who had fled California after killing
four unarmed men, antagonized Ellsworth's cowboys and
citizens alike, the latter numbering English-born gamblers Ben and Billy Thompson. After he had sparked a
fracas in which Billy Thompson shot Sheriff Chauncey
Whitney, Ellsworth finally dismissed Morco. He refused
to be disarmed and had to be shot dead by a police
colleague, J. C. Brown.

Morco was a far from isolated example. The number of
men who spent as much time on the run from the law as
they did wearing a badge is legion. "Mysterious" Dave
Mather, reputed to be a descendant of puritan theologian
Cotton Mather, had a career as a horse thief, train robber,
con man (selling "gold bricks" to gullible cowboys, an
enterprise in which he was partnered by Wyatt Earp), jail-
breaker and road agent, as well as serving as a policeman
in Las Vegas, New Kiowa in Kansas, and Dodge City. In
Dodge he quarrelled with Deputy Marshal Tom Nixon –
and shot him. (In 1888 Mather disappeared "mysteriously" and forever. Other lawmen who were prominent
badmen were Jim Miller (paid assassin), Buffalo Bill Brooks
(lynched as a horse thief), Lon Chambers (train robber),
Jim Clark (thief), John Webb (extortionist, murderer and
close friend of outlaw Dave Rudabaugh), Willard
Christianson (rustler and bank robber), and Texas's John

King Fisher (rustler), the last-named the West's gaudiest gunman. He was once spotted by the Texas Rangers decked out in a pair of chaps made from the skin of a tiger he had shot at a circus, a beaver hat, a silk shirt and a brace of ivory-handled guns. Also from Texas was "Longhaired Jim" Courtright who began a protection racket in Fort Worth, where he used to be sheriff, in which gambling joints were "policed" in return for a share of the takings. The diminutive, fastidiously dressed gambler Luke Short, who owned a third of the White Elephant Saloon, refused to pay. Courtright sent a warning; the two men met in February 1887, and Courtright pulled a gun. The hammer caught in Short's watch chain, giving Short time to pull his weapon and shoot Courtright three times. Courtright died within minutes.

On at least one occasion a lawman committed a major crime while actually in office. This was Henry Newton Brown of Caldwell, Kansas, who held up the bank in the neighbouring town of Medicine Lodge in May 1884, murdering the bank's president. Brown and his accomplices were chased by citizens, Brown being shot in the process. His cohorts were lynched. Before hiring on as Caldwell's town marshal, Brown had been a cattle rustler and had served as a "Regulator" alongside Billy the Kid during the Lincoln County War.

Such men as Brown, Courtright and Morco were tolerated in office if they did not abuse its privileges too outrageously, and above all kept order. So successful had Brown been at installing peace in Caldwell that only six months before his robbery of the Medicine Lodge bank, burghers had presented him with a new Winchester rifle and a silver plate commending his "valuable services to the citizens of Caldwell." In a similar vein, when outlaw and gunfighter John Daly gained control of the Nevada mining town of Aurora in the early 1860s (through the neat expedient of having an acolyte elected town marshal), the local newspaper, the *Esmeralda Star*, noted that the people bore this with "utter indifference": not least, because the first man John Daly – now appointed deputy marshal – shot was an unruly member of his own gang, one George Lloyd.

To "tame" towns, different lawmen had different methods. Brown used both a pistol and a rifle to kill rowdies in Caldwell. Abilene's Tom Smith employed his fists, spectacularly flooring town bully Big Hank and gunman "Wyoming Frank" on consecutive days in 1870. Shotguns loaded with buckshot were favoured by lawmen the West over, among them John "Don Juan" Slaughter of Apache County, Texas, and Oklahoma's Heck Thomas. However, to the consternation of lawmen those they "took alive" often escaped justice. Jails were rudimentary – where they existed at all – and inmates absconded with alacrity.

To be counted amongst the most unusual lawmen of the West was New Mexico's Elfego Baca. At the age of 19 Baca bought a mail-order badge, which he promptly used in October 1884 to "arrest" a cowboy called McCarty who was making Hispanics in the town of Frisco "dance" by shooting at their feet. After seizing the cowboy, Baca handed him over to the local justice of the peace. On the following day, however, 80 cowboys led by McCarty's rancher employer intercepted Baca; one of the cowboys shot at him. Baca ran into a jacal, a wood-and-mud hut, shoved the inhabitants out, and managed to close the door in the face of rifle-wielding cowboy Jim Herne. Baca then shot the cowboy through the door.

Herne's body was dragged away, and the cowboys began to shoot the jacal to pieces, keeping up volley after volley until dusk. The jacal, however, had a floor some 12 inches below ground level, and Baca was able to duck the bullets. From time to time, he fired back with an accuracy that killed three more cowboys and wounded others. At midnight, the exasperated cowhands demolished most of the building with a stick of dynamite; Baca survived, crouched in an opposite corner behind a portion of roof which had been caved in by rifle fire.

To the disbelief of the cowboys, Baca was still alive next morning. They saw smoke from the chimney of the jacal. Baca was cooking breakfast.

The shooting continued until late afternoon, when deputy sheriff Ross intervened. Baca surrendered at 6.00 p.m., having withstood the siege by 80 gunmen for 36 hours. A later examination of the jacal revealed that the door alone had 367 bullet holes in it.

After the "miracle of the jacal", Baca utilized his fame to secure various public posts, among them sheriff of Socorro County. One of his stratagems as a properly legal sheriff was to send letters to all the local fugitives telling them to surrender or suffer his wrath. A number of men actually complied. Baca died at the age of 80 having become one of New Mexico's leading lawyers.

Fighting Outlawry in Oklahoma Territory

Perhaps the most outstanding peace officers in the West were some of those who worked under Evett Nix, the US Marshal of Oklahoma Territory. A former grocer, Nix was appointed (to some amazement) Marshal of the Territory by President Grover Cleveland in July 1893. What the ex-grocer brought to the task was organizational skill, and under his direction 150 deputy marshals were put into the field with an iron determination to end outlawry in the Territory. Nix set high standards, telling the *Guthrie Daily News* that he would have "none but honest men around me". He added: "The time has gone for swashbucklers

who fence themselves round with revolvers and cartridges.
A revolver will be for business and not for show."

Nix's sceptics accused him of "searching the ranks of
democracy with a microscope to find this brand of Sunday school moralists from which to make sleuthhound
saviours of banks and express trains." The novice 32-year-
old marshal quickly proved them wrong. His deputies
included three of the greatest lawmen in the West, William
Mathew ("Bill") Tilghman, Chris Madsen and Henry
Andrew "Heck" Thomas. The trio worked in semi-inde-
pendence from their colleagues, hunting down major outlaws like the Doolin gang, and were quickly christened
the "Three Guardsmen".

Chris Madsen was an adventuring, red-haired Dane
who, before pinning on the badge of a deputy, had fought
in Italy for Garibaldi, in Africa for the French Foreign
Legion and in the West for the US Cavalry. A spell as
homesteader farmer had proved too tame and he accepted a commission for deputy US marshal, operating
from El Reno, Oklahoma. The next year he was transferred to Guthrie and was highly active in pursuing fugitives until the outbreak of the Spanish–American War,
when he joined the Rough Riders, a mounted regiment
organized by Theodore Roosevelt. After returning from
Cuba, Madsen re-entered law enforcement and in 1911
was appointed US Marshal for Oklahoma. Among those
brought to justice by Madsen were Dalton/Doolin gang
member Red Buck Weightman and train robber Felix
Young.

In a famous episode in Beaver City, Oklahoma, in 1893
Madsen entered a saloon to stop drunken revellers shooting the place up, disarming one man by seizing his pistol.
At this, another belligerent shouted: "I'm a son of a bitch
from Cripple Creek."

"I knew who you were," replied Madsen, "but I didn't

know where you were from." A third reveller tried to pull a gun, but Madsen was quicker, and winged him in the shoulder.

Like Madsen, Heck Thomas saw service as soldier, joining the Stonewall Jackson Brigade of the Confederate Army when he was 12. He went to Texas after the Civil War, joining the Rangers, and earning a commendation from the governor for the single-handed capture of the two Lee brother outlaws. Before serving under Nix, Thomas had worked as a deputy for Judge Parker in Indian Territory. It was Heck Thomas's shotgun that finally ended the career of outlaw Bill Doolin.

Bill Tilghman, the third of the Three Guardsmen, was already a renowned lawman before he came to Oklahoma, having served as the marshal of Dodge in 1884–6. When Oklahoma was opened up for White settlement in 1889 Tilghman took part in the land rush, but soon reverted to marshalling in the new Territory. Evett Nix offered this portrait of "Old Bill" Tilghman:

> Tilghman was one of the handsomest men I ever knew – six feet tall, he weighed about one hundred and eighty pounds, and every ounce of it was sinuous muscle. His kind blue eyes and his open countenance reflected good will and friendliness to all he met. I have never known a man who regarded his enemies more kindly than did Bill Tilghman – and I have never known a man who fought his enemies more bitterly or more effectively than did Bill Tilghman when circumstances demanded it. Looking into his soft blue eyes, it was very hard to believe that the same eyes had looked down the barrels of flaming six-guns and rifles and dealt death to a great many men. During his service as my deputy, more rewards were paid to him for captures than were ever paid to any officer in the same period of time in the history of the United States.

Bill Tilghman was to serve longer than any of the lawmen made famous by the clean-up of Oklahoma Territory, and was voted a state senator. In 1915, incensed at the portrayal of federal officers in a movie depicting the bandit career of Al Jennings (whom Tilghman had pursued), the retired lawman directed a filmic riposte, *The Passing of the Oklahoma Outlaws*. Secretary of the company which produced it was Chris Madsen, and the movie's underwriter was Evett Nix. The men saw themselves as setting the record straight.

Bill Tilghman died with his boots on. Aged 70, against the advice of friends, he became marshal of rowdy oil town Cromwell, Oklahoma. On the night of 21 November 1924, Tilghman heard a shot in the street and went to investigate. He found the offender and took his gun away. But the offender had a second gun, which he drew and shot the great lawman down.

The offender was a drunken federal prohibition agent.

The Legend and Life
of Wyatt Earp

Bill Tilghman was not the only ageing lawman to develop an interest in motion pictures. Wyatt Earp spent many of his twilight years in Hollywood, and even appeared as an extra in the 1916 Douglas Fairbanks feature *The Half Breed*. His admirers counted among them Western film stars Tom Mix and William S. Hart, both of whom were pall-bearers at Earp's 1920 funeral. Another of Earp's Hollywood admirers was the young John Ford, later to direct the Earp biopic *My Darling Clementine*. Thus Earp took a strong hand in the creation of his own legend, simultaneously enlarging and sanitizing a career in "town taming" which, in truth, had little to justify his posthumous reputation as one of the West's great heroes.

Wyatt Berry Stapp Earp came of pioneer stock, and was descended from a Virginian agrarian-lawyer clan who migrated westward in chain-like fashion, first to Monmouth, Illinois (where Earp was born on 19 March 1848), and then to Missouri, Kansas and by wagon train to South California.

Earp's early career was as a teamster in California, Arizona and Wyoming, where he also refereed prizefights in the railroad camps. On 10 January 1870 he married

Irilla H. Sutherland, the daughter of a neighbour of Earp's
Illinois grandparents. The marriage lasted less than a
year, when Irilla died in a typhoid epidemic. For some
time afterwards, Earp drifted aimlessly. Near the town of
Van Buren, Arkansas, he was caught horse-thieving, and
was only saved from hanging by the intervention of his
father. Nicholas Earp paid his son's bail – and then suggested he abscond.

Wyatt Earp then took up buffalo hunting in Kansas,
and during a visit to Ellsworth in 1873 was offered a job as
marshal. He refused. But in 1874 he arrived in Wichita,
then the boom town of the cattle trade, where his invalid
Civil War-veteran brother James was a bartender and
James's wife Bessie ran a brothel. With the buffalo fast
disappearing, Earp decided to hire on as a policeman,
serving under Sheriff Mike Meagher. Most of Deputy
Earp's duty consisted of patrolling Wichita's red light
district, Delano, and ensuring that the cowboys who
thronged the town observed the Deadline, the boundary
which they were not allowed to cross wearing firearms.
Among the transgressors Earp was obliged to arrest was
the giant, 220-pound Texas cattleman Abel "Shanghai"
Pierce. On this occasion, Pierce was too drunk to be dangerous. Earp himself was eventually kicked off the force
for fighting and for neglecting to turn in fines collected
from prostitutes.

In 1876 Earp moved to Dodge, then at the height of its
infamous reputation as the "Gomorrah of the Plains". Earp
served two periods on the town's police force, 1876–7 and
1878–9, rising to become assistant marshal. It was during
his sojourns in Dodge that Earp made friends with lawmen
Luke Short and Bat Masterson and joined the "Dodge City
Gang", a cartel which controlled the local liquor, gambling
and prostitution business. Another member of the Gang
was John Henry "Doc" Holliday, a tubercular sometime

dentist turned gambler. The son of a Confederate officer, the sad-faced alcoholic was mercurial in temper but an unrelenting racist. His first victims were two Negro boys who dared share a swimming-hole near his Georgia home. In Dodge he lived with – and was possibly married to – the prostitute Kate Elder, better known as "Big Nose Kate". According to some accounts, Holliday saved Earp's life in Dodge by disarming a rowdy cowboy.

Earp's law-enforcement achievements in Dodge were unremarkable, although on 26 July 1878 he indirectly killed his first man, a "hurrahing" Texas cowboy by the name of George R. Hoyt. Earp, aided by Jim Masterson, shot at Hoyt as the latter rode out of town. Hoyt fell off his horse, injured his arm and died of an infection a month later.

Hoyt was not just the first man Earp killed in Dodge; he was the last. A fracas with a saloon girl, however, did make the local *Times*:

> Miss Frankie Bell who wears the belt for superiority in point of muscular ability, heaped epithets upon the unoffending head of Mr. Wyatt Earp to such an extent as to provoke a slap from the ex-officer, besides creating a disturbance of the quiet and dignity of the city, for which she received a night's lodging in the dog house and reception at the police court next morning, the expense of which was about $20. Wyatt Earp was assessed the lowest limit of the law, $1.

Earp was less lucky in another fight in Dodge City. A cowboy called Red Sweeney beat him to a pulp in an altercation over a dance-hall girl.

While in Dodge Earp also acted as deacon of the Union Church.

In December 1879 Earp went to the silver camp of

Tombstone, Arizona, at the invitation of his brother Virgil, who was deputy US marshal. The town's funereal name came from prospector Ed Schieffelin, who had once been told that his grave was the only thing he would find in the sun-blasted Dragoon Hills; when, in 1877, he found instead thick veins of silver he decided to name his claim ironically: Tombstone. At the time Earp arrived, Tombstone was one of the most turbulent places in the Southwest, overflowing with miners attracted by the prospect of making $4 a day for a 10-hour shift.

Accompanying Earp to Tombstone was Celia Ann (Mattie) Blaylock, a laudanum addict who lived with him as his wife. Wyatt soon became deputy sheriff of Pima County, and his brothers Jim, Morgan and Warren also settled in the town.

The Earps and their wives formed a notably close-knit entity, all buying frame houses within a block of each other. They were Republican and civic-minded; they ran for public office and founded church congregations; they leaned heavily on each other for their economic advancement. The Earps also formed close associations with the town's business and upper-class community, including the publisher of the *Tombstone Epitaph*, mayor John P. Clum, mine magnate E. B. Gage and youthful Episcopalian minister Endicott Peabody (later the White House chaplain of Franklin D. Roosevelt) .

Showdown

It was this association, more than anything else, which led to the famous gunfight – not at, but near, the O.K. Corral. The business elite, who were predominantly Republican and Northern, turned to Virgil and Wyatt Earp and their gunfighting talents to pacify Tombstone and end its wild "man for breakfast" image. Most in need of "civilizing" was a miscellaneous, anarchic confederation of Cochise County small ranchers, rustlers and outlaws headed by "Old Man" (N. H.) Clanton and known as "the Cowboys". Other prominent members of the Cowboys – estimated to number anything between 50 and 300 – were Clanton's sons, Billy, Ike and Phineas, Curly Bill Brocius (alias William Graham), Pony Deal, John Ringo, and the brothers Frank and Tom McLaury. The Cowboys, who periodically rode into town for a drinking spree, unsettled Tombstone's elite because they undermined civic efforts to convince mining capitalists that the town was safe for investment. The profits at stake were enormous: $25 million dollars' worth of silver would be dug out of Tombstone between 1879 and 1883. The Earps – who were themselves speculating in mines and real estate – enthusiastically backed the civilizing mission, with an enthusiasm heightened by a series of personal clashes with the Clantons and McLaurys.

The first blood between the two factions came on 28 October 1880. In the evening, some of the Cowboy outlaws rode into town and started shooting up Allen Street. Fred White, the city marshal, stepped out to intervene and was shot – probably accidentally – by Curly Bill Brocius. Wyatt Earp pistol-whipped Curly Bill and threw him in jail.

Tension between the two sides increased dramatically. Accusations and threats flew back and forth. Earp telegraphed his Dodge City cronies Doc Holliday and Luke Short to join him, installing them as dealers in the Oriental Saloon and Gambling Hall, in which he had a quarter share. Shortly after, the Tombstone *Nugget*, a paper which sided with the Clantons, charged that Doc Holliday had led a raid on the Wells Fargo stage, and that the Earps were the masterminds behind it. The clinching piece of evidence seemed to come from Holliday's partner, Big Nose Kate, who signed an affidavit that Holliday had been involved in the affair. Later, Big Nose Kate withdrew the affidavit, possibly under pressure from Earp.

In June 1881 Old Man Clanton was killed on a rustling foray into Mexico, and his son Ike took over leadership of the Cowboys. Matters now hurtled towards their climax. Wyatt Earp and the teenage Billy Clanton had a heated exchange over the ownership of a horse. In a saloon on 25 October 1881 Ike Clanton and Doc Holliday met, and three times Holliday tried to get Ike Clanton to go for his gun. Ike insisted he was unarmed. The Earps and Clantons left the saloon bellowing threats at each other.

The gunfight came the next day, Wednesday 26 October 1881. Early in the morning the Earps were awakened with the news that the Clanton gang was gathering in town. Virgil Earp – who had recently been appointed city marshal – arrested Ike Clanton for carrying a weapon within city limits. Taken to police court by Virgil and Morgan Earp, Ike was fined 25 dollars. In a rage, Ike started berating Morgan Earp, who offered Ike a gun and suggested that they have it out, there and then. Ike declined. Tom McLaury, meanwhile, had literally collided with Wyatt Earp outside the police court, Earp responding by hitting McLaury over the head with the barrel of his pistol. Later the same morning, Wyatt and Frank McLaury taunted each other in the street.

The Earps held a council-of-war in Hafford's saloon, and determined on a showdown with the Clanton-McLaurys. Virgil took his brothers Wyatt and Morgan to his office and deputized them. Doc Holliday turned up with a shotgun and was similarly deputized. Realizing that trouble was brewing, John Behan, sheriff of Cochise County, intervened and offered to disarm the Clantons and McLaurys peaceably. The offer was brushed aside, probably because Behan was a friend of the Cowboy outlaws, whose votes he needed for his elected office, so could not be trusted.

The Earps and Holliday then went looking for their enemies. They found them in Fremont Street, next to the O.K. Corral. Lined up were Ike and Billy Clanton, Frank and Tom McLaury, and a friend of the Clanton's, Billy Clairborne. The Earps and Holliday carried on walking until there was a bare eight feet between the two groups. According to Behan, who trailed the Earps, Wyatt Earp started the battle by saying "You sons of bitches, you have been looking for a fight, now you can have one." The Earps' version was that Virgil called on the men to surrender, but Billy Clanton and Frank McLaury dropped their hands to their guns.

Neither version is accurate. Almost certainly the gunfight was initiated by the impetuous Doc Holliday, who raised his shotgun and fired at – and narrowly missed – Ike Clanton, Holliday trading on this notorious act for the rest of his life. After Holliday's shotgun blast, the Earps also began shooting. Frank McLaury fell almost immediately, shot in the stomach by Wyatt Earp. Morgan Earp, his coat holed from a bullet from Tom McLaury's Colt .45, fired at Billy Clanton, hitting him in the right arm, then in the chest, Clanton falling back against the photographic studio of Camillus S. Fly. Although dying, Billy managed to fire his gun twice. These bullets apparently wounded Virgil in the calf, and Morgan in the shoulder. Ike Clanton and Billy Clairborne, meanwhile, had run to the safety of Fly's doorway. Tom McLaury, who had taken shelter behind a horse, received a mortal blast from Holliday's shotgun when the horse reared up, exposing him. Seeing this, Tom's wounded brother Frank fired at Holliday, skinning his hip. Morgan Earp then killed Frank McLaury.

Suddenly, there was silence. The battle of the O.K. Corral was over. It had taken just 30 seconds.

There was considerable controversy afterwards as to whether the Clanton-McLaurys had actually intended to fight. Ike Clanton and Tom McLaury, at least, had been unarmed. Feelings against the Earps and Holliday ran high. The dead men – Frank McLaury, Tom McLaury and Billy Clanton – were dressed in their finest clothes and placed in the window of a hardware store with a sign stating: MURDER IN THE STREETS OF TOMBSTONE.

A 30-day court hearing finally exonerated the Earps and Doc Holliday. Judge Spicer ruled that they had acted "wisely, discreetly and prudentially to secure their own preservation" and "were fully justified in committing these homicides." However, Virgil's deputizing of his brothers and Holliday was frowned upon, and he was relieved of his post as city marshal.

Three months later Virgil was invalided for life in a night-time ambush on Allen Street, and in March 1882 Morgan Earp was assassinated as he played pool at the Campbell & Hatch Billiard Parlor.

An investigation by a coroner's jury ruled that Morgan had been killed by Frank Stilwell, Pete Spence and Florentino "Indian Charlie" Cruz, a *mestizo* woodcutter working for Spence. Stilwell and Spence were prominent members of the Cowboy outlaw faction.

The body of Morgan Earp was put aboard a train for burial at the family home in California. Accompanying him were all the Earp men, their families, along with Doc Holliday and three hardcase gunmen friends of Wyatt Earp's: Sherman McMasters, Texas Jack Vermilion and Turkey Creek Johnson.

The ostentatious departure from town was a ruse. At Tucson, Wyatt and Warren Earp, together with Holliday and the gunmen, detrained and began a campaign of vengeance for the dead Morgan Earp. Frank Stilwell and Florentino Cruz were both shot dead by the gang. Wyatt

Earp, along with his cohorts, was indicted for their murder. According to Earp's later testimony, he also shot Curly Bill Brocius, although this is doubtful. However, the killings effectively broke up the Cowboy-rustler faction in Cochise County. Ike Clanton disappeared into Mexico, later to be killed by a sheriff, while Pete Spence put himself under Behan's protective custody. Another of the Clanton faction, the Greek-quoting gunman John Ringo, was found dead, a presumed suicide.

After defeating the outlaw faction Earp left Tombstone, the murder indictment still hanging over him, and worked the gold camps as a gambler. His reputation as a card player was that he always had "some dishonest trick". At various times he was in Cripple Creek, Colorado, in Nevada and Alaska. Journeying with him was "artiste" Josephine Sarah Marcus, daughter of a prosperous German Jewish mercantile family from San Francisco, who had caught Earp's wandering eye in Tombstone. The couple later married. (The abandoned Mattie Blaylock Earp became a prostitute and died of an overdose in 1883.

An interruption to Earp's gambling occurred in 1883 when Luke Short asked for his help in Dodge City. A reforming shift in local politics had resulted in Short's Long Branch saloon being prosecuted for prostitution. Holliday and Bat Masterson were also wired. The arrival of Earp, Holliday and Masterson led to the so-called "Dodge City War" confrontation, though in fact not a shot was fired. The *Globe* reported, with a tone of civic satisfaction: "A new dancehall was opened on Saturday night where all the warriors met and settled their past differences and everything was made lovely and serene. All opposing factions . . . met and agreed to stand by each other for the good of trade. A not unlooked for result."

Three years later Doc Holliday died alone of tuberculosis in the sanitarium at Glenwood Springs, Colorado, on 8

November 1887. He was 35. That same year, Ike Clanton was killed by Deputy Sheriff J. V. Brighton while rustling cattle.

Earp himself gave up gambling some time in the 1890s, and retired to Los Angeles having made a small fortune from this career, plus his interests in mining. Shortly before his death, he assisted Stuart N. Lake in his biography, *Wyatt Earp, Frontier Marshal*. Published in 1931, two years after Earp died, the book providentially appeared at a time when the public was hungry for new Western heroes. It was also almost entirely fabricated. As Lake later admitted, he "put words into Wyatt's mouth because of the inarticulateness and monosyllabic way he had of talking." Subsequently, it has been proved that Lake even invented the famous "Buntline Special", the long-barrelled Colt supposedly given to Earp by admiring dime novelist Ned Buntline.

Texas Rangers, Pinkerton Detectives

Guardians of the Frontier

Something of the stature of the Texas Rangers in frontier mythology is attested to by the apocryphal story of the West Texas mayor who summoned the Rangers to quell a riot. The Rangers sent a single man, a Winchester rifle over his shoulder. The mayor protested that he had requested a company of men. "Why so you did," replied the Ranger, "but there's only one riot, ain't there?"

It was the early Texas colonialist Stephen F. Austin who first organized a body of armed mounted "watchmen". This was in 1826. The Rangers were more properly constituted in 1835, as 25 men whose task was to "range and guard the frontier between the Brazos and Trinity rivers." Soon after, their jurisdiction was extended westwards to the Guadalupe. Thus, the first rangers were scouts and fighters against the Indians and Mexicans. They furnished their own horses and saddles, submitted to their own discipline, and subsisted on $1.25 a day.

The Rangers, their numbers increased to 150, played a key role in the 1835–6 Texan Revolution and the ensuing defence of the Republic. Patrolling the vast frontier in small detachments of around 20 men (a company), some of which used German rather than English, Rangers intercepted Mexican raiders in the Southwest and Indian hostiles in the West with notable success. A company of Rangers led by Colonel Henry Karnes forced 200 Comanche to withdraw at Arroyo Seco in August 1837, and Rangers were heavily involved in the victories over the Comanche at Council House and Plum Creek in 1840.

This Indian-fighting period saw the rise of such legendary Ranger figures as Captain Samuel Walker – who gave Samuel Colt's .45 revolver its field trial – and Captain John ("Jack") Coffee Hays. As everyone allowed, Hays was recklessly brave. A Lipan chief described him as a man "not afraid to go to hell by himself." He was also capable of phenomenal endurance. On one notable occasion he joined a party of Delawares running (literally) after a band of Comanche who had stolen their horses. The foot chase was kept up for three days. It was Hays who commanded the regiment of Rangers who served under Zachary Taylor in the war with Mexico which erupted after Texas's 1845 entry into the Union.

After the Mexican war, the Rangers were officially disbanded, the Army insisting that it take over the role of protecting settlements in Texas against the Indians. Unofficially, the Rangers continued to exist under such men as William A. ("Big Foot") Wallace. A book about Wallace by Texas author John C. Duval, *Adventures of Big-Foot Wallace, the Texas Ranger and Hunter*, was so popular in the East that it was reprinted six times. Under public pressure, the governor of Texas reorganized the Rangers as a state Indian-fighting force, and they carried the war against the Native Americans deep into the southern plains. At the climax of the Rangers' 1860 campaign, Captain Sul Ross engaged the Comanche band of Peta Nocona, and rescued the White captive Cynthia Ann Parker. The reformed

Rangers were also active against Mexican bandits, who raided north of the border, a detachment under Rip Ford killing the famed Juan Cortina at Rio Grande City on 26 December 1860. Additional duties included the pursuit, capture and return of runaway slaves.

For their part in the cause of the Confederacy, the Rangers were disbanded by the Union at the close of the Civil War. Death and disorder were so rife in the state, however, that the Rangers were once again revived. In 1874 a Frontier Battalion was raised under Major John B. Jones to fight Indians, while a "Special Force of Rangers" under Captain Leander H. McNelly was detailed to suppress lawlessness along the border with Mexico. Since the Indians of the southern plains were all but defeated, and Mexican banditry on the decline, the new Rangers became an organization that dealt almost exclusively with erring Anglo-Americans, whether rustler, robber, thief or murderer. Badmen brought to justice included the racist gunfighter John Wesley Hardin, captured by Ranger Captain John Armstrong ("McNelly's Bulldog") at the train station at Pensacola, Florida. Lame from having once shot himself in the leg, Armstrong eased into Hardin's coach, drew out a .45 pistol and ordered Hardin and his companions to surrender. Hardin pulled a pistol, which became trapped in his suspenders. One of Hardin's friends, 19-year-old Jim Mann, got off a shot at Armstrong, but it only holed his hat. Armstrong shot Mann through the chest. Hardin then started kicking the Ranger, who finally pistol-whipped him into submission. Armstrong afterwards set up as a rancher on the $4,000 reward he got for delivering Hardin up to justice.

Another prominent outlaw tracked down by the Rangers was Sam Bass. Orphaned at 15, Bass drifted west from his Indiana home to become a cowboy at Denton, Texas. In 1875 Bass and a colleague, Joel Collins, drove a herd up the trail to Kansas, where – probably at Collins's instigation – they absconded with the owner's money. When this was lost in the gambling dens of Deadwood, Bass held up the Union Pacific train at Big Springs, Nebraska, taking $60,000 in gold. Later, he returned to Texas as a highway robber. Though only moderately successful at this, he was notably successful at eluding arrest. Efforts to storm his Cove Hollow hide-out were driven back by bullets. Eventually, he was betrayed by a henchman, Jim Murphy, who alerted the Rangers to a planned robbery by Bass of the bank at Round Rock. Five Rangers, led by Captain Lee Hall, ambushed Bass as he reconnoitred the town on 19 July 1878. Though shot in the spine, the outlaw was scooped to safety by fellow bandit Frank Jackson, and the two escaped into the evening. However, Bass proved unable to ride, and Jackson had to set him down just outside town. He was found next morning and taken into Round Rock, where he died the next day, his 27th birthday.

These successes aside, the Rangers of the post-War decades attracted a great deal of controversy. Their depredations on Hispanics on both sides of the border are well recorded, and on occasion they mounted something like invasions of northern Mexico, fighting sizeable skirmishes with Mexican forces and citizens, such as at Palo Alto and Las Cueces in 1875. One Ranger was once moved to boast: "I can maintain a better stomach at the killing of a Mexican than at the crushing of a body louse."

A number of Rangers were also outlaws rather than the pursuers of outlaws. Prime among them was James Miller, resident Ranger at Memphis, Texas, in the late 1890s.

Miller began his long career as a murderer and gunfighter in 1884 when, aged 17, he murdered his brother-in-law. There followed a known 12 other victims. He survived a number of gun battles by the simple expedient of wearing an iron breastplate. Outwardly he was a devout Methodist, and "Deacon Jim" spoke regularly at prayer meetings. Perhaps his most famous victim was Pat Garrett, the killer of Billy the Kid, whom Miller assassinated in February 1908 near Las Cruces, New Mexico. When Garrett stepped out of his buggy to urinate in the road, Miller opened fire from concealment, shooting Garrett in the head and stomach. He died instantly. By coincidence, Garrett had once served as a Texas Ranger himself.

The Rangers continue to exist as a small, elite force of criminal investigators. They still, when need arises, saddle up to hunt men in the brush country.

Men Who Never Sleep

When the Texas Rangers ambushed Sam Bass at Round Rock, they were not the only detectives on his trail. The much-robbed Texas and Pacific Railway had retained in the case the services of Pinkerton's National Detective Agency ("We Never Sleep"), the most significant of the private police forces in the West. Although the Pinkertons missed their badman this time, they would get others. They would also attract controversy, even hatred, in the course of doing so.

Founded by Allan Pinkerton, a Scots emigrant and ardent abolitionist (his Chicago home was used as a hiding-place by escaping slaves), the Agency gained fame just before the Civil War, when it foiled a plot to assassinate Lincoln. During the War it helped organize Union secret-service operations under the direction of General George B. McClellan. In the late 1860s and early 1870s the Agency grew rapidly, and played a major role in the labour–management conflicts of the Pennsylvania coalfields, famously breaking the labour terrorist organization, the "Molly Maguires".

Also giving rise to prominent cases was the Agency's involvement with Western railroad robbers. Pinkertons trailed the Reno brothers, the first in the world to hold up a train, apprehending John Reno in 1867, and William and Simeon Reno in Canada in 1868. (Extradited to the USA, William and Simeon were lynched by the Southern Indiana Vigilance Committee.) Another early target was the James–Younger gang, one which led to the death of a Pinkerton operative in March 1874 when he tried to infiltrate it. Shortly after this another Pinkerton detective, Louis J. Lull, was shot dead in a gunfight with Jim and John Younger. The Pinkerton bomb attack of January 1875 on the James cabin, in which the James boys' mother was seriously injured and their half-brother killed, brought the Agency to a low in popular opinion. Jesse James's hatred for Allan Pinkerton became an obsession. Once, the outlaw even went to Chicago to kill him. He failed, but told a friend that "I know God some day will deliver Allan Pinkerton into my hands." Pinkerton died in 1884. His would-be Nemesis was already two years under the sod.

By the time Pinkerton died, leaving the business to his sons William and Robert, the Agency had opened offices in Seattle, Kansas and Denver. Head of the Denver office was James McParland, the agent who had infiltrated the Maguires, while operatives included gunslinger Tom Horn and ex-Texas cowboy, Charles A. Siringo. The work of a Western operative for Pinkertons, as recalled in Siringo's memoir, *A Cowboy Detective*, included "testing" (spying on) train conductors, investigating the Ute Indian War in Utah for the government, undercover work in mines to expose thieves, detecting murderers, infiltrating unions, and chasing rustlers. Pursuing train and bank robbers was a staple Pinkerton activity. Aside from Sam Bass, the Agency was assigned to the case of the Texas outlaw gang headed by Rube and Jim Burrows, the Agency's detective work leading to the shattering of the gang in 1888. Further north, Pinkertons so persistently harassed the Wild Bunch that they drove them out of their Wyoming–Montana stomping ground, Butch Cassidy and the Sundance Kid eventually fleeing to Bolivia.

While some Pinkerton agents were chasing Western outlaws in the 1890s, others were employed by capital in the rash of labour wars that spread through the mines of Colorado, Utah, Nevada and Idaho. The "class struggle" in the West took on a violent, blood-red colour, with mining disputes exacerbated by the stand-up-and-fight frontier attitudes of the participants. Labour militants used dynamite to blow up mines and concentrators. Employers hired gunmen-thugs to guard their property and break up strikes. And they employed Pinkerton agents to infiltrate the unions.

The operative sent, in 1891, to the flashpoint of the Coeur d'Alene mining district in the Idaho panhandle was Charlie Siringo. His infiltration of the miners' union in Gem was almost of a piece with McParland's of the Molly Maguires a generation before, and would be one of the great escapades in Pinkerton history.

Arriving in the mining camp of Gem, Siringo took a job in the mine and joined the local union. This required him to take a Molly Maguire-type oath that "I would never turn traitor to the union cause; that if I did, death would be my reward." Enthusiastic and industrious, he was elected recording secretary.

Initially, the miners were not suspicious of Siringo:

My worst trouble was writing reports and mailing them. These reports had to be sent to St. Paul, Minnesota, where our Agency had an office, with my Chicago friend, John O'Flyn, as superintendent. There they were typewritten and mailed back to John A. Finch, Secretary of the Mine-Owners' Association, where all the mine-owners could read them.

The Gem Post Office was in the store of a man by the name of Samuels, a rabid anarchist and Union sympathizer; so for that reason I dare not mail reports there. "Big Frank" was the deputy post-master and handled most of the mail. He was a member of the Gem Miners' Union, consequently I had to walk down to Wallace, four miles, to mail reports; and for fear of being held up I had to slip down there in the dark.

Siringo sent out his reports for months, detailing the union's secret plans for a coming offensive against the mine-owners. When these plans were published in a local pro-employer newspaper, *The Barbarian*, the union realized that it had a spy in its midst. Suspicion came to rest on Siringo, whose frequent trips to Wallace to mail letters had been noted. His exposure coincided with the start of what he characterized as an "uprising" by the union against Coeur d'Alene mine-owners. The atmosphere was murderous. After being tipped off that militants were looking to kill him, Siringo fled to the store of Mrs Shipley, where he roomed, and holed up:

I had Mrs. Shipley keep the store door locked, and told her to not let any one in. I then went out in the back yard to see if the coast was clear in the vicinity of my hole in the fence. I looked through a crack in the fence and discovered two armed men hiding behind a big log. I then went into a storeroom adjoining the fence on the east, and through a crack saw my friend Dallas [a union militant] walking a beat with a shotgun on his shoulder. He was evidently guarding a rat in a trap, and I happened to be that rat.

In this storeroom I discarded my hat and coat and in

their place put on an old leather jacket and a black slouch hat. Then I got a saw and went into Mrs. Shipley's room, and next to the store wall, tore up a square of carpet and began sawing a hole through the floor. I sawed out a place just large enough to admit my body. This done, I replaced the carpet in nice shape, loosely, over the hole.

At first I had planned a scheme to barricade the head of the stairs with furniture and bedding and then slaughter all who undertook to come up the stairs. Had I carried out this plan, the newspapers would have had some real live news to record; but I hated to wait upstairs for business to come my way, hence made up my mind to go under the floor and do some skirmishing, which would at least keep my mind occupied.

The back part of my store building rested flat on the ground, and the front part was up on piles three feet high.

Finally I bade Mrs. Shipley and her little five-year-old goodbye, and dropped out of sight. Then Mrs. Shipley pulled her trunk over the hole as per my instructions.

In scouting around under the house, I could find no possible way to get out, except up under the board sidewalk on the main street. Through a crack the width of my hand, on the east side, I saw Dallas resting on his beat. He was leaning on his shot-gun. I up with my rifle and took aim at his heart, but before pulling the trigger, the thought of the danger from the smoke going up through the cracks and giving my hiding place away, flashed through my mind, and the rifle was taken from my shoulder.

Just then an explosion took place which shook the earth. It was up towards the Frisco Mill. The rifle shooting was still going on, but it soon ceased.

In about 20 minutes Mrs. Shipley pulled the trunk from the hole, and putting her head down in it, cried: "Oh, Mr. Allison [Siringo's cover name] run for your life. They have just blown up the Frisco Mill and killed lots of men and now they're coming after you to burn you at the stake, so as to make an example of Dickenson [for legal reasons Siringo was obliged to refer to Pinkertons as the Dickenson Agency in his narrative] detectives." Crawling near to the hole I asked Mrs. Shipley how she had found this out. She replied that Mrs. Weiss, a strong union woman, who was a friend of mine while I was in the union, had just told her when she went across the street to find out the cause of the explosion. I told Mrs. Shipley to keep cool and put the trunk back over the hole. It was explained to her that I could find no way to get out, hence must stay.

Soon I could hear the yelling of more than 1,000 throats as they came to get me. It wasn't long until the street was jammed with angry men. I was directly under the center of our store and could hear the leaders command Mrs. Shipley to open the door, but she refused to do it. Then they broke it down and the mob rushed in. I could hear Dallas' voice demanding that she tell where I was, but she denied having seen me since the night before. He told her that they knew better, as Miss Olsen had seen me crawl through the window, since which time a heavy guard had been kept around the house. I heard Mrs. Shipley ask why they wanted me. Then Dallas replied: "He's a dirty Dickenson detective and we intend to burn him at a stake as a warning to others of his kind." Mrs. Shipley asked why they didn't kill me yesterday when they had a good chance. To this Dallas replied: "The time wasn't ripe yesterday, but it is now and we will find him, so you might as well tell us or it will go hard with you." Mrs. Shipley then told them to do their worst, as she didn't know where I was. I felt like patting the lady on the back, as one out of 10,000 who wouldn't weaken and tell the secret with that vicious mob around her. I feared the child would tell, as he was bawling as though his little five-year-old heart would break.

Now I could hear "We'll find the———. He's in this

house," etc. Then a rush was made into Mrs. Shipley's bedroom and out into the back yard and also upstairs. I couldn't help but think of what a fine chance I was missing for making a world's record as a man-killer; for had I carried out my first plan, this was the moment as the rush was being made upstairs, when there would have been "something doing."

As I feared they might find the hole in the floor and then set fire to the building, I concluded to get out of there, even though I had to fight my way out.

The only opening was under the sidewalk, which was about a foot above the ground. I had no idea where it would lead me, but I thought of the old saying, "Nothing risked, nothing gained."

Finally I started east, towards the Miners' Union hall. The store buildings were built close together, except at my building where there was a narrow alleyway leading to the rear. It was in this narrow passage where Dallas had his policeman's beat that morning. I had to crawl on my stomach, "all same" snake in the grass; but I had to move very slowly as I was afraid of being seen by the angry men who lined the sidewalk as thick as they could stand. Some of the cracks in the sidewalk were an inch or more wide. After going the width of two store buildings, I stopped to rest, and while doing so, I lay on my back so as to look up through a wide crack. I could see the men's eyes and hear what they said. Most of their talk was about the "scabs" killed when they blew up the Frisco Mill with giant powder. Finally one big Irishman with a brogue as broad as the Atlantic Ocean, said: "Faith and why don't they bring that spalpeen out. I'm wanting to spit in his face, the dirty thraitor. We Emericans have got to shtand on our rights and show the worreld that we can fight." Of course I could have told this good "Emerican" citizen the reason for the delay in bringing me out to be burnt at a stake; and I could also have told him that he was then missing a good opportunity of spitting in my face, while alive, for my mind had been made up not to be taken until dead.

This was a hint for me to be moving, knowing that I was exploring new territory.

Another twenty-five feet brought me in front of a saloon, and here I found an opening to get under the building, which was built on piles and stood about four feet from the ground. In the rear I could see daylight. At this my heart leaped with joy. The ground was covered with slush and mud and there were all kinds of tree-tops, stumps and brush under this building.

In hurrying through this brush, my watch-chain caught and tore loose. On it was a charm, a $3 gold piece with my initials C. L. A. I hated to lose this, so stopped to consider as to whether I should go back to hunt it. While studying, I wondered if I was scared. I had to smile at the thought, so I concluded to test the matter by spitting; but bless you, my mouth was so dry I couldn't spit anything but cotton, or what looked like cotton. I decided that it was a case of scared with a big S. I had always heard that when a person is badly frightened he can't spit; but this was the first time I ever saw it tested.

A week or so later I bought the watch-chain and charm from a boy who had found it while the union had "kids" searching for me under these buildings on the day of the riot. When the chain was found, I suppose they figured that the bird had flown, all but this relic of his breast-feathers.

On reaching the rear of the saloon, I found plenty of room to get out in the open, but before making the break, I examined my rifle and pistol to see that they were in working order.

All ready, I sprung from under the house and stood once more in glorious sunshine. The Winchester was up, ready for action. Only three men were in sight and their backs were towards me. They stood at the corner of the saloon building, looking up a vacant space towards the main street. They had evidently been placed behind these buildings to watch for me, but in their eagerness to be at the burning, they were watching the crowd in the street, knowing that the movements of the mob would indicate when the "fatted calf" was ready for the slaughter. My first impulse was to start shooting and kill these three men, but my finer feeling got the best of me. It would be too much like taking advantage and committing cold-blooded murder.

I glanced straight south. There, in front of me, about fifty yards distant, was the high railroad grade which shut off the view from the Gem mill where I knew my friends awaited me. But to undertake to scale this high grade I would be placing myself between the two fires, for the chances were, my friends would take me for an enemy and start shooting.

Quicker than a flash the thought struck me to fool these three men and make them think I was going up to the top of the grade to get a shot at the "scabs."

A little to the left there was a swift stream of water flowing through a culvert under the railroad grade, and to avoid being shot by my friends I concluded to go through this and sink or swim.

I started in a slow run, half stooped like a hunter slipping upon game, as though intending to crawl up on the grade and get a shot at the enemy, my course being a few feet to the right of the boxed culvert. I didn't look back, as I knew my footsteps would attract the attention of the three men, and I didn't want them to see my face or to note that my movements were suspicious. When within a few feet of the rushing water, I made a quick turn to the left and into the culvert. Just then one bullet whizzed past my head. This was the only one shot fired. It was all I could do to stem the force of the water, which reached to my arm-pits. The Winchester was now in my left hand while my right extended forward holding on to the upright timber on the west wall of the culvert. After I had worked my way far enough into this culvert so that I was in the dark and out of sight of my enemy, I braced myself against an upright timber and turned round to look back. There in plain view, was three drunken Swedes trying to see me so as to get another shot. Now I held the winning hand, and raised my rifle to take advantage of my opportunity; but my heart failed me at the thought of murdering a drunken Swede, for I had found them to be a hardworking lot of sheep who were always ready to follow heartless Irish leaders. I also thought of the danger of shooting, as the flash from my rifle would indicate my whereabouts and shots might be fired in that direction. Although from the way these Swedes or Finlanders were staggering around, I didn't think they could shoot very straight. I began to work my way to daylight on the other side, a distance of about fifty feet. I would reach ahead and get hold of an upright timber and then pull myself forward against the raging torrent. I finally emerged from the culvert and found myself under a Swede's house, which was built over the opposite end of this culvert, with the entrance to the house fronting on the railroad track. On walking from under the house, which was built on piles, a Swede woman at her back door recognized me. She called me by name and asked what I had been doing under her house. Her husband had been one of my best union friends. I told her that I was just prowling around a little for exercise. She laughed.

Now I had to march across a 200-yard open space to reach the Gem mill and I had to take chances of being shot at by both sides.

On reaching the "scab" forts – high ricks of cordwood with port holes — I was halted by a voice behind the woodpile which said: Drop that gun you — and walk up here with your hands up." I replied that I was a friend. He answered: "It don't make a d—d bit of difference; if you don't drop that gun your head goes off." I dropped it, and with both hands raised, I walked up to the port hole which was made by a stick of the wood being pulled out. The fellow then told me to pull off my hat so he could see my face. I did so, and he said: "Are you that detective who came to our camp last night?" I replied yes. Then he told me to hurry and get behind the fort before the union — took a shot at me. It was a relief to get behind the fort and shake hands with the Thiel guards there.

Siringo's evidence convicted 18 union leaders, who received terms in penitentiary.

Labour matters continued to preoccupy the Denver offices of the Pinkertons. The new Western Federation of Miners battled mine-owners in Leadville (1894), Telluride (1901) and, most bitterly, at Cripple Creek (1894–1904). A dynamite attack on the Cripple Creek railroad station by union terrorist Harry Orchard left 13 strikebreakers dead. In 1905 the former governor of Idaho, Frank Steunenberg, was killed in a bomb attack, seemingly as punishment for calling in federal troops against striking miners at Coeur d'Alene. Pinkerton agents extracted a confession from Orchard, who in turn implicated officials of the Western Federation of Miners. A jury found Orchard guilty of the bombing, but other defendants, among them noted labour radical William "Big Bill" Haywood, were freed.

The charismatic Haywood went on to be a founder of the revolutionary labour union, the International Workers of the World ("Wobblies"), which garnered support far and wide across the West. Particular bastions of support were the logging camps of the Pacific Northwest and the mines of Montana, but the Wobblies organized many types of worker, including hop-pickers. A Wobbly-led hop-pickers' strike in 1913 in Wheatland, California, produced a gunfight between sheriffs and workers which left five dead. Two years later in Butte, Montana, a confrontation between the Wobblies and mine-owners resulted in Wobbly leader Frank Little being murdered. Little was one of the last victims of Western vigilantism. He was swung from the trestle at the end of a rope.

Pinkertons were involved in many of the conflicts, as guards, as union-busters, and as spies. The Agency's willingness to act on behalf of management was occasioned by its belief that unions were unpatriotic and did the workers more harm than good. But the mood of the public shifted, and the Pinkertons' somewhat heavy-handed methods (there were allegations of framing and forced confessions) set it behind the times. In 1937 Pinkertons abolished its industrial division, after Congress ruled that industrial spying was illegal.

Wild, Wild Women

Women were tamers of the West, not shoot-'em up perpetrators of wildness. When women began to arrive in raw cow towns and mining camps in significant numbers the invariable consequence was an outbreak of peace. "Streets grew passable, clean and quiet," recalled one prospector in Helena, Montana, on the coming of women, and "pistols were less frequently fired."

Women brought with them the perfume of civilization, the prospect of families and settlement. Respectable women worked as cooks, laundresses, schoolteachers and, above all, wives and mothers. By the mores of the time, they were not lumberjacks, railroad builders, doctors or miners.

And yet some women were not satisfied just to be "the Missus". To them, as to men, the West was a land of promise and possibility, the chance to fulfil long-damped aspirations. Thousands homesteaded their own land, and a few vied for jobs normally filled by men. Minnie Mossman captained steamboats on the Columbia, Nellie Cashman worked the West as a prospector, and the African–American Mary Fields, an ex-slave, drove a US mail coach.

And some women chose – or were obliged – to pass beyond all bounds of respectability into the *demi-monde*, or even into full-scale outlawry.

Most women who inhabited the *demi-monde* did so as prostitutes. Outside of St Louis, San Francisco and other large towns, the fabled *maison de joie* hardly existed. Nearly every settlement had a Painted Lady or two, but most prostitutes worked the women-hungry, wide-open, cow, mining, rail and garrison towns. Attitudes to prostitution in the West tended to be that it was an evil necessity; the ratio of males to females was hugely unbalanced. San Francisco was a prime example. Before the Gold Rush the population of the town consisted of 459 people, of whom 138 were women. After the discovery of gold, the migration of 1849 brought 65,000 men to the city – but just 2,500 women. Not until towns and regions had been settled for some time did births reduce the disproportion between the sexes. In the meantime, there was prostitution on a large scale; in 1880, Leadville, Colorado was recorded as having a brothel for every 129 inhabitants.

Prostitutes had lives of hardship and tragedy. Many were forced into prostitution by poverty, or by abandonment by their husbands. Suicide and disease were commonplace. So was violence. In consequence, many prostitutes went armed with knives or Derringer-type pistols. A gun made a prostitute a formidable combatant. "Soiled dove" Martha Camp chased a customer out of a brothel in Bodie, California, in 1881 and fired five shots at him. According to the local paper, the man's "hair stood on end, as he expected any second to be reduced to a state of perfect utility."

Elenor Dumont also worked Bodie as a prostitute, although she began her career as a gambler in Nevada City in 1854, where she was employed as a dealer in the largest gambling establishment in town. The novelty of a woman gambler created a sensation, and customers flocked to her table. But Dumont was possessed by a wanderlust, and joined the miners in the rushes to British Columbia, Montana, the Black Hills and Idaho. She committed suicide after losing $300 she had borrowed from a friend in a faro game.

The most celebrated woman gambler in the West was "Poker Alice" Tubbs. Born in England in 1851, the daughter of a schoolmaster, she came to America when she was 12 and at 19 married engineer Frank Duffield in Colorado. After he was killed in a mining accident, Alice took up teaching, and a more profitable dealing of cards in a saloon on a percentage basis. With a cigar in her mouth and a pistol about her person, she was to be seen in many a boom town. She was working for Bob Ford, assassin of Jesse James, when he was shot dead in Creede, Colorado, at which she moved on to Deadwood, working in a saloon alongside another gambler, William Tubbs. One day a drunken miner pulled a knife on Tubbs, but before the blade could be wielded "Poker Alice" shot the miner in the arm with her six-shooter. Inevitably, the pair of gamblers then married. When William Tubbs later died of pneumonia, Poker Alice tried sheep farming before drifting back to the card tables. In 1912 she opened a club near Fort Meade, South Dakota. This was successful until drunken soldiers tried to break in after hours. Fearing she was to be robbed, Poker Alice shot through the door, killing one of the men. At her trial, the judge let her go, declaring: "I cannot find it in my heart to send a white-haired lady to the penitentiary." She retired to a farm, dying at 79 during a medical operation.

With her cigar dangling from her mouth, Poker Alice was not the only unconformist woman to adopt male mannerisms or conventions. A number took to wearing male clothing, even impersonating men. Not the least reason for doing this was expressed by Elizabeth Jane Forest Guerin ("Mountain Charlie"), who periodically disguised herself as a man: "I could go where I chose, do

many things which while innocent in themselves, were
debarred by propriety from association with the female
sex." At the minimum, the donning of male garb placed a
woman so far outside expected standards that there was a
kind of safety in eccentricity.

Martha Jane Canarray or "Calamity Jane", was a
habitual wearer of male clothing, and according to her
own account was an army scout (for the army's premier
Indian fighter, General George Crook) and an army teamster. More likely her connection with the army was as
camp follower or prostitute, employed at E. Hoffey's "hog
farm" near Fort Laramie. She was also an alcoholic and
notorious liar, who claimed to be married to Wild Bill
Hickok. This is unlikely, although she probably knew him
in Deadwood. She does seem to have married a Clinton
Burke, by whom she had a daughter. Her tendency to
vagrancy and brawling saw her arrested several times in
mining camps around the West. Her origins are as obscure as the reason for her nickname. She was born anywhere between 1844 and 1852 in Missouri, and her
explanation for her soubriquet is that she once rescued a
wounded officer, who hailed her as "Calamity Jane, hero-
ine of the Plains." Her bravery as a nurse is a matter of
record; during an outbreak of smallpox in Deadwood she
was one of the few to stay behind and help tend the sick.
Towards the end of her life she was discovered down and
out, working in a brothel in the appositely named Horr,
Montana, by Josephine Blake, who persuaded her to take
part in the Pan-American Exposition in New York as
"Calamity Jane, the Famous Woman Scout of the Wild
West." In 1903, Canarray died in Terry, South Dakota.
Friends claimed that her last wish was: "Bury me next to
Bill [Hickok]." And she was.

Another cross-dresser was Flo Quick, who called herself "Tom King" and rustled cattle in Indian Territory in

the 1880s. Quick was a genuine outlaw. After rustling, she became the mistress of bank robber Bob Dalton, working as the Dalton gang's spy. As Eugenia Moore or Mrs Mundy, Quick befriended railroad employees, obtaining from them the information about trains the gang intended to hold up. It was Quick who rustled the horses the Daltons used in the Coffeyville disaster in 1892 in which Bob Dalton was killed. Quick then organized her own band before disappearing, although some reports told of her death in a gunfight.

Indian Territory in the 1880s and 1890s saw something of a flowering of women outlaws. The myth-covered Rose of the Cimarron – her real name seems to have been either Rosa Dunn or Rose O'Leary – became an outlaw to share the life of lover George Newcomb (who so frequently sang "I'm a wild wolf from Bitter Creek / And it's my night to howl" that he was nicknamed "Bitter Creek"). They met when Rose was 15. Allegedly she helped Newcomb escape from a gunfight in Ingalls, Oklahoma, in 1893, when the Doolin gang of which he was a member was trapped by a posse. Realizing that Newcomb was out of ammunition, she hid a gun and cartridge belt beneath her skirt and sneaked them across to where Newcomb was waiting. Newcomb was killed in a gunfight two years later, the assailants being Rose's brothers, who killed him for the $5,000 reward.

Jennie "Little Britches" Stevens and "Cattle Annie" McDougal were also female associates of Bill Doolin's gang of "Oklahombres". They started their careers in crime selling whiskey illegally to Indians in the Osage nation. After that, they tried cattle rustling and horse stealing, and aiding the Doolin gang in their bank robberies. Stevens and McDougal were finally arrested by deputy marshals Bill Tilghman and Steve Burke at a hide-out near Pawnee. The girls resisted arrest, Stevens grabbing a Winchester and jumping on a horse. Tilghman chased after her, ducking shots. Since the Code of the West did not allow Tilghman to shoot the female fugitive, he downed her horse, and fought Stevens to the ground.

The West's most infamous female outlaw was Belle Starr, the "Bandit Queen", also a denizen of Indian Territory. She was born Myra Belle Shirley in Missouri during the troubled era of the border wars. Her first lover was Cole Younger, of the James–Younger gang, who fathered her daughter, Pearl. Soon after, she had another child, Edward ("Eddie"), by Jim Reed. Like Younger, Reed had served as a guerrilla during the Civil War, and had developed a taste for plunder and the illegal pursuit of wealth. He had taken part in at least three of the James–Younger gang's raids. In 1873 Reed, accompanied by Shirley and another thief, journeyed to Oklahoma, where they tortured a Creek chief until he revealed the whereabouts of $30,000, this being the government's subsidy to the tribe. Such misdeeds brought the law onto Reed's trail, and he was obliged to leave Shirley.

When Reed was killed for the $4,000 bounty on his head, Shirley organized her own gang of outlaws in Indian Territory, mostly for the rustling of cattle and horses. In 1876 she took up with Native American outlaw Blue Duck and then with the part-Cherokee Sam Starr, whose surname she adopted, living with him on his small ranch – named by her Youngers Bend – on the Canadian River, which became a refuge for outlaws "on the dodge".

Belle Starr's first brush with infamy came in 1883, when she was charged by Judge Parker at Fort Smith with being the "leader of a band of notorious horse thieves." This was the first time a woman had ever been tried for a major crime in the Western District of Arkansas. Newspapers luridly raised her to celebrity status as "The Petticoat of the Plains" and "The Lady Desperado", and she played the part, posing for photographs in a plumed hat sitting on a horse (side-saddle), with a pistol strapped around her waist. Parker found her guilty as charged, and sentenced her to nine months' imprisonment.

On release, she carried on her illegal trade in horses, and graduated to robbery. In 1886, Belle Starr was again brought before Parker for horse-stealing, but the case was dismissed for lack of evidence. That same year, Sam Starr was killed in a drunken gunfight with an Indian deputy. After Sam Starr's death, Belle took another common-law husband, the Creek Indian outlaw Jim July. At one point, Belle Starr's banditry was of sufficient stature to have a $5,000 reward placed on her head "dead or alive".

Belle Starr was shot in the back by an assassin in 1889. The culprit was probably a neighbour, Edgar Watson, with whom she had quarrelled over land. The other suspect was her son, Ed. According to R. P. Vann, a former member of the Indian police, it was local knowledge that there were "incestuous relations between Belle and her son and that she complicated this with extreme sadism." By this version, Ed killed his mother to be free of her tyranny.

Belle Starr's career in crime was long, lasting almost 20 years. That of Pearl Hart was brief and absurd, but she gained fame for participating in the nation's last stagecoach hold-up. In 1898, while working as a cook in a mining camp, she was persuaded by a drunken miner, Joe Boot, to aid him in the robbery of the stage near Globe, Arizona. They grabbed $431 but then got lost, and a posse caught them three days later. Boot was sentenced to penitentiary for 35 years, Pearl Hart for five. After serving two and a half years, she was released – for good behaviour.

Part IV

The Indian Wars

5. The Indian Wars

Prologue

> ... these tribes cannot exist surrounded by our settlements
> and in continual contact with our citizens. They have
> neither the intelligence, the industry, the moral habits, nor
> the desire of improvement. They must necessarily yield to
> the force of circumstance and, ere long, disappear.
>
> *President Andrew Jackson (1832)*

There were 10 million Native Americans living in the
Americas when the White man landed in the 1490s. The
diseases he brought wiped out entire villages, even tribes.
The Indians had no immunity to the Europeans' microbes
(or even any indigenous, epidemic diseases to give back
to the invader). When the explorers Lewis and Clark met
the Mandan at their earth-lodge villages on the bluffs
above the Missouri in 1805 the Indians had already suffered one smallpox epidemic, communicated by Indians
in contact with the White settlements to the East. In 1837,
another smallpox holocaust descended on the Mandan.
There were 39 bewildered survivors. The Mandan, to all
intents and purposes, had ceased to exist. Other tribes
suffered similar catastrophes.

There was more. The White man wanted the Indians'
land. Sometimes he bought it, usually he just took it.
Thousands of Indians were killed by war and the famine
which resulted. For three centuries, the Indians suffered

pestilence, war and hunger, and fell back and back before the tide of White civilization.

By 1840, there were only 400,000 Indians left in North America. All the eastern tribes had been annihilated, subdued or forcibly removed to Indian Territory, west of the Mississippi. This was to be a permanent Indian domain, inviolable.

No sooner had the permanent Indian frontier been declared than it began to crumble. The westward movement of White settlement had a momentum behind it that could not be stopped by declarations. In 1843 the emigrant trains began crossing the West, invading the "permanent" Indian lands. The discovery of Californian gold sent thousands more stampeding through the Indian hunting grounds in an endless stream of covered wagons and carts, which devastated the grasslands and scared away the buffalo so necessary to the life of the Plains Indian. Angry and despondent, the Indians began to harass the emigrant trains, or exact tributes for the right to pass through their lands.

Government agents in the West began to fear that the desperate Indians would go on the warpath. "What then will be the consequences," wrote Thomas Fitzpatrick, a former trapper, to his superiors in Washington, "should twenty thousand Indians, well armed, well mounted, and the most . . . expert in war . . . turn out in hostile array against all American travellers?" To forestall this dread possibility, in September 1851 the government called a meeting of all the northern tribes at Horse Creek, 35 miles from Fort Laramie, a remote outpost on the Oregon Trail.

It was the greatest gathering of tribes in history, attended by 10,000 American Indians, camped in the valley in a forest of skin-tents known as tipis. The mighty Teton (from *Titowa*, "plains") Sioux were there, so were their time-honoured enemies, the Crow. Also in attendance were the Arikara, Shoshonis, Cheyenne, Assinboine, Arapaho, and the Gros Ventre. Colonel Thomas Fitzpatrick addressed the tribesmen, telling them that the Great Father was "aware that your buffalo and game are driven off, and your grass and timber consumed by the opening of roads and the passing of emigrants through your countries. For these losses he desires to compensate you." The compensation offered the tribes by the Great Father was $50,000 a year, plus guns, if the Indians would keep away from the trail and confine themselves to designated tracts of land. (Thus began the reservation system, though no one yet called it that.)

The Indians "touched the pen", and many went away in the belief that an age of harmony between the White and Red people was about to begin. Cut Nose of the Arapaho declared: "I will go home satisfied. I will sleep sound, and not have to watch my horses in the night, or be afraid for my women and children. We have to live on these streams and in the hills, and I would be glad if the Whites would pick out a place for themselves and not come into our grounds."

Two years later a similar council was held with bands of the Comanche and Kiowa in Kansas. They agreed to refrain from molesting emigrants on the Santa Fe Trail in return for the annuity of $18,000 in goods.

The treaties were doomed to failure. Invariably, the political organization of an Indian tribe did not allow a chief to speak for all his people. And some chiefs, anyway, did not fully understand what they had been required to give up: their freedom to roam on the wind, to hunt buffalo, and to wage war with their ancient enemies. Such freedom required immense space; the Blackfoot from Montana are known to have raided as far south as the Mexican province of Durango. More serious were the White man's failures. Congress almost immediately re-

duced the number of years the stipend would be paid.
Supplies delivered were inadequate. To avoid starvation,
the Indians were forced to range far and wide in pursuit of
a dwindling supply of game. Tension along the emigrant
trails increased. There were frequent instances of petty
thieving. To defend the emigrants, the Army sent more
troops west.

Nearly 40 years of war between the United States and
the Plains Indians was set off by an argument over a cow.
On 18 August 1854 a young Miniconjou Sioux warrior
called High Forehead butchered a lame cow that an emigrant on the Oregon Trail had either lost or abandoned.
Hearing this, the owner demanded that the Sioux pay him
$25 for his loss. An amiable Sioux leader, Bear That Scat-
ters, offered two cows as reparation. This was refused.
Furthermore, the Army at nearby Fort Laramie intervened to insist on High Forehead's surrender. The next
day, brash young Brevet Second Lieutenant John L.
Grattan, a West Pointer who had bragged that he could
handle the red hordes single-handedly, marched into the
Sioux camp accompanied by 31 men. Negotiations broke
down when Bear That Scatters refused to surrender High
Forehead, who was a guest in his village. Suddenly,
Grattan's patience snapped, and he ordered his men to
fire into the Sioux village at point-blank range. Bear That
Scatters fell mortally wounded. After a second or two of
silence, hundreds of Lakota warriors leaped into battle
and every White man in the force was killed. Grattan's
face was smashed to a pulp with stones.

One year later, Brigadier-General William S. Harney
was sent to punish the "hostile" Sioux and fell on a village
on Blue Water Creek in Nebraska. Eighty-six Indians were
killed, and the village razed to the ground. The Indians
were staggered, for never before had a village been destroyed by the Whites' army. Watching the massacre from

the safety of a hill was a young Sioux boy, Curly. Afterwards, he went into the Sand Hills to find a vision, and
when it came it was a vision of himself as a warrior aboard
a flying horse, both untouched by the bullets and arrows
which thickened the air. Later the boy's father helped him
understand the dream: he would be a warrior who never
fell in battle, a warrior who would lead his people against
the Whites. He would also be given a new name: Crazy
Horse.

The peace of the plains was broken. But before the full
fury of Whites could be loosed on the Indians, the United
States began to bloodily rip itself apart in the debate over
slavery. In 1860 seven states (South Carolina, Mississippi,
Florida, Alabama, Louisiana, Georgia, and Texas) had
passed ordinances of secession and formed the Confederate States of America, later extended to include Virginia,
North Carolina, Tennessee, and Arkansas. A year later,
North and South were at war.

The conflict between the Union and the Confederacy
was both a disaster and a respite for the Native Americans. Those closest to the Whites' turmoil, the settled
tribes located in Indian Territory (Oklahoma), were those
most affected by it. Under threats and entreaties, the
tribes were obliged to sign to the respective causes of the
North and South. The Cherokees, one of the Five Civilized
Tribes forced to move to Indian Territory in the 1830s and
to become agriculturalists (hence their "civilized" status
in the eyes of the Whites), signed an alliance with the
Confederacy. Cherokee chief, Stand Watie, organized a
regiment with himself at the head and fought with the
South in the victory over the Union at Wilson's Creek in
Missouri in August 1861. More tribes – the Choctaws,
Chickasaws, Osage, Senecas, and Shawnees – cast their lot
in with the South, hoping that it would offer them a better
deal in the long run. (A not altogether foolish hope: del-

egates from the Choctaw-Chickasaw, Creek-Seminole and Cherokee nations sat in the Confederate Congress throughout the war; the US had extended the prospect of Indian seats in Congress as early as 1778, but had never implemented it.) Several tribes had their own Union versus South civil war. In 1863 they were joined by the Cherokee, when the majority of that nation rejected Stand Watie's Confederate treaty. Along with the Whites in the Civil War, the Indians bled plenty, too.

Less adversely affected by the Civil War were the Indians of the Far West. When the conflict commenced, the Army's forces in the West numbered around 10,000 men. The majority were quickly summoned to the East, which would be the main theatre of the war. Eventually, these regulars were replaced by large numbers of volunteers, highly motivated young men, keen on adventure, and keenest of all to "crack it to the Indians."

But in the meantime, some of the tribes of the West enjoyed the breathing space. And some decided to take advantage of the reduction in numbers of "blue coats" to go on the warpath. Among them were the Apache in the dry lands of the Southwest. The series of bloody confrontations between Native Americans and Whites, which would determine the future of the West, had begun.

War Comes to the Land
of Little Rain

The People Against the White Eyes

The Apache arrived in the arid, rugged country of the Southwest in a time before memory. The land was already occupied, by the Comanche and the Zuni, who were ruthlessly driven out. Known to themselves as "N'de" or "Dine" (meaning "people"), the newcomers were known to others by the Zuni word for enemy, *apachu*. Like the Zuni and Comanche, the Spanish found them an implacable foe, impossible to conquer and resistant to the overtures of the Church's black-robed friars.

Most feared of the Apache tribes were the Western and Chiricahua Apaches, nomads who lived primarily by raiding and hunting. They were as hardy as the mountain environment from which they sprang. A Chiricahua brave was expected to be able to run-and-walk 70 miles a day. Horses could not keep up. Even when he was in his forties the warrior Geronimo, a member of the Bedonkohe band of the Chiricahua, still ran on raids, trotting endlessly hour after hour.

If the big-lunged mountain Apaches valued brawn and the ability to endure beyond anything their enemies could conceive, they esteemed another quality more: cunning. This was the greatest virtue to the Apache. It ranked even higher than courage.

At first, relations between the Apache and the Anglo-Americans were cordial. The Apaché, with their bows and arrows, hardly merited a mention in the annual reports of the War Department in Washington. For their part, the Apache were more interested in pursuing their hereditary opponents, the Comanche and Mexicans, than the few "White Eyes" prospecting for metals in their New Mexico–Arizona homeland.

The fragile peace, however, was soon broken. Characteristically, it was the Anglo-Americans who began the trouble. One day in the late 1850s Mangas Coloradas ("Red Sleeves"), a chief of the Mimbreno band of the Chiricahua, made a friendly visit to miners at Pinos Altos in south-western New Mexico. The miners tied him to a tree and lashed him unconscious with a bullwhip. Unsurprisingly, he went on the warpath. He also requested the help of his son-in-law, Cochise, the great Chiricahua warrior chief.

The six-foot-tall Cochise soon had his own grudge against the Americans. In early 1861, Cochise was accused of stealing a White boy named Ward from a ranch near Buchanan. The boy (who later became a government scout known as Mickey Free) had in fact been stolen by Pinal Apaches. A Second Lieutenant George Bascom of the 7th Cavalry refused to believe Cochise's protestations of innocence, and took Cochise and his family hostage. Cochise escaped by pulling his knife, slashing a gash in the tent wall and jumping through. In an effort to free his relatives, Cochise captured a stage driver and two Americans from a wagon train and offered Bascom an exchange of prisoners. Bascom refused. The affair ended with Cochise killing the Whites he had taken, and Bascom hanging

three Indian hostages. (Hanging was the worst form of
death for an Indian, because it shut him out from the
warrior's afterlife.)

And so Cochise joined Mangas Coloradas on the warpath. "I was at peace with the Whites," said Cochise,
"until they tried to kill me for what other Indians did; now
I live and die at war with them."

It was a good time for war. The Whites were beginning
to shoot each other in their civil conflict, and New Mexico
was stripped of its troops and its forts evacuated. Rang-
ing from their mountain strongholds, the Chiricahuas
brought swift-striking death to wagon trains, mines,
ranches and small settlements. Estimates of White dead
were as high as 150 within two months. Many were
tortured, some burned alive, others having small pieces
of their body cut away until they died from shock or loss
of blood.

Settlers fled for their lives to safer regions – if they
could find them. For the Apache were not the only people
laying claim and waste to the Southwest. Confederate and
Union forces began to manoeuvre and skirmish in the
region. In 1862, in an effort to seize the desert country for
the federal cause, the Union sent out 1,800 Californian
Volunteers under General James Carleton. Their eastwards
route lay through Apache Pass.

Alerted by his scouts, Cochise decided to ambush the
White soldiers in the gorge. He was joined by Mangas
Coloradas and 700 Apaches, the largest force the People
had ever raised. Many were armed with rifles, taken from
dead Whites.

On 14 July 1862, an advance party of 123 Californian
Volunteers entered the pass. The ambush should have
been deadly, but the Volunteers under Captain Thomas L.
Roberts had two mountain howitzers in tow. Quickly
Roberts trained these on the Apache positions. The Indi-

ans had never encountered shellfire before, and withdrew.

Mangas Coloradas, as he retreated, was shot in the chest. The wound was not fatal, but it caused him to tire of fighting. Less than a year after Apache Pass, he decided to take up the American offer of peace. The old chief walked trustingly and alone into Pinos Altos. Brevet General Joseph West ordered him seized, telling his guards: "I want him dead or alive tomorrow morning. Understand? I want him dead."

A miner walking about the camp related what happened next: "About 9 o'clock I noticed the soldiers were doing something to Mangas. I discovered that they were heating their bayonets in the fire and burning his feet and legs. Mangas rose upon his left elbow, angrily protesting that he was no child to be played with." Whereon the guards shot him dead. Afterwards, he was scalped and decapitated. The official euphemism for the event was "resisting arrest". Even other Army soldiers were appalled. General Nelson Miles declared Mangas Coloradas "foully murdered".

The fate of Mangas Coloradas only encouraged Cochise to stay on the warpath. Apache Pass had taught him a valuable, if harsh, lesson – never to confront well-armed troops in open combat. Henceforth, Cochise's war would be a guerrilla struggle, in which the Apache would come and go like the wind. He was joined by other Apache notables, among them the Warm Springs chiefs Victorio and Nana, and the warrior leader Geronimo. Soon the Gila River country of south Arizona was swept clean of ranchers. The exception was Pete Kitchen, who turned his hilltop adobe ranch into a fortress, and was left alone. Elsewhere Apache raids continued unabated.

On the Long Walk

Nor were the Apache the only Indians in the turquoise-skyed Southwest on the warpath. The evacuation of Fort Defiance had given the pastoralist Navajo – linguistic and cultural kindred of the Apache – the opportunity to do some profitable plundering. A single raid in 1863 netted them 20,000 sheep.

A crisis was upon the White man in the "land of little rain". Thus, when it became apparent that the Union's 1862 victory at Glorieta Pass in New Mexico (the largest Civil War battle in the Far West) had effectively ended the chances of Confederate control in the region, federal forces turned to fighting the Indians. Brigadier-General H. Carleton directed his old friend, ex-mountain man Colonel Kit Carson of the New Mexico volunteers, to invade the lands of the Apache and the Navajo. By the end of March 1863, Carson had rounded up more than 400 Mescalero Apaches and sent them to the new reservation at Bosque Redondo, a 40-mile square tract of semi-arid land next to the military outpost of Fort Sumner.

Next, Carson moved to subdue the Navajo, a nation 10,000 strong. His message to the Navajo was brief: "Go to Bosque Redondo, or we will pursue and destroy you. We will not make peace with you on any other terms."

Carson was as good as his word. After starving the Navajo into submission by destroying their livestock, crops and orchards, the Americans invaded their Canyon de Chelly citadel. In the spring of 1864 6,000 Navajo surrendered. They were marched 300 miles to the Bosque ("Hweeldi" in Apache), an event that became known to them as the "Long Walk". The land at Bosque Redondo was too poor to support the Indians incarcerated there. Navajo starved and fell ill. Many times was their healing chant, the "Blessing Way" sung, the concluding lines of which run:

> May it be beautiful before me
> May it be beautiful behind me
> May it be beautiful all around me
> In beauty may I walk
> In beauty it is finished.

Such words fortified not only the patient but also the whole people. The Navajo would endure to return to their homeland in 1868 and become one of the most populous Native American tribes.

Colonel Kit Carson, meanwhile, having obtained the surrender of the Navajo, had been sent hot-foot in 1864 to the southern plains, where Kiowa and Comanche raiders had stolen five boys from a wagon train on the Santa Fe trail. At Adobe Walls, an abandoned trading post in the Texas Panhandle, Carson and his 350 volunteers and 75 Ute scouts ran into a thousand Comanche and Kiowa warriors. Carson's force was saved by two howitzers. With two dead and ten wounded Carson claimed victory – and got out of the Canadian River valley as quickly as honour would let him.

If Carson intended to send the Kiowa and Comanche to Bosque Redondo he was disappointed. Proving similarly difficult to capture was Cochise and his Chiricahuas, who were trading atrocity for atrocity with the miners and army. The toll Cochise took was heavy, but not heavy enough. Whatever he did, White emigrants still came through the "land of little rain" and miners still dug for metal. "We kill ten; a hundred come in their place," Cochise lamented to his warriors.

For a long, bloody decade Cochise fought the White man, but when he saw it was to no avail he decided to make peace. Other Apache leaders, like Nana and Victorio, had already surrendered, after a relentless pursuit conducted largely by Black troopers. Yet while the army pursued him, Cochise seemed to have no option but to carry on fighting.

Then something happened which brought a softening in government attitude to the Apache. Early in the morning of 30 April 1871, a mob of Americans, Mexicans and Papago Indians massacred 128 unarmed Arivapa Apache near Tucson, in revenge for raids carried out by other Apaches. Twenty-nine of the Arivapa children were taken as slaves. Although the participants in the massacre were tried and acquitted in Tucson, Eastern humanitarians applied pressure on the government to stop such slaughter. Congress voted $70,000 for the "collecting of the Apaches of Arizona and New Mexico upon reservations, furnishing them with subsistence and other necessary articles, and to promote peace and civilisation among them." General George Crook was assigned to Arizona with orders to deal firmly but fairly with the Apache. A year later, Crook was succeeded by one-armed General Oliver O. Howard, who arrived with full powers to make peace. For help, Howard sought out Thomas Jeffords, the superintendent of mail between Tucson and Fort Bowie. The flame-haired New Yorker was the one White man Cochise called friend, a friendship begun when Jeffords had courageously ridden alone into Cochise's camp and asked the chief not to kill his drivers. In respect to Jeffords' personal courage, he did not.

The intensely moral General Howard won Jefford's approval, and the two went to meet Cochise in the mountains. After 11 days of negotiation, a deal was struck. Cochise agreed to stop fighting and enter a reservation in the Dragoon mountain if Jeffords was appointed agent for the Chiricahua. The terms were met. Also entering into the agreement was the warrior leader Geronimo, whose small band of Bedonkohe Apache had been virtually assimilated into the Chiricahua. Geronimo served as escort to Howard as he left the mountains, riding double on the general's horse. A war that had cost the United States 1,000 dead and $40 million was over.

Cochise was not privileged to enjoy his peace for long. In 1874, in his fifty-first year, he was taken mortally ill. He died with Jeffords by his side. Cochise's warriors painted him in yellow, black and vermilion, shrouded him in a red blanket, propped him on his favourite horse and took him deep into the mountains. His body was buried in a crevice whose location they never revealed.

The great chief of the Chiricahua Apache was dead, but the peace he agreed for his people endured.

For a while.

The Great Sioux Uprising

In the Civil War summer of 1862, the agricultural state of Minnesota looked to be one of the quieter places on the continent. The bulk of the internecine fighting was going on in the East and in the Missouri–Kansas border country, while the Indian frontiers were far away on the Great Plains and in the Southwest. The most unexpected event was a rising by the peaceful Santee Sioux who lived on a reservation along the Minnesota River.

The Santee (or eastern) Sioux had remained in Minnesota when their relatives migrated to the buffalo plains in the eighteenth century. Over time, the government had acquired all their land, save for a barren strip 150 miles long and 10 miles wide on the south side of the Minnesota River. The payment for the Santee's many land cessions, which totalled 26 million acres, was an annual government cash allotment that barely kept them alive.

In June 1862, the annuity failed to arrive. To make matters worse, cutworms had devastated the tribe's previous year's corn crop. Local merchants refused to extend credit, or to equip the Indians for their privilege of an annual summer buffalo hunt on the Dakota range. "If they are hungry," the trader Andrew Myrick said of the Santee Sioux, "let them eat grass or their own dung."

By August, the 12,000 Santee crowded on the reservation were starving. The 52-year-old leader of the Santee, Little Crow (Ta-oya-te-duta), tried to warn the Whites that trouble was coming: "We have waited a long time. We have no food, but here are stores, filled with food. We ask you: make some arrangement by which we can get food, or we will keep ourselves from starving." On 8 August, bands of Santee at the Upper Agency looted the government warehouse. But still nobody expected an uprising. It began with an incident that would have been trivial but for its bitter consequences.

On Sunday 17 August, a small group of Sioux warriors returned from an unsuccessful hunt in the "Big Woods" along the Mississippi. As they passed through the settlements, one found some eggs belonging to a farmer's hen. Another cautioned him against taking the property of a White man. The group then fell to arguing and boasting, with one warrior insisting that he would prove he was unafraid of the White man by killing one – and dared his comrades to do the same. Arriving at a farm where some families had gathered for a Sunday visit, the Santee warriors challenged the White men gathered there to a shooting contest. When the White men had emptied their rifles, the Indians turned on the hosts and killed three men and two women. The murderers then rode to the reservation and reported their crime to Little Crow. A council was called.

The Indians debated all night. Some chiefs, among them Wabasha and Wacouta, spoke for peace. So did Little Crow. "The White men," said Little Crow, "are like the locusts when they fly so thick that the whole sky is a snowstorm . . . We are only little herds of buffaloes left scattered." Some argued that the time for war was never better, with so many able-bodied Whites away on battlefields fighting each other. Finally, the council declared for war. Little Crow, to retain his leadership, put himself at the head of the hostiles. "Little Crow is not a coward," he said, "he will die with you."

At dawn the next day, Monday 18 August, scores of braves attacked the Lower Agency. "Kill the Whites! Kill all the Whites!" shouted Little Crow. Twenty-three White men were shot and stabbed. One of the first to die was Andrew Myrick, his body mutilated, his mouth stuffed full with prairie grass.

From the Lower Agency, bands of Santee fanned out to the Upper Agency and into the surrounding countryside. Whites were hauled from their homes and fields. Few had time to pull a gun. Men – unless judged to be friends – were summarily dispatched. Women were held captive and raped. "They came down upon us like the wind," one survivor remembered.

A few fugitives reached Fort Ridgely on the north side of the Minnesota River and raised the alarm. With more courage than judgement, the commander took out 47 of his men – more than half of his depleted force – to engage the Sioux. At the river, he ran into an ambush and his men were all but wiped out. The Santee lost one brave – their only casualty in the whole of the first day. Whites losses ran at 400.

By Wednesday 20 August, when Little Crow finally mounted an attack on Fort Ridgely, the post had been reinforced. (Among the reinforcements were the guards of the coach carrying the delayed annuity.) The defenders threw back the Santee, who lost over a hundred warriors. As one of the Santee said years later: "But the defenders of the fort were very brave and kept the door shut." Frustrated at the fort, Little Crow launched an all-out attack on the town of New Ulm. Throughout 23 August, Little Crow's men besieged New Ulm, despite withering fire from the militia. The town was reduced to ashes. Thirty-six Whites died. The survivors abandoned the town and picked their way eastward to Mankato.

The settlements of Western Minnesota and Eastern Dakota were now in a state of fear. Thirty thousand settlers evacuated their homes and fled to Mankato and other White population centres. "You have no idea," wrote General John Pope to the War Department, "of the uncontrollable panic everywhere in this country. The most horrible massacres have been committed; children nailed alive to trees and houses; women violated and then disembowelled – everything that horrible ingenuity could devise."

It took two weeks for Minnesota to calm down enough to organize a militia to take the field against the Santee. This was placed under the command of Colonel Henry Sibley, a former fur trader, who advanced towards the Santee at a snail's pace. The Indians continued their raids, adding more to their toll of dead Whites. By conservative estimate, the Santee eventually killed 500 Whites.

The Indians won several skirmishes with the slowly approaching militia. Then, on 22 September, after failing to spring a planned ambush, Little Crow was beaten in battle by the 1,600-strong militia near Wood Lake. The warring Santee fled back to the reservation, packed their tipis and debated what to do with their pitiful captives. Eventually, these were left in the care of those Santee who had not embarked on hostilities. Little Crow and most of his warriors left for the Plains.

If Colonel Sibley was slow to fight, he was quick to avenge. By October 2,000 Santee had been rounded up, many of them Santees from the Upper Agency who had refused to participate in the rising. Four hundred of the gathered Santee were tried by military commission, some cases receiving as few as five minutes. The trials ended with 307 Santee sentenced to die, who were hauled to Mankato for hanging.

Most Minnesotans were eager to see the convicted Indians hang, but one kept his humanity. Episcopal Bishop Henry B. Whipple appealed to President Lincoln for mercy: "I ask," he wrote, "that the people shall lay the blame . . . where it belongs, and . . . demand the reform of an atrocious Indian system which has always garnered for us . . . anguish and blood."

Lincoln commuted the sentences of those Sioux condemned to die merely because they had partaken of battle. Still, 38 were taken out into the chilly morning of 26 December and hanged from a special scaffold, constructed so that all the traps would drop by the cutting of a single rope. Those who died, their bodies jerking grotesquely in the air, included Cut Nose, who claimed he had killed Whites "till his arm tired." Alongside him were three innocent men accidentally put to death when their names were confused with those of the condemned. While waiting to die a warrior called Little Six (Shakapee) is said to have heard the shriek of a train whistle in the distance and said: "As the White man comes in, the Indian goes out."

Thereafter there were a few desultory raids by Santee still free and hostile, but in the summer of 1863 two settlers near Hutchinson, Minnesota, caught Little Crow picking raspberries in a field and shot him dead. They shot him not because he was Little Crow but because he was an Indian. When his body was identified, the Minnesota legislature paid $575 for Little Crow's scalp, and then put it on display in a museum. Another chief was caught and hanged at Fort Snelling.

The Santee reservation by the Minnesota River was then wiped off the map, and 2,000 Santee – hostile or otherwise – were herded into a tiny reservation along the Missouri River, alongside 3,000 Winnebago Indians. During the first winter, 400 Indians died of starvation and disease.

The Great Sioux Uprising – the biggest Indian insurrection since Wampanoag King Philip had set the Massachusetts frontier aflame in 1675 – was over. But the climactic struggle between the Indians and Whites had barely passed its first rounds.

Sand Creek

I have come to kill Indians, and believe that it is right and honourable to use any means under God's heaven to kill Indians.

Colonel John Chivington, 3rd Colorado Volunteers

The area around Pike's Peak in Colorado had long been rumoured to be rich in gold, and in 1858 a small group of prospectors hit pay dirt. The cry went up "Gold in Colorado!" and wagon trains of frenzied prospectors rolled west in wagons daubed with the defiant slogan "Pike's Peak or Bust!"

To the prospectors swarming into Colorado one thing was apparent: the region's Indians were an obstacle, possibly a dangerous one. They would have to go.

The Southern Cheyenne and the Arapaho were themselves relatively recent arrivals to the plains, both being Algonquin-speakers from the Great Lakes area. Not until the early 1800s had the Cheyenne accumulated enough horses to become a truly equine people of the interior plains. Their nomadic scattered lifestyle meant that the Cheyenne avoided some of the worst smallpox and cholera epidemics. In the mid-nineteenth century their population stood at around 20,000. A people with a highly elaborate moral code, the Cheyenne were relatively free of crime, and any transgressors were more likely to be rehabilitated than punished. But a murderer left undiscovered, they believed, would smell bad and keep away the buffalo.

The Cheyenne and Arapaho might have been late in getting to Colorado country, but they were determined to keep it. As more and more prospectors swarmed onto tribal land – more than 50,000 of them by 1859 – the Indians became resentful and hostile. Treaty commissioners managed to persuade some Cheyenne and Arapaho to move onto a small reservation in eastern Colorado, but the younger war leaders refused.

All through the winter of 1864 wisps of rumour of an Indian war floated up and down the Denver road. These were deliberately fanned by Major-General Samuel R. Curtis, Army commander of the Kansas and Colorado department, who wanted any pretext to drive the Indians out. So did Colonel John Chivington, the fiery Methodist-preacher-turned-soldier who had led the Union to victory at Glorieta Pass. Now commander of the District of Colorado, Chivington was eager to try out his new-found appetite for war on the Cheyenne.

Nothing Lives Long

The excuse to "punish" the Cheyenne and Arapaho came on 7 April 1864. Chivington reported to Curtis that the Cheyenne had raided 175 cattle from a ranch on the Smoky Hill trail. Later, a thorough investigation would find no evidence of Indian theft.

Chivington was in the field within days of reporting the "theft". In his pocket he had an order from Governor John Evans, another ruthless Indian-hater, to "burn villages and kill Cheyenne whenever and wherever found."

By early June, Chivington's brutal campaign had razed four unsuspecting Cheyenne villages. One of his junior officers had also shot Chief Lean Bear, a peaceful Cheyenne who had walked up to the White man proudly wearing a medal the Great Father in Washington had given him. Arapahoes, who had tried to intercede in a dispute between the Army and some Kiowa, were fired on. Soon half the Cheyenne and Arapaho in Colorado were on the warpath.

The first retaliatory blow was struck at a ranch outside Denver. A family named Hungate was murdered, their bodies mutilated. The corpses were taken to Denver and placed on display. The town went wild with fear and fury. Traffic on the trails was attacked, Cheyenne and Arapaho bands virtually cutting Denver off from the outside world. During three weeks in August, 50 people were killed on the Platte route alone.

With Denver near famine, the War Department authorized Governor Evans to raise a special regiment of Indian fighting volunteers who would serve for 100 days. The 3rd Colorado Regiment (the"Hundred Dazers") under the command of "the Fighting Parson" Colonel Chivington was still being mustered, however, when peace suddenly broke out.

Some of the Cheyenne chiefs had tired of war; some had never wanted it. Using the offices of George Bent, a half-White living with the Cheyenne, the chiefs sent a letter to Major Edward W. Wynkoop at Fort Lyon offering an end to hostilities:

> We held a counsel . . . and all came to the conclusion to make peace with you providing you make peace with the Kiowas, Comences, Arropohoes Apaches and Siouxs. We are going to send a message to the Kiowas . . . about our going to make [peace] with you. We heard that you [have]

some prisoners in Denver. We have seven prisoners of
you which we are willing to give up providing you give
up yours. There are three war parties out yet, and two of
Arropohoes; they have been out some time and expected
in soon. When we held this counsel there were few
Arropohoes and Siouxs present; we want news from you
in return. (That is a letter)

Signed BLACK KETTLE and Other Chiefs

Wynkoop, a decent and able officer, saw a chance to
avert bloodshed. He visited Black Kettle, persuaded him
to release four prisoners, and encouraged him to go to
Denver and consult with the Governor.

On 28 September, the genial and aged Black Kettle rode
into Camp Weld near Denver to talk peace. After conced-
ing his inability to control some of his younger warriors,
Black Kettle agreed to settle at Fort Lyon with those
Cheyenne and Arapaho who would follow him. There he
would be protected by Major Wynkoop. The Indian left
the meeting believing he had made a peace deal.

Peace was the last thing the Indian-hating Colonel
Chivington wanted. If he was to use his hundred-day
men he had to use them soon. He complained to General
Curtis about Wynkoop's conciliatory policy and got him
replaced at Fort Lyon by Major Scott J. Anthony. In the
presence of other officers at Fort Lyon, the newly arrived
Anthony told Black Kettle that he would continue to be
protected by the Army. Allegedly to enable the surrendered Cheyenne and Arapaho to do some hunting,
Anthony directed them to move their village to an almost
dry watercourse about 40 miles to the north-east: Sand
Creek.

Anthony had moved the Indians to a place where they
could be inconspicuously massacred. Chivington and
his 3rd Colorado Volunteers reached Fort Lyon on 28

November. Major Anthony and 125 men of his garrison joined them. Some officers protested violently when they learned what Chivington and Anthony intended to do. Chivington cursed them as spies and traitors, no better than Indians.

At daybreak on the clear frosty morning of 29 November 1864, Colonel Chivington and 700 soldiers approached Black Kettle's camp. When a junior officer again protested that the Cheyenne were at peace, Chivington roared back: "I have come to kill Indians, and believe that it is right and honourable to use any means under God's heaven to kill Indians." His troops were ordered to "Kill and scalp all, big and little; nits make lice."

The sleeping Indians were given no warning, no chance for talk. Chivington's men simply bore down on them, firing their rifles, slashing into the sleeping tents. There was confusion and noise. Black Kettle, unable to comprehend what was happening, ran up the Stars and Stripes outside his tent. Then a white flag of surrender. Still the killing continued.

Some of the Indians ran into the sand hills and frantically dug pits in the banks in which to hide. The troops pursued them, and shot into the pits. To prevent an escape, the Americans cut off the horse herd. Nevertheless, a few Indians ran as far as five miles to escape the slaughter – and were still cut down. A lost child crying for its family was used for target practice.

There was little chance for the dazed Cheyenne and Arapaho to fight back. They had surrendered most of their guns to Wynkoop days before. Those warriors who had arms and could use them fought desperately. Major Anthony himself said: "I never saw such bravery displayed by any set of people on the face of the earth than by these Indians. They would charge on the whole company singly, determined to kill someone before being killed themselves." Chief White Antelope refused to flee or fight. He stood in front of his tipi and sang his death song, "Nothing lives long / Except the earth and the mountains," until he was killed.

A few soldiers, almost all from the 1st Colorado, refused to join the slaughter, or the mutilation of the Indians' bodies which occurred afterwards. "It looked too hard for me," Captain Silas Soule wrote, "to see little children on their knees begging for their lives, having their brains beaten out like dogs."

Another soldier, Lieutenant James Connor, recorded:

> In going over the battleground, I did not see a body of a man, woman or child but was scalped, and in many instances, their bodies were mutilated in the most horrible manner. I heard of numerous instances in which men had cut out the private parts of females and stretched them over the saddlebows and wore them over their hats while riding in the ranks.

By the end of the day, 28 men and 105 women and children lay dead at Sand Creek. Among those who escaped was Black Kettle, his badly injured wife on his back.

When the soldiers returned to Denver the town went into a delirium of joy. "Colorado soldiers", the *Rocky Mountain News* declared, "have again covered themselves with glory . . . the Colonel [Chivington] is a credit to Colorado and the West." Cheyenne scalps were strung across the stage of the Denver Opera House during intermission, to standing applause.

On the Great Plains, the shock waves from Sand Creek rolled westwards. Already agitated by the Minnesota Sioux uprising, the tribes fell to anger and a desperate revenge. Plains Indians rarely fought in winter, but now they made an exception. In January 1865, a combined military expedition of Cheyenne, Northern Arapaho, Oglala and Brulé Sioux – 1,600 picked warriors and one of the greatest cavalry forces the world had ever seen – whipped into Colorado. Fort Rankin suffered severe losses. The town of Julesburg was sacked twice, the outskirts of Denver threatened. Seventy-five miles of the South Platte Trail was wrecked. Ranches and stations were burnt, wagon trains captured and more people killed than Chivington had slain at Sand Creek.

The Sand Creek massacre caused outrage in the East, and bolstered the movement for Indian reform. A Military Investigation Commission condemned Chivington and his soldiers, but the colonel escaped punishment because he had left the army. (The most damaging witness, Captain Silas Soule, was murdered before the Commission finished its business, probably with Chivington's connivance.) Congress approved the report, and added more testimony to it.

In July 1865, Senator James Doolittle of Wisconsin went out to Denver to argue the case for a peaceful solution to the Indian problem. The choice, he told a capacity crowd at the Denver Opera House, was to put the Indians on adequate reservations where they might support themselves, or to exterminate them. The audience, Doolittle later wrote, gave "a shout almost loud enough to raise the roof of the Opera House – 'Exterminate them! Exterminate them! Exterminate them!'"

Punishment

Three months before Senator Doolittle had the roof of the Denver Opera House raised on him, the Civil War had come to an end. On 9 April 1865, in the front parlour of Wilmer McLean's farmhouse at Appomattox, Virginia, Robert E. Lee surrendered to Ulysses S. Grant. Now the

North versus South conflict was over, Union officers turned their faces towards the land of the setting sun to unite the nation East and West.

Top of their agenda was "punishment" of the Sioux, Northern Cheyenne and Arapaho, whose rampage through Colorado had been followed by a mass raid on the great overland trail on the Platte and North Platte. In July 1865 3,000 warriors had fallen on the Platte Bridge (now Casper, Wyoming), wiping out a train of dismounted cavalry.

The Army began a determined effort to defeat the Indians of the North Plains, sending General Patrick E. Connor and 3,000 troops to destroy the Indians in their Powder River camps. Connor instructed his junior officers not to "receive overtures of peace or submission" but "to kill every male Indian over 12 years of age." Connor was a seasoned Indian fighter, having defeated the trail-harassing Shoshonis at Bear River (Idaho) in 1863, but he would not have his way in the Powder River country. All summer the Indians harried his columns, took his horses and vanished into the buttes before they could be engaged. Some of his detachments got hopelessly lost, the men died of scurvy and were lamed by cactus spines. Already exhausted by the Civil War, soldiers deserted by the drove.

General Connor was deprived of his command for failing to punish the elusive Indians. But before he left the northern plains he built a fort, Fort Reno, on a road which had recently been blazed to the goldfields of Montana by John M. Bozeman. The Bozeman Trail would be the subject of the next great fight between the Whites and the Cheyenne, Arapaho and their Sioux allies. A fight the Indians would win.

Red Cloud's War

They made us many promises, more than I can remember, but they never kept but one. They promised to take our land, and they took it.

Red Cloud (Makhpiya-Luta), Oglala Sioux chief

Fort Phil Kearny was established amid hostilities. No disaster other than the usual incidents to border warfare occurred, until gross disobedience of orders sacrificed nearly eighty of the choice men of my command . . . In the grave I bury disobedience.

Colonel Henry B. Carrington, US Army

The Fort Laramie council held in June 1866 was a magnificent spectacle. To either side of the fort, set between the Laramie and Platte rivers in the heart of Sioux country, tipis stretched for a mile or more, smoke wisping out of their tops into the sunshine. Hundreds of ponies were corralled, knots of Indians came and went, and from a staff at the corner of the sod parade ground the Stars and Stripes flapped languidly in the breeze. On a temporary platform sat officials of the federal government and the leading chiefs of the Cheyenne, Arapaho, and the Brulé, Miniconjou and Oglala sub-bands of the Teton Sioux.

Prominent on the platform was the 44-year-old Oglala chief Red Cloud (Makhpiya-Luta), a warrior with 80 coups to his name. For three years "Bad Faces" led by Red Cloud had been attacking parties of Whites travelling the Bozeman Trail to the Montana goldfields. The Trail ran through the heart of the Powder River country, the last unviolated buffalo range of the Sioux and their allies. The Laramie council had been called to bribe Red Cloud and the other warring bands into selling the road.

The talks began promisingly. In return for the safe passage of Whites on the Bozeman Trail, the government promised the Indians $75,000 a year and an assurance that their land would never be taken by force. Then Colonel Henry Beebe Carrington rolled into the fort at the head of a long column of wagons and men. When a chief asked where he was going, Carrington explained that he was to construct two more forts on the trail, both deep into Teton Sioux country. At this news, Red Cloud exploded with anger: "The Great Father sends us presents and wants us to sell him the road, but White chief goes with soldiers to steal the road before Indians say Yes or No! I will talk with you no more! I will go now, and I will fight you! As long as I live I will fight you for the last hunting grounds of my people!"

With that, Red Cloud stormed off the platform. Within days, the Army would realize the truth of Red Cloud's words.

"Character of Indian Affairs Hostile"

On 22 June, Colonel Carrington and the 700-strong Eighteenth Infantry, plus assorted civilian woodchoppers and a number of wives and children, marched out of Fort Laramie for the Powder River country. On the 28th, Carrington reached Fort Reno on the Bozeman Trail. The next afternoon Indians ran off nearly all the fort's horses and mules.

Security was tightened. The expedition went on, through a heat so profound that it caused the wheels of the wagons to shrink and fall apart. At Crazy Woman's Creek nine men deserted for the Montana goldfields. A detail sent after them was stopped on the Trail by a band of Cheyenne who refused to let them pass.

Still Carrington pressed on. At the fork to the Little Piney he pitched camp and started to build Fort Phil Kearny. The scout Jim Bridger, accompanying the expedition, argued against it: the hills on all sides shut out any view, and the nearest wood was five miles away. He was overruled by the military.

While Fort Phil Kearny was being built, Carrington dispatched two companies north to build a smaller stockade, Fort C.F. Smith, on the Bighorn. With Fort Reno, Carrington then had three forts to guard the Bozeman Trail. But his men were spread terribly thin.

Red Cloud used a familiar Indian strategy. There were no full frontal attacks. There were ambushes, lightning raids, and constant sniping. A steady attrition of White men and morale.

Some of Red Cloud's tactics, however, were dangerously novel. He even taught some of his warriors a few words of English and dressed them in captured blue uniforms, all the better to confuse the enemy when they pursued him.

By August, Carrington's soldiers at Fort Phil Kearny were being scalped and wounded at the rate of one per day. When the photographer-correspondent Ridgeway Glover of *Frank Leslie's Illustrated Paper* wandered away from the post he was found naked, his back cleaved open by a tomahawk (The naive, daydreaming Glover had survived a desperate ambush by 160 Sioux at Crazy Woman's Creek only days before and thought he was "Indian-proof".) But even soldiers inside the growing fort were not safe. One was shot as he sat in the latrine. The garrisons were too besieged to protect traffic. In his first five weeks in the Powder River country, Carrington reported that 33 travellers were killed on the Bozeman road.

Carrington was reduced to ever more desperate orders to tighten vigilance. After a sequence of attacks on his woodcutters, hay mowers and the driving off of the fort's beef herd, Carrington issued a special order on 13 September (to the Indians, the month of the "Drying Grass Moon"):

1. Owing to recent depredation of Indians near Fort Philip Kearny, Dak., the post commander [Ten Eyck] will issue such regulation and at once provide such additional escorts for wood trains, guard for stock and hay and the steam saw-mills as the chief quartermaster [Brown] may deem essential. He will also give

2. Instructions, so that upon Indian alarm no troops leave the post without an officer or under the antecedent direction of an officer, and the garrison will be so organized that it may at all times be available and disposable for exterior duty or interior defence.

3. One relief of the guard will promptly support any picket threatened at night, and the detail on posts should be visited hourly by a non-commissioned officer of the guard between the hours of posting successive reliefs.

4. Stringent regulations are enjoined to prevent camp rumors and false reports, and any picket or soldier bringing reports of Indian sign or hostilities must be required to report to the post commander or officer of the day or to the nearest commissioned officer in cases of urgent import.

5. Owing to the non-arrival of corn for the post and the

present reduced condition of the public stock, the quartermaster is authorized upon the approval of the post commander, to purchase sufficient corn for moderate issues, to last until a supply already due, shall arrive, but the issue will be governed by the condition of the stock, and will only be issued to horses unless the same in half ration shall be necessary for such mules as are daily in use and can not graze or be furnished with hay.

6. Reports will be made of all Indian depredations, with the results, in order that a proper summary may be sent to department headquarters.

7. Soldiers while on duty in the timber or elsewhere are forbidden to waste ammunition in hunting, every hour of their time being indispensable in preparing for their own comfort and the well-being of the garrison during the approaching winter.

More Indian attacks brought more instructions from Carrington to tighten defensive measures. The Commander was in a dithering panic, reduced to ever more obsessional treatises on security. A special order of 21 September 1866 read:

The fastenings of all gates must be finished this day; the locks for large gates will be similar, and the district commander, post commander, officer of the day, and quartermaster will alone have keys. Keys for the wicket gates will be with the same officers.

Upon a general alarm or appearance of Indians in force or near the gates, the same will be closed, and no soldier or civilian will leave the fort without orders.

No large gate will be opened, except the quartermaster gate, unless it shall be necessary for wagons. Stock must invariably pass in and out of that gate.

The west or officers' gate will not be opened without permission, even for wagons, unless for timber wagons or ambulances, or mounted men.

Upon a general alarm the employees in the sutlers' department will form at the store and wait for orders and assignment to some part of the interior defence, but will not be expected to act without the fort unless voluntarily, and then after sanction is given, and under strict military control.

All soldiers, however detailed or attached, or in whatever capacity serving, will, upon a general alarm, take arms and be subject to immediate disposal with their companies or at the headquarters or department with which serving.

All horses of mounted men will be saddled at reveille.

. It is also expressly enjoined that in no case shall there be needless running in haste upon an alarm. Shouting, talebearing, and gross perversion of facts by excited men does more mischief than Indians. And the duty of guards being to advise of danger, soldiers who have information must report to the proper officer, and not to comrades.

At the sounding of assembly the troops of the garrison not on daily duty will form in front of their respective quarters.

The general alarm referred to in foregoing paragraph will be indicated by the sound of the assembly, followed by three quick shots from the guard-house, which latter will be the distinction between the general alarm and the simple alarm for turning out the troops of the garrison.

This order will be placed upon a bulletin-board for early and general information.

Officers and non-commissioned officers are charged with its execution, and the soldiers of the 18th Infantry are especially called upon to vindicate and maintain, as they ever have, the record of their regiment.

This will require much hard work, much guard duty, and much patience, but they will have an honorable field to occupy in this country, and both Indian outrages and approaching winter stimulate them to work, and work with zeal and tireless industry.

Their colonel will with his officers share all, and no idling or indifference can, under these circumstances, have any quarters in the breast of a true soldier.

In addition to his instructions on fort security, Carrington kept up a steady stream of complaining missives to his superiors. A report to General Philip St George Cooke, Commander of the Department of the Platte, informed him:

Character of Indian affairs hostile. The treaty does not yet benefit this route [Some tribes did sign the 1866 Fort Laramie agreement] . . . My ammunition has not yet arrived; neither has my Leavenworth supply train . . . My infantry make poor riders . . . I am equal to any attack they [the Indians] may make, but have to build quarters and prepare for winter, escort trains, and guaranty the whole road from the Platte to Virginia City with eight companies of infantry. I have to economize ammunition . . . I sent two officers out on recruiting service, under peremptory orders from Washington, leaving me crippled and obliged to trust too much to non-commissioned officers . . .

Carrington's pleas fell on deaf ears. Cooke fully understood the impossibility of his Colonel's position.

But if Cooke was deaf and Carrington a ditherer, the special responsibility for the disaster that was to ensue lay elsewhere.

Slaughter at Lodge Trail Ridge

In November 1866 a young infantry captain named William Judd Fetterman joined Carrington's staff at Fort Phil Kearny. A dashing Civil War hero who had been breveted Lieutenant-Colonel, Fetterman had little respect for his cautious commanding officer, a former attorney who had served the conflict behind a desk as an administrator. Fetterman had even less regard for the Indians around the fort. "Give me a single company of regulars," he bragged "and I can whip a thousand Indians. With eighty men I could ride through the Sioux nation."

By December 1866, Red Cloud and the other senior chief of the Oglala Sioux, Man-Afraid-of-His-Horses (more accurately translated as "the mere sight of his horses inspires fear"), were ready to give Fetterman his opportunity to prove his boast. They were joined by Black Shield of the Miniconjou, Roman Nose and Medicine Man of the Cheyenne, and Little Chief and Sorrel Horse of the Arapaho. Around 2,000 warriors moved into the foothills around Fort Phil Kearny. For two weeks they tantalized the soldiers, riding on the skyline just out of rifle range, creeping around the fort at night howling like wolves, springing small attacks, but always keeping their main force hidden.

The soldiers' nerves were stretched to breaking point.

Then on 20 December the Sioux and their allies camped on Prairie Dog Creek and began the ceremonies which preceded battle. A hermaphrodite medicine man rode off over the hills and returned to tell of a vision in which he had caught a hundred soldiers in his hands. The warriors beat the ground with their hands in approval and selected the leaders for the next day's battle. The task of leading the all-important decoy party fell to a young warrior named Crazy Horse.

At daybreak on 21 December, the Indians moved into position. The decoy rode towards Fort Phil Kearny, while the remainder prepared an ambush on either side of Lodge Trail Ridge. The Cheyenne and Arapaho took the west side, and some Sioux hid in the grass opposite. Still more Sioux remained mounted, hidden behind rocks.

Meanwhile, at the fort, Carrington had sent out the customary train of wagons to cut wood. The morning was beautiful, with the snow around the fort sparkling in the brilliant sunshine, but as though he had some premonition of danger, Carrington attached an extra guard to the train. About eleven o'clock look-outs on top of Pilot Hill started signalling frantically that the wood train was under attack.

Carrington ordered a relief party of cavalry and infantry to assemble. As it was about to move out under the command of Captain J. W. Powell, Fetterman stepped before Carrington and demanded permission to lead the relief instead of Powell. Fetterman pointed out that because of his brevet rank of Lieutenant-Colonel he technically outranked Powell. For a second Carrington hesitated, then gave Fetterman the command.

Knowing Fetterman's rashness, Carrington warned him that the Indians were a cunning and desperate enemy. Then he gave him exact orders: "Support the wood train, relieve it and report to me. Do not engage or pursue the Indians at its expense. Under no circumstances pursue over Lodge Trail Ridge."

As the relief started to move out, Carrington sprang up onto the sentry walk by the gate and repeated his order to Fetterman: "Under no circumstances must you cross Lodge Trail Ridge." Fetterman acknowledged the order, and the relief moved quickly out of sight. Fetterman had with him 80 men – all he needed to "ride through the Sioux nation."

When Fetterman got to the wood train, the Indians had

apparently disappeared. But moments later, the decoy party under Crazy Horse rushed out of the brush, yipping and waving blankets. The soldiers opened fire, but the Indians merely cantered up close, taunting the White men. At least once, Crazy Horse dismounted within rifle range and admired the view, pretending that the soldiers were not there. Then the warriors began to retreat slowly in a zig-zagging path up the slope to Lodge Trail Ridge, always tantalizingly just out of reach.

The frustrated Fetterman ordered his men to follow them.

The trap worked perfectly. A little before noon, Fetterman's command followed Crazy Horse over Lodge Trail Ridge.

The earth must have seemed alive with warriors. Two thousand Plains Indians sprang from behind their cover, their cries of "Hoka hey, hoka hey" filling the chill air.

It was over in minutes. Two civilian Civil War veterans accompanying the relief were armed with 16-shot Henry rifles and managed, with several infantrymen, to form a defensive wall that blunted the first charge. Using downed ponies as breastworks they kept up a rattling fire. Dead Indians were ringed around them. Then they were overwhelmed.

Some of the infantry ran back up the slope to a rock formation and held off their attackers for a quarter of an hour before running out of ammunition. Fetterman and a Captain Fred Brown committed suicide, shooting each other in the head with their revolvers.

Above the infantry in the rock formation, a group of dismounted cavalry tried to get over the ice which covered the ridge top – and found Indians on the other side. Few Sioux or Cheyenne carried rifles but they fired up showers of arrows. As the cavalry slipped and scrabbled towards a cluster of boulders they were cut to pieces. A few knots of survivors took up position in the boulders.

Around this time, Indian scouts reported that soldier reinforcements were riding out from the fort. Desperate for a quick victory, the warriors charged the dismounted cavalrymen. It was now so cold that blood froze as it spurted from wounds. Among the last of the soldiers to die was the bugler Adolph Metzger, who beat off attackers with his bugle until it was a shapeless mass. A dog belonging to a cavalryman came running out of the rock. Even this was killed, a Sioux arrow through its neck.

When the reinforcements from the fort under Captain Ten Eyck reached the top of the ridge at 12.45 all sounds of firing had ceased. Looking down into the Peno valley they could see literally thousands of Indians moving about, some picking up the wounded and their 60 or so dead, others salvaging any of the 40,000 arrows fired which were still usable. A few Indians rode up towards the reinforcements, slapping their buttocks, and calling obscenities.

Gradually, the Indians began to move off westwards. As they cleared the battlefield, one of the reinforcements suddenly pointed to the Bozeman Trail:"There're the men down there, all dead!"

And they were. None of Fetterman's command survived. They had been annihilated. Warily going down to retrieve the bodies, Ten Eyck's men found them mutilated beyond their belief. In Colonel Carrington's official report, suppressed for 20 years after the event, there were no details spared:

Eyes torn out and laid on rocks; noses cut off; ears cut out; chins hewn off; teeth chopped out; joints of fingers, brains taken out and placed on rocks with other members of the body; entrails taken out and exposed; hands cut off; feet cut off; arms taken out from sockets; private parts severed and indecently placed on the person; eyes, ears, mouth and arms penetrated with spear-heads, sticks, and arrows; ribs slashed to separation with knives; skulls severed in every form, from chin to crown; muscles of calves, thighs, stomach, breast, back, arms and cheek taken out. Punctures upon every sensitive part of the body, even to the soles of the feet and palms of the hand.

All had been scalped, save for two, whose heads had been placed in buffalo-skin bags, a signal dishonour reserved by the Sioux for cowardly foe.

The so-called Fetterman Massacre so reduced the Fort Phil Kearny garrison that Carrington feared that his entire command might be destroyed. Despite a raging blizzard, a miner staying at the fort volunteered to ride the 235 miles to Fort Laramie to obtain reinforcements. This was John ("Portugee") Philips. He refused pay, but took one of the colonel's horses. Before riding off, Philips visited the pregnant wife of Lieutenant Grummond, killed alongside Fetterman, and told her: "I will go if it costs my life. I am going for your sake."

John Philips's ride, through snow and Indians, is an epic in the folklore of the frontier. With only hardtack to eat and temperatures reaching 20 below, he somehow made the 190 miles to Horse Shoe Station in four days, from where the news was flashed to Fort Laramie. For good measure, he rode on to Fort Laramie to report in person. He arrived on Christmas night, as the officers were holding a ball.

Less well known is that Carrington sent out another volunteer messenger from the fort, George Bailey, who also made it through the blizzards and hostile Native Americans, meeting up with Philips sometime before Horse Shoe Station. Both men arrived together at the telegraph office and later at Fort Laramie.

Within hours of their arrival, reinforcements were struggling towards Fort Phil Kearny. With them went orders relieving Carrington of his command.

These fresh troops did not intimidate the Sioux, who continued to besiege Fort Phil Kearny and virtually halt travel along the Bozeman Trail.

Victory Out of Defeat

In the late summer of 1867 there came another battle at Fort Phil Kearny. At dawn on 2 August Red Cloud and a thousand Sioux warriors, wearing their white and green and yellow warpaint, attacked a 36-man detail working under Captain James Powell at the pinery. Anticipating such a fight, Powell had taken the precaution of building an oval barricade of the large wooden boxes from the wagon beds. Thirty-two of the detail made it to shelter behind the wagon boxes. For four hours, to the vast surprise of the Sioux, the soldiers kept up an almost continuous fire. Braves fell in futile charge after charge.

Unknown to Red Cloud, the soldiers had the new breech-loading Springfield rifles instead of muzzleloaders. "Instead of drawing ramrods and thus losing precious time," recalled Sergeant Samuel Gibson, "we simply threw open the breech-blocks of our new rifles to eject the empty shell and slapped in fresh ones." These Springfield rifles, along with Powell's wagon boxes, enabled the work detail to hold off the Indians until reinforcements arrived. Years afterwards Red Cloud said he lost the flower of his fighting warriors in the Wagon Box Fight.

The day preceding the Wagon Box Fight, an attack by Cheyenne at Fort C.F. Smith — the Hayfield Fight – had also been beaten off with Springfields.

For weeks, Red Cloud believed he had suffered a fatal defeat. But the government in Washington had been so shocked by the previous disasters on the Trail – especially the Fetterman Massacre – that it wanted to make peace. A commission was sent out to Wyoming to draw up a treaty. Red Cloud refused to sign. Sensing his advantage, he demanded that the blue-coat soldiers abandon their forts in Sioux country. Wearied of a war that was costly and unpopular in the East, the government took the unprecedented step of agreeing to an Indian's terms. Forts C.F. Smith, Phil Kearny and Reno were abandoned in the summer of 1868.

As the soldiers departing Fort Phil Kearny looked back, they saw a band of Indians under Little Wolf set fire to the buildings.

When he saw that the posts had truly been evacuated, Red Cloud rode into Fort Laramie and signed the treaty. Under its terms, the government agreed to abandon the Bozeman Trail, and define the Powder River country as "unceded Indian territory" from which White persons would be excluded. Red Cloud had won his war to retain his people's traditional hunting grounds. In return, the Indians agreed to settle on a giant reservation in Dakota and cease hostilities. "From this day forward," the treaty began, "all wars between the parties to this agreement shall forever cease."

A pious hope. But peace of a sort held for eight years on the northern plains. And when it was finally broken, it was broken by the White man.

Blood on the Grasslands

"They have run over our country; they have destroyed the growing wood and green grass; they have set fire to our lands. They have devastated the country and killed my animals, the elk, the deer, the antelope, my buffalo. They do not kill them to eat them; they leave them to rot where they fall. Fathers, if I went into your country to kill your animals, what would you say? Would I not be wrong, and would you not make war on me?"

Bear Tooth

The Buffalo and the Iron Horse

White emigrants had been streaming into the trans-Mississippi West since the 1840s, along roads which disfigured the landscape and scared away the buffalo. To keep them in contact with the East, stagecoach lines and telegraph poles sprang up in the wilderness, stretching to Santa Fe, Salt Lake, Denver and beyond. But not until 1862 were the forces set in motion which would transform the Wild West beyond redemption. In that year, Lincoln's Congress passed the Homestead Act, which offered parcels of 160 acres of free land to anyone willing to work it. Millions took up the offer, and began pushing out into the

Great Plains. In the same year, Congress passed the Pacific Railroad Act, which made possible the first transcontinental railway.

The iron horse had already penetrated to Omaha. Now it would push westwards from Omaha into the wilderness, while a line would come eastwards from Sacramento, California to meet it. With the end of the Civil War in 1865, the pace of expansion quickened at a fantastic rate. National energies which had been directed North and South were now focused West. Emigration boomed. Demobbed soldiers and men desperate for work flooded to work on the transcontinental railroad. By the end of 1866, the Union Pacific was advancing into Nebraska at the rate of a mile a day. Another railroad, the Kansas Pacific, was started towards Denver, Colorado.

The railway was the engine of ultimate destruction for the Native American. The railway would bind East and West the plains across in bands of steel. It would make possible the settlement of the interior frontier, and it would give the Army an added mobility in the Indian Wars. And it would bring the buffalo to near extinction.

There were around 25 million buffalo on the High Plains before the White man came. A few nomadic pedestrian Indians followed the buffalo on their great seasonal migrations, killing the beasts en masse by stampeding them over a cliff, or by stalking them individually whilst disguised under a buffalo robe. Most Native Americans in aboriginal times, however, were part-time buffalo hunters, venturing out from the sheltered woodlands and tall grass prairies in fall and winter. In the fall, the buffalo was fat from summer grazing. Around February, its winter coat was thick and warm to wear. Men were the hunters, dogs (the Indians' only domesticated animal) and women the transport. A dog with *travois*, two tipi poles which trailed the ground and were attached to a collar around the animal's neck, could carry 75 pounds of meat.

The arrival of the horse changed everything. When in 1603 the Spanish began to settle in earnest along the Rio Grande, they forbade the Indians the use of the horse. Neither the Indians nor the horses were tractable to Spanish wishes. Horses escaped; Indians raided. By about 1640 the southern Apache were mounted, and not long afterwards the Kiowa were trading horses to the Wichita, and so the equine revolution proceeded north. The Comanche were horsed by about 1700, the tribes of the central Great Plains by the 1720s.

With the horse, the buffalo became an easy target. Tribes surged West to become horse-riding, exultant nomadic hunters of *bos bison Americanus*. The Teton (Western) Sioux, Assinboin, Cheyenne, Crow, Arapaho and others abandoned digging-sticks entirely ("We lost the corn," say the Cheyenne). Others, like the Osage, maintained static agricultural villages and rode out for a great fall buffalo hunt.

For those tribes typical of the new Plains culture, such as the Teton Sioux, the buffalo was almost everything. It was food and it was clothing. A dozen cured buffalo hides made a tipi home. Buffalo leather could also make war shields, kettles and even coracle-like boats. The brains in the skull, cracked open with a buffalo hoof, helped tan the hide. Horns were used for drinking cups, and ceremonial dress. Large bones were weapons, small ones awls and needles. Buffalo dung made "chips" for fires. The Blackfoot extracted no fewer than 88 commodities from the buffalo, excluding food.

Since Indians believed that the buffalo, like every animal, was an other-than-human-person, the beast had to give its consent to die. This was obtained by prayer and reverence. Intricate ceremonials preceded the kill.

Unknown to the Plains Indians, the buffalo on which they had based their lifestyle, culture and religion was already in crisis before the railroads came. At their peak there were probably 25 million buffalo on the Great Plains (50 million less than the traditional estimate), and by the early 1800s these were suffering competition from mustang and Indian horse herds for water and grazing. The cattle brought to the Plains by Native American raiders and White migrants gave the buffalo brucellosis and tuberculosis. Emigrant trails – which cut the immense herds in two – and White settlement on the edges of the grasslands obliterated areas of range which were critical in times of drought.

The buffalo only appeared to be infinite. By the mid-nineteenth century the animal was struggling to maintain its numbers. And then came the railroads.

The iron horse scared away the herds and destroyed the range. To feed the railroad crews with meat, the companies hired hunters to slaughter the conveniently placed bison. A discovery that buffalo hides made cheap machine belts for Eastern factories increased the demand for the animal's skin – which could now be shipped back on the railroads. Buffalo hunters galloped to the end of the line, and the carnage began.

A skilled marksman, using a heavy Sharps rifle and staying down wind from the herd, could kill – with luck – around 150 of the short-sighted animals per day. A former Pony Express rider and crack-shot called William F. Cody killed 4,280 buffalo for the Kansas-Pacific in eight months in 1867–8. This feat won him the soubriquet "Buffalo Bill". Hide hunters took an estimated 4,374,000 from the southern plains alone between 1872 and 1874. The Great Plains were being turned into a wasteland and a charnel-house.

Great Plains Indians began to attack the railroad, strik-

ing at Union Pacific grading crews, even speeding locomotives. Rails were ripped up, obstacles tied to the track.
Once, a group of braves tried to capture a moving locomo-
tive by pulling a rawhide lariat taut in front of it. Several
were pulled under the wheels. A more effective attack
came in the late summer of 1867.

On the night of 6 August 1867, the telegraph wire at
Plum Creek, Nebraska, went dead. William Thompson
and a crew of five went down the Union Pacific line in the
dark to investigate – and ran headfirst into a Cheyenne
barricade made from a section of ripped-up track. Within
moments the crew were dead, and Thompson had been
knocked unconscious. He woke to feel himself being
scalped, but feigned death. Lying inert, he witnessed another attack by the Cheyenne nearby. This time a freight
train came along and piled up on the barricade; the driver
and fireman were killed by the Indians, but four men
travelling in the caboose escaped. Still pretending death,
Thompson watched the Cheyenne loot the cars. When the
war party finally moved on, Thompson retrieved his
bloody scalp and stumbled back to Plum Creek, from
where he caught a train to Omaha. Among those who
visited the scalpless repairman there was the journalist
Henry Stanley: "In a pail of water by his side, was his
scalp, somewhat resembling a drowned rat, as it floated,
curled up, on the water. At Omaha, people flocked from
all parts to view the gory baldness which had come upon
him so suddenly."

Custer and the Cheyenne

As the attacks on the railroad increased, the Army turned
its attention to the central and southern plains. To protect
railcrews and emigrants in Kansas and Nebraska, the
irascible commander of the Military Division of the Mis-

souri, General William Tecumseh Sherman, wanted to remove all Indians from a wide corridor between the Platte and the Arkansas. Sherman was itching for war, complaining in 1866: "God only knows when, and I do not see how, we can make a decent excuse for an Indian war." Desultory attacks on the iron horses did not quite justify wholesale war on the Indians, but Sherman got his excuse when his subordinate, Major General Winfield Scott Hancock, burned a Cheyenne village because it was a "nest of conspirators". Scott added that it was not "of much importance" whether the villagers had actually committed depredations. Thus provoked, the Cheyenne took to the warpath. Sherman got his Indian War.

To fight the war against the Cheyenne, Sherman employed the talents of Hancock and another celebrated officer, George Armstrong Custer. Although Custer had graduated 34th of a class of 34 at West Point (and collected 726 demerits), he had gone on to establish a Civil War reputation as an able cavalry leader, being breveted Major-General of Volunteers at the age of 25. Sherman held Custer in high esteem, but was not blind to his failures:

> G. A. Custer, Lieutenant Colonel, Seventh Cavalry, is young, very brave, even to rashness – a good trait for a cavalry officer. His outstanding characteristics are his youth, health, energy and extreme willingness to act and fight. But he has not too much sense.

As if to prove the truth of Sherman's latter assessment, Custer mounted one of the most capricious and ineffectual cavalry campaigns seen on the plains. Pained at being separated from his wife, Libby, Custer became moody and erratic. Men were given brutal punishments for the slightest reason. Rather than engage the enemy he went buffalo-hunting. When his men, exhausted by four months of fruitless careering about the plains, began to desert, he sent out a posse with the order to "shoot them down, and bring none in alive."

Eventually, Custer broke off the campaign completely, and force-marched his men across Kansas so that he could be with Libby. Two men were killed by Indians en route but Custer refused to stop to bury them. A week after being reunited with Libby, Custer was arrested and charged with inhumane treatment of his men and abandoning his command. He was convicted on both counts, and suspended from his post for one year.

An expedition into Kansas headed by Hancock fared little better. In four months of active campaigning, Hancock's command killed four Indians, two of them friendly. The other two were Sioux, casualties in a fight that saw one of Hancock's detachments annihilated.

There were other Indian victories. On 26 June 1867, a war party of 300 Cheyenne and their Arapaho and Sioux allies descended on Fort Wallace in Western Kansas, where a company of the 7th Cavalry was stationed. "They [the Indians] came literally sailing," recalled Captain Albert Barnitz, "uttering their peculiar 'Hi! Hi! Hi!' and terminating it with the warwhoop – their ponies, gaily decked with feathers and scalplocks, tossing their heads high in the air, and looking wildly from side to side."

Seven soldiers died in the attack, including Sergeant Frederick Wyllyams, an English Eton graduate who had come West for adventure. Another Englishman, Dr William Abraham Bell, working for the Kansas Pacific Survey, came upon his countryman's body shortly afterwards and photographed it. Bell also recorded the scene in words:

> I shall minutely describe this horrid sight, characteristic of a mode of warfare soon – thank God – to be abolished. We shall have no difficulty in recognising some meaning in

the wounds. The muscles of the right arm hacked to the
bone speak of the Cheyennes; the nose slit denotes the
Arapahoes; and the throat cuts bear witness that the Sioux
were also present. I have not discovered what tribe was
indicated by the incisions down the thighs, and the lacera-
tion of the calves of the legs, in oblique parallel gashes.
Warriors from several tribes purposely left one arrow
each in the dead man's body.

Bell sent copies of his photograph to Washington so
that "the authorities should see how their soldiers were
treated on the Plains." Few in the 7th Cavalry forgot the
fate of Frederick Wyllyams.

Military policy was a self-evident failure. The Indians
on the northern plains had been even more successful by
this date, having wreaked havoc to the Bozeman Trail
and wiped out Fetterman's command.

A peace commission was established which met first
with the northern tribes at Fort Laramie, then in October
1867 with the central and southern plains tribes at Medicine Lodge Creek in Kansas.

More than 5,000 Indians were present at the council,
which was conducted with much pomp and ceremony.
On both sides. Soldiers drilled. Indians rode around in
milling circles, their horses painted for war. The only ones
who remained aloof were the Quahadi Comanche of the
Staked Plains, fearsome raiders led by the half-breed
Quanah. Indian chief after chief made eloquent, impas-
sioned speeches on behalf of their cause and their desire.

The Kiowa chief Satanta (White Bear), wearing a blue
officer's uniform coat given him as a present, told the
commission:

I love the land and the buffalo and will not part with it . . .
I want the children raised as I was. I have heard that you

> want to settle us on a reservation near the [Wichita] mountains. I don't want to settle. I want to roam over the prairies. There I feel free and happy, but when I settle down I feel pale and die . . . These soldiers cut down my timber; they kill my buffalo; and when I see that it feels as if my heart would burst with sorrow.

As for the commission's offer to build the Indians "civilized" homes, Satanta added: "This building of homes for us is all nonsense. We don't want you to build any for us."

At the end of the council some chiefs signed, and some did not. Black Kettle of the southern Cheyenne, despite the massacre of his people at Sand Creek, still wanted friendship with the Whites, and signed. So did Kicking Bird of the Kiowa and, after protestations, Chief Ten Bears of the Comanche. Just before he left, the ageing Satank, noted chief of the Kiowa, came up to the commissioners to bid them farewell. He stood there with his pony, and made a little speech that moved even the most Indian-hating of the White men gathered.

> I come to say that the Kiowas and the Comanches have made you a peace, and they intend to stick to it . . . We have warred against the White man, but never because it gave us pleasure . . . In the far distant past there was no suspicion among us. The world seemed large enough for both . . . But its broad plains seem now to contract, and the White man grows jealous of his Red brother . . . You have patiently heard our many complaints . . . For your sakes the green grass shall not be stained with the blood of Whites . . .

Little more than a year later, the ranges were running with White blood. Despite the hopes of Satank, Black Kettle, and other tribal leaders peace was impossible. The

Indians had promised to stay away from the trails and the railroads, but these things were not static. They spread over the hunting grounds almost by the day. And now the farmer had arrived, eating land with his plough and his vision of a land turned to agriculture. The iron horse and the sodbuster: these were the ultimate enemies. They had to be stopped.

During the summer of 1868, bands of hostile Indians attacked settlements and trails in western Kansas and Colorado, killing 124 people. By fall, the grasslands from Kansas to Texas were criss-crossed by war parties.

Following the disastrous campaigns of the previous year, Sherman replaced Hancock with his old colleague, General Philip H. Sheridan, a black-eyed, brilliant and profane cavalry officer. Sheridan authorized Major George A. Forsyth to enlist 50 volunteer frontiersmen who would give the Indians a taste of their own free-booting warfare. The result was the famous fight at Beecher Island in the Arikaree River, Colorado, where Forsyth's scouts withstood repeated assaults by 600 Indians for nine days. It was here that the legendary Cheyenne war chief Roman Nose (Woqini) was killed. Roman Nose had a black and red eagle-feather warbonnet whose supernatural ability to protect him from harm depended on his not eating food touched by metal. While besieging Forsyth he learned that his food had been taken from the fire with an iron fork. He was cut down early in the action.

Forsyth's stand at Beecher Island (named after one of his volunteers who was killed there, authoress Harriet Beecher Stowe's nephew, Frederick) was a singular bright episode for the Army. Elsewhere the picture on the central and southern plains was bleak. Sheridan called in the one officer he believed had the motivation to crush Indian resistance: George Custer. "If there was any poetry or romance in war he could develop it," said Sheridan of his protégé. In October 1867, the flamboyant Custer rejoined the 7th Cavalry and marched them into hostile country, determined to restore his glorious reputation.

On 23 November, Custer's Osage scouts picked up the trail of a war party of young men returning from a plundering raid in the Kansas settlements. The story of the ensuing "Battle of the Washita" – at least from the point of view of the 7th Cavalry – was later told by Edward S. Godfrey, one of Custer's lieutenants:

November 23rd—Reveille at 3 o'clock. Snowed all night and still snowing very heavily. The darkness and heavy snowfall made the packing of the wagons very difficult, but at dawn the wagons were assembled in the train and daylight found us on the march, the band playing, "The Girl I Left Behind me," but there was no woman there to interpret its significance. The snow was falling so heavily that vision was limited to a few rods. All landmarks were invisible and the trails were lost. "We didn't know where we were going, but we were on the way." Then General Custer, with compass in hand, took the lead and became our guide.

As the day wore on the weather became warmer and I have never seen the snowflakes as large or fall so lazily as those that fell that day. Fortunately there was no wind to drift the snow to add to our discomfort. They melted on the clothing so that every living thing was wet to the skin. The snow balled on the feet of our shod animals causing much floundering and adding to the fatigue of travel. About two o'clock we came to Wolf Creek, crossed to the right side of the valley and continued to march till we came to a clump of fallen timbers and there went into camp with our wagon train far behind. As soon as the horses were unsaddled everyone except the horse holders was gathering fuel for fires. The valley was alive with rabbits and all messes were supplied with rabbit stew. Our rawhide covered saddles were soaked. The unequal drying warped the saddle trees which subsequently caused that bane of cavalry – many sore backs. Snow, eighteen inches "on the level"; distance marched, about fifteen miles.

The snowfall ceased during the night. The sun rose on the 24th with clear skies and with warmer weather. The snow melted rapidly. The glare of the bright sunshine caused much discomfort and a number of cases of snowblindness. Some buffalo were killed and many rabbits. Some deer were seen. We camped on Wolf Creek. Distance marched, about 18 miles.

November 25th we marched some distance up Wolf Creek and then turned in a southerly direction toward the Canadian. As we approached the summit of the divide, the peaks of the Antelope Hills loomed up and became our marker for the rest of the day. We made camp late that evening on a small stream about a mile from the Canadian. The day's march had been tedious. The melting snows balled on our shod animals during the long pull to the divide. A number of horses and mules gave out, but were brought in late that night. Wood was very scarce, but usually the quartermaster sergeants would load some wood in the cook wagon when packing and they usually were on the lookout for fuel on the march.

At daybreak, November 26th, Major Elliott, with troops G, H, and M, some white scouts and Osage trailers, started up the north side of the Canadian to scout for a possible trail of war parties. The remainder of the command and the wagon train marched to the Canadian to cross to the south side. To "California Joe" had been given the task of finding a ford. The river was high and rising, current swift and full of floating snow and slush ice. After much floundering he found a practical ford. The cavalry crossed first and assembled on the plain. Owing to the quicksand bottom, each wagon was double teamed and rushed through without halting. A mounted man preceded each team and other mounted men were alongside to "whoop 'em up."

While this tedious crossing and parking was going on, General Custer and a number of officers went to the tops of the hills to view the country. The highest peak was about three hundred feet above the plain. Suddenly we were enveloped in a cloud of frozen mist. Looking at the sun we were astonished to see it surrounded by three ellipses with rainbow tints, the axes marked by sundogs, except the lower part of the third or outer ellipse which seemingly was below the horizon, eleven sundogs. This phenomenon was not visible to those on the plain below.

As the last of the wagons had crossed and the rear guard was floundering in crossing, someone of our group on the hills called out, "Hello, here comes somebody." But General Custer had already seen him and had focused his field glasses on the galloping scout, but he said nothing. It was a tense moment when Jack Corbin rode up and began his report.

Major Elliott had marched up the Canadian about twelve miles when he came to the abandoned camp of a war party of about one hundred and fifty; he had crossed the river and was following the trail which was not over twenty-four hours old, and asked for instructions. Corbin was given a fresh horse to return to Major Elliott with instructions to follow the trail till dark, then halt till the command joined him.

Officers' call was sounded and when assembled we were told the news and ordered to be prepared to move as soon as possible. One wagon was assigned to each squadron (two troops), one to Troop G and the teamsters, and one to headquarters; seven in all, and one ambulance under the quartermaster, Lieutenant James M. Bell. These were to carry light supplies and extra ammunition. I cannot recall of just what the limited supplies consisted. Each trooper was ordered to carry one hundred rounds of ammunition on his person. (They were armed with the Spencer magazine carbine and Colt revolver, paper cartridges and caps.) The main train guarded by about eighty men under the command of the officer of the day was to follow as rapidly as possible. For this guard men with weak horses were selected. Captain Louis M. Hamilton, a grandson of Alexander Hamilton, was officer of the day. He was greatly distressed because this duty fell to him and begged to go along to command his squadron, but was refused unless he could get some officer to exchange with him. Lieutenant E. G. Mathey, who was snowblind, agreed to take his place.

Soon the regiment was ready to move and we struck in a direction to intercept the trail of Elliott's advance. We pushed along almost without rest till about 9 p. m. before we came to Elliott's halting place. There we had coffee made, care being taken to conceal the fires as much as possible. Horses were unsaddled and fed. At 10 p. m. we were again in the saddle with instructions to make as little noise as possible, – no loud talking, no matches were to be lighted. Tobacco users were obliged to console themselves with the quid. Little Beaver, Osage Chief, with one of his warriors, had the lead dismounted as trailers; then followed the other Indian and white scouts with whom General Custer rode to be near the advance. The cavalry followed at a distance of about a half mile. The snow had melted during the day but at night the weather had turned cold and the crunching noise could be heard for a considerable distance.

After a couple of hours' march, the trailers hurried back for the command to halt. General Custer rode up to investigate when Little Beaver informed him that he "smelled

smoke." Cautious investigation disclosed the embers of a
fire which the guides decided from conditions had been
made by the boy herders while grazing the pony herds
and from this deduced that the village could not be far
distant. The moon had risen and there was little difficulty
in following the trail and General Custer rode behind the
trailers to watch the developments. On nearing the crest of
any rise, the trailer would crawl to the crest to reconnoiter,
but seeing Little Beaver exercise greater caution than usual
and then shading his eyes from the moon, the General felt
there was something unusual. On his return the General
asked, "What is it?" and Little Beaver replied, "Heap
Injuns down there." Dismounting and advancing with the
same caution as the guide, he made his personal investigation, but could only see what appeared to be a herd of
animals. Asking why he thought there were Indians down
there, Little Beaver replied, "Me heard dog bark." Listening intently they not only heard the bark of a dog, but the
tinkling of a bell, indicating a pony herd, and then the cry
of an infant.

Satisfied that a village had been located, the General
returned to the command, assembled the officers, and,
after removing sabres, took us all to the crest where the
situation was explained or rather conjectured. The barking of the dogs and the occasional cry of infants located
the direction of the village and the tinkling of the bells
gave the direction of the herds. Returning and resuming
our sabres, the General explained his plans and assigned
squadron commanders their duties and places. Major
Elliott, with Troops G, H, and M was to march well to our
left and approach the village from the northeast or east-
erly direction as determined by the ground, etc. Captain
Thompson, with B and F, was to march well to our right so
as to approach from the southeast, connecting with Elliott.
Captain Myers, with E and I, was to move by the right so

as to approach from a southerly direction. The wagons under Lieutenant Bell and Captain Benteen's squadron – H and M – had been halted about two or three miles on the trail to await the outcome of the investigations.

Just after dismissing the officers and as we were separating, General Custer called my name. On reporting, he directed me to take a detail, go back on the trail to where Captain Benteen and the wagons were, give his compliments to Captain Benteen and instruct him to rejoin the command, and Lieutenant Bell to hold the wagons where they were till he heard the attack which would be about daybreak. "Tell the Adjutant the number of men you want and he will make the detail. How many do you want?" I replied, "One orderly." He then said, "Why do you say that? You can have all you want." I replied that one was all I wanted – "to take more would increase the chances of accident and delay."

I delivered my messages and returned with Captain Benteen's squadron. The camp guard remained with the wagons.

Upon the arrival of Captain Benteen's squadron, Major Elliott proceeded to take position, also Captain Thompson and later Captain Myers.

Before the first streak of dawn, General Custer's immediate command as quietly as possible moved into place facing nearly east, Lieutenant Cooke's sharpshooters in advance of the left dismounted. General Custer and staff were followed by the band mounted. Captain West's squadron was on the right and Captain Hamilton's on the left, the standard and guard in the center. Troop K (West's) was on the right flank and I had command of the first platoon.

With the dawn we were ordered to remove overcoats and haversacks, leaving one man of each organization in charge with orders to load them in the wagons when

Lieutenant Bell came up. Following the General, the command marched over the crest of the ridge and advanced some distance to another lower ridge. Waiting till sunrise we began to feel that the village had been abandoned although the dogs continued their furious barkings. Then "little by little" we advanced. Captain West came to me with orders to charge through the village but not to stop, to continue through and round up the pony herds.

With all quiet in the early dawn, Major Elliott's command had reached a concealed position close to the village, but was waiting for the signal from headquarters. The furious barking of the dogs aroused an Indian who came from his lodge, ran to the bank of the Washita, looked about and fired his rifle. I was told that a trooper had raised his head to take aim and was seen by this Indian. With the alarm thus given, the command opened fire. The trumpeters sounded the charge and the band began to play "Garry Owen," but by the time they had played one strain their instruments froze up.

My platoon advanced as rapidly as the brush and fallen timbers would permit until we reached the Washita which I found with steep, high banks. I marched the platoon by the right flank a short distance, found a "pony crossing," reformed on the right bank, galloped through the right of the village without contact with a warrior, and then proceeded to round up the pony herds.

As I passed out of the village, Captain Thompson's and Captain Myers' squadrons came over the high ridge on my right. Both had lost their bearings during their night marching and failed to make contacts for the opening attack.

At the opening of the attack, the warriors rushed to the banks of the stream. Those in front of Custer's command were soon forced to retire in among the tepees, and most of them being closely followed retreated to ravines and behind trees and logs, and in depressions where they maintained their positions till the last one was killed. A few escaped down the valley. This desperate fighting was carried on mostly by sharpshooters, waiting for a head to show. Seventeen Indians were killed in one depression.

Lieutenant Bell, when he heard the firing, rushed his teams to join the command and while loading the overcoats and haversacks was attacked by a superior force and the greater part of them had to be abandoned. His arrival with the reserve ammunition was a welcome reinforcement.

While the fighting was going on, Major Elliott seeing a group of dismounted Indians escaping down the valley called for volunteers to make pursuit. Nineteen men, including Regimental Sergeant Major Kennedy responded. As his detachment moved away, he turned to Lieutenant Hale waved his hand and said: "Here goes for a brevet or a coffin."

After passing through the village, I went in pursuit of pony herds and found them scattered in groups about a mile below the village. I deployed my platoon to make the roundup and took a position for observation. While the roundup was progressing, I observed a group of dismounted Indians escaping down the opposite side of the valley. Completing the roundup, and starting them toward the village, I turned the herd over to Lieutenant Law who had come with the second platoon of the troop and told him to take them to the village, saying that I would take my platoon and go in pursuit of the group I had seen escaping down the valley.

Crossing the stream and striking the trail, I followed it till it came to a wooded draw where there was a large pony herd. Here I found the group had mounted. Taking the trail which was well up on the hillside of the valley, and following it about a couple of miles, I discovered a lone tepee, and soon after two Indians circling their ponies. A high promontory and ridge projected into the valley and shut off the view of the valley below the lone tepee. I knew the circling of the warriors meant an alarm and rally, but I wanted to see what was in the valley beyond them. Just then Sergeant Conrad, who had been a captain of Ohio volunteers, and Sergeant Hughes, who had served in the 4th U. S. Cavalry in that country before the Civil War, came to me and warned me of the danger of going ahead. I ordered them to halt the platoon and wait till I could go to the ridge to see what was beyond. Arriving at and peering over the ridge, I was amazed to find that as far as I could see down the well wooded, tortuous valley there were tepees – tepees. Not only could I see tepees, but mounted warriors scurrying in our direction. I hurried back to the platoon and returned at the trot till attacked by the hostiles, when I halted, opened fire, drove the hostiles to cover, and then deployed the platoon as skirmishers.

The hillsides were cut by rather deep ravines and I planned to retreat from ridge to ridge. Under the cavalry tactics of 1841, the retreat of skirmishers was by the odd and even numbers, alternating in lines to the rear. I instructed the line in retreat to halt on the next ridge and cover the retreat of the advance line. This was successful for the first and second ridges, but at the third I found men had apparently forgotten their numbers and there was some confusion, so I divided the skirmishers into two groups, each under a sergeant, and thereafter had no trouble.

Finally the hostiles left us and we soon came to the pony herd where the group we had started to pursue had mounted. I had not had a single casualty. During this retreat we heard heavy firing on the opposite side of the valley, but being well up on the side hills we could not see through the trees what was going on. There was a short lull when the firing again became heavy and continued till long after we reached the village, in fact, nearly all day.

In rounding up the pony herd, I found Captain Barnitz' horse, *General*, saddled but no bridle. On reaching the village I turned over the pony herd and at once reported to General Custer what I had done and seen. When I mentioned the "big village," he exclaimed, "What's that?" and put me through a lot of rapid fire questions. At the conclusion I told him about finding Captain Barnitz' horse and asked what had happened. He told me that Captain Barnitz had been severely and probably mortally wounded.

Leaving the General in a "brown study" I went to see my friend and former Captain, Barnitz. I found him under a pile of blankets and buffalo robes, suffering and very quiet. I hunted up Captain Lippincott, Assistant Surgeon, and found him with his hands over his eyes suffering intense pain from snowblindness. He was very pessimistic as to Barnitz' recovery and insisted that I tell him that there was no hope unless he could be kept perfectly quiet for several days as he feared the bullet had passed through the bowels. I went back to Captain Barnitz and approached the momentous opinion of the surgeon as bravely as I could and then blurted it out, when he exclaimed, "Oh hell! they think because my extremities are cold I am going to die, but if I could get warm I'm sure I'll be all right. These blankets and robes are so heavy I can hardly breathe." I informed the first sergeant and the men were soon busy gathering fuel and building fires.

In the midst of this, the general sent for me and again questioned me about the big village. At that time many warriors were assembling on the high hills north of the valley overlooking the village and the General kept looking in that direction. At the conclusion of his inquiry, I told him that I had heard that Major Elliott had not returned and suggested that possibly the heavy firing I had heard on the opposite side of the valley might have been an attack on Elliott's party. He pondered this a bit and said slowly, "I hardly think so, as Captain Myers has been fighting down there all morning and probably would have reported it."

I left him and a while later he sent for me again, and, on reporting, told me that he had Romeo, the interpreter, make inquiries of the squaw prisoners and they confirmed my report of the lower village. He then ordered me to take Troop K and destroy all property and not allow any looting – but destroy everything.

I allowed the prisoners to get what they wanted. As I watched them, they only went to their own tepees. I began the destruction at the upper end of the village, tearing down tepees and piling several together on the tepee poles, set fire to them. (All tepees were made of tanned buffalo hides.) As the fires made headway, all articles of personal property – buffalo robes, blankets, food, rifles, pistols, bows and arrows, lead and caps, bullet molds, etc. – were thrown in the fires and destroyed. I doubt but that many small curios went into the pockets of men engaged in this work. One man brought to me that which I learned was a bridal gown, a "one piece dress," adorned all over with bead work and elks' teeth on antelope skins as soft as the finest broadcloth. I started to show it to the General and ask to keep it, but as I passed a big fire, I thought, "What's the use, 'orders is orders'" and threw it in the blaze. I have never ceased to regret that destruction. All of the powder found I spilled on the ground and "flashed".

I was present in August 1868, at Fort Larned, Kansas, when the annuities were issued, promised by the Medicine Lodge Peace Treaties of 1867, and saw the issue of rifles, pistols, powder, caps, lead and bullet molds to these same Cheyennes.

While this destruction was going on, warriors began to assemble on the hill slopes on the left side of the valley facing the village, as if to make an attack. Two squadrons formed near the left bank of the stream and started on the "Charge" when the warriors scattered and fled. Later, a few groups were seen on the hill tops but they made no hostile demonstrations.

As the last of the tepees and property was on fire, the General ordered me to kill all the ponies except those authorised to be used by the prisoners and given to scouts. We tried to rope them and cut their throats, but the ponies were frantic at the approach of a white man and fought viciously. My men were getting very tired so I called for reinforcements and details from other organizations were sent to complete the destruction of about eight hundred ponies. As the last of the ponies were being shot nearly all the hostiles left. This was probably because they could see our prisoners and realized that any shooting they did might endanger them.

Searching parties were sent to look for dead and wounded of both our own and hostiles. A scout having reported that he had seen Major Elliott and party in pursuit of some escapes down the right side of the valley, Captain Myers went down the valley about two miles but found no trace.

A while before sunset, as the command was forming to march down the valley, the General sent for me to ride with him to show him the place from which we could see the village below. There was no attempt to conceal our formation or the direction of our march. The command in column of fours, covered by skirmishers, the prisoners in the rear of the advance troops, standard and guidons "to the breeze," the chief trumpeter sounded the advance and we were "on our way," the band playing, "Ain't I Glad to Get Out of the Wilderness." The observing warriors followed our movement till twilight, but made no hostile demonstration. Then as if they had divined our purpose there was a commotion and they departed down the valley.

When we came in sight of the promontory and ridge from which I had discovered the lower villages, I pointed them out to the General. With the departure of the hostiles our march was slowed down till after dark, when the command was halted, the skirmishers were quietly withdrawn to rejoin their troops, the advance counter-marched, joined successively by the organizations in the rear, and we were on our way on our back trail. We marched briskly till long after midnight when we bivouacked till daylight with the exception of one squadron which was detached to hurry on to our supply train, the safety of which caused great anxiety. I was detailed to command the prisoners and special guard.

At daylight the next morning, we were on the march to meet our supply train and encountered it some time that forenoon. We were glad that it was safe, but disappointed that Major Elliott and party had not come in. After supper in the evening, the officers were called together and each one questioned as to the casualties of enemy warriors, locations, etc. Every effort was made to avoid duplications. The total was found to be one hundred and three.

The Washita "battle" was one of many controversies which trailed in the wake of George Armstrong Custer. The village attacked was that of the unfortunate Black Kettle, whose tipi flew a white flag. Black Kettle and his wife were shot in the back as they tried to flee across the Washita, and died face down in the water. Contrary to the claims of the 7th Cavalry, the soldiers killed not 103 warriors but eleven. The rest of the dead were women, children and old men.

The destruction of Black Kettle's village was a Western tragedy, but it was not another Sand Creek. Black Kettle was the leading peace chief of the Cheyenne, yet his camp harboured warriors. The chief had also been informed that he would be attacked unless he surrendered to Sheridan. Black Kettle's village was a mixture of Indians who wanted war and Indians who wanted peace. It was the Indian nation in miniature.

Sheridan applauded Custer for the Washita battle, which appeared to have ended Indian resistance on the central and southern plains. All winter long, straggles of Indians appeared at Fort Cobb wanting to surrender. To encourage the recalcitrant, Custer summoned Cheyenne chiefs to a peace council – then seized three of them and threatened to hang them on the spot unless the tribe carried out his demands. More Indians surrendered and moved onto reservations. When the Comanche arrived at Fort Cobb, one of their chiefs introduced himself to Sheridan. "*Tosawi*, good Indian," he said. Sheridan replied: "The only good Indians I ever saw were dead."

In March 1869 General Philip Sheridan was able to report to the War Department that the tribes assigned to the Indian Territory were living quietly on their reservations.

Custer's victory at the Washita was not, as Sheridan thought, the end of the Indian war on the central and southern plains. But it was the beginning of the end.

The Struggle for the Staked Plains

Always Against Us

There was something about the Comanche and the horse. They were uncannily conjoined. Writing in the 1830s the frontier artist George Catlin, who regarded the Comanche as "homely", remarked that as soon as one of the tribe "lays his hand upon his horse, his *face*, even, becomes handsome, and he gracefully flies away like a different being."

All who witnessed the Comanche on horseback were amazed and scared in equal measure by their skill. A favourite Comanche feat was to hang under the neck of the horse to fire arrows or throw 14-foot lances. Some Comanche warriors could hang under the belly of the horse to shoot their bows. While many plains tribes rode to war and then got off and fought on foot, the Comanche disdained any form of pedestrian warfare or hunting. Raids and the taming of mustangs made the Comanche enormously rich in horses. An ordinary warrior often owned 250 horses, a chief a thousand.

Their equine prowess aside, the Shoshoni-speaking Comanche were originally mountain dwellers from the

north ("Comanche" is derived from the Ute *kohmachts,*
"always against us"), who arrived on the south plains as
late as 1700. Yet as nobody took to the horse like the
Comanche, their ability to fight a highly mobile warfare
won them a huge 240,000 square mile empire on the high
plains, from which they evacuated the eastern Apache,
the Navajo and others. The five main Comanche bands
also blocked the northward expansion of the Spanish,
confining them in the bulk to southern Texas. At the peak
of their power, in the early nineteenth century, the
Comanche were 20,000 strong. Their horses were almost
countless.

And then the Anglo-Americans started to appear in
east Texas. The Comanche had a reputation for belliger-
ence, but the Whites matched it. A long and venomous
war between the Anglo-Americans and the Comanche
began shortly after Texas won independence from Mexico
in 1836. Massacres and reprisals became commonplace on
both sides.

One of the first Comanche victories in 1836 was at
Parker's Fort, a stockaded cluster of homesteads in east-
central Texas. The Comanche raiders killed and scalped
the men, and ripped their genitals out. Some of the women
were raped, and five were borne off as captives, a practice
the Comanche adopted to offset their low birth rate. They
included the nine-year-old Cynthia Ann Parker. When
she was 18 Cynthia Ann became the wife of Chief Peta
Nocona of the Nocona band. Early in the marriage she
bore him a son Quanah ("Fragrant"). Another son, Pecos,
and a daughter, Topasannah ("Prairie Flower"), followed.

In December 1860, while the Nocona band were camped
near the Pease River and the men were off hunting buffalo, a force of 40 Texas Rangers and 21 US cavalry struck.
Cynthia Ann was recaptured and taken, with her daughter, back to the settlements. Cynthia Ann was welcomed

by her brother and her uncle. But she mourned for her sons and several times tried to ride away to join them. When her daughter died in 1864, Cynthia Ann starved herself to death.

Meanwhile, her sons, Quanah and Pecos, had suffered other tragedies. Their father had died from an infected arrow wound. Then Pecos died of disease, probably in one of the cholera epidemics that repeatedly decimated the Comanche.

With no ties to hold him Quanah joined the Quahadi, a particularly warlike and anti-White band of the Comanche. When the Civil War stripped Texan forts of US soldiers and sent 60,000 Texan men flocking to the Confederate colours, the Quahadi Comanche were in the forefront of the devastation of central Texas. Hundreds of settlers were killed, their homes burnt to the ground.

In the course of these Comanche Wars of the 1860s, Quanah rose to become a war chief of the Quahadi band, second only to Bull Bear, the main Quahadi leader. Quanah was famed for his exploits in war, and his unbending opposition to the Whites. During a debate with other Comanche chiefs he declared: "My band is not going to live on the reservation. Tell the White chiefs that the Quahadi are warriors."

Refusing to attend the Medicine Lodge peace talks of 1867, Quanah instead marauded Texas, always afterwards retiring to the Quahadi sanctuary of the Staked Plains, a hostile arid land in the Texas Panhandle in which the Whites showed little interest. There the Quahadi were joined by other holdout bands of Comanche and Kiowa who refused to take the White road offered at Medicine Lodge, such as that of Woman Heart. On the remote Staked Plains the Indians still had freedom to live in the old ways.

It was about the last place on the southern plains where they could do so.

Jumping the Reservation

Occasionally news of the Comanche and Kiowa who had signed the Medicine Lodge Treaty came to the Texas Panhandle. The news was not good.

Government rations on the barren Comanche–Kiowa reservation in Indian Territory were pitiful. The inhabitants resented the attempts to teach them to farm, and the intrusions of Whites and eastern Indians onto their lands. Most of all these free-riding hunters of the endless plains were unable to accept confinement, or forsake the calendar joys of the buffalo hunt. Before long, Kiowa and Comanche alike were jumping the reservation to hunt. Outside reservation limits they came into violent conflict with White settlers.

In spring 1871, Satanta (White Bear) led a hundred Kiowa and Comanche off the reservation. Some of their annuity goods had been diverted to Texans, and they decided to make up the loss with a raid. They also wanted to stop a railroad being built across their old and beloved hunting grounds. On the prairie they spotted a luckless mule train and swooped down on it. Seven teamsters were killed. The Indians then plundered the train and made off with 41 mules.

When he returned to the reservation, Satanta was summoned before General William T. Sherman, out in the West on a tour of inspection. Before Sherman, Satanta gave a defiant account of the raid. At this, Sherman gave a sharp command and soldiers, previously hidden, appeared at the windows behind him with their rifles levelled. Satanta pulled a carbine from beneath his blanket and pointed it at Sherman's heart. For a few, brief moments it looked as though Satanta and the chiefs with him would kill Sherman in a suicidal shooting match. The General's nerve held, however, and the chiefs put up their guns.

Satanta, Satank and Big Tree were arrested and sent to Texas to be tried for murder.

During the journey to Texas Satank, manacled hand and foot, began singing his death song: "O sun you remain forever, but we Ko-eet-senko must die, / O earth you remain forever, but we Ko-eet-senko must die." He made a grab for a rifle, but was shot before he could fire it. Satanta and Big Tree were tried and sentenced to death by the court in Jacksboro, Texas, in July 1871 but on the advice of Indian agents and the trial judge, who feared an Indian uprising if the chiefs were hanged, the sentences were commuted to life imprisonment.

But the Kiowas wanted Satanta, their great chief, free. When their entreaties failed, they began raiding. They captured an army ordinance train, drove off 127 mules from Camp Supply, and raided the home of a Texas family. Lone Whites on trails and in settlements were murdered.

Once again, the Kiowa were at war.

Invasion of the Staked Plains

The tribulations of the Kiowa alarmed and agitated the Quahadi Comanche. Chief Quanah resolved ever more strongly to resist the White man. He soon had the chance to show his resolution.

Determined to halt Quahadi raiding in Texas, the Army assigned Colonel Ranald Slidell Mackenzie to conquer the band and other holdouts operating from the Staked Plains. Unapproachable and merciless, Mackenzie was considered by Ulysses S. Grant to be the most "promising young officer in the Army". Like other Civil War heroes, however, he had much to learn about Indian fighting.

In September 1871, Mackenzie assembled 600 troopers for an invasion of the Staked Plains. But Quanah and Bull

Bear did not oblige Mackenzie with the frontal fight he wanted. Instead, they harried his columns and made reckless lightning thrusts, before wheeling away and vanishing. Often the war parties were led by Quanah himself. He made an impressive, unforgettable sight in battle. A cavalry officer who fought Quanah wrote in his memoirs:

> A large and powerfully built chief led the bunch on a coal black racing pony. His heels nervously working in the animal's side, with a six-shooter poised in the air, he seemed the incarnation of savage brutal joy. His face was smeared with black war paint, which gave his features a satanic look. A large cruel mouth added to his ferocious appearance. Bells jingled as he rode at headlong speed, followed by the leading warriors, all eager to outstrip him in the race.

Shortly after midnight on 10 October 1871 Quanah led a charge through Mackenzie's encampment, flapping buffalo skins and ringing bells to panic the cavalry's horses. The Quahadi ran off 70 mounts, including Mackenzie's own prized animal. When Mackenzie sent a detachment of troopers after the Comanche, the Indians unceremoniously beat them off.

The relentless Mackenzie kept after the Quahadi. But in mid-October blizzards caused him to end the mission. On the way home, Mackenzie chased two Comanche who were trailing the column – and got an arrow in the hip.

But the redoubtable Mackenzie was back in the field by March 1872, hunting the Comanche. He campaigned throughout the summer, and in September his scouts came across a camp of the Kotsoteka Comanche on McClellan Creek. Mackenzie and 231 troopers attacked, killing 23 warriors and taking 124 women and children captive.

Mackenzie's victory at the creek was a crippling blow to the Kotsoteka. Most of the band trickled to the reservation. Even the Quahadi lost their morale, and raiding almost ceased. A strange quiet descended on the west Texas frontier.

It held for almost two years, but in 1874 the South Plains War set the Panhandle afire.

Having stripped Kansas of buffalo, White hunters began to drift south in March 1874 and set up a base near the deserted trading post of Adobe Walls (where Carson had engaged the Comanche a decade before) on the South Canadian River. The presence of these buffalo hunters enraged the Indians, for it seemed the end of their world. The White hunters had to be fought.

Another cause of the war was the governor of Texas. In 1873 the Kiowa chiefs Satanta and Big Tree were released from prison. This was offset by the demand of the governor of Texas that five Comanche braves on the reservation be surrendered to him as punishment for a raid which had occurred on Texas.

The Comanche refused to give up five men to an unknown fate. Instead, they moved out on the plains. So did the Cheyenne, Arapaho and some of the Kiowa.

In the spring of 1874, Quanah called a great council of all the Indians holding out on the south plains. They met near the mouth of Elk Creek and debated, and held a medicine dance. Isa-tai (Rear End of a Wolf), a young Quahadi medicine man, prophesied that an all-out attack would drive the White man away. "The buffalo shall come back everywhere," said Isa-tai, "so that there shall be feasting and plenty in the lodges. The Great Spirit has taught me strong medicine which will turn away the White man's bullets."

Quanah probably thought Isa-tai a fraud, but saw how desperately the others wanted to believe his predictions.

He even allowed Isa-tai to organize a sun dance, not a ceremony the Comanche observed. After the celebration, the Indians agreed to launch a combined attack on the buffalo hunters at Adobe Walls. From there they would move north, raiding all the camps in Panhandle country.

Before dawn on 27 June 1874, 700 warriors moved through the darkness and took up positions in the timber at the edge of Adobe Walls Creek. Before them were the three adobe buildings of the camp, and 30 sleeping hunters.

The hunters would have been slain in their sleep but for the luck of a ridge pole which happened to snap just before daylight. The noise awoke the hunter Billy Dixon, who chanced to go outside. In the grey dawn he saw hundreds of warriors moving towards the camp and shouted the alarm.

The hunters, now alert, took up positions in the buildings, and staved off repeated assaults with their new long-range Sharps rifles, fitted with telescopic sights. A warrior was knocked off his horse by one of the hunters – who included the soon-to-be-famous lawman Bat Masterson – at a distance of nearly a mile. As Red Cloud had found in the Wagon Box Fight on the Bozeman Trail, numbers or even unlimited courage were no match for innovations in gun technology. Although Quanah led the warriors to the very doors of the stockade, so that they could beat upon them with their rifle butts, the Indians could not break in. After three days of siege, Quanah called the warriors off. He was injured in the shoulder, and many of the best braves were dead. Isa-tai's magic had failed to work.

The buffalo hunters had lost only three men, one of them killed by Quanah. When the Indians withdrew, the buffalo hunters decapitated the bodies of the warriors left behind and stuck their heads on the poles of the stockade.

For weeks following Adobe Walls, the Indians raided the southern plains from Texas to Colorado. To subdue them, the Army sent out columns from Fort Griffin, Fort Sill and Camp Supply. They adopted a scorched-earth policy to deny the warriors essential supplies, burning their camps and supplies, and killing their pony herds. In September 1874, at the vast chasm of Palo Duro – previously unknown to White men – Mackenzie routed a mixed camp of Comanche, Cheyenne and Kiowa, ransacking the village and slaughtering 1,000 ponies. Above all, the Army gave the Indians no rest, and pursued them all fall, all winter. Leading the pursuits were the 30 men who formed the Army's elite scout unit, the Seminole Negro Indians, descendants of slaves who had escaped to the Florida swamps. At first in small bands, and then in large numbers the Indians began to come in.

The last were the Quahadis. Not until April 1875 did the first Quahadi, half starved, arrive at the reservation. Quanah and 400 followers continued to hold out until they received a message from Mackenzie, which informed them that if they surrendered they would be treated honourably. If they held out any longer, he would exterminate them. To the astonishment of the messenger, Quanah personally guaranteed to lead in the last of the Comanche.

On 2 June 1875 Quanah arrived at Fort Sill with his band, and over 1,500 horses in tow. The days of the free Native American on the southern plains were over – for ever.

Quanah Parker Lives in Peace

For 30 years Quanah had fought the White man. Now he took up their road. He was fortunate to escape imprisonment, which was the fate of some Comanche and Kiowa chiefs (among them Satanta, re-arrested on a fake charge;

unable to endure prison, he committed suicide in 1876 by slashing his wrists and leaping from a window). After a period of model behaviour, Quanah was allowed to visit relatives of his mother, who made him welcome. He stayed with them, learnt some English and studied farm tasks.

As he had once led his people in war, he began to lead them in peace. He made a big business out of the grazing rights the Comanche owned, leasing pasturage to Texas stockmen like Charles Goodnight and Burk Burnett. Burnett built Quanah Parker – as Quanah now called himself, in deference to his White blood – a large ranch house near Cache, Oklahoma, which became known as the "Comanche White House". Wearing a business suit, Quanah Parker lobbied governments, argued legal cases and invested in the railroads. He served as a judge, and in 1902 was elected deputy sheriff of Lawton, Oklahoma. Six years later, he was elected president of the local school district, which he had helped to create.

To do his duty by the Comanche, Quanah Parker was prepared to take up White ways. Yet he seldom compromised his Comanche cultural and spiritual heritage; he was a principal proponent of the ceremonial use of peyote, a spineless cactus which produces "buttons" containing a hallucinogenic drug. Over time the peyote rite became the focus for the Indian religion known as the Native American Church.

Quanah Parker died of pneumonia on 22 February 1911. In keeping with Comanche tradition, a medicine man flapped his hands over the body of Quanah like an eagle flaps its wings – and so the chief's spirit was called to the afterworld.

Quanah Parker was buried next to his mother. Inside the White man's coffin, he was dressed in the full regalia of a Quahadi chief.

Little Big Horn

War Clouds Over the Black Hills

When the final war between the Sioux and the Whites came, it began in the Black Hills of Dakota, to the Sioux a special, hallowed place. Although they had only arrived in the land themselves a century before, the Sioux had come to regard the Black Hills as the most sacred place on earth.

Under the terms of the Treaty of 1868, which the victorious Red Cloud had secured from the government, the Black Hills were promised to the Sioux for "as long as the grass shall grow." They would also hold forever the Powder River Buffalo range.

The ink of the treaty was hardly dry before small clouds of war began to hover over the Black Hills and the other lands held by the Sioux. White homesteaders were outraged that good land had been given to the Indians. Twenty Sioux chiefs, including Red Cloud, travelled east to Washington DC to put their case to President Grant. The talks petered out without conclusion, but what Red Cloud saw of the White man's power in the East persuaded him that a military struggle against the US was fruitless. Red Cloud, on his return home, hung up his war lance for ever, and reluctantly agreed to move to an agency south of the Black

Hills. Many went with him and gave up the old way of life.

The decision of Red Cloud split the Sioux, for many also refused to leave the Powder River. Increasingly, the holdout Sioux began to look for guidance to a Huncpapa medicine man called Sitting Bull (Tatanka Iyotake), who was as stubborn as his name suggested. In boyhood Sitting Bull had been nicknamed "Slow", for his wilful deliberation, and this aspect about him had never changed. Almost as influential as Sitting Bull was the Oglala warrior Crazy Horse. Although many found Crazy Horse strange – he believed that he lived in the world of dreams, and he always went into battle naked save for a loincloth – he was a fearless and inspired warrior. Such was his utter suspicion of and contempt for the White man that he refused to have his photograph taken by their cameras.

As each year passed, more and more little clouds of war began to accumulate over the northern plains. The slaughter of the American buffalo was continuing apace, and threatening the last big herd, located in Montana–Wyoming. Settlers were edging onto Sioux lands. And then a second transcontinental railroad, the Northern Pacific, began to reach out into the Far West, with surveying parties entering the Yellowstone River region – Teton Sioux land – in 1873. In the summer of that year, bands of Sioux under Crazy Horse skirmished with the cavalry assigned to protect the surveyors. The White horse soldiers were from the 7th Cavalry and were led by George Armstrong Custer. After his victory at the Washita, Custer had thrown himself into the role of frontier Indian fighter, and dressed in buckskin, complete with tassels. Custer relished fighting Indians, but was also attracted to them, to their heroic glory and their freedom. He had even taken an Indian mistress, Mo-nah-se-ta, daughter of the Cheyenne leader Little Rock.

The skirmishes in the Yellowstone were sharp probing engagements, curtain-raisers to a bigger affair. Second Lieutenant Charles Larned described one in a letter home:

At early dawn on the 10th our efforts to cross [the Tongue River] commenced, and it was not until 4 in the afternoon that they were reluctantly relinquished, after every expedient had been resorted to in vain. The current was too swift and fierce for our heavy cavalry. We therefore went into bivouac close to the river bank to await the arrival of the main body, and slept that night as only men in such condition can sleep. We hardly anticipated the lively awakening that awaited us. Just at daylight our slumbers were broken by a sharp volley of musketry from the opposite bank, accompanied by shouts and yells that brought us all to our feet in an instant. As far up the river as we could see, clouds of dust announced the approach of our slippery foes, while the rattling volleys from the opposite woods, and the "zip," "zip" of the balls about our ears told us that there were a few evil disposed persons close by.

For half an hour, while the balls flew high, we lay still without replying, but when the occasional quiver of a wounded horse told that the range was being acquired by them, the horses and men were moved back from the river edge to the foot of the bluffs, and there drawn up in line of battle to await developments. A detachment of sharpshooters was concealed in the woods, and soon sent back a sharp reply to the thickening compliments from the other side. Our scouts and the Indians were soon exchanging chaste complimentary remarks in choice Sioux – such as: "We're coming over to give you h—l;" "You'll see more Indians than you ever saw before in your life," and "Shoot, you son of a dog" from ours. Sure enough, over they came, as good as their word, above and below us, and in twenty minutes our scouts came tumbling down the bluffs head

overheels, screeching: "Heap Indian come." Just at this
moment General Custer rode up to the line, followed by a
bright guidon, and made rapid disposition for the defense.
Glad were we that the moment of action had arrived, and
that we were to stand no longer quietly and grimly in line
of battle to be shot at. One platoon of the first squadron on
the left was moved rapidly up the bluffs, and thrown out
in skirmish line on the summit, to hold the extreme left.
The remainder of the squadron followed as quickly as it
could be deployed, together with one troop of the Fourth
Squadron.

On they came as before, 500 or 600 in number, screaming and yelling as usual, right onto the line before they
saw it. At the same moment the regimental band, which
had been stationed in a ravine just in rear, struck up
"Garry Owen." The men set up a responsive shout, and a
rattling volley swept the whole line.

The fight was short and sharp just here, the Indians
rolling back after the first fire and shooting from a safer
distance. In twenty minutes the squadrons were mounted
and ordered to charge. Our evil-disposed friends tarried
no longer, but fled incontinently before the pursuing squadrons. We chased them eight miles and over the river, only
returning when the last Indian had gotten beyond our
reach.

No less than a thousand warriors had surrounded us,
and we could see on the opposite bluffs the scattered
remnants galloping wildly to and fro. Just at the conclusion of the fight the infantry came up, and two shells from
the Rodman guns completed the discomfiture of our de-
moralized foes. Our loss was one killed, Private Tuttle, E
Troop, Seventh Cavalry, and three wounded. Among the
latter, Lieutenant [Charles] Braden, Seventh Cavalry, while
gallantly holding the extreme left, the hottest portion of
the line, was shot through the thigh, crushing the bone

badly. Four horses were killed and eight or ten wounded, and deserve honorable mention, although noncombatants. Official estimates place the Indian loss at forty killed and wounded, and a large number of ponies.

To the disappointment of the 7th Cavalry they were suddenly withdrawn from the Yellowstone. So were the railwaymen. Overbuilding on the Northern Pacific had caused the bank backing the company to collapse. Within days the entire US financial system was in collapse. Within months a million Americans were out of work.

The year 1873 was destined to be a bad year for America; it also saw drought on the Great Plains, and swarms of locusts that devoured the crops, even the paint on houses.

A desperate nation began to seize on desperate solutions. There were rumours of gold in the Black Hills, the Sioux's hallowed ground, the ground given to them "forever". In July 1874, Custer, 600 soldiers and several newspapermen left Fort Abraham Lincoln near Bismarck, Dakota, on an expedition to the Black Hills. Ostensibly the purpose of the expedition was scientific and exploratory. But as everyone knew, its real mission was to determine whether there was gold in the hills; accompanying the soldiers were two prospectors.

On 27 July 1874 the prospectors found traces of gold at French Creek. By the spring of 1875 the Black Hills were alive with the sound of thousands of illegal White picks. Red Cloud and the other reservation leaders furiously demanded that the Whites should be removed, and called Custer "The Chief of all the thieves." Equally furiously, Whites demanded that the Indians be removed:

This abominable compact [the Treaty of 1868] is now pleaded as a barrier to the improvement and development of one of the richest and most fertile sections in America.

What shall be done with these Indian dogs in our manger?
They will not dig gold or let others do it.

Yankton Press and Dakotian

The government tried to buy the Black Hills from the
Sioux for $6 million, or lease mining rights at $400,000 a
year. Red Cloud and the reservation Sioux met in council
and turned the offer down.

As soon as the negotiation failed, the White invaders
became totally brazen, laying out towns and organizing
local governments in the Black Hills. Then they demanded
troops to protect them.

Although the White settlers were acting illegally, Washington decided to remove the Indians instead. It was
easier. In December, President Grant signed an executive
order requiring all Indians in the "unceded land" to go
voluntarily on to reservations by 31 January 1876. If they
did not, they would be treated as "hostiles" and driven in.
By this order, the government seized the Powder River
country as well as the Black Hills.

News of the order was to be taken by messenger from
the agencies to the camps of Sitting Bull, Crazy Horse,
Gall, Rain-in-the-Face, Low Dog and the other Indians
living up on the buffalo ranges. Blizzards and snowdrifts
held up the messengers. Some camps never even received
the order.

When the deadline came and the Powder River camps
had not entered the reservation, the Secretary of War
received a brief dispatch: "Said Indians are hereby turned
over to the War Department for such action as you may
deem proper."

No sooner had the snows in the northern ranges begun
to thaw than General George Crook was in the field,
destroying a Sioux–Cheyenne camp on the Powder River.
Bad weather – including a blizzard so severe that the

mercury in the expedition thermometer froze – caused Crook to return to camp unsatisfactorily early.

Meanwhile, General Phil Sheridan began to plan a three-pronged assault on the "hostiles". One column, led by Colonel John Gibbon, would drive down the Yellowstone from Fort Ellis. Crook would move up through Wyoming and strike the Indians from the south. A third column, under General Alfred Terry and Colonel Custer, would head west out of Dakota.

Throughout the spring, White soldiers gathered for the big campaign. The Army had been drastically reduced in strength since 1866, down to 27,000 men, was beset by bullying and poor pay (a mere $13 a month for privates), and weakened by alcoholism and scurvy. Disease killed more troopers than did Indians. A frequent morale-lowering lament of troopers in the 1870s was that Indians had better rifles (they seldom did). Despite all this, the 7th Cavalry, full of veterans, considered itself an elite, and was almost as good as it thought it was. On 17 May 1876, Custer – his long hair cut short for the campaign – and the 7th Cavalry marched out of Fort Lincoln towards Indian country, the regimental band striking up the familiar tones of "The Girl I Left Behind Me".

While the White soldiers had been gathering, so had the Native Americans. From all over the northern plains Indians gathered in the Powder River country. For the first time in years, more Indians left the reservation than joined it, as thousands streamed to the buffalo ranges for a joyous summer hunt. And for a war, if it was necessary.

By late May, Sitting Bull's camp had swollen to more than 7,000 people, from the Teton Sioux (even some eastern Santee Sioux), Arapaho and other Northern tribes. Seldom before had so many Plains Indians come together.

During the second week of June, the great Indian camp moved up the Rosebud Valley to the head of Ash Creek.

Here they held a Sun Dance. Among those who sought vision was Sitting Bull, whose adopted brother, Jumping Bull, cut 100 pieces of flesh from his arms with an awl and a sharp knife: then Sitting Bull danced with eyes fixed on the sun for 18 hours until he fell unconscious. At length, a great vision came: he saw many soldiers falling into the camp upside down. "These dead soldiers are the gifts of God", said Sitting Bull.

Shortly after the Sun Dance was over, Cheyenne scouts rushed into the camp to report that White soldiers headed by "Three Stars" (General Crook) were in the valley of the Rosebud. The Indians decided to intercept him.

On the morning of 17 June Crook and his 1,300 men, including Shoshoni and Crow scouts (always particularly keen to fight the Sioux), halted for coffee. Suddenly there was firing up ahead and shouts of "Sioux! Sioux!" from the scouts, and then Crazy Horse and 1,500 Sioux and Cheyenne warriors were right on top of the soldiers. All day long the battle raged over the hills, the Indians preventing Crook forming a single strong front. This was the sort of war Crazy Horse liked best, small isolated fights, a chaos in which Western military theory had no application or point. By nightfall, Crook had lost 57 men and, short of ammunition, opted to withdraw back to base camp at Goose Creek. He was immobilized for the rest of the summer.

The Indians had just beaten Crook – the Army's best Indian fighter. After a triumphal four-day scalp dance, the great Indian village moved towards the Greasy Grass River – the stream the White man called Little Big Horn.

The Battle of the Greasy Grass

Up on the Yellowstone the other two columns of the Army's campaign met in conference aboard the steamer

Far West. A reconnaissance by the 7th Cavalry's Major Marcus A. Reno had located a great Indian trail leading towards Little Big Horn. General Terry, in overall command, decided to split his forces. He ordered Gibbon's infantry into the field, and sent Custer's fast-moving 7th Cavalry to pick up the Indian trail and follow it. There would be no escape for the Indians. They would be trapped between infantry and cavalry at Little Big Horn.

Custer drove his men relentlessly, a pace of 30 miles a day and more, hoping to defeat the Indians before the infantry could encounter them. On the second day out the cavalry hit the Indians' trail: it was over a mile wide. Ree and Crow scouts found scalps of Crook's soldiers which had been thrown aside. The scouts advised Custer to proceed with caution. He brushed them aside, and ordered his exhausted men to move on, towards the hills in the distance.

At dawn on 25 June, Custer's scouts climbed to the top of a mountain for a reconnaissance of the route ahead. As the light improved they could make out the Little Big Horn 15 miles away. And then they saw a pony herd which seemed to cover the distant land like a blanket. A second later they saw the hundreds upon hundreds of tipis, arranged in huge tribal circles, of the Huncpapas, the Miniconjous, the Oglalas, the San Arcs and the Cheyenne. There were nearly 7,000 Indians assembled before them, probably the greatest concentration ever of Plains Indians in one place.

Custer's scouts began singing their death songs. One told Custer that there were not enough bullets to kill all the Indians down there. Custer merely told his officers, "The largest Indian camp on the North American continent is ahead and I'm going to attack it."

A little after noon the 611 officers and men of the 7th Cavalry started down into the valley of the Little Big

Horn. Not knowing the terrain or the disposition of the enemy, Custer made a fateful decision. He would reconnaissance in force – split the regiment into several components, which could be employed separately or together as circumstances dictated. It made sense but it also weakened his attacking power. Thinking the Indians might try to escape, Custer sent Captain Frederick Benteen with about 125 troopers off to scout the hills on the south. Major Marcus Reno and his battalion was ordered to cross the Little Big Horn and attack the Indian village from the South. Custer and the rest of the regiment would proceed parallel to Reno and support his action.

Fording the Little Big Horn at around 2 o'clock, Reno began advancing along the open valley bottom. Ahead, around a timbered bend in the river, was an enormous cloud of dust, thrown up by hundreds of Indian war ponies' hooves, rising up into the blazing afternoon heat. Reno signalled a charge, and his command raced forward. Occasionally he threw glances behind, looking for Custer's support, but it was nowhere to be seen. Afraid of plunging into superior Indian numbers, Reno threw up his hand to halt the galloping charge which ground to a confused halt, with Reno then ordering the men to fight on foot. They began firing ragged volleys at milling horsemen in front of them.

Without informing Reno, Custer had changed his battle plan. Instead of supporting Reno's charge, he rode north, screened by hills, and circled the Indian village so that it was between him and Reno. Presumably he intended to strike into the village through a gap in the hills, thus confronting the enemy with attacks from two directions. Indians fleeing from Reno's attack would also be cut off.

Custer and his men probably never reached the Little Big Horn River. As they descended a coulée 1,500

Huncpapa warriors led by Gall rode screaming up to meet them. Custer's men began to fall back, trying to seek higher ground. Their situation was critical, but not entirely without hope – until Crazy Horse led a thousand Oglala and Cheyenne warriors up the ridge behind them. Custer had been outflanked by Crazy Horse, who had led his warriors out of the camp in a huge swinging arc to attack the cavalry from behind. The cavalry fought desperately. They shot their horses to form breastworks, vainly trying to find shelter from the overwhelming Indians. Some troopers fought to the last. Some tried to make a break for the river. Some probably killed themselves to avoid torture. The battle took an hour, perhaps slightly less. And then Custer's men were all dead.

A eye-witness view of "Custer's Last Stand" from the Indian side was later given by Two Moons, a Cheyenne chief:

Then the Sioux rode up the ridge on all sides, riding very fast. The Cheyenne went up the left way. Then the shooting was quick. Pop-pop-pop very fast. Some of the soldiers were down on their knees, some standing. Officers all in front. The smoke was like a great cloud, and everywhere the Sioux went the dust rose like smoke. We circled all round him – swirling like water round a stone. We shoot, we ride fast, we shoot again. Soldiers drop, and horses fall on them. Soldiers in line drop, but one man rides up and down the line – all the time shouting. He rode a sorrel horse with white face and white fore-legs. I don't know who he was. He was a brave man.

Indians keep swirling round and round, and the soldiers killed only a few. Many soldiers fell. At last all horses killed but five. Once in a while some man would break out and run towards the river, but he would fall. At last about a hundred men and five horsemen stood on the hill all bunched together. All along the bugler kept blowing his commands. He was very brave too. Then a chief was killed. I hear it was Long Hair [Custer], I don't know; and then the five horsemen and the bunch of men, may be forty, started toward the river. The man on the sorrel horse led them, shouting all the time. He wore a buckskin shirt, and had long black hair and mustache. He fought hard with a big knife. His men were all covered with white dust. I couldn't tell whether they were officers or not. One man all alone ran far down toward the river, then round up over the hill. I thought he was going to escape, but a Sioux fired and hit him in the head. He was the last man. He wore braid on his arms [sergeant].

All the soldiers were now killed, and the bodies were stripped. After that no one could tell which were officers. The bodies were left where they fell. We had no dance that night. We were sorrowful.

Next day four Sioux chiefs and two Cheyennes and I, Two Moon, went upon the battlefield to count the dead. One man carried a little bundle of sticks. When we came to dead men we took a little stick and gave it to another man, so we counted the dead. There were 388. There were thirty-nine Sioux and seven Cheyennes killed and about a hundred wounded.

Some white soldiers were cut with knives, to make sure they were dead; and the war women had mangled some. Most of them were left just where they fell. We came to the man with the big mustache; he lay down the hills towards the river. The Indians did not take his buckskin shirt. The Sioux said "That is a big chief. That is Long Hair." I don't know. I had never seen him. The man on the white-faced horse was the bravest man.

Three miles south of Custer, Reno had been badly mauled and retreated up a hill. Benteen arrived in time to save him, and the combined companies held out for another scorching day. Reno and Benteen would have their share of blame for the débâcle at Little Big Horn; Benteen, an able officer but public in his dislike of Custer, failed to respond to messages sent out by Custer to hurry to join him for the attack; Reno was indecisive, failed to keep a front at the river and failed to send Benteen, his subordinate, forward to a possible relief of Custer, whose battle he could hear.

Late in the afternoon of 26 June the exultant Indians withdrew, leaving behind their dead warriors on burial scaffolds, surrounded by a circle of dead ponies to serve the braves in the spirit land. The Battle of the Little Big Horn was over. Sitting Bull's vision had been good.

The next day Colonel Gibbon's infantry column arrived and found the ghastly piles of Custer's mutilated dead. "Long Hair" himself had been shot twice, once through the left temple, once through the heart. According to Kate Bighead, a Cheyenne woman who was on the battlefield, his ear was punctured to enable him to hear better in the afterworld.

The Sioux and Cheyenne had won an astounding victory. All five of Custer's companies, 225 men, had been killed. Reno and Benteen had lost 53 killed.

It took eight days for the news of the massacre to reach the town of Helena, Montana, and from there to be flashed by telegraph all over the world. Most Americans found out on reading their newspaper on the morning of 5 July, just a day after they had celebrated the centennial of independence.

Surrender

Yet, although the Indians won the battle, they lost the war. An enraged nation demanded immediate vengeance. All

reservations in the northern plains were placed under
military control. Congress passed a law compelling the
Sioux to hand over the Black Hills, the Powder River and
Big Horn mountains and to move onto reservations.

Throughout the rest of the year the free Indians of the
northern plains were harassed by Crook, Mackenzie,
Colonel Nelson A. Miles, and just about every seasoned
Indian fighter the Army could get into the field. Throughout the winter small bands of Sioux and Cheyenne limped
into the Red Cloud Agency.

On 6 May 1877 Crazy Horse led his lodges into Fort
Robinson, Nebraska, and surrendered. He gave his left
hand to Lieutenant W. P. Clark and said: "Friend, I shake
with this hand because my heart is on this side; I want this
peace to last for ever." Four months later he was dead.
Peace faction Indians and the Army regarded him as too
dangerous to be loose. On 6 September he was brought
under guard to the army compound at Fort Robinson.
Seeing that the soldiers intended to imprison him, Crazy
Horse tried to escape. There was a scuffle. An officer
called out, "Stab at the son of a bitch! Kill him!" A soldier
named William Gentle bayoneted Crazy Horse twice.

He was taken into the adjutant's office. He refused to
lie on the White man's cot, and died on the floor an hour
later.

Of the mighty Sioux nation only the Huncpapa band of
Sitting Bull and Chief Gall were not on the reservation.
They were across the border in Canada, where they hoped
to find sanctuary. Instead they found disease, diplomatic
intrigues, dissension and famine. Gradually they trickled
back across the border and into the reservation. In 1881
Sitting Bull himself finally gave up. At midday on 19 July,
near starving and dressed in rags, Sitting Bull rode into
Fort Buford in Dakota. With him were just 143 followers.

No Indians were spared in the backlash that followed

Custer's Last Stand. Although the Nez Perce ("Pierced Noses") had never killed a White man, they were ordered in 1877 to leave their homeland for a new reservation elsewhere in Idaho. They were given just 30 days to round up their stock and dismantle their homes. While they were doing this, a young Nez Perce whose father had been killed by Whites led a series of raids that took the lives of 18 settlers.

Fearing reprisals, Chief Joseph of the Nez Perce led 700 of his band into hiding in White Bird Canyon. After beating back an army detachment, he decided to lead his people to safety in Canada. Newspapers and politicians clamoured for the Nez Perce to be punished, for the Whites to be avenged. For 1,300 miles the Nez Perce walked, through Idaho, Wyoming, the Yellowstone (already a national park) and up towards the border, and as they did so they beat off army attack after attack. Only when Chief Joseph's "Long March" was in the snows of the Bear Paw Mountains, within 40 miles of Canada, did Colonel Nelson A. Miles manage to trap the Nez Perce. Chief Joseph surrendered after being promised that his people would be sent back to Idaho. "I am tired; my heart is sick," Chief Joseph told Nelson Miles. "From where the sun now stands, I will fight no more forever."

The Nez Perce were not sent home to Idaho. They were sent to Indian Territory, where many died. Nelson Miles protested, and eventually the Nez Perce went to a reservation in Washington.

After the Nez Perce, it was time for the Bannocks – the same Bannocks who had just scouted for Miles against the Nez Perce. When Congress failed to provide their promised rations, the starving Bannocks began fighting the settlers who had illegally occupied their camass (an edible plant of the hyacinth family) prairie. "I do not wonder," General Crook reported, "that when these Indians see their wives and children starving, and their last source of supplies cut off, they go to war. And then we are sent out to kill them."

After the Bannocks, it was the turn of the Utes. In 1879 Colorado citizens elected a governor whose platform was "UTES MUST GO". And so they did, forcibly banished to a strip of land in Utah that the Mormons thought too barren for human habitation.

All the Indians of the north and the plains were now on the White man's reservations. Only in the Southwest were there still Indians to be reckoned with.

Geronimo, Apache Tiger

The Invincible Leader

Five years had passed since the Chiricahua Apache under Cochise had entered the reservation. And gradually, imperceptibly, the peace had come undone.

When Cochise died in 1874 his son Taza became chief, tribal leadership being hereditary amongst the Apache. But Taza, if likeable, lacked authority, and larger numbers of Chiricahua warriors came under the influence of Geronimo, the warrior leader of the sub-band of Bedonkohe Apache who had become assimilated into the Chiricahua. The son of a Nednai chief who had renounced his chieftainship to marry into the Bedonkohe, Geronimo had been born One Who Yawns (Goyahkla). He had been given the name Geronimo by the Mexicans, for he had once fought them at Arispe – after they had murdered his family – with such terrifying ferocity that they prayed to St Geronimo for salvation. The name had stuck, and was used by Apache, Mexicans and White alike. Geronimo had the Power; it had visited him when he had grieved for his slain family. "No gun can ever kill you," the Power had told him. He was invincible.

Geronimo had grown tired of the monotony of reservation life, and begun to sneak off to indulge his old habit of raiding Mexico. The Mexicans complained bitterly, and in 1876 the Arizonans joined the outcry when two stage-coach attendants and a rancher were killed by drunken Apaches. (That the stagecoach attendants had gotten the Apaches drunk and tried to cheat them was conveniently ignored.) The Governor of Arizona, Anson P. Safford, demanded that Washington replace Thomas Jeffords as Apache Agent, while Tucsons's *Arizona Citizen* declared: "The kind of war needed for the Chiricahua Apaches is steady, unrelenting, hopeless, and undiscriminating war, slaying men, women and children, until every valley and crest and crag and fastness shall send to high heaven the grateful incense of festering and rotting Chiricahuas."

The murder of the three White men gave Washington a pretext to close the Chiricahua reservation, something it wanted to do anyway as part of its 1875 policy of "consolidation" of the reservations. The Apaches were all to be forced onto one overcrowded reservation at San Carlos. On learning of the consolidation plan, Geronimo, now aged 46, fled across the border to Mexico.

This first stint as a holdout was inauspicious. Early in 1877 he came out of Mexico, driving a herd of stolen horses, to visit the agency at Warm Springs (Ojo Caliente). The regime at Warm Springs was lax, and the place was used frequently as a refuge by "renegades" in their cross-border raids. News of Geronimo's whereabouts reached the Commissioner of Indian Affairs, who wired John Philip Clum, the young agent of the San Carlos reservation, and ordered him to arrest Geronimo. Clum immediately set out on the 400-mile journey to Warm Springs, accompanied by about 100 of his Apache Indian police.

After reaching Warm Springs, Clum sent a message to Geronimo and other "renegade" warriors, like Chief Victorio who had jumped the reservation, that he desired to talk. Having no reason to expect confrontation, the

Apache rode the three miles to the agency accompanied by their wives and children. Geronimo found Clum sitting on the porch of the adobe agency building, a dozen of his police around him. Clum opened the proceedings by accusing Geronimo of killing men and violating the agreement made between Cochise and General Howard. He told Geronimo he was taking him to San Carlos. Geronimo answered defiantly: "We are not going to San Carlos with you, and unless you are very careful, you and your Apache police will not go back to San Carlos either. Your bodies will stay here at Ojo Caliente to make food for coyotes." To emphasize the point, Geronimo hitched his rifle up in his arms.

At this moment Clum gave a prearranged signal, a touch of the brim of his hat; the doors of the commissary building burst open and 80 police charged out. Geronimo's thumb began to creep towards the hammer of his rifle, but he thought better of it and stood stock-still. Clum stepped forward to disarm the Apache. This was the only time that Geronimo was ever captured, and then it was by a trick.

Conveyed to San Carlos in shackles, Geronimo found the reservation worse than he had feared. Situated alongside the Gila River, much of it was low-lying, reaching temperatures of 110 degrees in summer. White settlers were already beginning to squat the best land. There were outbreaks of malaria and smallpox.

John Clum who, despite his deceit in the capture of Geronimo, was well-liked by many Apache, believed he could work with the People and keep them peaceful on the reservation. The Army, however, because of the concentration of Apache leaders at San Carlos, sent the cavalry to guard the reservation. John Clum was forced to disband his self-regulating Apache police. He resigned in protest, and went on to edit the Tombstone *Epitaph*.

Victorio fled San Carlos almost immediately, moving

back with his people to Warm Springs. The Army harassed them, and Victorio declared he would "make war forever" against the USA. He was killed in 1880 in a fight with Mexican soldiers.

Geronimo endured the reservation for a year. He had little choice, for much of the time he was incarcerated, an experience he thought "might easily have been death to me." As soon as he was able to he escaped to Mexico with a few other Chiricahuas. He returned voluntarily in 1880 following a bitter winter of starvation in the mountains, but again he did not stay long.

"The Apaches Are Out!"

During the spring of 1881, a religious movement arose among the reservation Apache which preached the end of the White man and the raising again of the old Apache order. In August, the agent sent a detachment of soldiers to arrest the spiritual leader of the movement, Noch-aydel-klinne. His followers attacked the troops; a pitched battle ensued, with dead on both sides. Army reinforcements were rushed in, and the rumour began to circulate that the Apache leaders would be arrested. More specifically, the rumours said that Geronimo – who had been sceptical about the new religion – was to be hanged. In September of 1881, in response to these rumours, Geronimo and the Nednai chief, Juh, along with 70 warriors, jumped the reservation and made for the Sierra Madre. Their route took them past Tombstone, where a posse including three of the Earp brothers tried to head them off, to no avail.

Six months later, in April 1882, Geronimo and his band returned to the reservation but not, this time, as captives. They rode in as self-declared liberators, and persuaded most of the remaining Chiricahuas and Warm Springs

Apaches to leave with them for Mexico. Near the border, at Horse Shoe Canyon, pursuing cavalry caught up with them. The warriors fought a stiff rearguard action, allowing the main body of women and children to cross into Mexico. Then disaster struck. A Mexican infantry regiment stumbled upon the Apaches, killing most of the women and children who were riding in front.

Among the warriors and chiefs who managed to escape were Naiche (a son of Cochise), Loco, Chato, and Geronimo himself. Embittered, they joined up with old Nana, chief of the Mimbrenos after the death of Victorio, to form a united guerrilla band of 80 warriors.

Over the next two years, Geronimo and the united band raided Mexican towns and villages with near impunity. The raiding life of the band was later described by Jason Betzinez, a young Chiricahua, in his memoir *I Fought with Geronimo*:

Preparations for the raid deep into Sonora consisted of making extra pairs of moccasins, cleaning our hair, sharpening knives, and cleaning and greasing guns. We had no tomahawks, arrows or spears. The Apaches never did have tomahawks and by 1882 arrows and spears were rarely used.

We established most of the young boys, women, and children on top of the mountain where they could keep a good lookout and take care of themselves. Mother and I went with the men at least part of the way. Our job was to bring back stolen beeves to our camp so that the women and children would have plenty to eat while the men were away.

After crossing a mountain range we bivouacked for the night. The next morning our leaders told us to travel close together because of the dense timbers, briars, and cactus. The trip was to be dangerous and difficult; it would be almost impossible to travel at night. We were nearly among the enemy now but kept on going to the vicinity of the nearest town. Then our men began scouting around for horses and mules while mother and I together with five young boys, waited on a hill top where we could see the surrounding country and watch out for signs of the enemy.

After a long and anxious wait, toward evening we were relieved to see our men coming, driving some horses. It had been a risky adventure for us. Even one Mexican cowboy spotting us would have meant serious trouble, we being without weapons.

The next day the men killed several head of cattle, which we cut up and loaded on horses. Late in the afternoon mother and I, together with five boys, started back toward the rest of our band. We traveled part of the night through the thick timber. In the morning we resumed our journey, our horses heavily laden with meat, arriving late in the afternoon within sight of camp. Some of the women came out to help us carry in the beef. As we climbed up the mountainside we were very careful not to leave tracks that would show. After we got to camp and unloaded the animals some of the boys drove the horses down to the river away from camp. We now had enough dried beef to last us for at least a month.

Meantime our men went on west to where a main road passed between several towns, south towards Ures, the then capital of Sonora. Where the road ran along the river through the timber was the locality in which the Apaches were accustomed to lie in wait for travelers especially pack trains laden with drygoods.

Our men were gone about fifteen days. Meanwhile we lived very quietly at camp. One day a woman standing in front of her tepee saw a white object approaching us in the distance. The women and children immediately became very excited and fearful, thinking that the enemy were coming. Two of us boys going out to investigate found that it was our warriors coming home with great quantities of dry goods, bolts of cloth and wearing apparel. When they arrived at the foot of the mountain they called up to us whereupon all the people in camp hurried down to meet them. We surely were glad to see them and they to see us. One thing we *didn't* see was scalps. The Apaches did not practice the custom of scalping a fallen enemy. There may have been exceptions to this but they were very, very rare. Concerning Geronimo I never knew him to bring in a scalp. Much nonsense has been written about this.

After our warriors returned, we hiked farther up the Yaqui River, camped for awhile, then again moved upstream. Here we had plenty of food and nothing to worry about. Nevertheless we were very careful not to disclose our presence because we were quite near a number of Mexican towns. Every day our men stationed lookouts on the hills. Our camp at this time was at the junction of the Bavispe and Yaqui Rivers.

The leaders decided to raid toward the northwest. This time we started off on foot leaving all the animals in the valley near the Bavispe River where there was plenty of good grass. We concealed in caves our saddles and the loot which the men had brought back from the earlier raid, as well as all our camp gear which we could not carry on our backs. We took only one mule, my big mule, on which Geronimo's wife and baby rode.

Our band moved straight west toward a Mexican town. Just when it appeared that we were going right on into the village the leaders stopped a few miles to the east. The plan was to avoid stealing any horses or mules while we were sneaking around in between these towns, two of which lay to the west and one to the east of our route.

From the last campsite the band turned northwest toward the mountains. Since we were about to cross the main road we were especially careful not to be seen or leave any sign that would put the soldiers on our trail. Our men knew that each town contained a garrison of troops. So we carefully covered our tracks.

We camped at the foot of a mountain a few miles from the road running between Buenavista and Moctezuma. Early next morning Geronimo told the men that they could now go out to look for horses and mules. They should drive in all that they could find, as we needed them for the expected move north into the mountains. About noon our men drove in quite a number of animals stolen from the Mexicans. We had a great time roping them and breaking them for the women and children to ride. My cousin roped a mule but it broke away from him. I chased it out into the prairie for nearly two miles. I nearly went too far. Suddenly I saw Mexican soldiers only a short distance away.

As I galloped back to the group of Apaches I heard my cousin shouting to me to hurry up, the enemy were coming along behind me. Meanwhile the Indians were taking up a position from which to attack the soldiers. As I sped over a low ridge I heard the shooting start. The Indians charged so fast toward the enemy that they failed to notice one soldier who was hiding in the bushes. This man shot and killed the last Apache to ride by him. The warriors, hearing the shot, came dashing back just in time to shoot the Mexican.

The band felt dreadfully sad over losing a warrior. He was a Warm Springs Apache who had no near relatives in the band with us.

Late that afternoon we started off to the west then camped at the foot of the mountains for supper. While we were thus engaged, a sentinel ran in to report that the

enemy were at the skirmish ground of that afternoon, not
far behind us. We moved out hastily into the foothills
where we remained in concealment during the night. In
the morning we saw the soldiers following our tracks and
approaching our hill. At once the warriors took up positions ready for a fight. But the Mexicans didn't attempt to
follow our trail up the mountainside.

Finally our men got tired of waiting, so we moved on,
traveling very fast right on into the night. We came to a
short steep canyon where we made camp and enjoyed a
good night's rest.

In the morning we set a course across the wide valley of
the Bavispe. Although our horses and mules were in good
shape we traveled slowly, enjoying the trip and the pleasant surroundings. That night we camped beside the Bavispe
River. The chiefs told the men not to shoot any deer
because the Mexicans might hear the firing.

This country looked as though it belonged to us. For
some days owing to the wise leadership of Geronimo we
had not been disturbed by an enemy. We crossed the river
and moved through the woods discussing the fact that the
country seemed to be full of deer and other game. In fact
the deer just stood and watched us pass. It seemed that
they had never been disturbed by anyone hunting them. A
person living in this favored spot would never have to go
hungry. There were plenty of wild animals and other
food, easily obtainable. But at this time the men all obeyed
Geronimo and didn't fire a shot. Besides, we still had
plenty of dried beef.

Arriving at our next objective we again settled down
for an indefinite stay. It was just like peacetime. We had
plenty to eat, good clothing taken from the stolen stocks,
and no enemies nearby. We were about thirty miles southeast of Fronteras.

During this period the women, assisted by some of the

boys, were gathering and drying the fruit of the yucca, preparing for a winter to be spent in the Sierras. It was in the late summer or early fall of 1882.

As well as raiding into Mexico, the Geronimo band attacked American settlements and ranches.

To stop the outrages, the Army once again called on George Crook ("Grey Wolf" to the Apache). On 4 September 1882 Crook assumed command at San Carlos and, on talking to the Apaches on the reservation, found that their grievances were justified. The reservation Apaches, he concluded, "had not only the best reasons for complaining, but had displayed remarkable forbearance in remaining at peace." He began a reform of the corrupt practices of White contractors and suppliers and set about re-establishing John Clum's Apache police.

Crook also gave much thought to the band of Apaches free in Mexico. He did not want another guerrilla war with the Apaches, especially in the rugged terrain of the sierras. Crook decided that he should meet with Geronimo and the other leaders, and that the best place to do this was in Mexico. But in order to cross the border, he had to wait for the Apaches to make a raid in the US. By international agreement, he could go into Mexico only in pursuit of renegade Apaches.

His justification came on 21 March 1883, when a renegade war party raided a mining camp near Tombstone. A few days later the same raiders killed federal judge H. C. McComas and his wife, and abducted their son. Crook, together with 50 soldiers and 193 civilian Apache scouts, trailed the renegades into Mexico. After searching for several weeks, the scouts located Geronimo's camp and captured the women and children, the men being on a raiding party. The Apache had believed that they were safe inside Mexico; Crook's capture of the camp was a stunning blow. Geronimo agreed to parley, and found Crook generous. Grey Wolf even allowed the Apache leader another two months of freedom, while he rounded up the rest of the Chiricahuas.

True to his word, Geronimo crossed the border voluntarily, although he stretched the two months to eight, arriving in February 1884. Before him he drove 350 head of cattle, stolen from the Mexicans. This seemed proper to Geronimo, who felt he was only supplying his people with meat. At San Carlos, Crook took a different view and confiscated the herd, ordered it sold and returned the proceeds to the original Mexican owners.

For more than a year things were quiet on the reservation, and Crook could proudly say that "not an outrage or depredation of any kind" was committed by the Apaches. Outside San Carlos, however, the citizens of Arizona were stirring up trouble. Newspapers contained lurid, and fabricated, stories about atrocities committed by Geronimo and called upon vigilantes to hang him. There was criticism of Crook for being too easy on the Apaches; some even suggested that he had surrendered to Geronimo in Mexico, and was now providing him with an easy life in return for the keeping of his scalp.

The stories made Geronimo uneasy. He also feared trouble from the reservation authorities for breaking the rule that prohibited the drinking of tiswin (corn beer), a pleasure the Apaches found unable to resist. Expecting the worst, Geronimo, Nana and 92 women and children, eight boys and 34 men departed for Mexico on the night of 17 May 1885. Before leaving, Geronimo cut the telegraph wire.

"THE APACHES ARE OUT!" warned the Arizonan newspapers two days later. Whites had little to fear, however, since Geronimo was trying to avoid any confrontation with them, and was hurrying his people towards

Mexico, not even stopping to make camp until they reached the safety of the Sierra Madre.

General Crook was detailed by Washington to apprehend the fugitive Geronimo, with orders to take his unconditional surrender or kill him. To fulfil his mission, Crook was obliged to mount the heaviest campaign in the Apache wars up to that date, with more than 2,500 cavalry troopers and 200 Indian scouts. (Some of these were old Apache cohorts of Geronimo, including Chato; the Apaches, understanding the boredom of reservation life, did not usually blame People who scouted for the Whites.)

Throughout the winter of 1885–6 Crook hunted Geronimo in the Sierra Madre, but having been surprised there before the Apache leader was more cautious. In January, Crook's force managed to discover and attack one renegade camp, although their quarry got away. But in March, Geronimo decided to surrender. Units of the Mexican Army, as well as the US cavalry, were combing the Sierra Madre for him. Caught between the Mexicans who only wanted to kill him and the Americans who might accept a surrender, Geronimo chose to meet with Crook at Cañon de los Embudos (Canyon of Tricksters), a few miles below the border.

When Crook arrived at the canyon, he was surprised to find neither Geronimo nor his braves looking particularly discouraged. "Although tired of the constant hounding of the campaign," Crook later recalled, "they were in superb physical condition, armed to the teeth, fierce as so many tigers. Knowing what pitiless brutes they are themselves, they mistrust everyone else."

He and Geronimo talked for two days, and Geronimo agreed once more to live on the reservation. "Do with me what you please," he said. "Once I moved about like the wind. Now I surrender to you, and that is all."

Despite his submission to Crook, within days Geronimo went fugitive. On the dark and rainy night of 28 March, as he and his surrendered Chiricahua band neared Fort Bowie, Geronimo, his young son Chappo, Naiche and 17 other warriors, and 18 women and children, slipped away from their escort. "I feared treachery," he later said, "and decided to remain in Mexico." A trader had got the hostiles drunk and filled them full of tales about how the local people were going to make "good injun" of them. It would be Geronimo's last break-out.

As a result of Geronimo's flight, the War Department severely reprimanded Crook for laxity and his over-indulgences towards the Indians. Crook resigned immediately, and was replaced by Brigadier-General Nelson A. Miles, whose orders were to "capture or destroy" Geronimo and his band of hostiles.

Miles managed to do neither, although his work amongst the Apaches would prove destructive enough. One of his first decisions was to transfer all the Mimbrenos and Chiricahuas on the reservations – including the scouts who had helped Crook – to Florida.

For the manhunt of Geronimo, Miles put 5,000 soldiers – a quarter of the entire army – in the field, and built 30 heliograph stations to flash messages from mountain to mountain, a system of communication well known to the Apaches, who had long before shifted from smoke signals to mirrors. Meanwhile, Geronimo raided almost at will. In April of 1886, he and his warriors crossed into Arizona and killed a rancher's wife, child and an employee. A short while later, Geronimo's war party killed two men outside Nogales, and then ambushed the cavalry sent in pursuit of them. Two troopers died. The Apaches suffered not a single loss. Geronimo would later say of this period, "We were reckless of our lives, because we felt that every man's hand was against us. If we returned to the reservation we would be put in prison and killed; if we stayed in Mexico they could continue to send soldiers to fight us; so we gave no quarter to anyone and asked no favours."

Throughout the summer of 1886 Miles pursued Geronimo and his 20 warriors, but to no avail. They seemed as elusive as ghosts. Finally, Miles decided to try another tack – he would negotiate with the enemy. His appointed emissary was Lieutenant Charles Gatewood, who had met Geronimo a number of times. Accompanying Gatewood were two scouts, Martine and Kayitah.

To make contact with the renegades, Gatewood headed across the border and wandered around, listening for word of the Apaches' whereabouts. Eventually, he discovered that Geronimo was sending women into the small town of Fronteras to procure mescal. He trailed one such woman out of Fronteras and deep into the Sierra Madre. It was the end of August 1886.

Gatewood sent Geronimo a message via his scouts, and the two met near a bend in a river. The Apache laid down his rifle and walked over to Gatewood ("Big Nose") shook his hand and asked how he was. But when they sat down to talk and smoke cigarettes in the Apache fashion, with tobacco rolled in oak leaves, Geronimo deliberately sat close enough to Gatewood for the lieutenant to feel his revolver.

Geronimo opened the council formally by announcing that he and his warriors had come to hear General Miles's message. Gatewood gave it to them straight. "Surrender, and you will be sent to join the rest of your friends in Florida, there to await the decision of the President as to your final disposition. Accept these terms or fight it out to the bitter end." At this Geronimo bristled, "Take us to the reservation [San Carlos], or fight!"

Gatewood then had to inform Geronimo that the reservation no longer existed, and that all the Chiricahuas had been removed to Florida, including members of Geronimo's own family.

The Apache were devastated by the news. They withdrew for a private council, which in the Apache way was democratic, with everyone having a voice. Perico, Fun, Ahnandia – all of them Geronimo's cousins – indicated that they wished to surrender so that they might see their families again. Geronimo still had a taste to fight on, but he was weakened by these defections. He stood for a few moments without speaking. At length he said, "I have been depending heavily on you three men. You have been great fighters in battle. If you are going to surrender, there is no use my going without you. I will give up with you."

Geronimo, the last of the Apache leaders, had finally surrendered.

There was a formal cessation of hostilities, signed at Skeleton Canyon. Brigadier-General Miles was in attendance, getting his first look at Geronimo: "He was one of the brightest, most resolute, determined looking men that I have ever encountered. He had the clearest, sharpest dark eye I think I have ever seen, unless it was that of General Sherman when he was at the prime of life . . . Every movement indicated power, energy and determination. In everything he did, he had a purpose."

The surrender ceremony was officially concluded on the afternoon of 4 September, and on the following day Miles flashed the news to the nation that Geronimo had finally given up arms. With a last glimpse at the Chiricahua mountains, Geronimo was taken to Fort Bowie, and from there transported, along with his hostile band, in a railway cattle car to San Antonio, Texas. From San Antonio Geronimo was shipped to Fort Pickens in Florida, a crumbling, abandoned fortification on Santa Rosa island, where he would start the first of his 23 years in captivity.

Learning to be White

Probably Geronimo was not surprised, after all these years of dealing with the White man, to find that he had been lied to. He did not, as General Miles had promised him, see his family on arrival in Florida, and instead spent two years in close confinement. To the great distress of Geronimo and the other male hostiles, the women and children of their band were taken from them and sent to Fort Marion, 300 miles across the state.

The warm and humid land of Florida, so unlike the dry country of Arizona and New Mexico, was not healthy for the Apaches. Eighteen died of a disease diagnosed as consumption within only a matter of months. Their children were sent away to a school in Carlisle, Pennsylvania, where they were to be readied for integration into White man's society. Our job, said the school's founder, is to "kill the Indian and save the man."

After two years of misery in Florida, the hostile warriors were transferred to Mount Vernon Barracks in Alabama. To their great joy, there they were finally reunited with their families, with Geronimo seeing an infant daughter Lenna for the first time. To those accustomed to seeing the Apache warlord as an "inhuman monster", the care he showed for his daughter was striking. One visitor wrote: "I had luck today . . . Saw Geronimo . . . He is a terrible old villain, yet seemed quiet enough today nursing a baby." Aside from family reunions, the pleasures to be found at Mount Vernon were few. The Apaches were put to work at hard labour. Their rations were pitiful. There were several outbreaks of tuberculosis and pneumonia. Many became depressed. Nineteen of the 352 Chiricahua prisoners died within eight months.

If it had not been for the efforts of a few White friends of the Apaches such as John Clum and George Crook, many more would have died at the barracks on the Mobile

River. In August 1894 the War Department was finally persuaded to move the Apaches back West, although not as far west as their original stomping grounds. They were sent to Fort Sill, in southern Oklahoma, which their old enemies, the Comanches and Cheyenne, generously offered to share with them.

Here the White men set about turning the Apache into dark-skinned White men. They were given small log houses, made to learn handiwork, made to garden, growing melons and cantaloupes on small patches of land, and made to farm. At one point, Geronimo was forced to learn how to be a cowboy. The Apaches, in fact, did well at raising cattle, but only moderately well at the other trades.

Something at which Geronimo excelled in captivity was selling himself. The Apache had always had a hard head for business and was soon making and purveying Geronimo souvenirs for the steady stream of visitors who dropped by to view him. One such visitor wrote:

> Geronimo has an eye to thrift and can drive a sharp bargain with his bows and arrows, and quivers and canes, and other work, in which he is skillful. He prides himself upon his autograph, written thus, G E R O N I M O, which he affixes to what he sells, usually asking an extra price for it. He had a curious headdress, which he called . . . his war bonnet . . . He seemed to value this bonnet highly, but finally in his need or greed for money, offered it for sale at $25.

In 1898, Geronimo met with General Miles at the Trans-Mississippi Exposition in Omaha, where the old warrior was the prime exhibit. He asked the former clerk to use his influence to allow him to return to Arizona.

"The acorns and piñon nuts, the quail and the wild

turkey, the giant cactus and the palo verdes – they all miss me," said Geronimo.

"A very beautiful thought, Geronimo," laughed Miles. "Quite poetic. But the men and women who live in Arizona, they do not miss you. Folks in Arizona sleep now at night. They have no fear that Geronimo will come and kill them. The acorns and the piñon nuts will have to get along as best they can without you."

Later that year Miles visited Geronimo at Fort Sill. The Army man again told Geronimo that he would not be allowed home. However, he did agree to Geronimo's request that he might be excused from forced labour because of his age. He was 69 years old.

In 1905 Geronimo was taken to Washington to ride in Theodore Roosevelt's inaugural parade. People bought his autographs for 25 cents as quickly as he could write them. Geronimo stole the show. Only the president himself attracted more attention.

When the parade was over, Geronimo was able to meet with Roosevelt. He took advantage of the occasion to plead for a return to Arizona:

Great Father, other Indians have homes where they can live and be happy. I and my people have no homes. The place where we are kept is bad for us . . . We are sick there and we die. White men are in the country that was my home. I pray you to tell them to go away and let my people go there and be happy.

Great Father, my hands are tied as with a rope. My heart is no longer bad. I will tell my people to obey no chief but the Great White Chief. I pray you to cut the ropes and make me free. Let me die in my own country, an old man who has been punished enough.

Roosevelt was sympathetic, but his reply was essentially the same as Miles's. The people of Arizona would not stand for it. He told Geronimo, "I am sorry, and have no feeling against you."

In the autumn of the same year, Mr S. M. Barrett, the White Superintendent of Education in Lawton, Oklahoma, secured permission from Roosevelt to interview Geronimo about his life. Geronimo related the tale in the Apache language to Asa Daklugie, the son of Juh, who translated it into English for Barrett to write down. More than anything in his old age Geronimo wanted to be allowed to return to the land of the Chiricahuas, and in telling his life story he politically left out most of his dealings with Americans. The book, *Geronimo's Story of His Life*, was dedicated to President Roosevelt.

By now Geronimo's years were piling up, and his rugged squat body showing signs of wear. Yet it took an accident to kill him. On a cold night in February 1909 he fell, drunk, off his horse and lay in a freezing creek all night. He developed severe pneumonia. He fought the illness for seven days, but it eventually overwhelmed him. Geronimo died at 6.15 in the morning of 17 February, and was buried the following day in Fort Sill's cemetery. He was about 80 years old, and still technically a prisoner of war.

He was never to realize his dream of returning to Arizona. But he was always proud that to finally subdue him and his band of 37 Chiricahua Apache it had taken 5,000 White soldiers.

Ghost Dancers

The whole world is coming,
A nation is coming.
The Eagle has brought the message to the tribe.
Over the whole earth they are coming;
The buffalo are coming, the buffalo are coming,
The Crow has brought the message to the tribe.

Ghost Dance Song

With the final capture of Geronimo in 1886 all great chiefs were within the reservations. Some, like Quanah Parker of the Quahadi Comanche, took up White ways, trying to do their best for their people by beating the Americans at their own games, like politics, real estate deals and money-making. Occasionally they won. Usually they lost. Every year the reservations got smaller, as did government allotments of beef and clothing. In 1889 drought came to the West; there was starvation on the reservations, and when measles struck the children they were too weak to resist.

It was a time for hope, a time to dream. A time to remember the buffalo which used to coat the plains, the chokecherries which used to hang by the mouthwatering bunch, and the freedom to roam over the range.

There were many shaman dreamers, but the most powerful was the Paiute Wovoka. Just before dawn on New Year's Day, 1889, far out in remote Nevada, the 34-year-old Wovoka fell ill. In his delirium he dreamed he visited the Great Spirit in heaven. There, he was told that a time was coming when the buffalo would once again fill the plains and dead tribesmen would be restored to their families. If the Indians refrained from violence, and if they were virtuous and performed the proper ritual dance – the Ghost Dance – they could hasten the coming of the new world, which would cover the old, and push the White men into the sea.

Some Indians, like the Kiowa and Comanche, were sceptical. But among the former tribes of the northern plains the Ghost Dance religion took a powerful hold. It spread wildly and rapidly across the reservations, from the Arapaho, to the Cheyenne, to the Wichita. In the winter of early 1890, a holy man of the Teton Sioux, Kicking Bear, brought the new gospel to Dakota.

The Sioux began Ghost Dancing in the spring, in secret ceremonies away from White Eyes. Adapting Wovoka's original ceremony to the Sioux Sun Dance, they danced around a sacred tree. At Kicking Bear's behest, the dancers also wore "ghost shirts" painted with magical symbols to keep away White bullets.

By mid-autumn of 1890, the Sioux were in something approaching a religious frenzy. Thousands of Sioux were now participating in the Ghost Dances, shuffling around in great circles, which speeded up until the exhausted dancers reached a state of delirious ecstasy where they saw the dead "come to life". Normal life on the reservations all but stopped. Even the schools were emptied, as the Indians spent all day dancing and chanting.

In October, Kicking Bear was invited by Sitting Bull to come to his isolated reservation at Standing Rock and teach the Huncpapa Sioux the Ghost Dance.

Sitting Bull's personal attitude to the Ghost Dance was one of disbelief. Yet, he considered that it would give succour to his people, and began to supervise personally the Huncpapa's dances.

The news that Sitting Bull, the great Sioux war leader and patriot, was Ghost Dancing caused White officials to panic. They already considered the situation out of control; with Sitting Bull involved they thought it might turn into an uprising.

On 17 November General Nelson Miles ordered troops to the Sioux reservations, including the all-Black 9th Cavalry and the late Custer's regiment, the 7th Cavalry. By December a third of the armed forces of the US was on alert. The former Indian agent Valentine McGillycuddy was dispatched by Washington to assess the gravity of the situation on the Sioux reservations. He went and saw, and counselled patience. "I should let the dance continue," he wrote to Washington. "The coming of the troops has frightened the Indians . . . . If the troops remain, trouble is sure to come."

Unfortunately, the government did not listen to McGillycuddy. Instead they listened to James McLaughlin, head of the Standing Rock Agency, who urged that Sitting Bull was dangerous and should be arrested. The government acceded, and McLaughlin sent 43 Sioux policemen up to Sitting Bull's cabins on the banks of the Grand River.

Just before daybreak on the dreary morning of 15 December 1890, the Sioux police surrounded Sitting Bull's home. Some of them had ridden with him at Little Big Horn. But now the Sioux were a divided and suspicious people. The police entered Sitting Bull's cabin, and the senior policeman, Lieutenant Henry Bull Head, found the old chief asleep on the floor. Waking him up, Bull Head brusquely informed him, "You are my prisoner. You must go to the agency."

At first, Sitting Bull agreed to go quietly. He sent one of his two wives to get his clothes, and asked one of the policemen to saddle his pony. But then the police began manhandling him and searching the house for weapons, something which upset Sitting Bull, for he then started cursing them. Meanwhile, more than 150 of Sitting Bull's most ardent followers had crowded around the police outside.

When Sitting Bull and Lieutenant Bull Head appeared outside the cabin, the situation became electric. People started shouting "You shall not take our chief!" As the 59-year-old Sitting Bull was pushed towards his pony, he suddenly declared that he was not going to Fort Yates and called upon his followers to rescue him. A brave named Catch the Bear shot Lieutenant Bull Head in the side. As he fell, he fired at Sitting Bull, hitting him in the chest. Almost in the same moment another policeman, Red Tomahawk, shot Sitting Bull through the head.

Sitting Bull was killed by his own people, as he had once been foretold by a meadowlark.

After Sitting Bull fell, a wild fight ensued in which police and Huncpapa (including women) fought and killed with guns, knives and clubs at point-blank range. The police, after suffering six dead, were only saved by the arrival of the cavalry.

Sitting Bull's body was taken away on a wagon and was buried in a pauper's grave.

Wounded Knee

Following the fight at Sitting Bull's cabin, some of his Huncpapa surrendered at Fort Bennett but some, half starving and half clad, fled to other reservations. Thirty-eight joined the Miniconjou Sioux chief, Big Foot, whose village was on the forks of the Cheyenne River. The Army

considered Big Foot another Ghost Dance trouble-
maker and he was under overt surveillance. Already disturbed by the supervision, Big Foot became deeply fearful
when the Huncpapa refugees told him of Sitting Bull's
death. Then troops were sighted nearby. Believing that he
was going to be murdered, Big Foot led his people – 333
men, women and children – out from their camp on the
night of 23 December. He headed south towards the Pine
Ridge Reservation, hoping to find protection with Red
Cloud.

The Army pursued the fleeing Indians, sending out
three regiments, including the 7th Cavalry. As the army
scoured the wintry prairie, Big Foot's band trudged south
and reached the Dakota Badlands.

At two o'clock in the afternoon of 28 December, the
Army caught up with Big Foot, now so ill with pneumonia that he was being carried in a wagon. He surrendered
without protest, and accepted a military guard. Since the
day was closing in, the Indians were directed to camp for
the night at a nearby creek, Wounded Knee. The troopers
took up positions in the surrounding hills to prevent any
escape.

While it was still dark, Colonel George A. Forsyth (of
Beecher Island fame) arrived with reinforcements from
the 7th Cavalry. By the morning of the 29th there were 500
troopers ringing the Sioux.

The day dawned bright and clear. Forsyth called all the
Sioux men and elder boys to stand in a semi-circle in front
of their tents. Numbering 106, they squatted on the ground,
wearing their bright-coloured Ghost Dance shirts. Troopers then began searching the tents for weapons.

Women began wailing. The men sitting in the council
circle immediately became alert. A shaman named Yellow
Bird jumped up and told warriors: "I have made medicine
of the White man's ammunition. It is good medicine, and

his bullets can not harm you, as they will not go through your ghost shirts, while your bullets will kill."

Forsyth ordered the shaman to sit down. Another officer, James D. Mann, warned his men: "Be ready; there is going to be trouble."

Two soldiers began struggling with a brave named Black Coyote, who refused to hand over his rifle. Then things happened with frightening speed. The holy man Yellow Bird threw a handful of dust up into the air, which the soldiers thought was a signal for an attack on them.

Four or five Sioux warriors pulled guns out from under their blankets. An officer was shot. And then all hell broke loose. Standing only eight feet away from the braves, a line of soldiers levelled their carbines and sent a volley into their ranks. Some warriors managed to shoot back, while from a low hill four Hotchkiss guns began to spew explosive shells into the scattering Sioux at the rate of a round a second. Tents were on fire, horses screaming in pain. In a few places warriors were fighting the soldiers with whatever they had to hand, and sometimes just their hands. Sioux women and children were trying to make it to a ravine, but the shells kept bursting around them. Maddened soldiers gave chase, killing groups of Indians as they huddled in the rocks and scrub cedar – or wherever they had run to. Dead women and children would be found strung out for three miles from Wounded Knee.

It is not known how many Sioux died at Wounded Knee. The smallest estimate is 153, but it may have been as high as 300. The Army suffered 25 casualties, some of them killed accidentally by their own side in the frenzy of firing.

In the darkening creek of Wounded Knee, where the snow was crimson with blood, a blizzard began to threaten. So the Sioux fallen, who numbered Big Foot, were left where they lay. Not until 3 January 1891 did a burial detail go back to collect the dead. Their bodies were frozen in grotesque positions, and like this they were thrown into a common grave.

The scene was so grisly that it moved some of the civilians in the burial party to tears: "It is a thing to melt the heart of a man, if it was of stone, [wrote one] to see those little children, with their bodies shot to pieces thrown naked into the pit."

The massacre at Wounded Knee caused the Sioux at the nearby Pine Ridge Agency to run off to the Badlands, where they gathered in a huge camp of 4,000 at White Clay Creek. When the 7th Cavalry went to probe the area, they became trapped by the Sioux in a valley. They were eventually rescued by the Black buffalo soldiers of the 9th Cavalry, who made an amazing forced march of 90 miles. General Miles then surrounded the Sioux, and made overtures of peace. The Indians were hungry and outnumbered – and disillusioned over the failure of the Ghost Dance shirts, most of which had been torn off and trampled underfoot.

Gradually, Sioux were coaxed out of the Big Badlands, without any more bloodshed. On 15 January, 1891, Kicking Bear and the last of the Sioux in the Badlands laid their rifles at the feet of General Nelson Miles at Pine Ridge Agency.

The Ghost Dance was over. And so were 300 years of resistance to the White man. A few individuals, even families, would hold out into the twentieth century, but there would be no more battles, no more war against the White man.

At Wounded Knee was buried the Indian's last bid for freedom as a people. An era had ended.

Part V

The Last Days of the West

Prologue

When did the West end? In 1893 – the year Sitting Bull's cabin was placed on display at the World's Columbian Exposition – a young historian called Frederick Jackson Turner stood up before an audience of his peers and read a paper entitled "The Significance of the Frontier in American History." Briefly and brilliantly, Turner explained that the frontier had been the most important factor in shaping the character and uniqueness of the American people.

He also said that the frontier was now closed, for ever.

Certainly the great spaces, which had once seemed limitless, had closed in. With the steady defeats of the Indians and their removal to the reservations, the settlement of the Great Plains had moved forward with astonishing speed. More than anything else, this enormous population movement tamed – and thus finished – the Wild West.

And yet Turner's imagery of the "closed" frontier did not quite match reality. Though the Census Bureau announced the frontier's "closing" in 1890, this meant only that a line could no longer be drawn to separate the zone of settlement from the wilderness. There was still plenty of "free" land to be grabbed. There would be land "rushes" into Oklahoma until 1911, the 1893 rush alone opening up 6 million acres of the Cherokee Strip.

Moreover, the frontier habit of violence had a 300-year momentum behind it; it could not simply be stopped dead. When Blacks and Native Americans allied under Chitto Hajo (Crazy Snake) to restore tribal government in Oklahoma it ended in a "rebellion" in 1909 which came complete with the sounds of rifle fire and death. Indians in Nevada were massacred as late as 1911. This was the family of Shoshoni Mike, who formerly lived in the mountains near Twin Falls, Idaho. When one of Mike's sons was murdered by a White horse thief, the Shoshoni family, in turn, killed the horse thief. This caused Shoshoni Mike to move to Nevada, where the family survived by killing cattle. When this was discovered, they fought a battle with four ranchers, who were all killed. Shoshoni Mike and his family then fled on horseback, but were chased nearly 300 miles by a posse. They were finally caught on 26 February 1911, and four Shoshoni men, two women and two children were killed by the posse. The four survivors (all children) were later sent to the Fort Hall reservation in Idaho.

The family of Shoshoni Mike had refused to submit to the reservation. There were other such "renegades", especially in Arizona. The famed Apache Kid, a former scout who turned "renegade", lived in the Sierra Madre, raiding Mexican and American settlements throughout the 1890s. Massai, a Chiricahua who fought with Geronimo in his last campaign, jumped Geronimo's prison train before it reached St Louis, Missouri, and then stole his way back to Arizona undetected. Since his family had been on the train and thus carried into exile in Florida, he seized a Mescalero Apache woman as his wife, and lived for many years by raiding the "Pinda-lick-o-yi" (White Eyes) in the traditional way. Finally he was killed, and his wife took his new family to live on the Mescalero reservation. Other Apaches are reported to have lived wild in the Sierra Madre until as late as 1935.

Meanwhile, Western outlawry in 1893 was still to have a heyday with the Wild Bunch of Butch Cassidy, while other – if lesser – bandits would be perpetrating Old West-type hold-ups for decades to come. Roy Daugherty ("Arkansas Tom Jones") was still robbing banks in the 1920s. And where there was Western outlawry, there was Western law. Vigilante committees were lynching until 1917. The legendary Bill Tilghman sported a tin star up to 1924, the year he was shot dead by a drunk outside Murphy's Restaurant in the oil town of Cromwell, Oklahoma.

And yet, if the West did not end abruptly in 1890, it was in the process of dying. Like the buffalo – of which only 12 were left alive in the USA in 1890 – its glory days were all behind it. As it receded into the past, so people found the need to celebrate its wildness, which grew ever larger in the imagination, helped by such spectacles as Buffalo Bill's Wild West Show, rodeo and the silver screen of Hollywood.

Settling the Great Plains

There seemed to be nothing to see: no fences, no creeks or trees, no hills or fields. There was nothing but land: not a country at all, but the material out of which countries are made.

Willa Cather

They who labor in the earth are the chosen people of God.

Thomas Jefferson

The Great Plains were the last frontier – a sea of grass, beautiful but unforgiving, stretching off to lonely horizons. Onto it, between the 1860s and 1890s, rolled the greatest population movement in US history, anxious to take up land given under the Homestead Act, land freed from the ownership of the Native Americans by money, guile or force of arms. More American soil was occupied and placed under cultivation between 1870 and 1890 than in the entire two and a half centuries since the landings at Jamestown. Some 430 million acres were claimed between 1870 and 1890.

For decades the plains had been ignored by westering settlers, who clung to the cherished American belief that timberland had the finest soil and that the land west of the 98th meridian was the Great American Desert. And then one day, all the timberland was used up, and sons of farmers were forced to look elsewhere to start up a place of their own. One such son, his name unknown to history, idly walked on to the land where the trees gave out and the prairie grass began, pulled up a root – and found to his disbelief that thick black soil clung to its roots. He dug down with his hands and came up with armfuls of fertile loam. One excited pioneer, Hubbel Pierce of Abbotsville, North Dakota, wrote back to his wife in 1879: "First the land is a black clay loam from two to three feet deep, the first plowing is rather hard [but] after one crop it is soft as can be, [and] any team [of horses] can work it."

Even so, the homesteaders faced a daunting task. There were almost no trees for lumber, little water, and few neighbours. The free 160 acres of plain was barely suffi-cient to support a family on a subsistence farming basis. When the grass on the prairie dried in summer it was liable to set alight. "It is a strange and terrible sight to see," wrote one pioneer, "to see all the fields a sea of fire. Quite often the scorching flames sweep everything along in their path – people, cattle, hay, fences. In dry weather with a strong wind the fire will race faster than the speediest horse."

Every season had its woes. Aside from fire, summer brought drought and plagues of grasshoppers which could eat a field of corn in hours. The Great Grasshopper Year of 1874 witnessed the insects landing in clouds 150 miles long and 100 miles wide. Union Pacific trains in Nebraska were forced to stop because the crushed insects made the wheels too oily to grip the track. Some Western states issued "Grasshopper Bonds" to help families who had been eaten out of their livelihoods.

In winter, the temperature on the plains frequently reached 40 below freezing. Blizzards came out of nowhere. In January 1888, 200 people died of exposure on the plains in one day, victims of a northeast snowstorm that arrived so quickly that children at one Dakota school were unable to get from the play yard into the safety of the schoolhouse. Nine were frozen to death.

Spring meant floods, fall more prairie fires. Tornadoes came at any time.

Many people were broken by the plains. A note found stuck to one deserted settler's home read: "250 miles to the nearest post office; 100 miles to wood; 20 miles to water; 6 inches to hell. Gone to live with the wife's folks."

Many pioneers, with courage and ingenuity, endured.

The prerequisite for the settler, after selecting and claiming his land, paying a $14 filing fee (at a land office anything up to 100 miles away), was shelter. Tents were blown away by the incessant wind, so pioneers dug holes in the ground, or in the side of a rise. When they had more time, they built sod huts, probably borrowing techniques from English turf shelters and Indian earth-covered lodges. Using a "grasshopper plow", and yoked oxen, plainsmen cut the turf into blocks – "Nebraska marble" – which they laid like giant bricks. Door, window, and timber for the sod roof were bought by mail order or from a distant town. A settler could erect a 24-foot long "soddy" in a week. Inside it was dark and dank, and insects and snakes dropped from the ceiling with alarming frequency. The sod house was also cheap (a 24-foot soddy might cost as little as $8 to build), warm in winter, cool in summer, bullet-proof, fireproof, and would last for a decade or more (sod houses were still common in Nebraska and Kansas until the 1930s). Some soddies were intricate and elegant, complete with wallpaper and lace curtains. Belgian Isadore Haumont built a magnificent sod "castle" in 1884, for only $500.

Where there was no firewood for heating and cooking, homesteaders used buffalo chips, cow chips ("prairie lignite"), mesquite sprouts, hay or sunflowers.

After a shelter was built, the sodbuster turned his or her mind to the farming by which they and their families would live. Essential was a supply of water. Nature forgot to provide enough, except on the western fringes of the plains, and eastern Texas and Kansas. Therefore farmers dug open wells, or hired professional diggers to do so; one professional digger, "Dutch Joe" Grewe, was reputed to be able to dig at 30 feet a day. The fee was 20 cents per foot. Many High Plains farmers had to dig down 200 feet before they found water (at least one had to go down to 500 feet). At first, water was raised by buckets or hand pumps, but in the late 1860s windmill manufacturers – especially Daniel Halladay in Chicago – began to develop a product suited to Western needs; it had small blades and a governor which reduced the pitch of the blades when high winds made them revolve too rapidly. The cost of such a windmill was high at $100, but by the 1890s they dotted the plains as the very symbol of sodbusting agriculture. Many were home-made, since instructions on how to make them were freely available. Popular with farmers with a shallow well was a "Jumbo", a fan-wheel in a box, made from old crates, gunny sacks, and salvaged farm machinery.

Even a windmill did not solve the water problem. Once a farmer had ploughed up the moisture-holding grasslands, he found that the earth baked dry and winds blew the topsoil away in huge dust clouds. "Real estate moved considerably this week," one Western newspaper wryly reported in 1880. To prevent this soil erosion, experimental farmer Hardy W. Campbell invented "dry farming", where farmers harrowed their fields after every rainfall, creating a dust mulch which would stop evaporation, thus keeping the water near the roots. The system worked and opened up some dry regions, but it had the distinct disadvantage of not working at all in unusually dry years.

Few homesteaders could afford machinery; most first

crops were put in with spade, hoes and mattocks. Flax
grew well in Dakota but beyond the line of the Missouri
wheat was found to thrive, and the country began to take
on a golden hue. Pioneers wanted a cash crop that would
give them a maximum return.

A major reason why pioneers wanted money was to buy,
or rent, the agricultural machinery that would make their
lives less back-breaking, and maximize the profitability
of their land. Reapers, threshers and grain separators
appeared in a bewildering variety of models in the wheat
country, the progenitor of them all being Virginian Cyrus
McCormick's revolutionary mechanical reaper, invented
in 1831. By 1880 combine harvesters were so advanced that
they cut the wheat and automatically tied it into sheaths. In
1840 it took around 233 hours of human labour to produce
100 bushels of wheat; in 1900, thanks to mechanization,
this had dropped to 108.

With luck, a pioneer would endure, and come to prosperity. But only with luck. A Kansas folksong sums up the
disillusion of many a homesteader:

How happy am I on my government claim
Where I've nothing to lose and nothing to gain,
Nothing to eat and nothing to wear,
Nothing from nothing is honest and square.
But here I am stuck, and here I must stay,
My money's all gone and I can't get away,
There's nothing will make a man hard and profane
Like starving to death on a government claim.

Those who stuck it out were joined by others, for the
settlers kept coming. Many were westering Americans
from the Old Northwest and the Mississippi Valley. A
million from these regions moved out onto the plains in a
single decade. Some were descendants of the farmers who

had hewn out the first American frontier back beneath the shadow of the Appalachians.

A significant number were Black farmers from the South and Texas, tired of prejudice, which had significantly increased with the end of Reconstruction in 1877. Henry Adams and Benjamin "Pap" Singleton organized an "Exodus" of Black people to Kansas and points west in the hope that they might find liberty. White plantation owners, anxious at the loss of cheap labour, hired gangs of thugs to stop them. One Black "Exoduster" had his hands chopped off by Whites who said, "Now go to Kansas to work!" Generally, the intimidation did not work. In one year alone an estimated 20,000 to 40,000 penniless Black men, women and children reached Kansas. They came up the Mississippi by boat, or made the long, slow walk up the Chisholm Trail. A Black community was founded at Nicodemus by Edwin McCabe, which thrived until the railroad passed it by. McCabe became the state auditor of Kansas, and thus the first Black man to hold a major political office in the West.

The whys and hows of the Black Exodus were cogently explained by Pap Singleton when called before a Senate Select Committee investigating the phenomenon on 17 April 1880 in Washington DC:

Q. [Senator Windom]: When did you change your home from Tennessee to Kansas?
A. [Benjamin Singleton]: I have been going there for the last six or seven years, sir.

Q. Going between Tennessee and Kansas, at different times?
A. Yes, sir; several times.

Q. Well, tell us about it.

A. I have been fetching out people; I believe I fetched out 7,432 people.

Q. You have brought out 7,432 people from the South to Kansas?
A. Yes, sir; brought and sent.

Q. That is, they came out to Kansas under your influence?
A. Yes, sir; I was the cause of it.

Q. How long have you been doing that – ever since 1869?
A. Yes, sir; ever since 1869.

Q. Did you go out there yourself in 1869, before you commenced sending them out?
A. No, sir.

Q. How did you happen to send them out?
A. The first cause, do you mean, of them going?

Q. Yes. What was the cause of your going out, and in the first place how did you happen to go there, or to send these people there?
A. Well, my people, for the want of land – we needed land for our children – and their disadvantages – that caused my heart to grieve and sorrow; pity for my race, sir, that was coming down, instead of going up – that caused me to go to work for them. I sent out there perhaps in '66 – perhaps so; or in '65, anyway – my memory don't recollect which; and they brought back tolerable favorable reports; then I jacked up 300 or 400, and went into Southern Kansas, and found it was a good country, and I thought Southern Kansas was congenial to our nature, sir; and I formed a colony there, and bought about 1,000 acres of ground – the colony did – my people.

Q. And they went upon it and settled there?
A. Yes, sir; they went and settled there.

Q. Were they men with some means or without means?
A. I never carried none there without means.

Q. They had some means to start with?
A. Yes; I prohibited my people leaving their country and going there without they had money – some money to start with and go on with a while.

Q. You were in favor of their going there if they had some means?
A. Yes, and not staying at home.

Q. Tell us how these people are getting on in Kansas?
A. I am glad to tell you, sir.

Q. Have they any property now?
A. Yes; I have carried some people in there that when they got there they didn't have 50 cents left, and now they have got in my colony – Singleton colony – a house, nice cabins, their milch cows, and pigs, and sheep, perhaps a span of horses, and trees before their yeards, and some 3 or 4 or 10 acres broken up, and all of them has got little houses that I carried there. They didn't go under no relief assistance; they went on their own resources; and when they went in there first the country was not overrun with them; you see they could get good wages; the country was not overstocked with people; they went to work, and I never helped them as soon as I put them on the land.

Q. Well, they have been coming continually, and adding from time to time to your colony these few years past, have they?

A. Yes, sir; I have spent, perhaps, nearly $600 flooding the country with circulars.

Q. You have sent the circulars yourself, have you?
A. Yes, sir; all over these United States.

Q. Did you send them into other Southern States besides Tennessee?
A. Oh, yes, sir.

Q. Did you do that at the instance of Governor St John and others in Kansas?
A. Oh, no, sir; no White men. This was gotten up by Colored men in purity and confidence; not a political Negro was in it; they would want to pilfer and rob at the cents before they got the dollars. Oh, no, it was the muscle of the arm, the men that worked that we wanted.

Q. Well, tell us all about it.
A. These men would tell all their grievances to me in Tennessee – the sorrows of their heart. You know I was an undertaker there in Nashville, and worked in the shop. Well, actually, I would have to go and bury their fathers and mothers. You see we have the same heart and feelings as any other race and nation. (The land is free, and it is nobody's business, if there is land enough, where the people go. I put that in my people's heads.) Well, that man would die, and I would bury him; and the next morning maybe a woman would go to that man [meaning the landlord], and she would have six or seven children, and he would say to her, "Well, your husband owed me before he died," and they would say that to every last one of them, "You owe me." Suppose he would? Then he would say, "You must go to some other place; I cannot take care of you." Now, you see, that is something I would

take notice of. That woman had to go out, and these little children was left running through the streets, and the next place you would find them in a disorderly house, and their children in the State's prison.

Well, now, sir, you will find that I have a charter here. You will find that I called on the White people in Tennessee about that time. I called conventions about it, and they sat with me in my conventions, and, "Old man," they said, "you are right." The White people said, "You are right; take your people away." And let me tell you, it was the White people – the ex-governor of the State felt like I did and they said to me, "You have tooken a great deal on to yourself, but if these Negroes, instead of deceiving one another and running for office, would take the same idea that you have in your head, you will be a people."

I then went out to Kansas, and advised them all to go to Kansas; and, sir, they are going to leave the Southern country. The Southern country is out of joint. The blood of a White man runs through my veins. That is congenial, you know, to my nature. That is my choice. Right emphatically, I tell you today, I woke up the millions right through me! The great God of glory has worked in me. I have had open-air interviews with the living spirit of God for my people; and we are going to leave the South. We are going to leave it if there ain't an alteration and signs of change. I am going to advise the people who left that country [Kansas] to go back.

Q. What do you mean by a change?
A. Well, I am not going to stand bulldozing and half pay and all those things. Gentlemen, allow me to tell you the truth; it seems to me that they have picked out the Negroes from the Southern country to come here and testify who are in good circumstances and own their homes and not the poor ones who don't study their own interests. Let them

go and pick up the men that has to walk when they goes, and not those who have money.

There is good White men in the Southern country, but it ain't the minority [majority]; they can't do nothing; the bulldozers has got possession of the country, and they have got to go in there and stop them; if they don't the last Colored man will leave them. I see Colored men testifying to a positive lie, for they told me out there all their interests were in Louisiana and Mississippi. Said I, "You are right to protect your own country," and they would tell me, "I am obliged to do what I am doing." Of course I have done the same, but I am clear footed.

Q. Now you say that during these years you have been getting up this colony you have spent, yourself, some $600 in circulars, and in sending them out; where did you send them, Mr Singleton?
A. Into Mississippi, Alabama, South Carolina, Georgia, Kentucky, Virginia, North Carolina, Texas, Tennessee, and all those countries.

Q. To whom did you send them; how were they circulated?
A. Every man that would come into my country, and I could get a chance, I would put one in his hand, and the boys that started from my country on the boats, and the porters in the cars. That is the way I circulated them.

Q. Did you send any out by mail?
A. I think I sent some perhaps to North Carolina by mail – I think I did. I sent them out by people, you see.

Q. Yes; by Colored people, generally?
A. Some White people, too. There was Mrs Governor Brown, the first Governor Brown of Tennessee – Mrs

Sanders, she was a widow, and she married the governor. He had 30 on his place. I went to him, and he has given me advice. And Ex-Governor Brown, he is there too.

Q. You say your circulars were sent all over these States?
A. Yes, sir; to all of 'em.

Q. Did you ever hear from them; did anybody ever write to you about them?
A. Oh, yes.

Q. And you attribute this movement to the information you gave in your circulars?
A. Yes, sir; I am the whole cause of the Kansas immigration!

Q. You take all that responsibility on yourself?
A. I do, and I can prove it; and I think I have done a good deal of good, and I feel relieved!

Q. You are proud of your work?
A. Yes, sir; I am! [Uttered emphatically.]

As the number of Black settlers in Kansas grew, the state passed laws forbidding them to settle within town limits. Many moved on to the mountain states and, especially, Oklahoma. Between 1890 and 1910, 25 Black communities were formed in Oklahoma, including the city of Langston, where Edwin McCabe – one of those who had moved on – was instrumental in forming a Black university.

More numerous than the "Exodusters" were the immigrants from outside the USA, from Europe, Canada (nearly 400,000 Canadians settled on the plains between 1880 and 1883), and from Russia. Usually foreigners settled in the northern states, where the climate reminded them of home, and close to others of their nationality. Sometimes whole communities were transplanted from Europe to the plains, like the pacifist German-speaking Mennonites from Russia who feared conscription. The Mennonites brought with them Turkey Red, a hard winter wheat that could survive plains weather, which transformed agriculture on the northern plains. (Another crucial immigrant import was the alfalfa seed that Wendelin Grimm brought with him from Bavaria.) At "Runnymede" in Kansas, promoter Ned Turnely set up a hotel for the dissolute sons of the British aristocracy, where they might learn frontiering and the open-air life; in fact they played tennis and ran to the hounds, chasing coyotes instead of foxes.

A homestead in the West was an appealing idea to many women, but no frontier was harder on them than the plains. They arrived as wives – sometimes by a form of mail order – and built homes, and endured drudgery and childbirth and a wind that cracked the skin of the face. For a bride from the East, the Great Plains came as a rude shock. Julia Gage, a native of Syracuse, New York, married Frank Carpenter in February 1882 and accompanied him to their homestead claim in Lamoure County, Dakota Territory (now North Dakota). A night in a frontier hotel in Ellendale proved an uncivilized tribulation:

The landlord showed us up stairs to a small room just large enough to contain two beds, one at the foot of the other. The foot bed contained a man, we were to occupy the other. The next room to ours was separated simply by studding, no lath, plaster or anything to shield us from the view of the man in that bed. So on through the house we could see the different occupants of the rooms. The windows in our room were broken, the door was minus. The landlord set the lamp on the floor (as there was no stand, chair, nothing but two beds). I asked him to take it down and we undressed in the dark, I simply taking off my dress and shoes and putting on my ulster. In the room the air was stifling. In the morning the man in the bed at the foot of ours and the one in the room adjoining seemed afraid to get up knowing a woman was so near. So I made the first move, slipping off my ulster and putting on my dress. There were no bathing arrangements in our room, each person washed in the office out of a tin wash dish, and *one* towel served for all. Soon after entering the dining room, a man, evidently the one who occupied the bed at the foot of ours, and who lay with his head covered with the bedding, entered the room.

On the tortuous road to their claim, they encountered mosquitoes.

With all the pain I ever suffered, I never endured such agony as I did that night. The mosquitoes numbered millions. The coulies were full of them. I wore a broad brimmed hat with the lower part tucked in the ulster, but it seemed hardly the least protection. I was bitten over my whole body not only through my gloves but through three thicknesses, ulster, dress, and wrapper sleeves; the miserable insects even found a small hole in the side of my shoes . . . But what I endured was nothing in comparison to what Frank went through, he having neither gloves, netting or any protection. Every few minutes he would jump out of the wagon, slapping the mosquitoes off from the mules, whose sides were so covered with them that their color could not have been told . . . Could we have driven fast, the little breeze thus produced would have made away with some of them . . . At last we reached our home . . . Frank had borrowed a tent, and as we entered it I sunk to the ground in exhaustion and immediately fell into a heavy sleep. Tired as Frank was he made a fire, boiled the tea kettle and steeped a strong cup of tea. He awakened me and after drinking a cup of tea, I again sunk into a heavy sleep, and there I lay until morning, with hat, dress, gloves &c all on.

To her dismay, Julia Gage Carpenter found that the nearest town, Edgeley, was a flimsy wooden affair, apparently only six weeks old. She came to hate the plains and the privations of pioneer life. By January 1884, during weather that reached 48 degrees below zero at noon, Carpenter was writing in her diary "I am *frantically* lonely. Can hardly endure it." Her diary continued in the same grim vein for years.

Unlike men, who occasionally went to town, women were confined to the sod house. Distance and the scarcity of population made companionship rare. When Ohio-born Sedda Hemry moved to Wyoming to marry a sheepherder she did not see another White woman for six months. Madness on the windswept plains was much higher amongst women than amongst men. "Pray for me," wrote Sarah Sim from Nebraska to her parents, "that I may overcome my present fear." Sim was severely melancholic, and for eight months bit herself and her children, smashed everything in sight and acted demented. When she tried to commit suicide her husband was obliged to tie her to the bed. She recovered.

Not all women were helpmates to men. Around 15 per cent of homesteaders in some states were lone women; and in some areas, women proved up on claims – that is, fulfilled the conditions for ownership under the Homestead Act – more often than men.

The shortage of women on the plains gave them a peculiar power. If a man wanted a wife, he often had to agree to her demands not to drink or to smoke. As the female population of the plains grew, so did the temperance movement. Carry Nation from Kansas went on hatchet-wielding forays which left a trail of smashed-up saloons behind her.

Temperance was not the only movement Western women were involved with. In Wyoming Territory in December 1869, for the first time on the continent, women were "invested with all the political rights, duties, franchises, and responsibilities of male citizens." Women thus had the vote in Wyoming 50 years before female suffrage was added to the US Constitution, this largely due to campaigning by the "Wyoming Tea Party" led by Esther McQuigg Morris, plus some astute politics by male legislators, who hoped to attract responsible woman settlers to the state, so offsetting the influence of the lawless (male) elements who had arrived to work on the railroads.

Yet, ultimately, the saga of the settling of the plains is not one of women or men, but of families. Children eased the isolation and provided more hands for the unceasing work. Western children joined the family labour force at an early age. By the age of seven a frontier boy would be expected to herd cattle, pick potatoes and plant corn. When he was older, his strapping muscles might be hired out to a neighbour to bring in some money to the family coffer.

Westerners were clannish by nature. They did things as a family – bad things as well as good. Much of the history of outlawry can be told in families: the James brothers, the Youngers, the Clantons, the Renos, the Doolins, and the Daltons.

And also the Logan brothers, who would organize the Hole in the Wall gang, and then join up with the Wild Bunch to produce the most effective bandit gang ever to roam the West.

The Wild Bunch

The operations of the Wild Bunch were at one time so bold
that during his term of office, former Governor Wells of
Utah suggested that the governors of Colorado, Wyoming,
and Utah unite in concentrated action to wipe out this
gang. The operations of the freebooters extended from the
Montana lines outward to the conjoining of Sweetwater,
Wyoming, Utah and Routt County, Colorado.

Denver Daily News, 1903

The Hole in the Wall was a desolate valley at the top of
Wyoming, and took its name from the gash in the cliff
which was its main entrance. Isolated, easy to defend,
with good grazing nearby, the Hole in the Wall was a
natural paradise for rustlers and wanted men. And it
became one.

Among the first to ride into the Hole in the Wall
were Harvey Logan, and his brothers Lonie and Johnny.
Orphaned in Missouri at an early age, the brothers wandered west, accompanied by a cousin, Bob Lee. When
the four reached Wyoming they joined a rustling gang
led by Flat Nose George Curry. In admiration of Curry,
the teenage Harvey Logan began to call himself "Kid
Curry". Under Flat Nose Curry's patronage, the Logans
started up a ranch with a stolen herd of cattle. During

the Johnson County range war of the early 1890s, they hired themselves as gunmen to the rustling Red Sash Gang, but after Nate Champion was killed withdrew from the fray.

On Christmas Eve 1894, a drunken Harvey Logan killed prospector Pike Landusky, founder of the town of that name. Landusky's stepdaughter was the mother of Harvey Logan's illegitimate child. Logan attacked without provocation, hitting the prospector's head against the floor; when Landusky tried to pull a gun, Logan was quicker, shooting the battered miner while he was on his knees.

After the shooting of Landusky, the Logan brothers fled inevitably to the Hole in the Wall, where they rejoined the rustling gang of Flat Nose Curry.

A year later, the Logans were involved in a shoot-out with a rancher called Jim Winters, in which Johnny Logan was killed. Though Harvey Logan entertained thoughts of revenge, his interest was more taken by the proposal of Robert LeRoy Parker, a rustler and outlaw who occasionally stayed at the Hole in the Wall. Parker, who used the alias "Cassidy", was organizing a gang to rob banks and trains. Logan joined him.

Parker was the descendant of Mormons who had emigrated to Utah with the second handcart procession, and had left home at 16 to become a rustler in the gang of a ruffian called Mike Cassidy (like Logan, Parker borrowed his pseudonym from the man who introduced him to crime). Parker had since robbed banks in Colorado's Denver and Telluride with the bandit gang of Tom and Bill McCarty, and spent two years in Wyoming State Penitentiary for cattle stealing. (The man who swore out the warrant leading to Parker's arrest, rancher Otto Franc, was later mysteriously shot to death.) Friends called Parker "Butch", because he once worked in a Rock Springs butcher shop, while his Pinkerton file described him as having the "looks of a quarter breed Indian".

It was on his release from the Wyoming Penitentiary in January 1896 that the affable Parker drifted to Brown's Hole, a desperado haven at the junction of Utah, Colorado, and Wyoming, and on to the Hole in the Wall and began to form the notorious "Wild Bunch" of outlaws. Aside from Harvey Logan as "Kid Curry", the gang included – at various times, for riders came and went – Ben "The Tall Texan" Kilpatrick, Harry Tracy, Lonie Logan, Tom Ketchum and his brother "Black Jack" Ketchum (who also led a celebrated band of his own), Bill Carver, Elza Lay, and Tom O'Day. A prominent member of the gang, and Parker's closest associate, was Harry ("Sundance Kid") Longbaugh, a Pennsylvanian who had migrated to Wyoming as a teenager, and served a jail sentence in the Sundance Penitentiary for horse theft. He was recruited to the Wild Bunch while cowboying on the Bar FS ranch in Wyoming.

The Wild Bunch in Action

In April 1897 the Wild Bunch made their first raid, holding up the mining camp at Castle Gate, Utah, and taking $8,000 from the paymaster. This was followed by a number of other moderate hold-ups, among them a hold-up of the First National Bank in Winnemucca, Nevada, in 1900, before the gang pulled off a sequence of spectacular train robberies.

The Union Pacific was a favourite target. On the night of 2 June 1899 the Overland Flyer was stopped at Wilcox Siding, Wyoming, by a red lantern placed on the track. The Wild Bunch climbed aboard. Their endeavours were unhappily witnessed by one Robert Lawson, a mail clerk on the Flyer:

As soon as we came to a standstill, Conductor Storey went forward to see what was the matter and saw several men with guns, one of whom shouted that they were going to blow up the train with dynamite. The conductor understood the situation at once and, before meeting the bandits, turned and started back to warn the second section. The robbers mounted the engine and at the point of their guns forced the engineer and fireman to dismount, after beating the engineer over the head with their guns, claiming that he didn't move fast enough, and marched them back over to our car.

In a few moments we heard voices outside our car calling for Sherman and looking out saw Engineer Jones and his fireman accompanied by three masked men with guns.

They evidently thought Clerk Sherman was aboard and were calling him to come out with the crew. Burt Bruce, clerk in charge, refused to open the door, and ordered all lights extinguished. There was much loud talk and threats to blow up the car were made, but the doors were kept shut. In about 15 minutes two shots were fired into the car, one of the balls passing through the water tank and on through the stanchions.

Following close behind the shooting came a terrific explosion, and one of the doors was completely wrecked and most of the car windows broken. The bandits then threatened to blow up the whole car if we didn't get out, so Bruce gave the word and we jumped down, and were immediately lined up and searched for weapons. They said it would not do us no good to make trouble, that they didn't want the mail – that they wanted what was in the express car and was going to have it, and that they had powder enough to blow the whole train off the track.

After searching us they started us back and we saw

up the track the headlight of the second section. They asked what was on the train, and somebody said there were two cars of soldiers on the train. This scared them and they hastened back to the engine, driving us ahead. They forced us on the engine, and as Dietrick moved too slowly they assisted him with a few kicks. While on the engine, Dietrick, in the act of closing the furnace door, brushed a mask off one of the men, endeavoring to catch a glimpse of his face. The man quickly grasped his mask and threatened to "plug" Dietrick.

They then ran the train ahead across a gully and stopped. There were two extra cars on the train. They were uncoupled. Others of the gang went to the bridge, attempting to destroy it with their giant powder, or dynamite, which they placed on the timbers. After the explosion at the bridge they boarded the engine with the baggage, express, and mail cars, went for about 2 miles, leaving the extra cars.

Upon arriving at the stopping place they proceeded to business again and went to the express car and ordered the messenger, E. C. Woodcock, to open. He refused, and the outlaws proceeded to batter down the doors and blew a big hole in the side of the car. The explosion was so terrific that the messenger was stunned and had to be taken from the car. They then proceeded to the other mail car, occupied by Clerks O'Brian and Skidmore and threatened to blow it up, but the boys were advised to come out which they did.

The robbers then went after the safes in the express car with dynamite and soon succeeded in getting into them, but not before the car was torn to pieces by the force of the charges. They took everything from the safes and what they didn't carry away they destroyed. After finishing their work they started out in a northerly direction on foot.

The men all wore masks reaching below their necks and of the three I observed, one looked to be 6 foot tall, the others being about ordinary sized men. The leader appeared to be about 50 years old and spoke with a squeaky voice, pitched very high.

Flat Nose Curry and the Sundance Kid made camp near the Powder River. While eating supper, they were attacked by a posse led by Sheriff Joe Hazen of Converse County. In a running gunfight, Logan shot Sheriff Hazen, fatally wounding him with a rifle bullet through the stomach. Though the Powder was swollen and turbulent, the bandits swam it, losing the posse, and picking up horses from a friendly rancher on the north fork.

The Bunch's escapades were often followed by gang vacations, to such retreats as New Orleans, Denver and Fort Worth. The Wild Bunch liked to pose for photographs, jauntily wearing derby hats and smiles, gold watch chains tucked into vest pockets. Between hold-ups, Parker sometimes hid out in the respectable, ordinary ranks of society; he worked as a cowboy, Great Lakes sailor, and as a waiter on the steamer from Seattle to Los Angeles.

Late in the evening of 29 August 1900, the Wild Bunch struck No. 3 Train of the Union Pacific just as it passed the station at Tipton, Wyoming. The driver was ordered at gunpoint to halt the train, and when it had ceased motion, the express and mail cars were uncoupled. By coincidence, the messenger inside the express car was Woodcock, the same messenger the Wild Bunch had dynamited at Wilcox Siding. Again Woodcock refused to open the car. Finally he was persuaded to do so, and the safe was blown with three charges of dynamite ("Kepauno Chemical Co., Giant Powder"). The bandits secured $5,014 in cash.

After the Tipton hold-up, the Union Pacific organized a special mobile posse under its Chief Special Agent

T. T. Kelliher, which was also given use of its own train, outfitted with stalls and a loading ramp for horses. The train was held in permanent readiness, to be sent wherever and whenever the Wild Bunch next struck.

They did so at 2.30 p.m. on the summer's afternoon of 3 July 1901, robbing a Great Northern Railroad train in Montana. According to the later Pinkerton report:

> One man [of the Wild Bunch] boarded the blind baggage car as the train was leaving Malta, Montana, and shortly before reaching the place of robbery, crawled over the engine tender and "covered" the engineer and fireman with a revolver and compelled them to stop the train near a bridge from under which two men came, armed with Winchester rifles. Two men, one on each side of the train, with rifles prevented passengers and others from interfering with the other man who marched the engine men ahead of him to the express car, which was entered and the safe opened by the use of dynamite.
>
> After robbing the express car, the bandits mounted horses and rode away.

The haul was large: $40,000 in notes from the Bank of Montana.

A hundred-man posse chased after the Wild Bunch, who now included a new female member, Laura Bullion ("Della Rose"), who had formed a relationship with Ben Kilpatrick. By the time they reached Texas, the Wild Bunch had thrown off the posse and celebrated with a drinking spree in Fort Worth and San Antonio. A bicycle-riding craze was sweeping the West in 1901, and Parker endlessly rode up and down the red light district of Fort Worth.

But Parker also had more serious matters on his mind. With the detectives of the Union Pacific, Pinkertons and the law closing in, he understood that his days as a Wild West outlaw were numbered. In 1902 he parted company with the Wild Bunch and fled to South America, via an extended vacation in New York. Joining him in Uruguay were Harry Longbaugh, and Longbaugh's mistress, Texan prostitute Etta Place.

The trio moved to Argentina, where they operated a cattle and sheep ranch at Chibut, trailing their herds to the meat-hungry miners of neighbouring Chile. This idyll lasted for four years, before the outside world began to close in again. Also, Etta Place began to suffer from attacks of appendicitis, and in 1907 Longbaugh escorted her to Denver for an operation. A bartender who tried to stop him shooting up a saloon was himself shot by Longbaugh, although not mortally. After this they returned to South America, but relocated to Bolivia, where Longbaugh and Parker began to rob payroll shipments and banks, working at the Concordia Tin Mine in between times. Their crimes in South America amounted to a mere handful.

And then, as legend has it, there was a gunbattle between the *bandido yanquis*, who had just hijacked a money-laden mule train, and Bolivian soldiers in the town of San Vincente. Longbaugh then shot the *capitan* out of his saddle; Parker – who had never killed anyone before – shot another soldier. They quickly retreated inside a restaurant, piling up tables and chairs before them. They ran short of ammunition, and when darkness fell Longbaugh made a dash across the plaza to their mules, and grabbed their Winchesters and cartridge belts. As Longbaugh ran back he was shot. Parker managed to pull him inside, suffering a wound himself. Parker held out for a while, but at about 10 p.m. he shot the badly wounded Longbaugh in the head, donned the uniform of a slain soldier and escaped into the night. After facial surgery, he returned to the USA as William

Thadeus Phillips, a mechanical engineer from Des Moines, Iowa. He married, his Phillips Manufacturing Company prospered, he became an Elk and a Freemason. In the 1920s and 1930s he made nostalgic trips back to the Hole in the Wall country, even renewing an acquaintanceship with former mistress Mary Boyd Rhodes. During the Great Depression, his business went under. Robert LeRoy Parker, alias "Butch Cassidy" and "William T. Phillips", died of cancer at the county poor farm at Spangle, near Spokane, in 1937.

That is one version of what befell Parker and Longbaugh in South America. Another, as described in a manuscript William T. Phillips wrote entitled "The Bandit Invincible", has Parker, Longbaugh and two accomplices attacking a mule train on a track outside La Paz, and then being ambushed by Bolivian cavalry. There was a sharp fight, during which the accomplices and Longbaugh were shot. Before he died, Longbaugh told Parker that he had legally married Etta Place, and asked him to give her his money belt. When darkness fell, Parker shot at a noise in the brush, killing another soldier, and crawled away to safety, and eventually to America.

In other accounts of Parker and Longbaugh's Latin American exile, both escape back to the USA to live under assumed names and identities. Or both die in the little square at San Vincente.

The truth of what happened to Butch Cassidy and the Sundance Kid may never be known. There *was* a battle in San Vincente in November 1908 in which two North Americans were killed. Probably they were not Parker and Longbaugh. Parker, at least, seems to have made it back to the USA, to live under an assumed name, William T. Phillips. His sister certainly thought so. Not least because he paid her a surprise visit in 1929.

Business (Almost) as Usual

After Parker and Longbaugh left for South America, most of their old Wild Bunch confederates carried on with business as usual. Or, at least, as far as they were able in a world of telegraphs, telephones, spreading settlements, growing railroads and the combustion engine.

Harvey "Kid Curry" Logan – after returning to Wyoming to kill rancher Jim Winters, who had shot his brother Johnny five years earlier – wounded three deputies in a gunfight at Knoxville, Tennessee, in December 1901, but was captured by a posse with dogs. He made a daring escape from the "escape-proof" prison at Columbus, Ohio, and tried to join Parker and Longbaugh in South America, but was unable to get out of the country. Logan was by now one of the most wanted men in America. In June 1904, he held up the Denver & Rio Grande railroad at Parachute, Colorado, but the safe yielded only a few dollars. Pursued by a posse, Logan and his accomplices were cornered in a small canyon near Glenwood Springs. Wounded by a bullet as he tried to take cover, Logan was asked, "Are you hit?"

"Yes," gasped Logan, "and I'm going to end it here." He committed suicide by a shot to the head. Rumours persisted for years that he managed to escape to South America.

Tom O'Day was captured by Sheriff Frank Webb in Casper, Wyoming, with a herd of stolen horses in 1903, and sentenced to jail.

Harry Tracy shot his brother-in-law in an argument in July 1902, and a month later battled it out with a posse at Davenport, near Washington. Badly injured, he jammed a revolver to his head and committed suicide.

Ben Kilpatrick ("The Tall Texan") was still holding up trains as late as 1912. On the afternoon of 14 March in that year, Kilpatrick and accomplice Nick Grider stopped the Southern Pacific just outside Dryden, Texas. Everything seemed to be going in the traditional manner. The mail and express car were detached and run a mile up the track. Kilpatrick, however, allowed himself to be distracted by the messenger, David Trousdale, who battered him over the head with an ice pick. He died moments later.

And so ended the last old-style train robbery in the history of the West.

The Saga of Tom Horn

> I can never believe that the jolly, jovial, honorable and
> whole-souled Tom Horn I knew was a low-down mis-
> erable murderer.
>
> *Al Sieber, Chief of Scouts*

After their failed invasion of Johnson County in 1892, the
Wyoming cattle barons adopted a low-key – but deadly
– approach to the problem of rustlers. They hired the
talents of the gunman named Tom Horn, who would shoot
rustlers for a price, leaving a trademark of two stones
under the victim's head. When Horn passed on, the long
wave of Wyoming range war violence ended with him.

Like many gunfighters, Horn was born and reared on a
farm. After a whipping from his father at the age of 14, he
ran away to the West. He worked for the railroad, then the
Overland stage company as a driver, and by 1876 he had
signed on with the army as a scout. His career as a scout
in Apache country was heroic, and in 1885 he succeeded
the celebrated Al Sieber as civilian chief of scouts. Horn
played a part in the final capture of Geronimo, and when
that campaign was over he hired out his ability with a
gun in the Pleasant Valley War. Later, he was sheriff of
Yavapai County, Arizona, and occasionally worked a gold
claim near Tombstone.

In 1890 Tom Horn joined the Pinkerton Detective Agency in Denver, and captured the outlaw Peg Leg McCoy. Two years later, Horn enlisted as a range detective with the Wyoming Stock Growers' Association, and helped recruit the gunmen who fought in the Johnson County War against the homesteaders and rustlers. He may have even been a member of the cattle baron invasion force himself.

After the Johnson County War, Horn signed on with the Swan Land and Cattle Company, at that time managed by Scotsman John Clay. According to Clay, Horn hardly spoke, and would sit for long periods silently smoking cigarettes and braiding horsehair ropes. On the company's books, Horn was listed as a horsebreaker, but his real job was to assassinate troublesome rustlers.

For the next three years, Horn roamed the ranges for the Swan Land and Cattle Company and for other big ranches. When a rancher suspected someone of rustling, they would summon the thin-faced, balding killer and he would set about organizing an ambush. As the testimony in his later trial showed, he was a methodical and patient assassin. He would move into an area under an assumed identity, get to know the victim's habits, and then wait for hours in the rain or cold or sun, chewing on raw bacon, waiting for the perfect shot. "Killing is my business," Horn remarked on occasion. He always worked alone, made his kills with a high-powered rifle, was scrupulous in collecting up any evidence of his crime, and always left the two-stone signature.

Horn's murder of Matt Rash at Cold Springs Mountain, Colorado, on 8 July 1900 was typical. Calling himself James Hicks, Horn drifted into Rash's neighbourhood and began spying on the rustler. Early in the afternoon of 8 July, Rash finished a lunch of steak and potatoes and then stepped outside his cabin. Horn then fired from concealment, hitting Rash three times, the rustler stumbling back inside.

Horn meanwhile collected his cartridge shells, and then raced off to collect his fee, a flat $600.

After killings, Horn would go to Cheyenne or Denver to let off steam in a drinking spree. Usually reserved, Horn would become talkative and boastful when drunk.

When the Spanish–American War broke out in 1898, Horn rejoined the army and went to Cuba as master of a pack train.

By spring 1901, Horn was back in Wyoming and took a job with John Coble, who owned a large ranch north of Laramie near Iron Mountain. Coble suspected homesteaders on the fringe of his ranch of stealing stock. Employing his usual method, Horn patiently scouted the area and the people. Among those he met was Glendolene Kimmel, the Iron Mountain schoolteacher. Kimmel boarded with a family called Miller, who were conducting a feud with a neighbouring homesteader, Kels P. Nickell. Victor Miller and Kels Nickell had quarrelled over a land boundary, which had resulted in Nickell wounding Miller with a knife. For his protection, Miller had started carrying a shotgun; but this had accidentally discharged, killing one of Miller's own sons. Miller blamed Nickell for the accident.

Meanwhile, Horn's employer, John Coble, had informed him that he also considered Nickell a nuisance and wanted him eliminated, not least because he was a sheepman.

At about 3.30 p.m. on 18 July 1902, two shots rang out on the Powder River Road near Cheyenne, Wyoming. Lying dead was 14-year-old Willie Nickell, who had died as he tried to open a gate to the family sheep camp to get a hay wagon through. He had been wearing his father's hat and coat.

Miller and his friend Tom Horn were immediately suspected of the crime, but Horn produced an alibi that he had been on the train between Cheyenne and Laramie at the time of the shooting. The Miller family, plus Glendolene

Kimmel, swore that Miller had been home the day Willie Nickell was killed. Kimmel had developed an affection for Horn; when she realised that her testimony placing Miller at home on the day of the murder endangered Horn, she withdrew it.

Willie Nickell's slaying deeply shocked the Iron Mountain community. A thousand-dollar reward was posted for the capture of the perpetrator. The case remained unsolved, however, until deputy US marshal Joe Lefors appeared at Iron Mountain, questioned everybody, and was soon on the trail of Tom Horn. Lefors knew Horn and believed that he must have killed the boy by accident. Tracking Horn to Denver, Lefors discovered the hired killer on one of his periodic drunks. Lefors plied him with more drink, and extracted what sounded like a confession to Willie Nickell's killing. The confession was overheard by eavesdropping deputies, who recorded it in shorthand.

The confession was used to arrest Horn the next morning. Coble and the other stockmen rallied to Horn's assistance, and managed to get the trial postponed until October 1902.

Tom Horn's trial was front-page news the West over. He denied the confession obtained under the influence of alcohol, and without this the prosecution had no real evidence. Nevertheless, Joe Lefors's short record of Tom Horn's conversation was enough to persuade the jury that he was guilty of murder in the first degree.

Horn did not expect to hang. He was confident that the cattle barons would obtain a new trial for him. This proved impossible. Friends did, however, pay a young cowboy to be arrested and confined in Cheyenne jail, so that Horn could give him an escape plan. The cowboy lost his nerve, and told the local newspaper of the plot.

Horn broke out anyway, jumping Deputy Sheriff Richard Proctor in the morning of 9 August 1903. Horn and another escapee, Jim McCloud, made their way outside into the jail corral, McCloud took the only horse, leaving Horn to make a run for it on foot. He was chased by a citizen named O. M. Eldrich, alerted by the shrieks of police whistles. Eldrich fired several shots at Horn, one of them grazing him on the head. The citizen then wrestled Horn to the ground, and a gang of lawmen arrived to take him back to jail.

Tom Horn was scheduled to hang on 20 November 1903. Two days before, as he sat in his cell, alternately writing his autobiography and braiding a horse-hair rope, he chanced to look out of his cell window. Scrawled in the snow was the message: KEEP YOUR NERVE.

There were frantic last-moment attempts by Glendolene Kimmel and the Wyoming stockmen to save Horn. Despite these pleas, he was hanged, as scheduled, on the morning of 20 November 1903. Horn never named his employers.

Ironically, the crime for which Horn swung is one he did not, on the balance of probability, commit. Glendolene Kimmel "born and reared midst the comforts and refinements of civilisation" as she wrote in her statement on Horn's behalf, declared on oath that the Millers had tried to throw suspicion for the deed onto Horn. She knew this for hard fact, because they had told her so. Even if Kimmel's statement is dismissed because of her bias towards Horn, the question remains: would an experienced bounty hunter like Horn have mistaken a boy – even if wearing his father's coat and hat – for a man he knew by sight?

Certainly there was no material evidence to tie Horn to Willie Nickell's death, save for a "confession" given in a spell of drunken bragging. The attempts of the cattle barons to free him prove nothing; they would have tried to protect Horn anyway, out of loyalty, and out of a need to keep all his deeds committed on their behalf

– not necessarily the killing of Willie Nickell – under wraps.

Almost a century on, the Horn case remains the subject of intense debate in Wyoming and elsewhere in the West.

Wild West Shows
and Rodeos

In America, Wild West shows and organized rodeos appeared even before the frontier and the open range disappeared. Probably the first live show exhibiting scenes from the West occurred in 1837, at the opening of artist George Catlin's Indian gallery at the Stuyvesant Institute on Broadway, when Ioway chief Keokuk and an assembly of Fox and Sioux Indians shot arrows and performed war dances. Contests in which working cowboys showed off their skills also had a long past; they were a part of the round-up before the great drives up the Chisholm Trail, while the first town to hold a rodeo was Santa Fe, in 1846, witnessed by Irish novelist Mayne Reid: "They contest with each other for the best roping and throwing, and there are horse races and whiskey and wines." Such contests involved Anglos and *vaqueros*, the *vaqueros* drawing on a Mexican tradition of equestrian display and competition which traces back to the days of the Conquistadors.

But it was only under the auspices of former Pony Express rider and buffalo hunter William F. ("Buffalo Bill") Cody that Far West shows and rodeos became an entertainment for millions.

Wild West Shows

In 1872 Buffalo Bill, Texas Jack Omohundro and the dime novelist Ned Buntline (Edward Judson) appeared in a stage melodrama written by Buntline entitled "The Scouts of the Prairie". It was lambasted by critics, with the *Chicago Times* commenting: "It is not probable that Chicago will ever look on the like again. Such a combination of incongruous dialogue, execrable acting . . . intolerable stench, scalping, blood and thunder . . ." Audiences, however, loved it. The stage show toured for years, with Cody occasionally breaking off to scout for the army in the Indian Wars, even killing a Cheyenne sub-chief, Yellow Hand, in battle at War Bonnet Creek. Cody's theatrical stock rose even higher.

The success of the stage show gave Cody a grander idea: a frontier extravaganza to play in large outdoor arenas. He got his chance to test the idea in 1882, when the citizens of his local town, North Platte in Nebraska, decided to organize an "Old Glory Blowout" to celebrate the Fourth of July. As a famous figure, showman and local rancher, Cody was inevitably asked to take charge as Grand Marshal. He came up with a rip-snorting bill which included shooting contests and even a herd of buffalo. Moreover, since North Platte was in cowboy country, he organized roping and riding contests under the title "Cowboys' Fun". He made cowboys into entertainment.

So successful was North Platte's "Old Glory Blowout" that Cody took it on the road the next year, only on a bigger scale. When he advertised for cowpunchers to join his show as "actors" so many applied that he had to arrange competitions to select the best. His first full-scale version of the "Wild West" (he thought the term "show" lacked dignity) took place at the Omaha Fair Grounds on 19 May 1883. The event was billed as "The Wild West,

Hon. W. F. Cody and Dr. W. F. Carver's Mountain and
Prairie Exhibition." Aside from Buffalo Bill himself and
several other marksmen, it featured amongst many other
acts an attack on the Deadwood Stage, the Pony Express,
and a "grand, realistic battle scene depicting the capture,
torture and death of a scout by savages." The brightest star
of the Cow-Boys' Fun section was Cody's own ranch hand,
Buck Taylor, who could seemingly ride and rope anything.
The closing spectacle was "A Grand Hunt on the Plains,"
with buffalo, elk, deer, mountain sheep, wild horses and
longhorns.

The show was a smash hit and toured for three decades, constantly adding to its repertoire of acts, and
often incorporating real characters and events from the
frontier years. Custer's Last Stand and Wounded Knee
were both dramatized, as was the Charge at San Juan
Hill by Teddy Roosevelt and his Rough Riders during
the Spanish–American war. Sitting Bull joined the show
in 1884, Sioux Ghost Dancers participated in 1891, and
Geronimo played the circuit in 1906.

One convention which was maintained was that the
trick-shooting sensation Annie Oakley, "Little Sure Shot"
("Watanya cicilia") as she was dubbed by Sitting Bull,
appeared as the second act, after Cody himself. Oakley,
who was born Phoebe Ann Moses to a Quaker family
from Darke County, Ohio, was idolized by audiences for
her ability to shoot cigarettes out of men's mouths and
splitting playing cards from 30 paces. She once broke 943
out of 1,000 glass balls thrown in the air, using a .22 rifle.

The success of Buffalo Bill's Wild West in America was
soon repeated in Britain and Europe. In 1887 in London
the Deadwood Stage, driven by Buffalo Bill, carried four
kings and the Prince of Wales to the arena. During the 1890
tour of Italy, a Wild West delegation was blessed by Pope
Leo XIII.

Buffalo Bill's show was not the only Wild West show in town. Gordon W. ("Pawnee Bill") Lillie, a scout who had worked as the interpreter for the Pawnee in Buffalo Bill's 1883 show at Omaha, set up his own Pawnee Bill's Historical Wild West Exhibition and Indian Encampment. His wife, Mae Lillie, was the female sharpshooting act. Pawnee Bill's was the only Wild West to rival Buffalo Bill's in grandeur or success, but the 4-Paws Wild West, Hardwick's Wild West and the Miller Brothers 101 Ranch Wild Wes' were all popular. Even Frank James and Cole Younger tried to cash in on the phenomenon with a show of their own in 1903.

Although Buffalo Bill Cody made millions from his show, he also lost them in unwise investments. According to Annie Oakley: "He was totally unable to resist any claim for assistance . . . or refuse any mortal in distress . . . and until his dying day he was the easiest mark . . . for every kind of sneak and gold-brick vendor that was mean enough to take advantage of him."

Buffalo Bill's Wild West had to be rescued by Pawnee Bill in 1908 and the new joint show became "Buffalo Bill's Wild West and Pawnee Bill's Great Far East Combine." But the new show only lasted for five years and closed in 1913, burdened by debts. The public had become sated and disillusioned with Western shows, hundreds of which toured the country. Many were started by Buffalo Bill's ex-partners, and were mere pale, offputting imitations of the original.

Buffalo Bill retired to his ranch, dying in 1917. Pawnee Bill went to work in rodeo, which was booming.

Rodeos

By the time Buffalo Bill's Wild West took its final bow, major competitive rodeo events with cash prizes had become annual occurrences in Salinas, Calgary, Cheyenne and Pendleton, Oregon. The Pendleton Roundup featured 1,000 American Indians performing war dances and pony parades. Nez Perce cowboy Jackson Sundown, who claimed to be a nephew of Chief Joseph, won many of the competitions. In 1916, at the age of 50, he won the Pendleton Championship, making a sensational ride on his horse Angel. The same year, rodeo was brought East with the New York Stampede, held in Brooklyn.

Most of the rodeos began as efforts by local towns to boost tourism and business. Cheyenne launched its Frontier Days in 1897, with a large rodeo component in a mixed programme of Wild West exhibitions. Pendleton planned its cowboy "round-up" in 1910, with such events as "roping, racing, and relays, by cowboys, Indians and cowgirls; steer roping, maverick races, steer bulldogging, riding bucking horses, steers, bulls, buffaloes, and cows; stagecoach racing, Indian ceremonial and war dances, trick riding, mounted tug of war, the grand parade, and that wonderful finale, the wild horse race." During the 1920s, however, rodeo evolved and slimmed down to its present form, with five main events: bareback horse racing, bull riding, calf roping, saddle bronc riding and steer wrestling ("bulldogging").

Roping cattle and riding unbroken horses were events derived directly from the work of the cowboy. But bull riding and bulldogging were added to rodeo simply because they looked spectacular. Bulldogging was popularized in the early 1900s by the Miller 101 Ranch from Oklahoma, especially its Black cowboy star Bill Pickett, who would jump from his horse onto a running steer, grab its horns, and twist its neck until the nose came up, at which point he would bite its lip, forcing it to a halt. Pickett thought up the trick after watching ranchers' bulldogs, used to flush cattle out of thickets, immobilizing them by biting their sensitive upper lips. Bulldogging has endured as a rodeo sport, although humane groups protested at Pickett's personal method and it was banned by the teens. Until he became famous Pickett had to dress as a Mexican toreador since many rodeos did not admit Black contestants. Zack Miller, owner of the sprawling 101 Ranch in Oklahoma, described Pickett as "the greatest sweat and dirt cowhand that ever lived – bar none."

Pickett was the second renowned African-American in rodeo, the first being Nat Love, who entered the rodeo at Deadwood City in 1876. He won several roping and shooting contests and recalled: "Right there the assembled crowd named me 'Deadwood Dick' and proclaimed me champion roper of the Western cattle country."

At first, rodeo riders were as poor as the cowboys from whose ranks they came. They travelled a huge circuit from the Mexican border up to Canada, from New York to California, existing only on the prize money they won – if any. Unlike cowboys, rodeo riders were successful at unionizing themselves, founding the Cowboy's Turtle Association in 1936 (so-called because a turtle "doesn't get anywhere unless it sticks its neck out"). This became the Rodeo Cowboys Association in 1945 and the Professional Rodeo Cowboys Association in 1974. They won an important victory over management in 1955 when their point system and standings became the measure for naming rodeo world champions.

Like cowpunching, rodeo was originally a male province. But by the early twentieth century many stockmen's daughters were translating skills learned on the family ranch into celebrity in the rodeo arena. The first female to enter a rodeo show was Bertha Kaepernick, who took part in both the wild horse race and the bucking bronc contest in Cheyenne's first Frontier Days in 1897. Prairie Rose Henderson was the first female headliner. She was refused entry in the bucking bronc contest at the Cheyenne Frontier Days in 1901 until she pointed out to judges that there was nothing in the rule book which forbade her trying. Her ride was magnificent and created such notoriety that other rodeos soon included a women's bronc riding contest. Among the other cowgirls in early rodeo were Prairie Lilly Allen and Kitty Canutt; trick riders Tillie Baldwin and Lottie Vandreau; trick roper Florence LaDue; and steer wrestler Fox Hastings. Teddy Roosevelt was so impressed by Oklahoma rancher's daughter Lucille Mulhall when he saw her performing in 1900 that he declared her to be a "cowgirl" – the first time the term was used. Mulhall starred in her father's Wild West show before working in rodeo, and after rodeo she became a star of silent Western movies.

Mulhall was far from the only star of rodeo to enter Hollywood. So did Tom Mix and Will Rogers, both of them Bill Pickett's assistants. Western cinema also drew heavily on the themes and imagery of the Wild West show.

The Wild West show, the rodeo, the Western movie, and the cowboy novel are all means by which the West has become mythologized, distorted, caricatured, made larger than – and sometimes smaller than – life, debased.

The West no longer lives in reality, only in the world of the imagination, and in the memory preserved by history.

The legacy of the West, meanwhile, lies all around. It can be seen in the democratic independence of the American character; equally it can be seen in the poverty-stricken reservations of the Native Peoples. Perhaps only the West, that promised land of beautiful immigrant dreams and cruel tragedies, could produce such good and such ill.

Afterword

Shoot! The American West in the Movies

The West was scarcely dead in the dust before someone came along with a movie camera to make myth of it. And money too.

In September 1903 the grandly named American Mutoscope and Biograph Company issued forth *Kit Carson*, the first true Western movie. Three months later, Edison released the better known *The Great Train Robbery*, a ten-minute extravaganza in which a mail carriage was robbed, a posse got up, the bad guys gunned down. Audiences loved it, and the fledgling companies of the new movie medium – Mutoscope, Edison, Lubin, Vitagraph – cranked out follow-up Western reelers as fast as they could turn the camera handle. It was the beginning of a cinematic gold rush, a bonanza that over the course of the next century would usually gush, sometimes trickle, but never quite dry up.

These early Westerns didn't come out of clear blue nowhere. They drew heavily on the stock stories and characters of the pop culture West as emblazoned in decades of Beadle & Adams dime novels, songs, and

Wild West shows. Stage shows, too, had their influence: *The Great Train Robbery* had been theatre before it had been celluloid; the greatest Western star of the silent era, William S. Hart, first came to notice in the 1905 stage play *The Squaw Man*.

The other vein to be tapped by the makers of early Western movies was the real West itself. While the first Westerns were shot at east coast studios, in 1907 the Selig-Polyscope Company of Chicago sent a film crew way out West to shoot *The Girl from Montana*, which made heavy use of the local scenery. A trend for authentic locations was set. It was confirmed forever in 1909 when the Bison Company arrived in California. More studios followed . . . and so was Hollywood born.

California had more than scenery: it had real Westerners. For bit parts in the first Hollywood Westerns, unemployed cowboys used to be rounded up from Los Angeles' dirt-floor saloons for a dollar a day and lunch. Not just cowboys, either. A few authentic Old West heroes and villains had their moment in the movies. Robber Al Jennings and Sheriff Bill Tilghman reconstructed their past in 1908's *The Bank Robbery*. Buffalo Bill Cody starred in *The Adventures of Buffalo Bill* (1917). Wyatt Earp was a near fixture around Hollywood lots declaiming on how the West had been won, and featured in 1919's *The Half-Breed*. Reputedly, Earp gave director John Ford the just-so version of the gunfight at the OK Corral, as patented in Ford's *My Darling Clementine* from 1946.

The West and the movies were made for each other. The camera loved the landscape west of the Mississippi better even than the brushes of Seth Eastman and Albert Bierstadt loved it. Motion pictures, by definition, need action. What could surpass the spectacles – the gunfights, the wagon trains across the Plains, the stampedes, the cavalry charges – of the real and pot-boiled West?

Nothing. It is perhaps small wonder that nearly one quarter of the movies made in America in 1909 were Westerns.

That same year also saw the emergence of the first Western star in the pugnacious shape of Gilbert M. Anderson (aka Max Aronson). Beginning with *Bronco Billy's Redemption*, Anderson played the "good bad man" (a ne'er-do-well redeemed by the heroic saving of, usually, a woman or child) in a slew of nearly 200 films. Anderson did something more than shine celestially. He also made the cowboy the Western hero *sans pareil*. Before Anderson, the heroes of Western movies had tended to be those of old-style Western literary fiction, the trapper and scout. After Anderson, the cowpoke ruled, a happenstance not entirely unconnected to the phenomenal success of Owen Wister's 1902 novel *The Virginian* and the growing popularity of rodeo. There was also the small fact that a cowboy looked stylish on film in a way that a man wearing furs never can.

The ascendancy of the cowboy on the silver screen was only proven when the next Western star, William S. Hart, adopted cowpuncher persona. And the next, Tom Mix. But whereas Hart, raised on the old frontier, brought authenticity and moralism to his films, Mix – whose career was at its zenith in the 1920s – opted for sheer escapist entertainment. Authenticity versus Fantasy. Always would the Western be pulled between them, to and fro, to and fro.

Even in the same moment. If Tom Mix's glitzy daredevilry was one flavour with the Jazz Age audience, another was the epic Western. Producers such as D. W. Griffith at Biograph had already shown what could be done with big production values and bigger vision in such spectaculars as *The Battle of Elderbush Gulch* (1913). But the first epic really to roll was Paramount's *The Covered Wagon* of 1923, based on Emerson Hough's novel, which followed an emigrant train going westwards in the 1840s. The theme was mighty (the conquest of the West), the budget vast ($782,000 – about $10 million at contemporary prices), the panoramas sweeping (it was filmed on location in Utah) and the length almost unprecedented (it was a ten-reeler, twice as long as the average feature).

A small stampede of historical epics followed, among them John Ford's railway-building extravaganza, *The Iron Horse* (1924, which used as extras the same "coolies" who had worked on the real transcontinental constructions), William S. Hart's Oklahoma land-rush tale *Tumbleweeds* (1925), and *The Vanishing American* (1926), this last based on Zane Grey's story about reservation Indians. There might have been more, but the epics required expenditure that unnerved studio heads. Down at the lot, meanwhile, "oaters" based around a particular Western star – Mix, Hart, Hoot Gibson, Tim McCoy, Ken Maynard, Buck Jones, Harry Carey – coined in the money nicely with little risk thank you. The oater got a further filip in the mid-1930s with the advent of the "double-bill", which required a filler for the bottom half of the programme. Oaters fitted the wanted notice perfectly and they rolled off the conveyor-belt of Hollywood at bewildering pace. In 1934 Hollywood produced 76 Westerns; a year later its annual production had more than doubled to 145 Westerns. The Taj Mahals of Hollywood's moguls were built on the back of the humble "B" (for Bottom of bill) Western, a star-based American morality play in which the guy in the white hat gunned down the villain in the black one. And was made on the cheap. The budget for the Westerns Marion Morrison (aka John Wayne) made for Monogram in the middle of the 1930s was $5,000 a pop. Wayne, at least, didn't have to sing, for this was also the era of the singing cowboy, epitomized by Republic studio's Gene Autry. A former "hillbilly" recording artist, Autry was installed at Republic in place of the unpredictable Ken Maynard and almost instantly topped *Motion Picture Herald*'s annual poll of the major money-making Western stars, staying in the top slot from 1937 to 1943. Many tried to emulate Autry, but only Tex Ritter and Republic stablemate, Roy Rogers (*né* Leonard Slye) offered serious dollar-spinning competition.

While the Bs boomed, A Westerns hit hard times in the 1930s, a direct result of the flopping at the 1930 box-office of RKO's *Cimarron* – ironically enough the only Western to win Best Picture at the Academy Awards until *Dances with Wolves* in 1990 – and Fox's *The Big Trail*. Not until 1939 with John Ford's *Stagecoach*, filmed in what would become Ford's signature backdrop, Monument Valley in Arizona, and *Jesse James* did the A Western come out all guns blazing, for a decade and more of glory.

The return to Hollywood town of the A Western was no coincidence. There was a new breed of athletic star – Tyrone Power, James Stewart, Henry Fonda and, especially, Errol Flynn – needing action screen parts, and when Cecil B. de Mille, whose first Western had been *The Squaw Man* in 1914, decided to have another shot at the genre others were sure to follow suit. Especially when, as with *Union Pacific* (1939) and *Northwest Mounted Police* (1940), he made lucre at the box-office.

More than any of this, the Western had grown up and got meaningful, become a mirror into which Americans might look and see something of their past, but also their present. It was more than coincidence that many of the new crop of Westerns were either biopics of American outlaws (*Jesse James*) or pageants of frontier progress (*Union Pacific*). Their common evil was money-grubbing capitalist barons who did down poor folk, even driving them to become outlaws (such as the James boys). The parallel with the Depression of the 1930s was plain for audiences to see.

Something else audiences were getting a glimpse of in the A Western was psyche and sex. Up to Howard Hughes's *The Outlaw* starring Jane Russell, released in 1943, women in Westerns were either absent or simpering symbols of civilization (the "gentle tamers"). Russell paraded a sexual desire unknown in Western movies ("What are the two reasons for Jane Russell's rise to stardom?" quipped the film's poster over a still of her décolletage), with the heat turned up further by *Duel in the Sun* (1946). What was acceptable taste in movieland West was changed forever.

But the film that truly blazed the trail for the A Western was not *Stagecoach* or *The Outlaw* or *Union Pacific* but *The Ox-Bow Incident* from 1942. Based on Walter van Tilburg Clark's novel, the *Incident* pictured a less than pretty West where townsfolk were given to lynching hysteria. There was no easy White v Black morality, "civilization" was hardly worth the fighting for, and there was not even a galahad-with-a-six to do it. And the folks had all sorts of neuroses. The Western was turned on its head.

Thereafter the trend towards "adult" Westerns trotted, cantered and by the 1950s was galloping apace. Gregory Peck found a town full of malice in *The Gunfighter* (1950). Gary Cooper encountered much the same in *High Noon* (1952). James Stewart played an angst-ridden lawman in *The Naked Spur* (1953), directed by Anthony Mann, probably the Western director most influenced by "film-noir". Nicholas Ray's *Johnny Guitar* (1954) lit into mob rule. Henry Fonda and Anthony Quinn came close to something like homosexuality in *Warlock* (1959).

Not, of course, that the "traditional" Western was driven out of town. The B Western continued untroubled and unchanged, until killed off by the emergence of Western series on TV in the mid-1950s. The mythic Old West (or was it the true Old West?) where a man had to do what he had to do to tame the wilderness and the wild-blooded was evoked unforgettably in *Shane* (1952). And John Wayne would not have become the icon of cowboy movies if he hadn't ridden uprightly through *Fort Apache* (1948) and *Rio Bravo* (1959).

Yet even the stalwart John Wayne had a share of 1950s angst, starring as the fractured hero of Howard Hawk's *Red River* (1948) and John Ford's *The Searchers* (1956). When the Duke had to play it tortured, it was a certain sign that the times were moving to a different drum beat.

As all manner of film commentators noted in learned journals of the 1950s, that age's paranoias (the Cold War, McCarthyism, youth rebellion) had found their place in the Western. *High Noon* and *Johnny Guitar* were implicit attacks on the witch-hunts of Joe McCarthy. *The Man Behind the Gun* (1953) took the opposite side of the street, and gave dire warnings to root out the red from under the bed. Nicholas Ray's *The True Story of Jesse James* (1957) put inter-generational conflict plot centre – as had the director's *Rebel Without a Cause* (1955) – which was just the right place for the new phenomenon of "teenagers". There were obvious Cold War parables to be found in the cavalry movies *Arrowhead* (1953) and *Drum Beat* (1954). After *Broken Arrow* (1950), however, any film that portrayed Injuns as bad was fighting the wind.

American Indians had not had a good time out in the cinematic West. Aside from some sympathetic treatment in early silent movies which tended to romance, such as *Ramona* (1910) and *A Squaw's Love* (1911), the lot of the Indian had been faceless savagery for 40 years. Delmer Daves's *Broken Arrow* made a stand against anti-Indian racism, and made a difference. A true historian of the West, Daves presented authentic Indian culture. Influenced by the contemporary civil rights movement he also gave out a message of co-existence between the races. That the studio insisted on Whites playing Indian roles and on the killing-off of the Indian princess (played by Debra Paget) before miscegenation could occur hardly lessened the movie's impact. A whole flurry of pro-Indian movies was knocked out by Hollywood, among them *Apache* (1954, starring Burt Lancaster) and *Taza, Son of Cochise* (1954, starring Rock Hudson) and John Ford's *Cheyenne Autumn* (1964), his last Western and something of apology for the cinematic crimes he'd committed against the Indians as far back as *Stagecoach*. Six years later the Western finally faced up to the real historical massacre of the Indian, with the release of *Soldier Blue*, which reconstructed the slaughters at Sand Creek and Wounded Knee, and *Little Big Man*, which focused on the mayhem at Washita. When, in 1973, Marlon Brando refused to accept an Academy Award in protest at Hollywood's treatment of Native Peoples, the pro-Indian uprising reached a kind of culmination.

It was too little, too late. By 1973 Hollywood was barely making any Westerns, let alone pro-Indian ones. Whereas 130 Westerns had been produced in 1950, just 16 Westerns came out of Tinseltown in 1973. The reasons weren't hard to guess. Over the 1950s and 1960s audiences had become sated with oaters on the silver and small screens. Demographics, too, took a hand. As studios had long known, the major audience for Westerns were rural folk. In an increasingly urban America, the Western found fewer takers. Moreover, even as late as the 1950s men and women who had actually fought on the frontier were still to be found on rocking-chairs on porches, yarning about chasing the 'Pache and building sod houses. By the next decade the last of the Old West survivors had gone, and with them went the living links to the frontier era. Their passing was acknowledged by a passel of End-of-the-West-Westerns in the 1960s, beginning with Sam Peckinpah's almost perfect *Ride the High Country* (aka *Guns in the Afternoon*) of 1962, which found Joel McCrea and Randolph Scott as aged gun-fighters escorting a payroll at the very moment the motor car arrived out West. There were similar laments to the gone West in *Lonely Are the Brave, The Man Who Shot Liberty Vallance, The Good Guys and Bad Guys* and *Monte Walsh.*

Arguably, though, the real truth behind the fall of the Western was none of the above. For 50 years the Western had got along by adapting to the mood of the people who bought the tickets. In the 1960s the people were cynical. You can do pretty much anything with a Western, save make it cynical.

Of course, some tried. Notably the Italian director Sergio Leone. After importing a minor Western TV star, Clint Eastwood, in 1964 Leone embarked on a cycle of Cinecitta-made Westerns featuring a "Man With No Name", an amoral and guileful mercenary who was almost superhumanly useful with a revolver. Leone's "dollars trilogy" (*A Fistful of Dollars, For A Few Dollars More* and *The Good, the Bad and the Ugly,* all released in the USA in 1967) made an aesthetic of violence, which was lovingly choreographed and played out to the almost operatic soundtracks of Ennio Morricone. You didn't need the eyes of an eagle to see that everybody involved had their tongues in their cheek. The limitations of the "Spaghetti Western" were nicely pointed up by the career of Leone himself. As soon as Hollywood came knockin' on Signor Leone's door with a wagonload of bucks, he made an almost entirely traditional-type Western, the epic *Once Upon a Time in the West.* Clint Eastwood followed the same path. Once back in Hollywood, he made oaters that retained Leone's stylistics but used the old, tried and tested Western formula: the man with the gun commits violence for personal or societal redemption. The more Westerns Eastwood made after *Hang 'Em High* (1968), the more "normal" his oaters became, especially when he warmed the director's chair too, such as on *The Outlaw Josey Wales* (1976) and *Pale Rider* (1985).

Put another way, nobody really wanted to make Spaghetti Westerns. They wanted to make real ones.

Only the opportunities for doing so were scarcer and scarcer. Eastwood himself largely departed Westerns for cop movies, somehow personifying the crime flick's long expropriation of Western elements. (After all, what is a cop but a sheriff gone to town?) And then, there was only one Western star left standing: John Wayne. The Duke made his final screen appearance in *The Shootist* (1976), playing a dying gunfighter in a dying West. The movie began with clips of Wayne's earlier films; it ended with Wayne's character dead on a bar-room floor. The Western might be belly up, *The Shootist* seemed to declare, but Wayne held true to cowboy virtue and valour throughout. Three years later Wayne himself was dead of cancer.

The next year they finally wrote the Western's obituary. The catastrophic failure of Michael Cimino's $50 million *Heaven's Gate* ensured that studio executives would bankroll no more oaters. In truth, Cimino's panoramic recounting of the Johnson County War was not so bad as some would have, and even approached John Fordian heights in its visual panache, but it was overlong and underplayed. And nobody much bothered to go to see it.

The Western, though, hadn't quite ridden off into the sunset. There were sporadic sightings (*Silverado* and *Pale Rider* in 1985, the "brat-pack" re-enactment of the Billy the Kid saga, *Young Guns*, in 1988) and then in 1989, the return of the Western was confirmed. On the silver screen's poor sister, TV, a CBS mini-series based on Larry McMurtry's *Lonesome Dove* attracted 40 million viewers a night. Always a nose to the wind, Hollywood executives took note and stumped up the funds for the personal project of hot star Kevin Costner. Released in 1990, *Dances with Wolves*, a movie notably sympathetic in its portrait of Native Americans (complete with Lakota sub-titles) was a sure-fire hit and the first Western to win the Oscar for best picture since *Cimarron*. Any doubts about the Western's comeback were quelled by the success of Eastwood's *Unforgiven* in 1992, which featured the star as a reformed gunslinger (turned pig farmer) enticed out of retirement for the bounty on a cowboy who sliced up a prostitute. It also won Best Picture. And suddenly there were Westerns galore.

What this new posse of Westerns had in common was a desire to debunk. So it was that Wyatt Earp was cut down to significantly human size in *Tombstone* (1993) and *Wyatt Earp* (1994). There were feminist takes on the West in *The Ballad of Little Jo* (1993), *Bad Girls* (1995, in which Andie McDowell, Drew Barrymore, Madeleine Stowe and Mary Stuart Masterson played saloon gals turned gunslingers) and *The Quick and the Dead* (1995, again with a woman as shootist). There was a Black revisionist West in Mario Van Peeble's *Posse*, the first significant Afro-American Western since the blaxploitation oater pics of Jim Brown and Fred Williamson back in the early 1970s.

Revisionist and debunking certainly, but all these movies made as much myth as they de-mythologized. After all, Belle Starr and Rose of Cimarron aside, woman gunfighters were as rare as blue moons in the historical West.

Who cares? Everybody, after all, eventually gets the West-U-Like in the movies.

It's now almost 100 years since that ten-minute reeler, *The Great Train Robbery*, started the epic story of the West in cinema. Or put another way, the West has survived in Hollywood almost three times as long as the "Wild West" – classically defined as the mid-1860s to mid-1890s – survived in reality. That tells much about the Western. Some of this phenomenal longevity can be accounted for in sly shifting accommodation to the *zeitgeist*, but there is something transcendental at work, too. The great theme of the Western is Civilization v Nature (played out in a score of variants such as Cowboys v Indians, Settlers v Gunslingers), where the conflict is resolved by a moment's action by an individual with a smoking gun. Order is made from chaos. Not in a biblical, godlike way, but in an all too recognizably human way.

When push comes to shove, when it's time to reach for your gun, people go to the Westerns to find a place where things seemed simpler, where life has more meaning and excitement than industrial society (be it the din of Henry Ford's conveyor belt, the "tap-tap" of the word processor in Silicon Valley), where a single person might have importance, be a hero, be their dream.

Pretty much the same reasons, then, that folks went to the real West.

The history of the Western never really comes to an end. There's always a sequel.

Appendix I:

Chronology of the American West

---

c. 30,000 BC   First humans enter North America, via land bridge over the Bering Straits.

AD 1400   Aboriginal population reaches 5 million.

AD 1000   Pueblo communities of Acoma and Hopi established.

1492   Columbus lands in the Bahamas.

1513   Ponce de Leon discovers Florida.

1521   Gregorio de Villalobos ships cattle from Caribbean to Mexico.

1528   Survivors of Panfilo de Narvaez's expedition to Florida blown ashore on the Texas coast – the first Europeans to see the American West. After numerous adventures four of the expedition, including Black Moorish servant Estevan, reach Mexico on foot in 1536.

1534   Jacques Cartier explores Gulf of St Lawrence.

1539–42   Francisco Vasquez de Coronado leads Spanish expedition from Mexico, penetrating as far into the West as Arizona and Kansas.

1542   Spanish explorer de Soto buried in the Mississippi.

1598   Juan de Onate founds Spanish settlements in northern New Mexico.

1607   English colonialists establish permanent settlement at Jamestown, Virginia.

1608   Quebec founded.

1620   English Pilgrims settle at Plymouth.

1637   Pequots of Connecticut battle English colonialists in a failed bid to retain hunting grounds.

1650   Captain Abraham Wood leads expedition along the Piedmont's Roanoke Valley.

1664   English seize New Amsterdam and rename it New York.

1669   John Lederer explores Blue Ridge Mountains.

1670s   Tidewater in Virginia and Maryland almost fully settled.

1671   Thomas Betts and Robert Fallum enter the Great Appalachian Valley via the Staunton River.

1675   Uprising by Wampanoag chief King Philip kills 600 New Englanders, but Wampanoags and their Narragansett allies are then slaughtered and enslaved.

1680   Revolt of the Pueblos.

1681–2   Sieur de La Salle sails down the Mississippi to Gulf of New Mexico.

1689–97   King William's War between France and England.

1700   Comanche established on Southern Plains.

1702–13   France loses Nova Scotia, Newfoundland and Hudson Bay to England in Queen Anne's War.

1744–8   King George's War between England and France results in stalemate.

1748   Jose de Escandon grazes the first cattle in what will become Texas.

1750   Dr Thomas Walker leads surveying party into "Kentucke".

1754–63   French and Indian War ends in victory for Britain, and places a third of the American continent in her hands.

1763   British Government issues Proclamation limiting White settlement to east of Appalachian crest in a bid to appease American Indians.

1769   Daniel Boone explores the Bluegrass region of Kentucky.

1775   American Revolution begins; Judge Richard Henderson purchases large tract of Kentucky from Cherokee; Daniel Boone clears the Wilderness Road from the Cumberland Gap to the Kentucky River, founding Boonesborough at its terminus.

1777   Shawnee raids against White settlements in Kentucky reach their peak.

1779   Retaliatory campaign by Generals Clinton and Sullivan razes 40 Iroquois towns in the Mohawk Valley.

1783   By the terms of the Treaty of Paris America is granted independence from Britain.

1785   Congress approves Ordinance to survey the old Northwest as a prelude to the public auction of its land.

1787   Northwest Ordinance passed by Congress, establishing process by which US territories can achieve statehood.

1790   Miami chief Little Turtle inflicts defeat on US force under General Arthur St Clair, killing 900.

1792   Kentucky enters the Union.

1794   General "Mad Anthony" Wayne wins the Battle of Fallen Timbers against the Miamis.

1795   Spain yields Yazoo Strip to United States in the Treaty of San Lorenzo.

1803   Ohio becomes a state; President Thomas Jefferson purchases Louisiana from France for $15 million, doubling the size of the USA.

1804–6   "Voyage of Discovery" led by Captains Meriwether Lewis and William Clark explores Louisiana Purchase.

1805–6   Lieutenant Zebulon Pike leads expedition along upper Mississippi as far as Leech Lake.

1806–7   Zebulon Pike explores Colorado and the Southwest; John Coulter becomes the first White man to see the Yellowstone.

1809–11   Tecumseh of the Shawnee campaigns for Native American unity and independence but is defeated by General William Henry Harrison at Tippecanoe, Indiana.

1811   The *New Orleans* journeys from Pittsburgh to New Orleans, inaugurating the great era of Western steamboating; the National Road links the East and the Ohio Valley; Astoria founded near the mouth of the Columbia River.

1812–15   War of 1812 between Britain and USA ends with no clear advantage to either side, although a Creek uprising is decisively defeated by the Americans at Horseshoe Bend, in the Mississippi Territory.

1819   The United States acquires Spanish Florida for $5 million.

1820   Major Stephen Long leads expedition to the Red River country.

1821   Mexico secures independence from Spain; William Becknell opens the Santa Fe Trail; Stephen F. Austin founds an Anglo colony in Texas.

1823   Mike Fink killed by Talbott after drunken shooting match.

1825   William Ashley establishes a rendezvous for fur trappers on the Green River, Wyoming; the Creek Nation cedes remaining lands to Georgia; the 363-mile long Erie Canal between Albany on the Hudson River and Lake Erie is completed at the cost of $7 million; trapper Jim Bridger discovers the Great Salt Lake.

1826   Stephen F. Austin organizes a corps of "watchmen", the beginnings of the Texas Rangers.

1827   Jedediah Smith makes first crossing of the Sierras.

1828   Cherokee nation surrenders its lands in Arkansas and agrees to relocate west of the Mississippi; Andrew Jackson elected president.

1830   John Jacob Astor secures agreement with the Blackfeet allowing his American Fur Company to trap beaver in their territory.

1832   Nathaniel Wyeth and other emigrants make pioneering journey to Oregon; Andrew Jackson re-elected president.

1834   Protestant mission established in Willamette Valley, Oregon.

1835   Samuel Colt of Connecticut patents revolving gun. Texas Revolution begins.

1836   Siege of the Alamo, February–March; Texas secures independence from Mexico after the 18-minute Battle of San Jacinto, April.

1837   Michigan admitted to the Union, January; smallpox epidemic devastates Indian tribes of the West, including the Mandan, of whom only 39 survive; last great fur trappers' rendezvous, Green River, June; Seminole nation defeated in Battle of Lake Okeechobee.

1838   Some 38,000 Cherokee are driven from Georgia to the West along the "Trail of Tears".

1842   The Seminole, the last of the Indian tribes remaining in the Southeast, lose their long guerilla war and agree to removal from Florida, although a few bands remain hidden in the Everglades; Oregon Trail established, a 2,000-mile route from Independence, Missouri, to the Pacific Northwest; a branch of the route will take pioneers to California.

1844   Telegraph invented by Samuel B. Morse; Joseph Smith killed by Illinois mob.

1845   Texas annexed by United States.

1846–8   United States declares war on Mexico, eventually gaining land in Texas and California.

1846   "Bear Flag Revolt" led by John Frémont secures California from Mexico for the USA: pioneer party led by George Dunbar becomes trapped in high sierras and resorts to cannibalism.

1847   Mormons arrive in Utah.

1848   James W. Marshall discovers gold at Sutter's Mill, California; Treaty of Guadalupe Hidalgo ends Mexican–American War, and adds 1.2 million square miles to USA.

1849   Gold rush of miners (dubbed "forty-niners") to California begins; Mormons attempt to form theocratic state of Deseret.

1850   California enters the Union.

1851   San Francisco's first vigilance committee formed.

1852   California mines yield $81 million in gold.

1857   So-called "Mormon War" sees nearly a sixth of the US Army dispatched to Utah; Fancher wagon train massacred by Mormons and Indians at Mountain Meadows.

1858   Overland stage route opened by John Butterfield.

1859   Gold rush to Pike's Peak, Colorado; "the Comstock Lode" discovered in Nevada.

1860–5   Civil War between North and South results in troops on Western frontier being recalled.

1860   Smith & Wesson pioneer metal gun cartridges; Bannock and Shoshoni Indians attack Otter–Van Orman wagon train, killing 18 pioneers; the Pony Express commences service; transcontinental telegraph line completed.

1861   Kansas admitted to the Union.

1862   Battle of Apache Pass between California Volunteers and Apache under Cochise and Mangas Coloradas, July; Homestead Act gives citizens over 21 the right to 160 acres of public domain; Little Crow leads uprising of Santee Sioux in Minnesota, with the Santee eventually defeated by superior force of militia at Wood Lake, September.

1864   Navajos make the "Long Walk" to Bosque Redondo; a punitive expedition led by Kit Carson is saved in a battle with the Comanche at Adobe Walls in the Texas Panhandle after deploying two howitzers; massacre of Southern Cheyenne at Sand Creek, Colorado, November; "road agent" Henry Plummer hanged by Montana vigilantes.

1865   President Abraham Lincoln assassinated; John Batterson Stetson establishes shop in Philadelphia specializing in headware for the range country; James Butler Hickok duels with Dave Tutt in Springfield, Missouri, July.

1866   Thieves (including Jesse and Frank James) raid bank at Liberty, Missouri, February; the Reno brothers rob a train at Seymour, Indiana; Fort Laramie Council between Government and Northern Plains tribes, June; Texan ranchers Charles Goodnight and Oliver Loving begin blazing the cattle trail to the Northern Plains which will bear their name; Red Cloud's Sioux ambush 80 officers and men near Fort Phil Kearny on the Bozeman Trail in the Fetterman Massacre, named after the arrogant army captain who led the command.

1867   More than 35,000 cattle driven up the Chisholm Trail to Abilene, Kansas; Alaska purchased by USA from Russia.

1868   Government to abandon forts along the Bozeman Trail, tacitly admitting that the Sioux are the victors in "Red Cloud's War"; Roman Nose of the Cheyenne dies in a skirmish with volunteer scouts at Beecher Island; Colonel George A. Custer and the 7th Cavalry massacre Black Kettle's Cheyenne near the Washita River, Indian Territory.

1869   Transcontinental railroad completed; Wyoming extends franchise to women.

1871   Mass shoot-out in a saloon in Newton, Kansas, leaves five dead; Marshal Wild Bill Hickok kills gunfighter/gambler Phil Coe in Abilene, Kansas.

1872–3   Modoc War, northern California, sees 165 Indians led by Captain Jack stand off vastly superior force of US Army until a series of pitched battles forces the Modoc to capitulate.

1873   Joseph Glidden invents barbed wire.

1874   Apache chief Cochise dies; buffalo hunters at Adobe Walls rebuff Comanche attack; Custer leads expedition to determine whether gold exists in the Black Hills of the Sioux.

1875   President Grant appoints Judge Isaac Parker (the "Hanging Judge") to the Western District Court, the jurisdiction of which includes Indian Territory (Oklahoma); Quanah Parker, chief of the Quahadi Comanche, agrees to accept reservation life.

1876   Custer and 7th Cavalry defeated by Sioux and

allies at Little Big Horn, June; "Wild Bill" Hickok assassinated in Deadwood, August; the James–Younger gang routed by citizens in their attempted robbery of the First National Bank in Northfield, Minnesota, September.

1877   Black American "Exodusters" found Nicodemus in north-west Kansas; after a relentless army campaign Sioux war leader Crazy Horse surrenders in May but is killed two months later; Chief Joseph of the Nez Perce surrenders after fighting for nearly 1,000 miles in his attempt to flee to Canada.

1878   Lincoln County War in New Mexico; Texan outlaw Sam Bass killed by Rangers at Round Rock; Marshal Ed Masterson mortally wounded attempting to disarm drunken cowboys in Dodge City, Kansas.

1880   Cattle ranching established throughout the Great Plains; California gunfighter Walter J. Crow kills five men in the "Mussel Slough Shoot-out" on behalf of Southern Pacific Railroad.

1881   James S. Brisbin publishes *The Beef Bonanza, or How to Get Rich on the Plains*; outlaw Billy the Kid is shot by sometime friend Pat Garrett at Fort Sumner in New Mexico, July; gunfight near the O.K. Corral in Tombstone, Arizona, between Earp brothers (with Doc Holliday) and Clanton gang, October; Sitting Bull, the Sioux victor of the Battle of Little Big Horn, surrenders after leaving sanctuary in Canada.

1882   Jesse James assassinated by Bob Ford, April.

1883   Cowboys in Texas Panhandle strike for higher wages; Buffalo Bill Cody begins his Wild West show; bison hunted almost to extinction.

1884   Vigilantes led by grandee rancher Granville Stuart

virtually clear Montana range of horse and cattle thieves.

1885   Fifty-one Chinese massacred by miners at Rock Springs, Wyoming.

1886–7   Blizzards decimate cattle on the northern ranges; the "Beef Bonanza" ends.

1886   General Nelson A. Miles accepts the surrender of Apache warrior leader Geronimo; feud between Graham and Tewksbury families sparks off the Pleasant Valley War, Arizona.

1887   Dawes General Allotment Act begins break-up of reservation lands.

1889   First land rush into Oklahoma, formerly the Indian Territory; celebrated female outlaw Belle Starr is murdered; Montana, Washington, North and South Dakota admitted to the Union, November.

1890   US Census announces the closing of the frontier; Idaho and Wyoming admitted to the Union, July; Sioux Ghost Dancers massacred by units of the 7th Cavalry at Wounded Knee Creek, South Dakota, and Indians at the nearby Pine Ridge Reservation flee in panic, December.

1891   Sioux Indians surrender to Nelson Miles and return to Pine Ridge, January; gold and silver rush to Cripple Creek, Colorado.

1892   Range war in Johnson County between large stock growers and alliance of homesteaders and cattle rustlers; Dalton gang of bank robbers ride to disaster at Coffeyville, south Kansas; historian Frederick Jackson Turner delivers his seminal paper "The Significance of the Frontier in American History."

1896   Al Jennings begins – and ends – his risible career

as a road agent in Oklahoma; Bill Doolin, "King of the Oklahoma Outlaws", killed by deputy marshal Heck Thomas while resisting arrest, August.

1898   The Wild Bunch reaches the apex of its career; Pearl Hart and Joe Boot commit the last hold-up of a stagecoach in Western history.

1901   Major oil field found at Spindletop, Texas; Butch Cassidy of the Wild Bunch, accompanied by the Sundance Kid and Etta Place, flees to South America via New York.

1903   Kid Curry, Wild Bunch member, commits suicide as police storm his hideout; range detective and hired killer Tom Horn is executed in Wyoming; first true Western movie, *Kit Carson*, is released; three months later *The Great Train Robbery* was released.

1905   Ex-Governor Frank Stuenenberg assassinated in Caldwell, Idaho.

1907   Oklahoma admitted to the Union.

1908   Pat Garrett murdered.

1909   Geronimo of the Apache dies; professional assassin Jim Miller lynched.

1911   Massacre of Shoshoni Indian family in Nevada; last land rush into Oklahoma.

1912   Ben Kilpatrick ("The Tall Texan") is killed during the hold-up of a train at Dryden, Texas.

1913–14   Strike by United Mine Workers in Colorado ends in Ludlow Massacre.

1913   Riot of hop-pickers, Wheatland, California; Buffalo Bill's Wild West show closes, burdened by debts.

1916   Henry Starr killed attempting to rob the People's National Bank at Harrison, Arkansas.

1917   Striking mineworkers deported from Bisbee, Arizona, by owners and vigilantes; International Workers of the World (IWW) leader Frank Little lynched by vigilantes in Butte, Montana; 18,000 people attend funeral of Buffalo Bill Cody, Denver, Colorado.

1919   Massacre of IWW activists at Centralia, Washington.

1924   Killing of Marshal Bill Tilghman in Cromwell, Oklahoma.

1929   Wyatt Earp and cattleman Charles Goodnight die.

1935   Last of the "bronco" Apaches living in the Sierra Madre gives up the old, free life.

Appendix II: Bibliography

The library of Western Americana is vast, and any bibliography necessarily selective. Among the most influential works and those which informed the preceding pages are:

Abbott, Edward C. and Helena Huntingdon Smith, *We Pointed Them North: Recollections of a Cowpuncher*. New York: Farrar & Rinehart, 1939

Adams, Andy, *Cattle Brand*. Boston: Houghton, 1906

—— *Log of a Cowboy*. New York: Airmont, 1969

Alderson, Nannie T. and Helena Huntingdon Smith, *A Bride Goes West*. Lincoln: University of Nebraska Press, 1942

Alter, J. Cecil, *James Bridger: Trapper, Frontiersman, Scout and Guide*. Columbus, OH, 1951

Ambrose, Stephen E., *Crazy Horse and Custer: The Parallel Lives of Two American Warriors*. New York: Penguin, 1975

Andrist, Ralph K., *The Long Death: The Last Days of the Plains Indians*. New York: Collier Books, 1964

Applegate, Jesse, *A Day with the Cow Column in 1843*. Chicago: Caxton, 1934

Arnold, Oren, *Hot Irons: Heraldry of the Range*. New York: Macmillan, 1940

Atherton, Lewis, *The Cattle Kings*. Bloomington, 1961

Baber, D. F., *The Longest Rope: The Truth about the Johnson County Cattle War*. Caldwell, ID: Caxton, 1940

Baldwin, Leland D., *Steamboats on the Mississippi*. American Heritage, 1962

Barnes, William C., *Story of the Ranger*, Washington, DC: US Department of Agriculture, 1926

Barth, Gunther, *Bitter Strength: A History of the Chinese in the United States, 1850–1887*. Berkeley, 1964

Bartlett, Richard A., *The New Country: A Social History of the American Frontier 1776–1890*. New York: Oxford University Press, 1974

Bergon, Frank (ed.), *The Journals of Lewis and Clark*. New York: Penguin, 1989

Betzinez, Jason (with W. S. Nye), *I Fought With Geronimo*. New York: The Stackpole Company, 1959

Billington, Ray Allen, *Westward Expansion: A History of the American Frontier*. New York: Macmillan, 1974

Bourke, John G., *An Apache Campaign in the Sierra Madre*. New York: Scribner's, 1886

Breakenridge, William M., *Helldorado*. Boston: Houghton, 1928

Breihan, Carl W., *Badmen of the Frontier Days*. New York: McBride, 1957

—— *Great Lawmen of the West*. New York: Bonanza Books, 1963

Brininstool, Earl A., *Trail Dust of a Maverick*. New York: Dodd Mead, 1914

Brisbin, James S., *The Beef Bonanza*. Philadelphia: Lippincott, 1881

Brown, Dee, *The Fetterman Massacre*. London: Barrie & Jenkins, 1972

—— *The Gentle Tamers: Women of the Old West*. New York: Bantam Books, 1974

—— *Hear That Lonesome Whistle Blow – Railroads in the West*. New York: Holt, Rinehart, 1977

—— *Bury My Heart at Wounded Knee: Indian History of the American West*. London: Arena Books, 1987 (reprint)

Brown, Richard Maxwell, *No Duty To Retreat: Violence and Values in American History and Society*. New York, 1991

Burdick, Usher L., *Marquis de Mores at War in the Bad Lands*. Fargo, ND, 1929

Burns, Walter Noble, *The Saga of Billy the Kid*. Garden City, NY: Doubleday, 1926

Canton, Frank M., *Frontier Trails: The Autobiography of Frank M. Canton* (edited by E. E. Dale), Boston: Houghton, 1930

Capps, Benjamin, *The Great Chiefs*. Alexandria, VA: Time-Life Books, 1975

Carrington, Frances C., *My Army Life*. Philadelphia: Lippincott, 1911

Casey, Robert J., *Pioneer Railroad*. New York: Whittlesey House, 1948

Clancy, Foghorn, *My Fifty Years in Rodeo*. San Antonio: Naylor Co., 1952

Clay, John, *My Life on the Range*. Chicago: privately printed, 1924

Cody, William F., *Buffalo Bill's Own Story of His Life and Deeds*. Chicago: Homewood Press, 1917

Connell, Evan S., *Son of the Morning Star*. New York: Harper, 1984

Cook, James H., *Fifty Years on the Old Frontier*. New Haven: Yale University Press, 1923

Corey, Elizabeth, *Bachelor Bess: The Homesteading Letters of Elizabeth Corey, 1909–1919* (ed. Philip L. Gerber). Iowa City: University of Iowa Press, 1990

Cronon, William, "Revisiting the Vanishing Frontier: The

Legacy of Frederick Jackson Turner," *Western Historical Quarterly* 18:2 (April, 1987)

Cruse, Thomas, *Apache Days and After*. Caldwell, ID, 1941

Cunningham, Eugene, *Triggernometry: A Gallery of Gunfighters*. New York: Press of the Pioneers, 1934

Curtis, Natalie, *The Indians Book*. New York: Harper & Brothers, 1907

Custer, George A., *Wild Life on the Plains and Horrors of Indian Warfare*. St Louis, 1891

Dale, Edward Everett, *The Range Cattle Industry*. Norman: University of Oklahoma Press, 1930

—— *Cow Country*. Norman: University of Oklahoma Press, 1942

Dalton, Emmett and Jack Jungmeyer, *When the Daltons Rode*. Garden City, NY: Doubleday, 1931

Davis, Britton, *The Truth About Geronimo*. New Haven: Yale University Press, 1929

De Voto, Bernard, *Across the Wide Missouri*. Boston: Houghton Mifflin, 1947

—— *Course of Empire*. Boston: Houghton Mifflin, 1952

Debo, Angie, *A History of the Indians of the United States*. Norman: University of Oklahoma Press, 1970

—— *Geronimo*. London: Pimlico, 1993 (reprint)

Dick, Everett, *Vanguards of the Frontier*. New York: Appleton-Century, 1941

—— *The Sod House Frontier*. New York: Johnsen, 1954

—— *Tales of the Frontier: From Lewis and Clark to the Last Roundup*. Lincoln: University of Nebraska Press, 1964

Dimsdale, Thomas J., *The Vigilantes of Montana*. Norman: University of Oklahoma Press, 1953

Dinsmore, Wayne, *The Horses of the Americas*. Norman: University of Oklahoma Press, 1978

Dobie, J. Frank, *On the Open Range*. Dallas: Southwest Press, 1931

—— *The Longhorns*. Boston: Little, Brown, 1941

Drago, Henry Sinclair, *Great American Cattle Trails: The Story of the Old Cowpaths of the East and the Longhorn Highways of the Plains*. New York: Dodd, Mead & Co., 1965

Duffus, R. L., *The Santa Fe Trail*. New York: Tudor Publishing Co., 1930

Durham, Philip and Everett L. Jones, *The Negro Cowboys*. Lincoln: University of Nebraska Press, 1965

Duval, John C., *Adventures of Big Foot Wallace*. Macon, GA: J. W. Burke & Co., 1885

Dykstra, Robert R., *The Cattle Towns*. New York: Alfred A. Knopf, 1968

Edwards, J. B., *Early Days in Abilene*. Abilene, 1938

Elman, Robert, *Badmen of the West*. Secaucus, NJ: Ridge Press, Inc., 1974

Faulk, Odie B., *Land of Many Frontiers*. New York: Oxford University Press, 1986

Fee, Chester A., *Chief Joseph, the Biography of a Great Indian*. New York, 1936

Forrest, Earle R., *Arizona's Dark and Bloody Ground*. Caldwell, ID: Caxton Printers Ltd., 1952

Frazier, Ian, *Great Plains*. New York: Penguin (US), 1989

Frewen, Moreton, *Melton Mowbray and Other Memories*. London: Jenkins, 1924

Fulton, Maurice, *Lincoln Country War*. University of Arizona, 1968

Gard, Wayne, *Frontier Justice*. Norman: University of Oklahoma Press, 1949

—— *The Chisholm Trail*. Norman: University of Oklahoma Press, 1954

Gardiner, Dorothy, *West of the River*. New York: Thomas Y. Crowell, 1963

Gardner, Charles M., *The Grange: Friend of the Farmer*. Washington, DC: National Grange, 1949

Garrett, Pat F., *The Authentic Life of Billy the Kid*. Santa Fe: New Mexican Printing and Publishing Co., 1882

Goetzmann, William H., *Exploration and Empire: The Explorer and the Scientist in the Winning of the American West*. New York: Alfred Knopf, 1966

Graham, William A., *The Story of the Little Big Horn*. Harrisburg, PA, 1941

Greeley, Horace, *An Overland Journey from New York to San Francisco in 1859*. New York: Saxton, Barker & Co., 1960

Grinell, George B., *The Fighting Cheyennes*. New York, 1915

Hagedorn, Herman, *Roosevelt in the Bad Lands*. Boston: Houghton, 1921

Haley, J. Evetts, *Charles Goodnight, Cowman and Plainsman*. Boston: Houghton, 1936

Hampsten, Elizabeth, *Read This Only to Yourself: The Private Writings of Midwestern Women, 1880–1910*. Bloomington: Indiana University Press, 1982

Hardin, John Wesley, *The Life of John Wesley Hardin – Written by Himself*. Seguin, TX: Smith & Moore, 1896

Harris, Frank, *My Reminiscences as a Cowboy*. New York: Boni, 1930

Hassrick, Royal B., *Cowboys: The Real Story of Cowboys and Cattlemen*. London: Octopus Books Ltd., 1974

—— *The Colourful Story of the American West*. London: Octopus Books, 1975

Havighurst, Walter, *Annie Oakley of the Wild West*. London: Robert Hale Ltd., 1955

Hawgood, John A., *The American West*. London, 1967

Hebard, Grace R. and Earl A. Brininstool, *The Bozeman Trail*. Cleveland, 1922

Hendricks, George D., *The Bad Man of the West*. San Antonio: The Naylor Company, 1942

Hiesinger, Ulrich W., *Indian Lives: A Photographic Record*

from the Civil War to Wounded Knee. Munich/New
York: Prestel-Verlag, 1994

Hill, Tom and Richard W. Hill, Sr, *Creation's Journey*.
Washington: Smithsonian Institution Press, 1994

Hine, Robert V., *The American West*. Boston: Little,
Brown, 1973

Holliday, J. S., *The World Rushed In: The California Gold
Rush Experience*. New York: Simon & Schuster, 1981

Hollon, W. Eugene, *Frontier Violence: Another Look*. New
York: Oxford University Press, 1974

Horan, James D., *Women of the West*. New York: Bonanza
Books, 1952

—— and Paul Sann, *Pictorial History of the Wild West*.
London: Spring Books, 1961

Hough, Emerson, *The Story of the Cowboy*. Gregg, 1970

—— *The Story of the Outlaw*. New York: Outing
Publishing Co., 1907

Howard, Helen A., *Saga of Chief Joseph*. Caldwell, ID: The
Caxton Printers, 1965

Howard, Robert West, *The Great Iron Trail*. New York:
Putnams, 1962

Hunter, J. Marvin, *Trail Drivers of Texas*. Argosy-
Antiquarian Ltd., 1963 (reprint)

—— and Noah H. Rose, *The Album of Gunfighters*.
Bandera, TX, 1951

Hutton, Paul Andrew (ed.), *The Custer Reader*. Lincoln:
University of Nebraska Press, 1992

Ise, John, *Sod and Stubble*. Lincoln: University of
Nebraska Press, 1967 (reprint)

James, Will, *Lone Cowboy*. New York: Scribners, 1930

—— *Cow Country*. New York: Scribners, 1931

Jeffrey, Julie Roy, *Frontier Women: The Trans-Mississippi
West, 1840–1880*. New York: Hill and Wang, 1979

Jennewein, J. Leonard, *Calamity Jane of the Western Trails*.
Huron, SD: Dakota Books, 1953

Jensen, Joan M., *With These Hands: Women Working on the Land*. New York: McGraw-Hill, 1981

Jensen, Richard E., R. Eli Paul and John E. Carter, *Eyewitness at Wounded Knee*. London: University of Nebraska Press, 1991

Jordan, Teresa, *Cowgirls*. Lincoln: Bison Books, University of Nebraska Press, 1992

Josephy, Alvin M., *The Nez Perce Indians and the Opening of the Northwest*. London: University of Nebraska Press, 1980

Katz, William Loren, *The Black West*. Seattle: Open Hand Publishing, 1992

Kelly, Fanny, *My Captivity among the Sioux Indians*. The Citadel Press, 1973

Kesey, Ken, *Last Go Round*. London: Black Swan, 1995

Krakel, Dean F., *The Saga of Tom Horn*. Laramie: Powder River Publishers, 1954

Lake, Stuart N., *Wyatt Earp, Frontier Marshal*. Boston: Houghton, 1931

Lamar, Howard R. (ed.), *The Reader's Encyclopedia of the American West*. New York: Crowell, 1977

Lavender, David, *The American Heritage History of the Old West*, 1965

Leckie, William H., *The Buffalo Soldiers*. Norman: University of Oklahoma Press, 1967

Lewis, Jon E., *The Mammoth Book of the Western*. London: Robinson, 1991

Limerick, Patricia Nelson, *The Legacy of Conquest: The Unbroken Past of the American West*. New York: W. W. Norton, 1987

Lomax, John A. and Alan Lomax, *Cowboy Songs and Other Frontier Ballads*. New York: Macmillan, 1938

Love, Nat, *Life and Adventures*. New York: Arno Press, 1968 (reprint)

McCoy, Joseph G., *Historic Sketches of the Cattle*

Trade (ed. Ralph P. Bieber). Glendale, CA: A. H. Clark, 1940

McGrath, Roger D., *Gunfighters, Highwaymen and Vigilantes*. Berkeley: University of California Press, 1984

McHugh, Tom, *The Time of the Buffalo*. New York: Alfred A. Knopf, 1972

McLaughlin, James, *My Friend The Indian*. Lincoln: University of Nebraska Press, Bison Books, 1989 (reprint)

McLoughlin, Dennis, *Wild and Woolly: An Encyclopedia of the Old West*. New York: Doubleday, 1975

Mails, Thomas E., *Mystic Warriors of the Plains*. New York: Doubleday, 1972

Marks, Paula Mitchell, *And Die in the West: The Story of the O.K. Corral Gunfight*. New York, 1989

Marshall, James, *Santa Fe: The Railroad that Built an Empire*. New York: Random House, 1945

May, Robin, *The Story of the Wild West*. London: Hamlyn, 1978

Mayer, Lynne Rhodes and Kenneth E. Vose, *Makin' Tracks*. New York: Praeger, 1975

Meeker, Ezra, *Ventures and Adventures of Ezra Meeker*. Seattle: Rainier Publishing Co., 1908

Mercer, Asa Shinn, *The Banditti of the Plains, or the Cattlemen's Invasion of Wyoming*. San Francisco: Grabhorn Press, 1935

Miles, Nelson A., *Personal Recollections and Observations*. Chicago: Werber, 1896

Miller, Nyle H. and Joseph W. Snell, *Why the West Was Wild*. Topeka, 1963

Mooney, James, *The Ghost Dance-Religion and the Sioux Outbreak of 1890*. Chicago, 1965

Morgan, Dale, *Jedediah Smith and the Opening of the West*. Indianapolis: Bobbs-Merill, 1953

—— (ed.), *Overland in 1846*. Georgetown, CA: Talisman Press, 1963

Murray, Keith A., *The Modocs and Their War*. Norman: University of Oklahoma Press, 1959

Myers, John Myers, *Bravos of the West*. Lincoln: Bison Books, 1995 (reprint)

Myres, Sarah L., *Westering Women and the Frontier Experience, 1800–1915*. Albuquerque: University of New Mexico, 1982

Niehardt, John G., *Black Elk Speaks*. Lincoln: University of Nebraska Press, 1979

O'Connor, Richard, *Bat Masterson*. London: Alvin Redman Ltd., 1958

O'Neal, Bill, *Encyclopedia of Western Gunfighters*. Norman: University of Oklahoma Press, 1979

Parrish, Randall, *The Great Plains*. Chicago: McClurg, 1907

Payne, Doris Palmer, *Captain Jack, Modoc Renegade*. Portland, OR, 1938

Petersen, Karen Daniels, *Plains Indian Art from Fort Marion*. Norman: University of Oklahoma Press, 1971

Poe, John W., *The Death of Billy the Kid*. Boston: Houghton, 1933

Prassel, Frank R., *The Western Peace Officer: A Legacy of Law and Order*. Norman: University of Oklahoma Press, 1972

Raine, William Macleod, *Famous Sheriffs and Western Outlaws*. New York: Doubleday, 1929

Rascoe, Burton, *Belle Starr*. New York: Random House, 1941

Rawling, Gerald, *The Pathfinders*. New York: Macmillan, 1964

Ray, Clarence E., *The Dalton Brothers*. Chicago: Regan. Publishing Brothers, n.d.

Reader's Digest, *Story of the Great American West*.

New York: The Reader's Digest Association, Inc., 1977

Reiter, Joan Swallow, *The Women* (*The Old West*). Alexandria, VA: Time-Life Books, 1978

Remington, Frederic, *Crooked Trails*. New York: Harper, 1898

Rhodes, Eugene Manlove, *Good Men and True*. New York: Holt, 1910

Riegel, Robert Edgar, *Story of the Western Railroads*. New York: Macmillan, 1926

Riley, Glenda, *The Female Frontier: A Comparative View of Women on the Prairie and the Plains*. Lawrence, 1988

Ripley, Thomas, *They Died With Their Boots On*. New York: Doubleday, 1935

Roach, Joyce Gibson, *The Cowgirls*. University of North Texas Press, 1990

Rodman, W. Paul, *Mining Frontiers of the Far West 1848–1880*. New York: Holt, Rinehart and Winston, 1963

Rosa, Joseph G., *The Gunfighter: Man or Myth?* Norman: University of Oklahoma Press, 1969

—— *They Called Him Wild Bill: The Life and Adventures of James Butler Hickok*. Norman: University of Oklahoma Press, 1974

Ross, Marvin C., *The West of Alfred Jacob Miller*. Norman: University of Oklahoma Press, 1951

Russell, Charles M., *Studies of Western Life*. New York: Albertype Company, 1890

—— *Trails Plowed Under*. Garden City, NY: Doubleday, 1928

Russell, Don, *The Lives and Legends of Buffalo Bill*. Norman: University of Oklahoma Press, 1960

Sabin, Edward Legrand, *Wild Men of the Wild West*. New York: Thomas Y. Crowell, 1929

Sandoz, Mari, *Crazy Horse*. New York, 1942

—— *The Cattlemen*. Hastings, 1958

Santee, Ross, *Cowboy*. Hastings, 1964

Savage, W. Sherman, *Blacks in the West*. Westport, CT:
  Greenwood Press, 1976

Schaefer, Jack, *Heroes Without Glory*. London: Mayflower,
  1968

Schissel, Lilian, Vicki L. Ruiz and Janice Monk,
  Western Women: Their Land, Their Lives. Albuquerque:
  University of New Mexico Press, 1988

Seidman, Laurence I., *Once in the Saddle*. New York:
  Facts on File, 1994

Settle, William A., *Jesse James Was His Name*. Columbia:
  University of Missouri Press, 1966

Shaw, Anna Howard, *The Story of a Pioneer*. New York:
  Harper and Brothers, 1943

Shirley, Glenn, *Shotgun for Hire: The Story of "Deacon"
  Jim Miller, Killer of Pat Garrett*. Norman: University of
  Oklahoma Press, 1970

Sibald, John, "Camp Followers All," *The American West*,
  2:2 (1966)

Siringo, Charlie, *A Texas Cow Boy; or, Fifteen Years
  on the Hurricane Deck of a Spanish Pony*. Chicago:
  Umbdenstock & Co., 1885

—— *A Cowboy Detective*. Lincoln: University of Nebraska
  Press, 1988 (reprint)

Slatta, Richard W., *Cowboys of the Americas*. New Haven:
  Yale University Press, 1980

Smith, Helena Huntington, *The War on Powder River*.
  New York: McGraw-Hill, 1966

Smith, Henry Nash, *Virgin Land: The American West as
  Symbol and Myth*. Cambridge, MA: Harvard University
  Press, 1950

Sonnichsen, C. L., *Roy Bean, Law West of the Pecos*. New
  York: Macmillan, 1943

—— *I'll Die Before I Run*. New York: Harper, 1951

Spence, Lewis, *The Illustrated Guide to North American Mythology*. London: Studio Editions, 1993

Spicer, Edward H., *A Short History of the Indians of the United States*. New York, 1969

Sprague, William Forrest, *Women and the West*. Arno Press, 1972

Steckmesser, Kent Ladd, *The Western Hero in History and Legend*. Norman: University of Oklahoma Press, 1965

Stegner, Wallace, *The Gathering of Zion: Story of the Mormon Trail*. New York: McGraw-Hill, 1964

Stempel, Penny, *Annie Oakley*. Bristol: Parragon, 1995

Stewart, Elinor Pruitt Rupert, *Letters of a Woman Homesteader*. Lincoln: University of Nebraska Press, 1961

Still, Bayrd, *The West: Contemporary Records of America's Expansion Across the Continent 1607–1890*. Capricorn Books, 1961

Streeter, Floyd B., *Prairie Trails and Cow Towns*. Boston: Chapman and Grimes, 1936

Sutley, Zack T., *The Last Frontier*. New York: Macmillan, 1930

Swift, Louis F., *The Yankee of the Yards: The Biography of Gustavus Franklin Swift*. Chicago: A. W. Shaw, 1937

Taylor, T. U., *Bill Longley and His Wild Career*. Bandera, TX: Frontier Times, 1925

Thrapp, Dan L., *Al Sieber*. Norman: University of Oklahoma Press, 1964

Tilghman, Zoe A., *Outlaw Days*. Oklahoma City: Harlow Publishing Co., 1926

Turner, Frederick Jackson, *The Frontier in American History*. New York: Holt, 1920

Turner, Geoffrey, *Indians of North America*. New York: Sterling Publishing, 1992

Tuska, Jon, *Billy the Kid: A Handbook*. Westport, CT: Greenwood Press, 1983

Twain, Mark, *Roughing It*. New York: New American Library, 1962 (reprint)

Unruh, John D., *The Plains Across: The Overland Emigrants and the Trans-Mississippi West 1840–1860*. Urbana: University of Illinois Press, 1979

Utley, Robert M., *Frontiersmen in Blue: The United States Army and the Indian 1848–1865*. New York: Macmillan, 1965

—— *Billy the Kid*. Lincoln: University of Nebraska Press, 1989

Vestal, Stanley, *Sitting Bull*. Norman: University of Oklahoma Press, 1957

Wallace, Charles, *Mrs Nat Collins, the Cattle Queen of Montana*. St James, MN: C. W. Foote, 1894

Wallace, Lew, *Lew Wallace: An Autobiography*. New York: Harper's, 1906

Ward, Don and J. C. Dykes, *Cowboys and Cattle Country*. New York: Harper & Row, 1961

Ward, Fay E., *The Cowboy at Work*, Hastings, 1958

Waters, Frank, *The Earp Brothers of Tombstone*. New York, 1960

Webb, Walter Prescott, *The Texas Rangers*. Boston: Houghton, 1935

Wellman, Paul I., *The Trampling Herd*. New York: Carrick & Evans, 1939

—— *A Dynasty of Western Outlaws*. Lincoln: University of Nebraska Press, 1986 (reprint)

Welsch, Roger L., *Sod Walls*. Purcells, Inc., 1968

White, Richard, "Outlaw Gangs of the Middle Border: American Social Bandits," *Western Historical Quarterly* 12 (October, 1981)

Wiltsey, N. B., *Brave Warriors*. Caldwell, ID: The Caxton Printers, 1964

Winther, Oscar O., *The Transportation Frontier 1865–1890*. New York: Holt, Rinehart, 1964

Wister, Owen, *The Virginian*. New York: Macmillan, 1925
Younger, Cole, *The Story of Cole Younger, By Himself*.
    Chicago: Hennerberry Company, 1903

Appendix III:

The American Indian Nations of North America

Here are listed 300 and more tribes and sub-tribes, and their primary area of settlement. Some of the tribes are long gone, their existence only remembered in place names and consumer goods.

Abitbi (Sub-Arctic)
Abnaki (Eastern Woodlands)
Accohannock (East Coast)
Achomawi/Atsugewi (Northwest Plateau)
Alabama (Southeast)
Aleut (Alaska)
Alsea (Northwest Coast)
Apache (Southwest)
Arapaho (Great Plains)
Arikara (Great Plains)
Assiniboin (Great Plains)
Atakapa (Southeast)
Atsina (Great Plains)
Attiwandaronk (Eastern Woodlands)
Bannock (Great Basin)
Beaver (Sub-Arctic)
Bella Coola (Northwest Coast)
Biloxi (Southeast)
Blackfoot (Great Plains)
Caddo (Great Plains)
Cahuilla (California)
Calusa (Southeast)
Caribou (Sub-Arctic)
Carrier (Sub-Arctic)
Catawba (Southeast)
Cayuse (Northwest Plateau)

Chemehuevi (Great Basin)
Cherokee (Southeast)
Cheyenne (Great Plains)
Chickasaw (Southeast)
Chicora (Southeast)
Chilcotin (Northwest
    Plateau)
Chinook (Northwest Coast)
Chipewyan (Sub-Arctic)
Chitimacha (Southeast)
Choctaw (Southeast)
Chumash (California)
Coahuiltec (Southwest)
Cocopa (Southwest)
Coeur d'Alene (Northwest
    Plateau)
Coharie (Eastern
    Woodlands/Southeast)
Comanche (Great Plains)
Conoy (East Coast)
Coos (Northwest Coast)
Costanoa (California)
Cowlitz (Northwest Coast)
Cree (Sub-Arctic)
Creek (Southeast)
Crow (Great Plains)
Delaware (East Coast)
Dieguno (California)
Dogrib (Sub-Arctic)
Edisto (Southeast)
Erie (Eastern Woodland/
    Great Lakes)
Eskimo (Sub-Arctic/
    Arctic Circle)
Esselen (California)

Eyak (Northwest Coast)
Flathead (Northwest
    Plateau)
Fox (Eastern Woodlands/
    Great Lakes)
Gabrielino (California)
Gitskan (Northwest Coast)
Goshute (Great Basin)
Gros Ventres of the Prairie
    (Great Plains)
Gros Ventres of the River
    (Great Plains)
Haida (Northwest Coast)
Haisla (Northwest Coast)
Halchidhoma (Southwest)
Han (Sub-Arctic)
Heiltsuk (Northwest Coast)
Hohokam (Southwest)
Hopi (Southwest)
Houma (Southeast)
Hupa (California)
Huron (Eastern Woodland/
    Great Lakes)
Illinois (Eastern Woodlands)
Ingalik (Alaska)
Inupiaq (Alaska)
Iowa (Great Plains)
Iroquois (including Mohawk,
    Oneida, Onondaga,
    Cayuga, Seneca) (Eastern
    Woodlands/Great Lakes)
Jemez (Southwest)
Kalapuya (Northwest Coast)
Kalispel (Northwest Plateau)
Kansa (Great Plains)

Karankawa (Great Plains)

Karok (California)

Kaw (Great Plains)

Keres (Southwest)

Kickapoo (Eastern
Woodlands/Great Lakes)

Kiowa (Great Plains)

Kiowa-Apache (Great Plains)

Klamath (Northwest Plateau)

Klikitat (Northwest Plateau)

Koyukon (Alaska)

Kutchin (Sub-Arctic)

Kutenai (Northwest Plateau)

Kwakiutl (Northwest Coast)

Lillooet (Northwest Plateau)

Lipan (Great Plains)

Luiseno (California)

Mohegan (East Coast)

Mahican (East Coast)

Maidu (California)

Makah (Northwest Coast)

Malisit (East Coast)

Mandan (Great Plains)

Maricopa (Southwest)

Mascouten (East Coast)

Massachuset (East Coast)

Mattabesic (East Coast)

Menomini (Eastern
Woodlands/Great Lakes)

Metoac (East Coast)

Miami (Eastern Woodlands)

Micmac (East Coast)

Minga (Eastern Woodlands)

Missouri (Great Plains)

Miwok (California)

Modoc (Great Plains)

Mojave (Southwest)

Mono (California)

Montagnais (Sub-Arctic)

Mountain (Sub-Arctic)

Nansemond (Southeast)

Narragansett (East Coast)

Naskapi (Sub-Arctic)

Natchez (Southeast)

Navajo (Southwest)

Nespelem (Northwest
Plateau)

Netsilik (Arctic Circle)

Nez Perce (Great Plains)

Notka (Northwest Coast)

Ojibwa (Eastern Woodlands/
Great Lakes)

Okanagan (Northwest
Plateau)

Omaha (Great Plains)

Osage (Great Plains)

Oto (Great Plains)

Ottawa (Eastern
Woodlands/Great Lakes)

Paiute (Great Basin)

Palus (Northwest Plateau)

Pamlico (East Coast)

Pamunkey (Southeast)

Papago (Southwest)

Patwin (California)

Pawnee (Great Plains)

Pennacook (East Coast)

Penobscot (East Coast)

Pequot (East Coast)

Pericu (California)

Pima (Southwest/Mexico)
Plains Cree (Great Plains)
Plains Objiwa (Great Plains)
Pomo (California)
Ponca (Great Plains)
Potawatomi (Eastern
  Woodlands)
Powahatan (East Coast)
Quapaw (Southeast)
Quileute (Northwest Coast)
Quinault (Northwest Coast)
Salinan (California)
Salish (Northwest Coast)
Santee Sioux (East Coast/
  Great Plains)
Sarsi (Great Plains)
Sauk (Eastern Woodlands/
  Great Lakes)
Secotan (Eastern Woodlands)
Sekani (Sub-Arctic)
Seminole (Southeast)
Seri (Southwest)
Serrano (California)
Shasta (California)
Shawnee (Eastern
  Woodlands/Great Plains)
Shoshoni (Great Basin)
Shuswap (Northwest
  Plateau)
Skidi (Great Plains)
Slave (Sub-Arctic)
Sobaipuri (Southwest)
Spokan (Southwest)
Susquehanna (Eastern
  Woodlands)

Sutaio (Great Plains)
Taensa (Southeast)
Tagish (Sub-Arctic)
Tahltan (Sub-Arctic)
Tanaina (Alaska)
Tanoan Pueblos (Southwest)
Tekesta (Southeast)
Teton Sioux (Great Plains)
Thompson (Northwest
  Plateau)
Timucua (Southeast)
Tionontati (Eastern
  Woodlands)
Tlingit (Northwest Coast)
Tobacco (Eastern
  Woodlands/Great Lakes)
Tolowa (Northwest Coast)
Tonkawa (Great Plains)
Tsetsaut (Sub-Arctic)
Tsimshian (Northwest Coast)
Tubatulabal (California)
Tunica (Southeast)
Tuscarora (East Coast)
Tutchone (Sub-Arctic)
Tutelo (Eastern Woodlands)
Umatilla (Northwest
  Plateau)
Ute (Great Basin)
Walapai (Southwest)
Wampanoag (Eastern
  Woodlands)
Wappinger (Eastern
  Woodlands)
Washo (Great Basin)
Wenro (Eastern

Woodlands/Great Lakes)

Wind River Shoshoni (Great Basin)

Winnebago (Eastern Woodlands/Great Lakes)

Wintun (California)

Wishram (Northwest Plateau)

Witchita (Great Plains)

Wiyot (California)

Yakima (Northwest Plateau)

Yakutat (Northwest Coast)

Yana (California)

Yankton Sioux (Eastern Woodlands/Great Plains)

Yaqui (Southwest/Mexico)

Yavapai (Southwest)

Yellowknife (Sub-Arctic)

Yokuts (California)

Yuchi (Southeast)

Yuma (Southwest)

Yurok (California)

Zuni (Southwest)

Index

Abbott, Teddy Blue   173, 177, 180,
   190–1, 224
Abilene   155, 156–8, 173–4
Adair, John and Cornelia   203–4
Adams, Andy   161, 163, 167–70,
   195, 252–4
Adobe Walls   350, 411, 412
Alamo   67–72, 520
alcohol   175
Allison, Clay   271
American Civil War   152, 251,
   281, 317, 343–4, 347, 365, 521
American Fur Company   53, 58
American War of
   Independence   24–8
Anderson, Gilbert M. (aka Max
   Aranson)   505
Apache   345–8, 350–2, 431–49,
   460, 527
Apache Kid   276, 460
Apache Pass   347–8, 522
Arapaho   360, 361, 363, 375
Arikara   56
Ashley, General H.   55, 56
Astor, John Jacob   53, 54,
   57–8, 520
Astoria   53, 54
Austin, Moses   62
Austin, Stephen F.   62–3, 64, 66,
   150, 313, 519
Autry, Gene   506–7
Averill, Jim   237–8

Baca, Elfego   xiv, 298–9

Bailey, George   378–9
Bannock   86, 429–30
barbed wire   204
Bass, Sam   315–16
Batts, Thomas   10
Bean, Judge Roy   260–1
Bear Flag Revolt   112–13, 521
beaver   50–2, 58
Becknell, William   59–60
Beckwourth, James P.   55, 57
Beecher Island   390
Beef Bonanza   152–70; 196–205,
   226, 525
Bent, Charles and William   60
Benteen, Captain Frederick   424,
   426–7
Big Foot   453–4, 455
Billy the Kid see Bonney, William
   H.
Bisbee   267, 527
Black Americans
   cowboys   177, 188
   farmers   467
   gold miners   117–18
   outlaws   274–6
   soldiers   274–5, 452, 456
Black Bart see Bole, Charles
Black Hills of Dakota   xiii, 126,
   415, 419–20
Black Kettle   362, 363, 364, 389,
   403, 404
Blackfeet   41–2, 52, 57, 58,
   341, 383
"The Blessing Way"   4, 349–50

Bole, Charles 138, 269, 278–9
Bonney, William H. (Billy the
    Kid) 207–21, 524
Boone, Daniel 21–2, 23, 27,
    33, 517
Boonesborough 22, 26–7
Boot Hill 174
boots and spurs 192
Bosque Redondo 349
Bowie, Jim 67, 69, 70, 71, 72
Bozeman Trail 366, 368, 380
Brannan, Sam 113, 116
Brant, Joseph
    (Thayendanegea) 26
Bridger, Jim 55, 58, 59, 80–1, 108,
    369, 519
Brisbin, James S. 197, 524
Britain
    colonialism 7–9
    and the War of
        Independence 24–8
broncbusting 185–6
Brown, Henry Newton 297
Buck, Rufus 277–8
buffalo 382–4
Buffalo Bill see Cody, William F.
Buffum, Edward 266
bunkhouses 186–7
"Buntline Special" 312
Burrows, Rube and Jim 319
Butch Cassidy see Parker,
    Robert LeRoy
Butterfield, John 135

Calamity Jane see Canarray,
    Martha
California 115, 521
California Gold Rush 113–18
Canarray, Martha (Calamity
    Jane) 332
Candy Ponting, Tom 150–1
Canton, Frank 237, 238, 242
Carpenter, Julia Gage 468–70
Carrington, Colonel Henry 367,
    368, 369, 370, 371, 373, 375,
    378, 379
Carson, Kit 58, 59, 80, 228, 349,
    350, 522
Cartier, Jacques 6, 50–1, 514

cattle
    Beef Bonanza 152–70,
        196–205, 226, 525
    branding 183–4
    bulldogging 499–500
    castration 184
    cattle/sheep feuds 228–32
    cutting out 182
    drives 161–70
    introduction to America 147
    mavericks 184
    river crossings 165–6
    round-ups 181–4
    rustling 236, 481, 482
    stampedes 164
    Texas Longhorn 150, 151
    tick fever 151–2
cattle barons 200–1
cattle towns 171–80
Central Pacific 143
Champion, Nathan 239, 240–3,
    245–7
Cherokee 23, 25–6, 343, 344
Cherokee Bill 274–5
Cheyenne 359–65, 375, 385,
    427, 428
Cheyenne Club 200–1, 204, 226
Chinese 118, 143, 525
Chinook 84
Chiricahua Apache 345, 347, 350,
    431–45
Chisholm Trail 157, 523
Chivington, Colonel John 359,
    360–1, 362, 363, 365
Christie, Ned 276–7
chuckwagons 162
Clantons 307, 308, 309–10,
    311–12, 524
Clark, George Rogers 27–8
Clark, William 52
    see also Lewis and Clark
        expedition
Clay, John 201
Clements, Arch 282
closing of the frontier 459, 525
Clover, Sam T. 239, 241–2
Clum, John P. 262, 432, 433, 446
Cochise 346–7, 348, 350–2, 523
Code of the West 252–6, 259–60

Cody, William F. (Buffalo
    Bill) 138, 258–9, 384, 495,
    496–8, 504, 524
Colorado 119
Colt revolvers 257
Columbus, Christopher 5,
    147, 514
Comanche 314, 350, 405–14
Cornstock Lode 119
Concord coach 135
Connor, General Patrick E. 366
Coronado, Francisco Vasquez
    de 6
Cortina, Juan Nepomuceno 279
Coulter, John 42, 52, 518
Courtright, "Longhaired Jim" 297
cowboys
    broncbusting 185–6
    dress code 149, 191–4
    life on the range 186–91,
        226–7
    life on the trail 161–70
    rodeos 494, 498–501
    unionization 187–8
    violence 172, 175, 178–80,
        295
    working cattle 181–4
Crazy Horse 343, 374, 376, 416,
    422, 425, 428, 524
Cripple Creek 126, 525
Crockett, Davy 71–2
Croghan, George 15
Crook, General George 351,
    420–1, 422, 428, 429–30, 440–1,
    442, 443, 446
Crow, Walter J. 252, 524
Crow xiii, 57
Cumberland Gap 20, 22
Custer, Colonel George
    Armstrong 126, 386–7,
    390–1, 395, 396, 400–1, 404,
    416, 419, 421, 423, 424, 426,
    427, 523

Dalton brothers 290–1, 292,
    333, 525
Daly, John 297–8
Dart, Isom 274
Daugherty, Roy 461

Daves, Delmer 509
Davis, Captain Jonathan R. 252
de Onate, Juan 6, 7, 227, 516
de Soto, Hernando 6, 516
de Vaca, Cabeza 5
Delaware 26, 28
Deseret 108, 109
disease 8, 339
Dodge City 159, 172, 174,
    304–5, 311
Donner Party 82, 96–102
Doolin, Bill 279, 291, 292, 301,
    333, 525–6
dry farming 465–6
Duffield, George 164–5
Dumont, Elenor 330–1

Earp, Morgan 308, 309, 310
Earp, Virgil 306, 308, 309, 310
Earp, Wyatt 303–12, 504, 513, 527
Eastwood, Clint 511–12, 513
Edgar, Henry 120–6
Ellsworth 159, 172, 173, 174, 296
European colonialism 4–11
"Exodusters" 467, 524

Fallam, Robert 10
Farnham, Thomas Jefferson 79
Fetterman Massacre 376–8, 522
Fetterman, William Judd 374, 375
Fink, Mike 129–30, 519
Finley, John 20, 21, 22
firearms 256–9
    Colt revolvers 257
    Kentucky rifle 13, 256
    Springfield rifle 379
    Winchester rifle 258–9
Fisher, John King 296–7
flatboats 128
Florida 5, 18, 519
Fonda, Henry 507, 508
Ford, Bob 288–9, 331
Ford, John 507, 509, 510
Forsyth, Colonel George A. 390,
    454, 455
Fort Laramie Council
    (1866) 367–8, 522
Fort Phil Kearny 369, 370–5, 378,
    379, 380

Fredonia Revolt (1826) 64–5
Frémont, John 59, 80, 521
Frewen, Moreton 199
frontier spirit xi–xii
fur trade 21, 50–9

gambling 174, 175, 330, 331
Garrett, Pat 217, 218, 220–1, 317, 526
German immigrants 11, 74
Geronimo 3–4, 345, 348, 351–2, 431–5, 437, 439, 440–9, 489, 526
Ghost Dance 451–2, 456
Glover, Ridgeway 369–70
Godfrey, Edward S. 391–403
gold prospecting 112–27, 359, 419, 521, 525
Goodnight, Charles 159–60, 162, 187, 188, 202, 203, 204, 527
Goodnight–Loving Trail 160, 522
Great American Desert 46, 48
Great Appalachian Valley 10, 11
Great Blizzard (1886–7) 223–5
Great Grasshopper Year (1874) 463
Great Plains 462–70
Great Sioux Uprising 353–8
Greenwood, Caleb 59
Gros Ventre 55, 341
Guerin, Elizabeth Jane 189, 331–2
gunfights 252, 254–5
guns see firearms

Hardin, John Wesley 271–3, 315
Harpe, Micajah and Wiley 269
Hart, Pearl 335, 526
Hart, William S. 505, 506
Hastings, Lansford W. 97–8
Hays, Captain John Coffee 314
Haywood, William 327
Hearst, George 119
Henderson, Judge Richard 23, 517
Henderson, Prairie Rose 500–1
Henry, Andrew 55, 56
Hickok, James Butler 157–8, 174, 256–6, 258, 272, 332, 522, 523
highway robbery 138, 264, 268–9

Hodges, Ben 275–6
Hole in the Wall 478, 479
Holladay, Ben 138, 142
Holliday, Doc 304–5, 307–8, 309, 310, 311
Homestead Act (1862) 232, 381, 522
homesteaders 232–3, 463–77
Horn, Tom 245, 274, 318, 489–94
horses 195
  horse breaking 185–6
  horse stealing 84, 87, 233, 260
  introduction to America xiv, 6, 383
  saddles, bridles and bits 194
Houston, Sam 65, 66–7, 73, 75
Hudson's Bay Company 51

Iliff, J. W. 159
immigrants 11–12, 74, 467–8
Indian Territory 261, 340, 343
Indians see Native American Indians
International Workers of the World 327–8, 527
Iroquois 16–17, 26

James, Frank 281, 287, 289, 498
James, Jesse 270, 279, 281–9, 318, 507, 522, 524
James, Will 232
James–Younger gang 283–8, 318, 524
Jamestown 8, 147, 516
Jayhawkers 153
Jefferson, Thomas 33, 34–5, 44, 518
Jeffords, Thomas 351, 432
Jennings, Al and Frank 292–3, 504, 525
Johnson County War 239–44, 245, 504
Johnson, John 133
Joseph, Chief 429, 524

Kaepernick, Bertha 500
keelboats 129
Kelley, Hall Jackson 78

Kentucky 20–3, 29, 518
Kentucky rifle 13, 256
Kicking Bear 451, 456
Kilpatrick, Ben 479–80, 526
Kiowa 350, 409
Koch, Peter 131–3

labour wars 319, 327–8, 526–7
law enforcement
 Indian police 262–3
 lawmen 180, 261–2, 294–302,
  304–12
 Pinkerton's Detective
  Agency 263, 285,
  317–28, 484
 private police forces 263
 rangers 262, 313–17
 vigilantism 117, 212, 233–6,
  237–8, 239–44, 263–7, 328,
  461, 524
lawmen 180, 261–2, 294–302,
 304–12
Lederer, John 10, 516
Ledyard, John 34
Lee, Jason 79
Lemmons, Bob 188
Leone, Sergio 511–12
Lewis and Clark
 expedition 35–43, 518
Lewis, Meriwether see Lewis and
 Clark expedition
Lillie, Gordon W. (Pawnee
 Bill) 498
Lincoln County War 211–15, 524
Lisa, Manuel 52–3
Little Big Horn 423–7, 523
Little Crow 354, 355, 356,
 357, 522
Little, Frank 328, 527
livestock associations 204
Logan brothers 478–80, 483, 487
Long Drive (1866) 152–4
long hunters 20–1
Long, Major Stephen
 Harriman 47–8
Long Walk (1864) 349, 522
Longbaugh, Harry (Sundance
 Kid) 480, 485–7
Longley, William P. 273–4

Louisiana Purchase 33, 518
Love, Nat 500
Loving, Oliver 159–60
lynch-law 237–8, 263–4, 266

Mackenzie, Colonel
 Ranald 409–10, 413, 428
Mackenzie, Murdo 200
Madsen, Chris 291, 300–1, 302
mail and freight services 134–42
Malone, Washington 150–1
Mandan 38, 339, 499
Mangas Coloradas 346, 347, 348
Manifest Destiny xiii, 77
marshals see lawmen
Massai 460
Masterson, Ed 295–6, 524
Masterson, William B.
 ("Bat") 257–8, 304, 311, 412
Mather, Dave 296
Maverick Act 236–7
McCabe, Edwin 467
McCoy, Joseph 155–6, 176
McDougal, "Cattle Annie" 333
Medicine Lodge peace talks
 (1867) 388–9
Mercer, Asa Shinn 244
Mexico 61, 62, 64, 65
Miami 31–2
Miles, General Nelson A. 348,
 429, 443, 444, 445, 447, 448,
 452, 456, 525
Miller, Alfred Jacob 58–9
Miller, Jim 296, 316–17, 526
miners' strikes 262, 327, 526
missions 6–7
Mississippi River 45
Missouri River 36
"Molly Maguires" 317, 319
Morco, John 296
Morgan, Middy 189
"Mormon War" 111, 521
Mormons 80, 103–111, 521
Morrison, Marion (John
 Wayne) 506, 509, 512
Mountain Meadows
 Massacre 110, 111
Mountain Men 56–7
Mulhall, Lucille 493

Murieta, Joaquin 271
Mussel Slough Shoot-out 252,
    524

Nacogdoches 62, 64
Nana 348, 350, 435, 441
Natchez Trace 268
Native American Indians
    army scouts 413, 422
    in the Civil War 343–4
    Ghost Dance 451–2, 456
    Indian police 262–3
    Indian Wars 31–2, 342–80,
        386–445
    inter-tribal conflict xiii
    outlaws 276–8
    prehistory 3–4
    reservation system 341
    in the War of
    Independence 25–8
        White-Indian mutual
            aid 83–4
    see also individual tribes e.g.
        Apache
Nauvoo 80, 104, 105
Navajo 349–50
Newton "General
    Massacre" 178–9
Nez Perce 428–9
Nickell, Willie 491–4
Nix, Evett Dumas 269–70, 291–2,
    299–300, 302
Northwest Ordinance
    (1787) 29–30, 518

Oakley, Annie 489, 490
Ohio 32, 497
Ohio Valley 15, 18, 19
O.K. Corral gunfight 306,
    309–10, 524
Olmstead, Frederick Law 74–5
Oregon 79–80
Oregon Trail 79, 80, 114
Otter–Van Orman wagon
    train 86–7
outlaw dynasties 289–93
outlaw-heroes 270, 271, 273
outlawry 268–93
overlanders 78–95

Palo Duro 202–3, 413
Parker, Cynthia Ann 314, 406–7
Parker, Judge Isaac 261, 275, 334,
    335, 523
Parker, Robert LeRoy (Butch
    Cassidy) 479–80, 484–6, 487
Parker's Fort 406
Pawnee 46, 85
Peacemaker (Colt revolver) 257
Pekinpah, Sam 510–11
Pennsylvania 11
Phillips, John 378–9
Pickett, Bill 499–500
Piegan 41–2
Pike, Zebulon Montgomery 44–7,
    518
Pike's Peak 46, 48, 359
Pinkerton's Detective
    Agency 263, 285, 317–28, 484
pioneers see overlanders
Plains Indians xiii–xiv, 342, 364,
    384–5, 423
Pleasant Valley War 229–31, 525
Plummer, Henry 264, 522
Pontiac Rebellion 18, 20
Pony Express 137–8
Prairie Schooner 81
Proclamation of 1763 (limiting
    White settlement) 19, 24, 517
prostitution 117, 176–7, 330
Pueblo uprising (1680) 7

Quahadi Comanche 388, 407,
    409–13
Quanah Parker 388, 406, 407, 409,
    410, 411–12, 413–14, 450
Quick, Flo 332–3

railroads 142–4, 382, 384–5
ranching 196–201
range wars 206, 211–15, 525
Ray, Nick 239, 240
Red Cloud 367, 368, 369, 374,
    379–80, 415–16, 419, 420
Red Light districts 174
Reed, James 96, 98, 101
religious migrants 8, 103
    see also Mormons
Remington, Frederic 182

Reno brothers 283–4, 318, 501
Reno, Major Marcus 423, 424, 426–7
river traffic 128–34
road agents *see* highway robbery
Rocky Mountain Fur Company 55–6, 58, 78
rodeos 495, 498–501
Rogers, Major Robert 17, 18
Roman Nose 374, 390, 523
Roosevelt, Theodore 448–9, 501
Rose of the Cimarron 333
Rose, Louis 70–1
Russell, Charles M. 225
Russell, Jane 508
Russell, William H. 136–7
Ruxton, George 56–7

St Vrain, Ceran 60
Salt Lake City 108, 110
San Antonio 66, 67
San Francisco 113, 116–17, 330
San Francisco Committee of Vigilance 263–4
San Jacinto, battle of 73–4
San Juan 6
Sand Creek Massacre 362–4, 510, 522
Santa Anna 65, 66, 67, 68, 71, 72, 73, 74
Santa Fe 47, 59–60
Santa Fe Trail 60, 519
Santee Sioux 353–7, 522
Satank 389, 409
Satanta 388–9, 408, 409, 411, 413–14
Scioto Company 30–1
Scotch–Irish immigrants 11–12
Seven Years' War 15–18
Shawnee 23, 26–7, 28, 47
sheep farming 227–32
Sheridan, General Philip H. 390–1, 404, 421
sheriffs *see* lawmen
Sherman, General William T. 386, 408
Short, Luke 304, 307, 311
Shoshoni 39–40, 86
Shoshoni Mike 460

Sieber, Al 481
silver mining 126, 307
Sioux 38, 342, 353–7, 369–78, 379, 415–27, 428, 451–6, 522
Siringo, Charles 318, 319–27
Sitting Bull 416, 422, 428, 451–3, 497, 524
Slade, Jack 264–5
slavery 72, 118, 315
Slye, Leonard (Roy Rogers) 507
Smith, Jedediah 55, 519
Smith, Joseph 103–4, 105
Smith, Tom 298
sod houses 464–5
Springfield rifle 379
Staked Plains 201–2, 407, 409–10
Starr, Belle 276, 282, 290, 334–5, 525
Starr, Henry 293, 526
steamboats 130–1, 134
stetsons 191–2
Stevens, Jennie "Little Britches" 333–4
Stewart, James 507, 508
stock detectives 236
Stuart, Granville 200, 225, 233–6
Stuenenberg, Frank 327, 526
Sublette brothers 55, 78
Sundance Kid *see* Longbaugh, Harry
Sundown, Jackson 499
Sutton–Taylor feud 272
Swan Land and Cattle Company 198, 226, 490

Taylor, William E. 88–95
telegraphy 137–8
temperance movement 470–1
Teton Sioux 38
Texan Revolution 65–72
Texas 62–75, 149, 152, 520
Texas Longhorn 150, 151
Texas Panhandle 201–2
Texas Rangers 313–17, 519
Thomas, Heck 276, 291, 292, 298, 300, 301
Thompson, William 385
Tilghman, Bill 291–2, 293, 300, 301–2, 333–4, 461, 504, 527

Tombstone 126, 306–10
train robbery 283–4
Travis, William B. 65, 66, 67, 68–9, 70, 71
Treaty of Paris (1783) 29, 518
Tubbs, "Poker Alice" 331
Tunstall, John Henry 207, 210–11
Turner, Frederick Jackson 459
Twain, Mark 116, 138–42, 264–5

Union Pacific 143, 474–6
US 7th Cavalry 391–403, 416, 417–19, 421, 423–7, 452, 454–5
Utah 109, 111
Ute 430

vaqueros 148, 149, 188–9
Victorio 348, 350, 433–4
vigilantism 117, 212, 233–6, 237–8, 239–44, 263–7, 328, 461, 524
violence in the West 251–67
Virginia 7–8, 29
"Voyage of Discovery" 34–43, 518
Wagon Box Fight 379
wagons 81
walkdowns (gunfights) 254–5
Walker, Captain Samuel 314
Walker, Dr Thomas 20, 517
Wallace, Lew 216–17, 220
Wallace, William ("Big Foot") 314
Wampanoags 8, 516
War of 1812 47, 53, 54
Washington, George 15–16, 24, 26, 31, 32
Washita battle 391–403, 510
water supplies 465
Watson, Ella 237–8
Wayne, General Anthony 32, 518
Wayne, John see Marion Morrison
waystations 138–42
Wells Fargo 142
wells and windmills 465

Western movies 503–14
Western Trail 159
whiskey 175
Whitman, Marcus 80
Wichita 159, 304
Wild Bill Hickok see Hickok, James Butler
Wild Bunch 279, 319, 480–5, 487–8
Wild West shows 495, 496–8, 526
Wilderness Road 21, 22, 269
Willamette Valley 79
Winchester rifle 258–9
Wolcott, Major Frank 239, 241, 242, 243
women in the West 329–35
    cowpunchers 189
    cross-dressing 331–2
    female suffrage 471, 502
    gamblers 330, 331
    homesteaders 468–70
    outlaws 332–5
    prostitution 117, 176–7, 330
    rodeo riders 492–3
Wood, Abraham 10, 516
woodhawks 131–3
woodlanders 12–13
Wounded Knee Massacre 454–6, 510, 525
Wovoka 451
Wyeth, Nathaniel 78, 499
Wyllyams, Frederick xiii, 387–8
Wyoming Stock Growers' Association 204, 236, 238, 244, 490

Yazoo Strip 33, 518
Yellowstone National Park 52
Young, Brigham 104, 105–6, 107–8, 109, 110
Younger, Thomas Coleman (Cole) 282, 283, 287, 288, 289, 334, 498

Zunis 6, 345